# Russian Business Power

This book examines how the connections between the Russian state, business community, and organized crime influence Russia's foreign and security policies, including its relations with the countries of the former Soviet Union, the European Union, Asia, and the Middle East. While earlier studies have focused separately on Russian foreign policy, the evolution of the business sector, or the growing crime problem, this book integrates these topics to gain a deeper understanding of how Russia's domestic evolution affects relations with its neighbors. It brings together, in an overarching conceptual framework, the impact of large corporations such as Gazprom and LUKoil, and small business networks active in the shadow economy of separatist regions in Georgia, the porous Russian–Kazakh border, and the Far East. Individual chapters analyze key sectors in the Russian economy, including energy, arms, banking, forestry, and drugs. By focusing on Russian business in all its forms, this book provides new insights into larger questions of conflict resolution and the role of the private sector in international and security relations.

**Andreas Wenger** is professor of International Security Policy and director of the Center for Security Studies at ETH Zurich (Swiss Federal Institute of Technology). His main research interests are in security and strategic studies and the history of international relations. **Jeronim Perović** is a senior researcher at the Center for Security Studies at ETH Zurich. He works on contemporary aspects of Russian foreign and security policy, energy politics in the Caspian, regionalism in Russia, and Soviet–Yugoslav relations. **Robert W. Orttung** is associate research professor at the Transnational Crime and Corruption Center of American University and a visiting scholar at the Center for Security Studies at ETH Zurich. His interests are Russian regional politics, business–state relations, corruption, organized crime, and terrorism.

# Routledge transnational crime and corruption series

Published in association with the Terrorism, Transnational Crime and Corruption Center, American University, Washington, DC

## 1 Russian Business Power
The role of Russian business in foreign and security relations
*Edited by Andreas Wenger, Jeronim Perović, and Robert W. Orttung*

# Russian Business Power

The role of Russian business in foreign and security relations

**Edited by Andreas Wenger,
Jeronim Perović, and
Robert W. Orttung**

Routledge
Taylor & Francis Group

LONDON AND NEW YORK

First published 2006
by Routledge
2 Park Square, Milton Park, Abingdon, Oxon OX14 4RN

Simultaneously published in the USA and Canada
by Routledge
270 Madison Ave, New York, NY 10016

*Routledge is an imprint of the Taylor & Francis Group, an informa business*

Transferred to Digital Printing 2009

© 2006 Selection and editorial matter, Andreas Wenger, Jeronim Perović
and Robert W. Orttung; individual chapters, the contributors

Typeset in Times by Wearset Ltd, Boldon, Tyne and Wear

*British Library Cataloguing in Publication Data*
A catalogue record for this book is available from the British Library

*Library of Congress Cataloging in Publication Data*
A catalog record for this book has been requested

ISBN10: 0-415-37478-2 (hbk)
ISBN10: 0-415-54569-2 (pbk)
ISBN10: 0-203-09972-9 (ebk)

ISBN13: 978-0-415-37478-1 (hbk)
ISBN13: 978-0-415-54569-3 (pbk)
ISBN13: 978-0-203-09972-8 (ebk)

We dedicate this book to our children: Andrina and Ariane Wenger; Luis and Lorenz Strologo-Perović; and Nicole and Joseph Orttung. Hopefully they will be able to resolve some of the difficult issues they will inherit from our generation.

# Contents

| | |
|---|---|
| *List of figures* | ix |
| *List of maps* | x |
| *List of tables* | xi |
| *List of contributors* | xii |
| *Acknowledgments* | xvi |
| *List of abbreviations* | xvii |

**PART I**
**Introduction**                                                                1

1  **Russian business power as a source of transnational conflict and cooperation**     3
   ANDREAS WENGER

2  **The role of business in Russian foreign and security relations**      22
   ROBERT W. ORTTUNG

**PART II**
**Russian energy: regional power and dependency**      45

3  **Russian energy companies and the enlarged European Union**      47
   HEIKO PLEINES

4  **Russian energy companies in the new Eastern Europe: the cases of Ukraine and Belarus**      67
   MARGARITA M. BALMACEDA

5  **Russian energy companies in the Caspian and Central Eurasian region: expanding southward**      88
   JERONIM PEROVIĆ

6  **Russia, Iraq, and Iran: business, politics, or both?**                    114
    CAROL R. SAIVETZ

7  **Russian and transnational energy companies: conflict and
   cooperation in Pacific Russia**                                           133
    MICHAEL J. BRADSHAW

**PART III**
**Beyond energy: emerging business networks and human
security**                                                                    155

8  **Russian business, the arms trade, and regional security**               157
    ROBERT W. ORTTUNG AND BORIS DEMIDOV

9  **Russian banks and Russian diplomacy: occasionally rather
   embarrassing**                                                            175
    WILLIAM TOMPSON

10  **The drug trade in Russia**                                             196
    LOUISE I. SHELLEY AND SVANTE E. CORNELL

11  **Uncharted territory: Russian business activity in Abkhazia
    and South Ossetia**                                                      217
    ERIK R. SCOTT

12  **Timber in the Russian Far East and potential transborder conflict**   239
    JOSH NEWELL

    *Index*                                                                  260

# Figures

| | | |
|---|---|---|
| 2.1 | State-business relations in various sectors of the Russian economy | 38 |
| 7.1 | Projected oil consumption to 2020 | 138 |
| 7.2 | Projected gas consumption to 2020 | 139 |
| 12.1 | Russian timber exporters to China, 1998–2002 | 243 |
| 12.2 | Timber production in the Russian Far East, 1960–2001 | 249 |
| 12.3 | Russian timber exports to Northeast Asia, 1993–2002 | 251 |

# Maps

| | | |
|---|---|---|
| 5.1 | Caspian gas pipelines | 94 |
| 5.2 | Caspian oil pipelines | 94 |
| 7.1 | Potential oil and gas pipelines in NE Asia | 142 |
| 11.1 | Major contraband trade routes in Georgia | 224 |
| 12.1 | Administrative regions of the Russian Far East | 240 |
| 12.2 | Russian timber export to Northeast Asia, 2002 | 250 |

# Tables

| | | |
|---|---|---|
| 3.1 | Russia's main trading Partners, 2003 | 47 |
| 3.2 | Russian exports to the EU-15 by product groups, 2001–2003 | 48 |
| 3.3 | Russia's major exporting companies | 53 |
| 3.4 | Gazprom's investments in EU-25 countries | 54 |
| 3.5 | LUKoil's investments in EU-25 countries | 54 |
| 3.6 | Yukos's investments in EU-25 countries | 55 |
| 5.1 | Russia's share in CIS country trade volumes, 2004 | 92 |
| 5.2 | Oil and gas reserves for selected countries | 93 |
| 5.3 | LUKoil's participation in Caspian oil and gas projects | 103 |
| 7.1 | The energy mix in Northeast Asia, 2003 | 135 |
| 7.2 | Patterns of LNG supply into Northeast Asia, 2003 | 136 |
| 7.3 | Reserves of the key East Siberian fields | 141 |
| 7.4 | Mid-2005 status of the Sakhalin projects | 145 |
| 7.5 | Sakhalin Energy's LNG deals | 146 |
| 8.1 | Earnings of top Russian Weapons Producers, 2004 | 159 |
| 9.1 | Selected balance-sheet indicators for the Russian banking sector | 176 |
| 12.1 | Disparities in trade statistics for logs, 2002–2003 | 247 |

# Contributors

**Margarita M. Balmaceda** divides her time between Seton Hall University, New Jersey, USA, where she is associate professor at the John C. Whitehead School of Diplomacy and International Relations, and Harvard University, where she is an associate of the Davis Center for Russian and Eurasian Studies and the Harvard Ukrainian Research Institute. She received a PhD in Politics from Princeton University (1996), and postdoctoral training at Harvard University. She has published widely on Russian, post-Soviet, and East European energy and foreign policies, including as editor/coeditor of *On the Edge: The Ukrainian–Central European-Russian Security Triangle* (Central European University Press, 2000), *Independent Belarus* (Harvard University Press, 2002), and a special double issue on energy in Eastern Europe of the German journal *Osteuropa* (2004). She has taught, and conducted field research on energy and foreign policy issues in Russia, Hungary, Ukraine, Belarus, and Germany. She is currently working on a book called "Understanding the Comparative Management of Energy Dependence in Central-East Europe." Balmaceda has been awarded a Humboldt Fellowship to continue work on this issue at Giessen University, Germany, in 2005 and 2006.

**Michael J. Bradshaw** is professor of Human Geography and head of the Department of Geography at the University of Leicester, UK. His PhD is from the University of British Columbia, Canada. He is also an Honorary Senior Research Fellow in the Centre for Russian and East European Studies at the University of Birmingham and an Associate Fellow of the Russia and Eurasia Programme at the Royal Institute of International Affairs in London. His research is on the economic geography of Russia, with a particular focus on the Russian Far East and energy relations with Northeast Asia. His publications include *Regional Economic Change in Russia* (with Philip Hanson) (Edward Elgar, 2000) and *The Russian Far East and Pacific Asia: Unfulfilled Potential* (RoutledgeCurzon, 2001).

**Svante E. Cornell** is research director of the Central Asia–Caucasus Institute and Silk Road Studies Program, a Joint Transatlantic Research and Policy Center affiliated with Johns Hopkins University-SAIS and the Department of

Eurasian Studies, Uppsala University. He is also editor of the *Central Asia–Caucasus Analyst*.

**Boris Demidov** was the general manager and Anti-corruption Resource Center coordinator of Transparency International, Russia, from 1999 to 2004. Since June 2004, he has served as a guide on the Development Gateway Governance topic page (http://topics.developmentgateway.org/governance) and co-guide for the Business Environment topic page. His publications include a survey for the US State Department of all foreign and domestic anticorruption projects conducted in Russia in 1999–2001 and planned for 2002. He also contributed a chapter dealing with corruption to the volume *Dynamics of Russian Politics: Putin's Reform of Federal–Regional Relations* (Rowman & Littlefield, 2005). Among his latest publications are a coauthored high school textbook on civics and *Anti-corruption Documents and Instruments*, a collection of Russian and international materials. Demidov was a lead social scientist for the Center for Public Integrity Global Access Project, released in March 2004. Since October 2002, he has been editing the monthly Current Highlights releases for the ABA/CEELI No Bribes website (www.nobribes.org). Since May 2005, he has produced the Anti-Corruption Review for the former Soviet Union and East European Countries (available at the Development Gateway's Governance webpage).

**Josh Newell** is a PhD candidate in the Department of Geography at the University of Washington. His research centers broadly around the environmental, social, and economic impacts of post-Soviet transition in the Russian Far East. He recently coauthored (with Paula Vandergert) the article "Illegal Logging in the Russian Far East and Siberia" for *International Forestry Review* and is the author of *The Russian Far East: A Reference Guide for Conservation and Development* (Daniel & Daniel, 2004).

**Robert W. Orttung** is associate research professor at the Transnational Crime and Corruption Center of American University, Washington, DC, and a visiting scholar at the Center for Security Studies at the Swiss Federal Institute of Technology (ETH) in Zurich. Orttung is the editor of the Russian Regional Report, a biweekly newsletter that tracks political and economic developments in Russia's 89 regions (http://www.isn.ethz.ch/news/rrr/). He is the editor/author of: (co-edited with Peter Reddaway) *The Dynamics of Russian Politics: Putin's Reform of Federal Regional Relations,* 2 volumes (Rowman & Littlefield, 2003 and 2005); *The Republics and Regions of the Russian Federation: A Guide to Politics, Policies, and Leaders* (M. E. Sharpe, 2000); (with Laura Belin) *Russia's 1995 Parliamentary Elections: The Battle for the Duma* (M. E. Sharpe, 1997); and *From Leningrad to St. Petersburg: Democratization in a Russian City* (St. Martin's Press, 1995). He earned his PhD in Political Science from UCLA in 1992 and a BA in Russian Studies from Stanford University in 1986.

**Jeronim Perović** is a senior researcher at the Center for Security Studies at

ETH Zurich (Swiss Federal Institute of Technology). He was a visiting scholar at the Davis Center for Russian and Eurasian Studies at Harvard University in 2003–2005, a short-term scholar at the Kennan Institute of the Woodrow Wilson International Center for Scholars in 2002, and an international student at the Russian State University for the Humanities in Moscow in 1995–1996. Perović studied history, political science, and Russian literature at the University in Zurich, where he received his PhD in 2000. Perović is author of the monograph *Die Regionen Russlands als neue politische Kraft* (Russia's Regions as a New Political Force) (Peter Lang, 2001). He has coedited several books, including (coedited with Kurt R. Spillmann, Andreas Wenger, and Derek Müller) *Russia's Place in Europe: A Security Debate* (Peter Lang, 1999). His work on contemporary aspects of Russian foreign and security policy, energy politics in the Caspian, regionalism in Russia, and Soviet–Yugoslav relations has appeared in *Journal of Cold War Studies, Geopolitics, Demokratizatsiya, Osteuropa, Europa Regional, the Journal of Political History and Culture of Russia*, and *Aussenpolitik: German Foreign Affairs Review*.

**Heiko Pleines** is a researcher at the Forschungsstelle Osteuropa (Research Centre for East European Studies) in Bremen, Germany. He has published extensively on lobbyism, political corruption, and economic policy making in Russia. He also works as an analyst of the post-Soviet energy sector.

**Carol R. Saivetz** is a research associate at Harvard's Davis Center for Russian and Eurasian Studies and a member of the Department of Government, where she teaches courses on Russia and the Middle East. She served as executive director of the American Association for the Advancement of Slavic Studies between 1995 and 2005. She has written widely on Soviet and now Russian policy in the Middle East. In addition, she has written about the politics of Caspian oil and the question of Russia's policies toward the other post-Soviet states. Her most recent publications include: "Plus Ça Change: Russia's Foreign Policy in 2004," *Post-Soviet Affairs* 21, no. 1, January 2005; "Russian Policy toward Iran and Iraq: A Complicated Balance," *Post-Soviet Affairs* 20, no. 1, January 2004; and "Perspectives on the Caspian Sea Dilemma: Russian Policies since the Soviet Demise," *Eurasian Geography and Economics* 44, no. 8, December 2003. She is currently working on a book tentatively entitled "Explaining Russian Foreign Policy: Domestic Politics and International Relations," to be published by Rowman & Littlefield.

**Erik R. Scott** is a graduate student in history at the University of California, Berkeley. He has traveled extensively in the Caucasus and from 2002 to 2004 managed the Transnational Crime and Corruption Center's programs in Georgia. He is currently working on Georgia and the Georgian Diaspora in the Soviet period.

**Louise I. Shelley** is the founder and director of the Transnational Crime and Corruption Center (TraCCC), and a leading expert on organized crime and

corruption in the former Soviet Union. Her expertise includes money laundering and illicit financial flows, human smuggling and trafficking, national
security issues, the use of information technology by international crime
groups, and the linkages between organized crime and terrorism. Since 1995,
Shelley has run programs in Russia, Ukraine, and, more recently, in Georgia
with leading specialists on the problems of organized crime and corruption.
She is the author of *Policing Soviet Society* (Routledge, 1996), as well as
numerous articles and book chapters. Shelley is a professor at American University's School of International Service.

**William Tompson** is senior economist for the Newly Independent States of the
former Soviet Union, and Southeastern Europe, in the Economics Department
of the Organisation for Economic Co-operation and Development (OECD).
He is on leave from Birkbeck College, University of London, where he is
professor of Politics. Tompson is the author of *Khrushchev: A Political Life*
(Macmillan/St Martin's, 1997) and *The Soviet Union under Brezhnev*
(Longman, 2003), as well as numerous articles and book chapters on Soviet
and Russian politics and economic policy. Together with Rudiger Ahrend, he
prepared the fifth *OECD Economic Survey of the Russian Federation*, which
appeared in July 2004.

**Andreas Wenger** is professor of International Security Policy and director of
the Center for Security Studies at ETH Zurich (Swiss Federal Institute of
Technology). He holds a doctoral degree from the University of Zurich and
was a guest scholar at Princeton University (1992–1994), Yale University
(1998), the Woodrow Wilson Center (2000), and, recently, at the George
Washington University (2005). His main research interests are in security and
strategic studies and the history of international relations. Wenger has published, *inter alia*, in the *Journal of Cold War Studies*, *Cold War History*,
*Presidential Studies Quarterly*, *Vierteljahrshefte für Zeitgeschichte*, *Defense
and Peace Economics*, and *Osteuropa*. He is author of *Living with Peril:
Eisenhower, Kennedy, and Nuclear Weapons* (Rowman & Littlefield, 1997),
coauthor of *International Relations: From the Cold War to the Globalized
World* (Lynne Rienner, 2003) and *Conflict Prevention: The Untapped Potential of the Business Sector* (Lynne Rienner, 2003), and recently coedited *War
Plans and Alliances in the Cold War: Threat Perceptions in the East and the
West* (Routledge, 2006) and *Transforming NATO in the Cold War: Chal-
lenges beyond Deterrence in the 1960s* (Routledge, 2006). Wenger is the del-
egate for the Master of Advanced Studies in Security Policy and Crisis
Management of the Department of Humanities, Social and Political Sciences
at ETH Zurich and responsible for the International Relations and Security
Network – ISN (http://www.isn.ethz.ch).

# Acknowledgments

This book evolved out of an attempt to shed light on an area that hitherto has received little attention. We were interested in the role of business in Russia and in the larger contribution of business in fostering conflict and/or promoting cooperation. The research was originally undertaken for a conference intended to review the role of business in Russia and in the country's relations toward its neighbors to the west, south, and east of its borders. The Center for Security Studies organized the conference, which met in closed session at ETH Zurich (Swiss Federal Institute of Technology) in June 2004. The three editors then focused on the conceptualization of a book and selected the most appropriate papers from among the contributions prepared for the conference.

The original texts were first reviewed, and then rewritten according to a set of questions drawn up by the editors. The results were discussed at a second conference in March 2005, on the basis of which the chapters were once again reviewed, and finally edited according to the editors' guidelines. We went through this process to emphasize a comparative perspective across a wide range of business activities and geographical areas and to bring overall coherence to the book. Hopefully, the resulting chapters illuminate some of the main issues and complexities that explain the international consequences of the rise of Russian business power in its various forms.

Along the way, we naturally incurred many debts. We would particularly like to thank the conference participants who provided useful comments to the authors in preparing the resultant chapters. They were Tor Bukkvoll, Gerald Easter, Graeme P. Herd, Andrew Jack, Bobo Lo, Andrey Makarychev, William Pridemore, Sergei Prozorov, Peter Rutland, and Alexei Zudin. We are also grateful to Jennifer Gassmann for excellent logistical support in Zurich. Naturally, all of these advisers could not save us from our own mistakes and we take full credit for them.

# Abbreviations

| | |
|---|---|
| AAC | annual allowable cut |
| ACG | Azeri–Chirag–Guneshli |
| APEC | Asia-Pacific Economic Cooperation |
| ARB | Association of Russian Banks |
| bbl | barrels |
| bbl/d | barrels per day |
| bcm | billion cubic meters |
| bn bbl | billion barrels |
| BONY | Bank of New York |
| BP | British Petroleum |
| BTC | Baku–Tbilisi–Ceyhan (pipeline) |
| CAST | Center for the Analysis of Strategies and Technologies |
| CBR | Central Bank of Russia |
| CIS | Commonwealth of Independent States |
| CMEA | Council for Mutual Economic Assistance |
| CMTC | Committee for Military and Technical Cooperation with Foreign Countries |
| CNPC | China National Petroleum Corporation |
| CPC | Caspian Pipeline Consortium |
| CSIS | Center for Strategic and International Studies |
| DEA | Drug Enforcement Administration (United States) |
| EADS | European Aeronautic Defense and Space Company |
| EIA | Energy Information Administration |
| ENL | Exxon Neftegaz Ltd. |
| ETG | Eural Trans Gas |
| EU | European Union |
| FATF | Financial Action Task Force |
| FDI | foreign direct investment |
| FIG | Financial-Industrial Group |
| FIMACO | Financial Management Company |
| FSB | Federal Security Service |
| GDP | gross domestic product |
| GDR | German Democratic Republic |

| | |
|---|---|
| IAEA | International Atomic Energy Agency |
| IEA | International Energy Agency |
| IEEJ | Institute of Energy Economics, Japan |
| IFC | International Finance Corporation |
| IMF | International Monetary Fund |
| IMU | Islamic Movement of Uzbekistan |
| LNG | liquefied natural gas |
| m bbl | million barrels |
| MID | Russian Ministry of Foreign Affairs |
| mt | million tons |
| mtoe | million tons of oil equivalent |
| mtpa | million tons per annum |
| MVD | Russian Ministry of Internal Affairs |
| NE | Northeast |
| OECD | Organization for Economic Co-operation and Development |
| OSCE | Organization for Security and Co-operation in Europe |
| PCA | Partnership and Cooperation Agreement |
| PPP | purchasing power parity |
| PSA | production sharing agreement |
| RF | Russian Federation |
| RFE | Russian Far East |
| RFE/RL | Radio Free Europe/Radio Liberty |
| SCP | South Caucasus Pipeline project |
| SIPRI | Stockholm International Peace Research Institute |
| SMNG | Sakhalinmoreneftegaz |
| SOCAR | State Oil Company of the Azerbaijan Republic |
| tcf | trillion cubic feet |
| tcm | trillion cubic meters |
| TNK | Tiumen Oil Company |
| TraCCC | Transnational Crime and Corruption Center |
| UAE | United Arab Emirates |
| UES | Unified Energy System |
| UFG | United Financial Group |
| UNCTAD | United Nations Conference on Trade and Development |
| VAT | value added tax |
| VTB | Vneshtorgbank |
| WTO | World Trade Organization |
| WWF | World Wildlife Fund |

# Part I
# Introduction

# 1 Russian business power as a source of transnational conflict and cooperation

*Andreas Wenger*

This book describes the role of Russian business in all its manifestations and its impact on Russia's foreign and security relations. Russian business power reflects a domestic situation shaped by the rise of powerful business networks, both legal and illegal, and by the fact that Russia's integration into the world is increasingly driven by economic factors. The new perspective is in what the book tells us about two important topics that are addressed in the subsequent chapters: The first is the distinct link between Russia's legitimate and criminal business development and the evolution of the Russian state and its foreign relations. The second is the impact of Russian business power on the balance of transnational conflict and cooperation in Russia's foreign relations.

The book is distinct in focusing on the link between the development of new patterns of interaction among the Russian state, a powerful business community, and organized crime networks and their impact on the dynamics of conflict and cooperation within Russia and along its borders. Most of the existing literature focuses either on foreign and security relations or on business development, but does not bring these two topics together. Several existing books discuss the dilemmas of Russia's foreign and security policies, shaped by the gap between the aspirations of a political elite focused on upholding the image of a great power and the political, economic, and social realities of a fundamentally weak state.[1] Likewise, there are several studies on the evolution of Russian business within the context of a domestic transformation marked by strong recentralization efforts since Vladimir Putin's rise to power.[2]

Examining the role of Russian state representatives, businessmen, and organized crime groups and their international operations raises a host of questions: To what extent are Russian corporations acting in the interests of the Russian state and to what extent are they simply pursuing normal business interests? How effective has the state been in using corporations to pursue larger political goals and exert influence over its neighbors? What is the role of organized crime in foreign operations of the Russian state and business and as a separate entity? And, most importantly, do Russian business operations abroad lead to more violent conflict between or within countries or do they promote mutually beneficial exchange and increase regional stability? The subsequent chapters of the book will address these questions.

## Business and conflict in a globalizing world

The book's focus on the impact of Russian business power on the security environment along Russia's borders is part of an emerging, more general research agenda that focuses on the link between business and conflict.[3] The growing interest in the multifaceted nexus between business interests and political stability comes as a reflection of two global trends that dominated the evolution of an increasingly pluralist international system after the end of the Cold War: On the one hand, the twin forces of globalization and localization led to the empowerment of business as an international actor.[4] On the other hand, the changing nature of conflict meant that deadly conflicts would have to be dealt with in the context of a broadening concept of international security.[5] With business intrinsically involved in conflict-related matters, new forms of governance patterns in the area of the peaceful transformation of violent conflicts are in demand.

Over the past decade, the role of business as an international actor increased considerably. To a large extent, the increased importance of business was the result of an accelerated transfer of assets and services from public to private hands and a dramatic expansion of transborder flows of capital, services, goods, ideas, and people as a result of the opening of national markets to foreign investments. More than ever before, business actors are deeply involved in world politics – however, with ambiguous and sometimes even contradictory effects on the balance of conflict and cooperation in international affairs. Few would dispute that economic growth and opportunity, generated by private enterprises, are essential to the reduction of poverty and the enhancement of social and political stability. Conversely, big companies, especially from the extractive industries, are frequently accused of harming the social and ecological interests of local communities, backing repressive regimes or deliberately prolonging conflict in order to pursue their parochial financial agendas.[6]

For many businesses, the general shift from a national economic focus to an international and global economic perspective and their own increasing geographic diversification of interests and operations have meant that they tend to find themselves confronted with conflict situations much more frequently. On the one hand, businesses are much more likely to be adversely affected by the transnational impact of faraway conflicts, and they are also more likely to have business interests in conflict-prone areas. In addition, many private actors – so-called business mercenaries and war entrepreneurs – take on the function of security providers. This new phenomenon has fueled concerns with regard to the legitimacy and accountability of their activities, reinforcing a predominantly negative perception of the link between business and conflict.[7]

In the early 1990s, the triumph of the market and the ever-increasing interdependence of world economic and financial forces were largely praised as mitigating conflicts. Yet such liberal views in favor of global governance and security were soon upset by the sobering realization that globalization does not necessarily foster global security. The very unevenness of globalization increases inequalities between and within states, and contributes to instability in regions that are shaped by processes of marginalization and fragmentation. The fact that borders have become more porous not only provides economic opportunity, but also increases the complexities of proliferation and export control issues and of the fight against transnational organized crime or terrorist networks.

Today's security risks no longer emanate predominantly from powerful states, but rather from warring social groups operating in weak and failed states. In reaction to the changing nature of conflict, state actors have been forced to seek new ways of providing peace and stability and to modify their conceptions of security. Proponents of human security acknowledge that while the security of states has improved in recent years, the security of various peoples and citizens has declined considerably. Human security – in contrast to a narrow concept focusing on the security of the state – stands for a broadened security notion that complements military and political measures for ensuring security with efforts at prevention of conflict by social, economic, and ecological means.[8]

As a consequence of these developments, there is an emerging debate about the need for new forms of governance patterns in dealing with the root causes and process factors of entrenched violent conflicts. While business actors, for good reasons related to sovereignty and political legitimacy, will not replace the state as the primary player in the area of war and peace, they are bound to increasingly supplement it when it comes to the socioeconomic aspects of peace building. In the West, this debate is shaped by public actors and institutions that recognize their limitations in dealing with new risks of a primarily political, social, cultural, economic, and ecological nature. The focus is on building partnerships and on those business qualities that can effectively complement the preventive efforts of public and civil society actors. The response from private actors, so far, has been one of restraint, since businesses tend to see their interests as unrelated to the (supposedly public affairs) issues of political risk management and transformation of deadly conflicts.[9]

## Russian business and transnational conflict

The Russian case with regard to the link between business and conflict is different from this Western perspective in two important respects: Looking at the domestic situation in Russia, the state has not yet established a stable regulatory framework for business, as well-established Western democracies have. In Russia, the line between the state and business and between legitimate business and organized crime is often blurred.[10] The rules of the game for business frequently change, depending on the balance between key political players. While the Western focus has been on the horizontal redistribution of power away from the nation-state, Russian perceptions have been dominated by the disintegration of centralist state structures and the potential negative consequences of such developments on Russia's status, influence, and position in Eurasia and on a global level. The power vacuum caused by the economic crisis of the 1990s and the inability of the state to implement structural reform – and not the forces of economic globalization – have dominated Russia's search for a new equilibrium of power.

. When Russia turns away from its inner crisis and addresses potential risks from outside the country, traditional problems seem at least as important as the newly globalized risks – despite the fact that Russia's political class increasingly recognizes the importance of "nontraditional" security threats. Unequal military balances along Russia's European and Asian borders transform into a feeling of weakness on the grand geopolitical chessboard. More importantly, Russian elites focus on acute dangers with regard to border problems and regional stability in the Caucasus, in Central Asia, and in the Far East. The mix of anti-Russian tendencies in some of Russia's own regions in the North Caucasus and in many of its neighboring countries, fragile domestic stability in the Commonweatlh of Independent States (CIS) countries, and a threat of Islamic fundamentalism, often exaggerated, but nonetheless serious, make for a highly complex and fragile situation, especially in view of the energy issues involved.

Russia's more traditional approach to security reflects its limited integration into the cooperative structures of an economically interdependent Western world. The rise of Russian business power across its borders is shaped by the dilemma between Russia's relative economic and institutional weaknesses and its Great (military) Power legacy. While the Western debate about power in the information age is founded in Joseph Nye's distinction between "hard" and "soft" power – the latter reflecting influence that depends less on territory, military, and natural resources than on information, technology, and institutional flexibility – Russia's foreign and security policy debate is dominated by a more traditional perception of power, vested in the territorial state as the single source of sovereignty and brought to bear through geopolitics and geo-economics.[11]

While Russia is no longer a superpower, it remains an extremely important factor – as much for its weakness as for its strengths – in addressing the nuclear, biological, and chemical weapons legacy of the Cold War; in securing regional stability in Eastern Europe and the Balkans, in the Caucasus and in Central Asia, as well as in the Middle and the Far East; and in managing transborder security issues such as terrorism, organized crime, drug trafficking, money laundering, and migration. Within this larger context, this book aims at understanding how and in what ways Russia's murky alliances between state structures, powerful businessmen, and criminal groups reduce or increase the basis for transnational conflict within Russia and along its borders.

## Organization and overview of the book

The book is divided into three parts – the first focusing on business–state interactions, the second reviewing energy dependencies and the role of Russian business power across different geographical areas, and the third analyzing the impact of emerging business networks in a variety of economic sectors on Russia's diplomacy, security, and capacity to deal with nontraditional human security issues. In theoretical and conceptual terms, we argue that the distinct kinds of relations established between the Russian state and Russian business in all its forms have an important impact on promoting conflict and cooperation on Russia's borders. While business obviously is a very heterogeneous sector, the state is not a homogeneous actor either. The state is strong in some sections of the economy, but weak in others.

The organization of the book reflects the key distinction we draw between the energy sector and the other sections of the Russian economy. Energy is not only by far the most important sector of the Russian economy, but also the most relevant example of the growing influence of business power in Russia's foreign and security relations. In the energy area, there is basically a structured relationship between a strong state and a highly centralized business community. In contrast, there is a generally weak, often highly corrupt state working with an amorphous business community in the other sectors addressed in this book. This distinction allows for new conclusions on the impact of Russian business power as a source of transnational conflict and cooperation.

Introducing the first part, Robert Orttung explains why the book conceptualizes "business" in the widest possible meaning as including both legitimate companies and organized crime. He notes that Russia's powerful business groups were formed through an extremely controversial process of privatization in a largely lawless environment. Characterized by opaque ownership structures and property rights, business in Russia depends on the highly personalized, and often highly corrupt, access of key individuals to state structures. While there is no doubt that business groups have a significant influence on the Russian state and its foreign relations, it is often difficult to analyze who is manipulating whom, given the blurring of state structures and business, in both its legitimate and its criminal forms.

Russia has one of the most concentrated economies in the world. In discussing its sectoral structure, Orttung differentiates among state-owned monopolies in natural gas, electricity, and oil pipelines that dominate the economy; a small group of large private companies comprising a very powerful business elite; and small and medium-sized businesses that operate in the shadows but play a significant transborder role. He consolidates his findings into a typology of state–business interaction that provides the basis for the analysis of the subsequent chapters. In the energy sector, a strong state can exert considerable influence on a concentrated business community. While in this sector state and business work often hand in hand to increase their influence across borders, in other sectors a much weaker state has only very limited influence on the foreign operations of what is a highly amorphous business community.

The foreign operations of Russian business, dominated by actors in the natural resources sector, have expanded dramatically over the past decade, with a geographic emphasis on the transition economies in the post-Soviet space. Often state and corporate interests overlap in that both want to expand markets and increase the dependence of other countries on Russian resources and

Russian business. At the same time, Orttung draws attention to the fact that state and business interests in Russia's foreign relations sometimes diverge. While the state seeks to maintain complete control of the country's infrastructure, companies would prefer to control the key assets of the full production cycle themselves. And while the state has an interest in selling Russian energy resources below market prices, businesses look for safe havens outside the country to park their assets in order to reduce their vulnerability against the state. More generally, the Kremlin perceives an independent business sector as a potential threat to its ability to mobilize political opposition.

The contribution on the energy trade between Russia and the European Union introduces part II of this volume. Heiko Pleines describes a case in which Russian oil and gas exports have not caused any major disputes between the two sides. On the contrary, he notes, energy is one of the major cooperation-promoting factors in EU–Russian relations. Russian business power operates in a framework of an energy trade that is stabilized both by mutual benefit in an area of great economic importance and by mutual dependency on a pipeline infrastructure constructed in Soviet times. While the EU is Russia's most important partner in foreign economic activities, the EU countries depend on a stable energy supply from Russia. And while the European Union hopes to diversify its energy supplies in the future, Russia's planned pipeline projects are focused on non-European markets.

Within this overall stable framework, Pleines discusses two instances in which the interests of Russian energy companies caused some friction at the level of state interaction. Both of these instances are related to the interest of Russian energy companies to enter the EU downstream market as a means of increasing their profits through sales to the end consumer, using investment in new EU member countries as an entry ticket. Exports to the EU are the major source of income for Russian oil and gas companies. This sales structure is closely linked to state policies, since the Russian government keeps domestic energy prices artificially low and since most CIS countries have accumulated immense debts for Russian energy supply.

The first example is linked to the European Union's intention to develop a comprehensive regulatory framework for the energy trade with Russia, using Russia's World Trade Organization (WTO) entry as leverage. In this case, Pleines notes, energy companies successfully lobbied the Russian state through Gazprom's close links to the government to protect their interests against EU demands for liberalization. The Russian state rejected EU demands as an unwarranted intervention into its domestic affairs and supported the interests of the Russian energy companies as being in the national interest. The second example is linked to attempts of Russian energy companies to invest in the new EU member states. Pressure by the Kremlin on behalf of the Russian companies backfired in this instance, because the new EU member countries interpreted it as proof that Russia, in a union of politics and business, was trying to dominate the former socialist countries. While both examples to a certain degree reflect conflicting perceptions about the forces that drive international relations in a globalizing world, disagreement was contained within the framework of a balanced political partnership.

The complex connections between energy dependence and integration issues in the post-Soviet space is the subject of Margarita M. Balmaceda's account of the role of Russian energy companies in the new Eastern Europe. While Russia seemingly has the upper hand because it supplies energy to Ukraine and Belarus, there is a mutually dependent relationship between the countries, because Russia currently needs Ukraine and Belarus to ship its energy to the West and for domestic political reasons. Russian business power offers the Kremlin the opportunity to pursue its goal of reintegration in the post-Soviet space at the bilateral level of economic and business links, rather than through a variety of weak multilateral institutions like the Commonwealth of Independent States. In economic terms, the growing involvement of Russian energy companies is a stabilizing factor at least in the short term, given that Ukraine and Belarus need Russian energy to keep their industries working. In political terms, however, it complicates an already fragile political landscape, with somewhat different effects in Ukraine as compared with Belarus.

In the case of Ukraine, Balmaceda notes, Russian energy companies have dramatically expanded their influence, resulting in *de facto* Russian control of the oil production and sales chain since 2003. Russian success in acquiring Ukrainian energy assets reflects the calculations of former president Kuchma that the Soviet-built infrastructure in Ukraine can work profitably only as part of a larger market in the post-Soviet space. Russia's state and corporate interests coincided in that both wanted to secure a stable and low-priced transit of Russian oil and gas and contain the influence of Western institutions and businesses. Nevertheless, the Orange Revolution comes as a reminder that, given the pro-Western orientation of Ukraine's leadership, there are limits to how much Russia can exploit the energy dependence of a country that is critical to a stable export of Russian energy to Europe.

The case of Belarus is different, because real economic integration with Russia in the energy sector has not yet taken place. Once again, Balmaceda notes, Russian state and corporate interests work hand in hand: both the Kremlin and Gazprom want to safeguard transit while maintaining political influence. However, serious disagreements over energy supply have increased lately, as the suspension of gas deliveries in 2004 indicates. Although President Aleksandr Lukashenko depends on cheap Russian energy to keep himself in power and the economy of his country afloat, he has proven surprisingly resistant to Russian pressure for privatization of key energy assets. The Kremlin is faced with an authoritarian politician who cannot accept an independent economic power base and shrewdly manipulates the issue of energy interruption as a populist tool to accuse Russia of obstructing the reintegration process the two countries claim they want to achieve. Insofar as Gazprom acts as a tool of state policy and supports the Lukashenko regime, it is bound to reinforce long-term instability in a country with an unclear political future. By helping to keep Lukashenko in power, Russian companies are simply postponing the inevitable crash of an untenable political and economic system in Belarus.

What applies to Eastern Europe is reinforced by the impact of Russian business power in the Caspian and Central Eurasian region. Jeronim Perović demonstrates that Russia has set out to recapture some of its influence with an increasing emphasis on economic means. Russian corporations from the energy sector have emerged as powerful players throughout the region. After more than ten years of disengagement, Perović notes, Russia's relations with these countries, which are plagued by economic weakness and a highly asymmetric dependency on Russian energy and pipelines, have improved markedly. Overall, Russia's economic engagement played a stabilizing role, as it helped to reestablish economic ties, which were severely disrupted after the collapse of the Soviet Union. At the same time, however, as in the case of Belarus, Russian business engagement provided support for the authoritarian regimes of the region, since it allowed them to strengthen their grip on power. Thus, the fact that Russia does not condition its economic engagement on domestic reform or international business standards helps to undermine rather than promote the development of free market practices and democratic institutions that are a precondition for structural economic and social change and for long-term stability.

Russia's important role in the region derives from the relative weakness of its southern neighbors, rather than from its own strength. The Kremlin's increasingly assertive policy of economic engagement, Perović observes, was prompted by outside influence in the form of Western investment in Caspian oil and gas extraction and transportation projects, on the one hand, and the stationing of US troops in Central Asia in the wake of 9/11 on the other. Most conflictive issues in the expansion of Russian business power are linked to Moscow's pipeline policies, rather than to the behavior of Russia's private companies. Gazprom seeks to control as much infrastructure as possible in order to benefit economically from the resale of Central Asian gas. This corporate behavior coincides with the Russian state's interest in gaining political leverage in the region. Russia is unwilling to expand the capacity of pipelines. As a result, the gas trade is highly politicized, with rewards and sanctions determined at a bilateral level through the monolithic structure of Gazprom.

Business expansion, Perović concludes, is more likely to result in conflict if the primary goal is control. In contrast, the expansion of RAO Unified Energy System (UES) into Georgia was driven by economic logic and an interest in a functioning electricity market. This project succeeded in rationalizing a grid with big problems. The fact that the quality of power improved considerably made it a win–win situation for all parties involved, though Georgians fear that Russia's control of their power supply could give the Kremlin leverage over Georgian policies. In the oil sector, LUKoil's behavior is guided by profitability and cost/benefit calculation, reflecting the fact that, in view of increasing Western engagement, Russia is no longer in control of oil flows. Russian state policies, however, remain ambiguous. Although Moscow understands that it has to develop a more cooperative approach, it continues to assert control over oil companies by setting pipeline quotas. In doing so, Russia is playing a delicate game, because its southern neighbors might start to look for export alternatives.

Discussing Russia's relations with Iraq and Iran, Carol R. Saivetz addresses a part of the world in which the extent of mutual Russian state and corporate interests is far less clear than in the post-Soviet space. This difference reflects the fact that these two countries are outside Russia's immediate sphere of influence and not linked to Russia by a Soviet-built infrastructure. As a result, Saivetz notes, the Kremlin often pursues a less than coherent and rather vague policy toward these countries, papering over the contradictory nature of its geopolitical as opposed to financial interests. When Russian companies move into the Middle East, Africa, or North America, the Russian state seems to be more willing to let them operate independently.

In the case of Iraq, in the period leading up to and during the US intervention, geopolitical and economic considerations seemingly coincided. In the context of pervasive feelings in Moscow that Putin had gained nothing for his support of US efforts in Afghanistan, Russia's Iraq policy became a way to undercut US unilateralism. This effort to limit the United States went in parallel with LUKoil's interest in securing its contract from Saddam Hussein's government to develop the West Qurna-2 field. In contrast, the coincidence between geopolitical and economic goals is less than clear-cut in the post-war period. According to Saivetz, Russia needs to curry favor both with the United States and with the Iraqi government if Russian companies are to have a chance of participating in Iraqi reconstruction. At the same time, while it wants neither a US defeat nor a civil war, the Kremlin has an interest in managed instability that constrains US unilateralism. However, such instability limits the ability of Russian corporations to work in Iraq because of their inability to assure the safety of their workers.

In Iran, the main actor is Russia's state-controlled nuclear power industry rather than a private company like LUKoil. While ties with Iran represent a means of countering, within limits, the Bush administration's unilateralism in the Middle East, Iran is also a large market for Russian arms, metals, and nuclear technology. Russia has a strong short-term financial interest in promoting the export of its nuclear power technology. But in the long term, Saivetz warns, pushing for the completion of the nuclear reactor at Bushehr could create a potentially unstable situation that could undermine Russia's national security. The exports of the Russian Atomic Energy Agency, Rosatom, could ultimately help Iran to build a nuclear weapon. Such a development would clearly not be in the interest of the Russian state. Moreover, Saivetz concludes, it would have negative repercussions for Russia's relations with the West.

In examining the case of the Northeast Asian energy trade, Michael J. Bradshaw demonstrates that state–business conflict within Russia undermines transnational energy cooperation in Pacific Russia. Battle over control of Russian energy exports resulted in costly delays in building the capacity to meet Northeast Asia's rapidly expanding energy needs. This failure to deliver energy supplies, Bradshaw argues, increases tension insofar as it pits Chinese against

Japanese energy needs. At the same time, it represents a missed opportunity, given the obvious complementarities between the needs of resource-rich Russia and resource-poor Northeast Asia. If Russia were to become a major supplier of oil and gas in the region, its improved economic position not only would help to defuse fear of Chinese dominance, but could also promote bilateral and multilateral cooperation between state and private actors, reducing the regional potential for conflict.

Although Russia sees the construction of new oil pipelines to Asia as an anchor for the development of the East Siberian region, the priority in recent years was clearly for the reestablishment of the state as primary actor through the destruction of leading private oil companies and the creation of state champions, such as Gazprom and Rosneft. Bradshaw analyzes how Gazprom, using its monopoly and its ties to the state, blocked the development of international projects and maneuvered itself into a position whereby it can influence the scale and the sequencing of Russian energy exports to Northeast Asia. At the same time, the relationship between the state and the private sector (in this case both domestic and foreign) in the oil and gas industry deteriorated markedly. Clearly, the Kremlin wanted strategic control over the development of energy relations with Northeast Asia.

Time is of the essence, however, and the window of opportunity to establish a mutually beneficial energy partnership in the Russian Pacific while the market is still there might close soon. According to Bradshaw, the current focus on an integrated plan that will demand massive investment and bilateral agreements between Russia and countries like China and South Korea bodes ill for the future. Russian state monopolies will have to partner with foreign oil majors to gain access to technology, project management skills, and possibly project financing. Given the current conditions, it is unclear, however, whether the foreign oil companies still want to invest in Russia.

Introducing Part III of this volume, Robert Orttung and Boris Demidov discuss an area of the Russian economy that can compete globally. The current success of the Russian arms industry might be short-lived, however, because the state has not articulated a way for Russian companies to innovate new technologies. As a result of the collapse of domestic sales in the early 1990s, the output of the Russian defense industry was to a large degree determined by foreign purchases, with China and India as the main consumers of Russian arms. Since Putin came to power, the state has increased domestic military purchases and tightened state control over all weapons exports. It is unlikely, Orttung and Demidov hold, that the restructuring of domestic arms manufacturers into large, vertically integrated holding companies will improve the sector's performance.

Although the state has extensive formal control over arms exports, in practice its influence is limited because of the extensive corruption throughout the sector. Orttung and Demidov point out that neither the state nor the weapons producers seem to benefit from the sales. Profits are swallowed by middlemen, leaving no money to fund the urgently needed transformation of an outdated Russian military. Arms sales are driven by a simple money-making logic, but they do not provide long-term development for Russian industry.

An arms industry with a doubtful future, a system of opaque state control of arms exports, widespread corruption throughout the sector, and painstakingly slow military reform are all factors bound to limit the Russian state's capacity to deal successfully with nontraditional security risks. In addition, many arms sales, Orttung and Demidov note, have the potential to increase conflict along Russia's borders. Although the sales of off-the-shelf, obsolete weapons to China seem to provide temporary support for Russian manufacturers, they cannot last and are considered risky because China could eventually pose a threat to Russian security.

William Tompson starts his chapter reminding the reader that the Russian banking sector remains overwhelmingly focused on the domestic market. Russian banks have been neither a source of serious transnational conflict, he finds, nor an important instrument for advancing Russia's foreign policy agenda. At the same time, the weakness of the banking system complicates Russia's integration efforts into the international economy. Unless Russia's elite is prepared to give up the short-term rents that can be gained by manipulating an opaque and undergoverned financial sector, Russia's banking system, Tompson concludes, is likely to remain a drag on economic growth and a source of periodic embarrassment abroad.

The banks have never been a particularly powerful lobby, and since the 1998 financial crisis they have become even less politically prominent. The unreformed state of the sector, however, suits many powerful domestic actors. Russia's banks tend to be tools of other interests rather than independent, profit-oriented businesses. The banking sector is small and fragmented, dominated by federal and regional state structures and characterized by opaque ownership. In stark contrast to Central Europe, there is still little foreign involvement. Conversely, Russian banks have little serious interest in overseas expansion. The most active Russian banks abroad are closely associated with Gazprom and UES.

The story of the banks' role in Russia's diplomacy is a story about their weakness rather than their strength. The sector's failings, highlighting Russia's financial fragility and its dirty business environment, have done considerable damage to the country's image. As an example, Tompson points to the considerable role of Russia's banks in the flight of capital out of the country. Although the prospect of sanctions forced Russia to adopt a new law on combating money laundering, it remains an attractive jurisdiction for individuals and groups interested in laundering the proceeds of criminal activities.

Louise I. Shelley and Svante E. Cornell examine the drug trade as a form of business within Russia and beyond its borders. The enormous and rapid rise in narcotics flows across Russia and the considerable strength of trading networks, they note, come as another demonstration of the state's weakness. Widespread corruption throughout the law enforcement system makes it difficult for the state to exert control over the illegitimate economy. Even worse, the state's own agents – soldiers, police officers, border guards, customs officers – are heavily involved in the drug trade. By not dealing with domestic drug addiction and by the complicity of state agents in the drug trade, Shelley and Cornell conclude, the Russian state is undermining its own security and its capacity to deal successfully with nontraditional security threats.

The globally increasing problem of drug trafficking and consumption has disproportionately affected the countries of the former Soviet Union, owing to weak state institutions, ineffective law enforcement and border controls, a high level of corruption, and a rise of entrenched regional conflicts generated by the demise of the Soviet Union. Shelley and Cornell emphasize that the growing reach of traffickers along Russia's borders and within the country expands the basis for conflict in Russia's relations with the outside world. There is an important link between drugs and violent conflict. The failure of the Russian state to address the drug trade contributes to prolonging regional conflicts, for example in Chechnya and in Afghanistan, and provides funding to separatist and terrorist groups thriving on war economies.

In discussing Russian business activity in Abkhazia and South Ossetia, regions seeking to secede from Georgia, Erik R. Scott analyzes a disturbing example of where Russian business in a conflict-affected country finds itself identified as part of the problem rather than as a potential agent of positive change. The residents in parts of the South Caucasus are faced with entrenched low-intensity conflicts that threaten territorial integrity and contribute to the criminalization of the region's economy by fostering widespread contraband trade. These conflicts have led to situations of *de facto* sovereignty for ethnic groups in Nagorno-Karabakh, Abkhazia, and South Ossetia. The murky status of these statelets means, Scott argues, that they are not only uncontrolled politically, but unregulated by the global financial system.

The continued involvement of Russian licit and illicit business constitutes the main source of economic sustenance and the political legitimacy for the regimes in place there. The economies of Georgia and Russia are closely linked, thanks largely to Soviet trade and transport networks. Russia's economic involvement is characterized by a fundamental asymmetry in which a few politically well-connected Russian actors have a major economic impact. Russian business and the state have a mutual interest in projecting their influence in the countries of the former Soviet Union. The Kremlin increasingly relies on economic, rather than military, leverage to achieve its foreign policy goals in the region. Russia's unwillingness to crack down on unregulated economic activity with the statelets along its borders occurs in the context of tacit political support for the secessionists. According to Scott, Russia essentially has it both ways, claiming officially to back Georgian territorial integrity while allowing some Russian small businesses to support separatist regimes.

In the short term, Scott concedes, the informal economy that has grown up in the absence of formal economic institutions has proven a stabilizing force. This, however, comes at a heavy cost: The criminalization of these entrenched conflicts lays the ground for future instability. The local economies represent postconflict versions of globalized war economies in which low-level violence is directed at establishing and maintaining control of contraband trade networks to fund further operations and enrich a few leaders. For there to be any chance for conflict resolution, Scott argues, the economic interests of Russian business elites active in the statelets must first be addressed. Their interest in prolonging the conflict is a major impediment to a lasting peace settlement. Legitimizing some licit contraband trade may be a first step in providing incentives for future cooperation. The authorities could then focus their efforts on cracking down on the illicit trade in small arms and drugs.

Economic globalization and the rise of the Asian markets are fundamentally reshaping the economic structure of the Russian Far East away from its traditional role as raw materials supplier for Russia's European core toward becoming a resource periphery for Northeast Asia. In examining Russia's reaction to this rapidly changing economic environment, Josh Newell argues that an unstable center–periphery relationship and corrupt state–business alliances pose serious limitations to the development of an economically stable Russian Far East. Putin's primary economic strategy, shaped by the geopolitical goal of counteracting Chinese influence, is to restitch the region to European Russia through a series of oil and gas pipeline projects. Currently, however, the oil and gas sector plays a relatively minor role in the economy of the Russian Far East. Far more important, according to Newell, are fishing, mining, and forestry, in terms of both jobs and revenues. Dealing with these sectors, in contrast to the energy sector, presents a difficult challenge to Moscow, because small and medium-sized enterprises are the primary actors in these industries.

Out of a chaotic privatization process in the early 1990s there emerged a complex network of actors within state institutions, timber companies, traders, and organized crime. These murky alliances, Newell argues, enabled the forestry sector to maintain some stability during a period of tremendous social, economic, and political upheaval. Yet over time, these corrupt alliances evolved into institutionalized norms, depriving Russia of much-needed tax revenues, jobs, and improvement of the quality of forest management and use. Moreover, the window of opportunity for the development of an internationally competitive wood-processing sector might be rapidly closing. Russia runs the danger of getting bogged down in an unsustainable development model: Russian companies supply the logs, while Chinese businesses process them into semifinished and finished goods for domestic use and export. Unstable property rights and ownership regimes, Newell concludes, prove hostile to long-term private-sector stability within the Russian Far East.

The extensive black market also negatively affects Russia's relations with its Northeast Asian neighbors. Rife corruption in the Far Eastern forestry sector, Newell argues, broadens the basis for conflict with China. Rising public resentment about exports of jobs and lost profits across borders could undermine the current stability. Perceived economic dominance by China may reinforce long-held concerns about Chinese migration. Against this background, timber-sector reform presents itself as a means to increase security and stability along Russia's eastern borders.

## Conclusions

In conceptual terms, Russia's political elites recognize that the country's main security threats stem from its internal development and that economic recovery alone will provide the basis for a long-term revival of Russia. In practice, however, both Russia's capacity to deal with nontraditional security threats and the depth and quality of its structural integration into a globalized world remain seriously hampered by an unfinished and unstable regulatory environment and by opaque and often highly corrupt alliances among state representatives, businessmen, and organized crime groups. Russia's domestic transformation continues to have significant implications for the peaceful management of political conflict at all levels.

### The energy sector: state-controlled business power and regional stability

This book stresses the important distinction between the energy sector and the other sectors of the Russian economy in assessing the impact of Russian business power on the balance of transnational conflict and cooperation. In the area of energy, a structured relationship between a strong state and an increasingly centralized business community translates into mutual interest in expanding Russia's economic and political power across its borders. Clearly, it is the energy sector that dominates the rapid expansion of the foreign operations of Russian business. Business power in this sector is vested in the state as the single source of sovereignty, and is brought to bear through state-owned or state-controlled monopolies and basic infrastructure dependencies going back to Soviet times. Even large private companies like LUKoil have little choice but to take state wishes into account.

The state wants extensive control over the energy sector because energy is perceived as strategically too important to be left to the market. While such state control is not unusual for resource-rich countries, the balance of control has clearly shifted away from the private sector toward the state in Russia, as recent instances of heavy-handed state intervention against private oil companies have made clear. Overall, this development tends to bode ill for the chances of transnational energy cooperation. Russia's private energy companies are more likely to globalize and invest outside the country, seeking bigger profits. At the same time, their move abroad often must be understood as part of a strategy to keep their assets out of reach of the Russian state. Conversely, state-owned companies tend to be more static and less reform oriented. The very fact that they do not need additional "protection" makes them also more prone to corruption.

The chapters dealing with energy issues in this book lead to two clear conclusions. The first is that business power promoted cooperation in the stable framework of EU–Russian relations and played an economically stabilizing role in the post-Soviet space, given the economic instabilities and the general social and political weakness of the post-Soviet transition countries. Improving stability in the former Soviet area in particular is no small achievement in view of the considerable economic, social, and political upheaval and the amount of violent conflict that the former states of the Soviet Union have witnessed. However, while the EU–Russian energy trade occurs in the framework of mutual dependencies and a balanced political relationship, Russia's energy trade in the post-Soviet space evolves in the framework of asymmetric power relationships with its neighbors – an issue that will be further addressed below.

The second conclusion, however, is less encouraging: the short-term stability promoting effects of business power, due to an emphasis on state control over energy resources, may well undermine the long-term political stability in the New Eastern Europe and in the Caucasus and Central Asia. It is asymmetric dependency – symbolized most visibly in a highly politicized management of the pipeline infrastructure – rather than a clear vision of regional order that allowed Moscow to increase its influence across its borders. The fact that Russian business power in the area of energy operates without an agenda for structural economic and social reform complicates the already very fragile political landscape of these regions.

The approach of this book to review energy dependencies across different geographical areas will draw the reader's attention to the fact that the role of Russian business power in the area of energy depends not only on the domestic context, but also on the particular characteristics of any given regional environment. In fact, Russian energy companies play a different game in different regions. The case of the EU–Russian energy trade demonstrates that in the context of a balanced and stable political relationship, Russian energy companies are able to provide services on a fairly professional and relatively transparent basis, thereby broadening the basis for cooperative engagement across borders. Mutually robust state and corporate interests compel the Russian state to seek compromise with its energy companies when their foreign interests cause friction in terms of Russia's foreign relations. Within the context of a stable institutional environment, it is in the interest of both the Russian state and Russia's energy companies to find a compromise with the EU countries rather than let interest conflicts escalate into wider identity conflicts.

In contrast to Russian–EU relations, the energy trade in the post-Soviet space is highly politicized, reflecting an asymmetric power relationship between Russia and its neighbors on the one hand, and the geopolitics and geo-economics of global energy security on the other. What Russia and its energy companies want is political influence and market share. In economic terms, the foreign operations of Russian energy companies promote stability insofar as most CIS countries depend on a functioning energy market with Russia in terms of domestic consumption and their economic survival (revenues through export or transit tariffs); in political terms, however, they tend to create tension because they are inseparable from the Kremlin's drive to control the regional market and dominate the post-Soviet space. Although there is a high level of convergence between state and corporate interests, the potential for political tension as a result of Russian energy operations across borders is higher in the case of the state-owned monopolies in the field of gas (Gazprom) and oil pipelines (Transneft) than in the case of private companies. Where Russia controls uncontested monopolies, it has no incentive to compromise.

While asymmetric energy dependencies give Russia a relative advantage over most CIS states, they do not in any easy way translate into concrete foreign policy achievements. The manipulation of blurred borders between businesses, both legal and illegal, and state structures to further foreign policy goals is a two-way street, as the case of Belarus under Lukashenko demonstrates. Happily, growing international investment, multiple pipeline options, and increasing Russian reliance on CIS resources have helped to moderate the Russian state's behavior. Russian companies have to adapt as well, and are increasingly forced to invest in international projects or alternative pipeline projects.

Despite some positive signs in other areas, the case of the Far Eastern energy trade is one of missed opportunities. This failure reflects state priorities that for a long time neglected Moscow's relations to both the Russian Pacific and its Asian neighbors. Only now is Russia beginning to think strategically about energy options, and it is an open question whether it will succeed in establishing a workable framework for a future energy trade between resource-rich Pacific Russia and resource-poor Northeast Asia. So far, the balance sheet is mixed at best: The state–business battle over control of Russian energy brought transnational energy cooperation in Pacific Russia to a standstill. In addition, weak state capacity and opaque state–business relations are obstacles to the establishment of a mutually beneficial energy partnership, thereby increasing the potential for tension in Northeast Asia.

### *The other sectors: murky business alliances and long-term instability*

In the nonenergy sectors of the economy, murky business alliances among state structures and criminal groups tend to undermine long-term stability within Russia and along its borders. The status quo reflects the fact that these sectors are marked by a generally weak, often highly corrupt state and an amorphous business community, including legitimate as well as illegitimate actors. The consolidation of the regulatory environment in most of these sectors has been slow. More often than not, the social and institutional environment is less than conducive for structural economic reform. The level of corruption and the number of politicians and oligarchs with a criminal past will clearly have to be reduced before Russian business power can become a more positive force of social and economic change.

The three relevant conclusions that can be drawn from the chapters of Part III of this book all point to the negative impact of Russian business power on the dynamics of transnational conflict and cooperation. The first is that corrupt state–business alliances seriously limit Russia's capacity to develop a stable economic system, as demonstrated by the case of timber in the Russian Far East. More generally, the unfinished and unstable nature of Russia's domestic institutions makes it unlikely that Russia will be able to use its energy export revenues successfully to develop sustainable growth patterns and an advanced manufacturing and high-tech industry. Russia therefore runs the risk of being integrated into the world economy as an energy and raw material producer, increasing the basis for political instability within and across its borders.

The second conclusion is that the distinct link between the Russian state and Russian business in all its forms seriously limits Russia's capacity to deal with nontraditional security threats. Widespread corruption makes it impossible for the state to control the illegitimate economy. The fact that the state's own agents are heavily involved in the illicit trade with drugs and corrupt arms sales undermines Russia's security and its capacity to address transborder issues like migration pressure, transnational terrorism, or the illegal flow of money.

The third conclusion is that Russia's inability and unwillingness to control unregulated economic activity across its borders prolong violent conflict in parts of the fragile states south of Russia's borders and broaden the basis for political conflict in the Far East. Russia is currently unable to do much about these problems because of its limited state capacity. More troubling is the seeming lack of interest among top policy makers to take effective measures to deal with this weakness.

### Russian business power: institutional weakness versus Great Power status

The rise of Russian business power across Russian borders remains troubled by the dilemma between Russia's institutional weakness and its Great Power legacy. On the one hand, Russia's institutional weakness feeds into many nontraditional cross-border security problems, in which Russia's often corrupt business-state alliances are heavily involved. The Russian state either has too little capacity or is not willing to deal with these complex problems. On the other hand, Russia's claim to its Great Power status – apart from its membership in the UN Security Council and its nuclear arsenal – is closely tied to its energy resources. As a consequence, the Russian state values control over Russian energy companies and over energy assets (reserves and pipelines) in the former Soviet republics not only in a narrow economic sense, but also in a much broader geopolitical context.

The dilemma between Russia's institutional weakness and its Great Power legacy is mirrored in the contradictory impact of Russian business power on the balance of transnational conflict and cooperation. Although there is evidence for a generally stabilizing role of the Russian energy trade along its southern borders, there are clear cases, for instance in Abkhazia and South Ossetia, in which the interests of Russian business prolong entrenched low-level regional conflict. Clearly, the potential for violent conflict emanates from the domestic political, social, and economic turmoil within the countries of these regions themselves, rather than from Russia's economic engagement. At the same time, it is fair to say that corrupt business–state alliances severely limit the cooperative potential of Russian business power.

We see the same dynamic at work in the Russian Far East. The Russian state concentrates on gaining strategic control over energy resources as an anchor for the development of the East Siberian and Far East regions and as a basis for building an energy partnership with Northeast Asian states. At the same time, extensive black market structures in the economically far more important sectors of fishing, mining, and forestry undermine economic growth within Russia and broaden the basis for conflict in Russia's relations with its neighbors. Clearly, the potential for transnational energy cooperation depends also on the foreign policies of countries like China, Japan, and South Korea and on investment decisions of foreign oil majors. Once again, however, it is obvious that state–business conflict within Russia severely limits the cooperative potential of Russia's business power.

The basic problem for Russia's business power is that the state is primarily concerned with the short-term challenge of establishing strategic control over the energy sector, and neglects the long-term challenge of building a stable regulatory environment for doing business. Yet the institutional inability and political unwillingness to expand the regulatory environment into the nonenergy sectors of the Russian economy has its price: the fact that Great Power energy politics overshadows the management of nontraditional cross-border security problems complicates Russia's relations with those parts of the Western world that are most directly engaged in cooperative endeavors to limit transnational risks. At the same time, local and regional actors opt for greater control over local security issues, causing further problems for the management of regional crises and transnational security threats.

A vicious circle is thus at work here: The longer these nontraditional security problems accumulate unchecked, the higher the risk that they could undermine Russia's security and give rise to increased regional instability. The murky state–business relationship in Russia seriously limits the potential of Russian business power as an agent of positive change in the dynamic context of conflict and cooperation within Russia and along its borders.

## Notes

I would like to thank Robert Orttung, Jeronim Perović, and Victor Mauer for their comments on previous drafts of this chapter.

1 See, for example, Bobo Lo, *Vladimir Putin and the Evolution of Russian Foreign Policy*, London: Blackwell, 2003; Bobo Lo, *Russian Foreign Policy in the Post-Soviet Era: Reality, Illusion and Mythmaking*, London: Palgrave, 2002; Gabriel Gorodetsky, ed., *Russia between East and West: Russian Foreign Policy on the Threshold of the Twenty-first Century*, London: Frank Cass, 2003; Robert H. Donaldson and Joseph L. Nogee, *The Foreign Policy of Russia: Changing Systems, Enduring Interests*, Armonk, NY: M. E. Sharpe, 2002; Michael Mandelbaum, *The New Russian Foreign Policy*, New York: Council on Foreign Relations, 1998; Celeste A. Wallan-

der, ed., *The Sources of Russian Foreign Policy after the Cold War*, Boulder, CO: Westview, 1996; Neil Malcolm, *Internal Factors in Russian Foreign Policy*, Oxford: Oxford University Press, 1996.

2 See, for example, Timothy Frye, *Brokers and Bureaucrats: Building Market Institutions in Russia*, Ann Arbor: University of Michigan Press, 2000; David E. Hoffman, *The Oligarchs: Wealth and Power in the New Russia*, New York: Public Affairs, 2002; Vadim Volkov, *Violent Entrepreneurs: The Use of Force in the Making of Russian Capitalism*, Ithaca, NY: Cornell University Press, 2002; Thane Gustafson, *Capitalism Russian-Style*, Cambridge: Cambridge University Press, 1999; Marshall I. Goldman, *The Piratization of Russia: Russian Reform Goes Awry*, London: Routledge, 2003; Chrystia Freeland, *Sale of the Century: Russia's Wild Ride from Communism to Capitalism*, New York: Crown Business, 2000; Rose Brady, *Kapitalizm: Russia's Struggle to Free Its Economy*, New Haven, CT: Yale University Press, 1999; and David Satter, *Darkness at Dawn: The Rise of the Russian Criminal State*, New Haven, CT: Yale University Press, 2003.

3 See, for example, Allan Gerson and Nat J. Colletta, *Privatizing Peace: From Conflict to Security*, Ardsley, NY: Transnational Publishers, 2002; Jan Nelson, *The Business of Peace: The Private Sector as Partner in Conflict Prevention and Resolution*, International Alert, Council on Economic Priorities, and the Prince of Wales International Business Leaders Forum, 2000; Virginia Haufler, "Is There a Role for Business in Conflict Management?" in Chester A. Crocker, Fen Osler Hampson, and Pamela Aall, eds., *Turbulent Peace: The Challenges of Managing International Conflict*, Washington, DC: United States Institute of Peace Press, 2001, pp. 659–675.

4 See, for example, Joseph S. Nye and John D. Donahue, eds., *Governance in a Globalizing World*, Washington, DC: Brookings Institution Press, 2000.

5 On the widening concept of international security, see Barry Buzan, Ole Waever, and Jaap de Wilde, *Security: A New Framework for Analysis*, Boulder, CO: Lynne Rienner, 1998.

6 See, for example, Scott Pegg, "The Cost of Doing Business: Transnational Corporations and Violence in Nigeria," *Security Dialogue* 30, no. 4, 1999, pp. 473–484; Jedrzej George Frynas, "Political Instability and Business: Focus on Shell in Nigeria," *Third World Quarterly* 19, no. 3, 1998, pp. 457–478.

7 See P. W. Singer, "Corporate Warriors: The Rise of the Privatized Military Industry and Its Ramifications for International Security," *International Security* 26, no. 3, 2001/2002, pp. 186–220; Damian Lilly, *The Privatization of Security and Peacebuilding: A Framework for Action*, London: International Alert, September 2000.

8 On the notion of human security, see United Nations Development Programme, *Human Development Report 1994: New Dimensions of Human Security*, New York: Oxford University Press, 1994; Roland Paris, "Human Security: Paradigm Shift or Hot Air?" *International Security* 26, no. 2, 2001, pp. 87–102.

9 See, for example, Andreas Wenger and Daniel Möckli, *Conflict Prevention: The Untapped Potential of the Business Sector*, Boulder, CO: Lynne Rienner, 2003.

10 See, for example, Peter Rutland, ed., *Business and the State in Contemporary Russia*, Boulder, CO: Westview Press, 2001.

11 See Joseph S. Nye, "Soft Power," *Foreign Policy* 80, 1990, pp. 153–171; Robert O. Keohane and Joseph S. Nye, "Power and Interdependence in the Information Age," *Foreign Affairs* 77, no. 5, 1998, pp. 81–94; Joseph S. Nye and William A. Owens, "America's Information Age," *Foreign Affairs* 75, no. 2, 1996, pp. 20–36; Joseph S. Nye, *Soft Power: The Means to Success in World Politics*, New York: Public Affairs, 2004.

# 2 The role of business in Russian foreign and security relations

*Robert W. Orttung*

Since the collapse of the Soviet Union, Russia has developed a powerful business community and a potent network of transnational organized crime groups. These new actors are having a significant impact on the evolution of the Russian state and its foreign relations.[1] The scope of these new entities is extensive, including well-known gigantic energy and metals companies, small-scale businesses involved in exporting logs illegally across Russia's porous borders, and organized crime groups working in Russia and a variety of other countries. Moreover, Russian businessmen are now active in the policy-making processes of neighboring countries.

Several examples show the breadth of these new relationships:

- Gazprom supplies 25 percent of Europe's natural gas;
- Yukos purchased the only oil refinery in the Baltic states in 2002;
- On 1 June 2004, Georgian president Mikhail Saakashvili appointed Kakha Bendukidze, an ethnic Georgian who rose to become one of Russia's top businessmen, as state minister for economic reform in Georgia;
- Increasingly larger supplies of narcotics from Afghanistan are flowing into Russia for local customers and on to the West as part of the global drug trade.

This analysis combines legal and illegal business, because in contemporary Russia it is increasing difficult to draw a bright line between the two. Many of Russia's current companies got their start in the murky underworld of the shadow economy and continue to maintain ties to it. Likewise, many criminal enterprises now are seeking to launder their previous earnings through the legitimate economy and the political system. Since large sums of money flow back and forth between the legitimate and illegitimate economies, it is impossible to understand one without taking into account the other. Naturally, these processes affect, and are affected by, the state. Corruption of state institutions touches all sectors of the economy and it is necessary to take this factor into account as well.

The state–business–crime nexus is not restricted to domestic Russian politics since it has an enormous impact across Russian borders. To understand Russia's relations with its neighbors and other parts of the world, it is necessary first of all to understand how the Russian state interacts with business in all of its legitimate and illegitimate incarnations. Today it is impossible to separate the state from business corporations and crime groups in Russia. They are in a continual process of manipulating each other and affecting the country's foreign relations in myriad ways, some of which are described in this volume.

The first section of this chapter provides an overview of what constitutes Russian business today. The discussion then defines some of the key characteristics of Russian business that distinguish it from the business communities of other countries. The third section looks at the congruent and opposing interests of the Russian state and business in terms of foreign policy. The final section lays out a typology of state–business interactions that serves as an organizing theme for the subsequent chapters in the book. This typology distinguishes between the energy sector and the other parts of the Russian economy, focusing on the strength of the state and the coherence of the business community. This background information leads into the case studies of the book, which show how business in Russia affects the level of conflict and cooperation in Russian foreign relations.

## What is Russian business? Legitimate and illegitimate components

In this book, we conceptualize "business" in the widest possible meaning as including both legitimate companies and organized crime, since the division between the two is often blurred in Russian reality. Using this definition of business allows us to bring together in one book subjects that are not ordinarily discussed simultaneously, such as LUKoil and the drug trade in Russia. Looking at the full spectrum of these various forms of business makes it possible to better assess the impact of Russian business on Russia's overall foreign relations.

When Russia became an independent country at the end of 1991, it had essentially no independent business community. However, through an extremely controversial process of privatization during the early 1990s, Russia formed powerful business groups that now influence key areas of state policy. These groups have evolved considerably through the economic crisis of 1998, the ascent of Putin to Russia's presidency, and the arrest of Mikhail Khodorkovsky, Russia's most successful businessman, but they remain key players.[2] A host of small and medium-sized enterprises have also developed over the past few years. At the same time, organized crime has grown dramatically as a separate entity and through links to legitimate business.

Private companies and well-defined crime groups with transnational ties did not exist during the Soviet period and have only begun to assert themselves in the past 15 years. While economic interests have always been present in the policy-making process, the appearance of legally defined corporations and tightly organized crime groups has created concrete institutions that can articulate and lobby for specific corporate and criminal interests in the Russian halls of power. These entities also take action abroad, with or without the consent of the Russian state.

### Legitimate business

Russian business appeared shortly before the collapse of the Soviet Union. The Soviet leader, Mikhail Gorbachev, permitted the establishment of *kooperativs*, independent small businesses, in the late 1980s. Soon banks appeared which were able to accumulate vast fortunes by taking advantage of the spiraling inflation unleashed by the decision of acting Prime Minister Yegor Gaidar's government to liberalize prices. The bankers were able to use their insider access to the Yeltsin administration eventually to obtain some of the most valuable and profitable oil and metals enterprises that had been owned by the Russian state.[3] The overall economic situation was extremely unstable, however, and the financial crisis of 1998 eliminated many Russian firms that had grown rich speculating on Russian debt markets. The 1998 crisis ultimately helped the Russian economy, because the value of the Russian ruble dropped by 75 percent in relation to foreign currencies, giving Russian business an incentive to switch from unproductive speculation to manufacturing real goods, as imports were now much more expensive. However, despite this stimulus, continued reform of the Russian economy, has largely been put on hold thanks to the high price of oil, which brings windfall profits to Russia and reduces the urgency of introducing needed structural changes.

Today, Russia has one of the most concentrated economies in the world: the 22 largest business groups control about 40 percent of Russian industry.[4] These large firms are divided into two groups: state-owned monopolies, and private firms. State-owned monopolies in natural gas (Gazprom), electricity (Unified Energy System – UES), and oil pipelines (Transneft) dominate the economy. President Putin has sought to strengthen state management of these firms, achieving only mixed results, as indicated by the low share price of firms like Gazprom compared to other energy companies on international markets. A group of large private companies, such as Yukos, LUKoil, Sibneft, Norilsk Nickel, Base Element, Alfa Group, and a handful of others, round out a tiny but powerful elite. These firms often have close ties to the high state officials, but the state's effective destruction of Yukos shows what can happen when these relations go sour.

Small business is important for this analysis of business and Russia's foreign behavior, because some small businesses play a significant transborder role. This sector of the Russian economy largely operates in the shadows and has not grown nearly as fast as its counterparts in Eastern Europe.[5] These businesses seek to avoid the onerous registration requirements that greedy bureaucrats impose on them, and shakedowns by organized crime groups.[6] As a result, debate rages over the number of small businesses in Russia. Official Goskomstat figures suggest that expansion of the small business sector leveled off in 1995 and that the sector has grown very slowly since then.[7] Other observers argue that visible changes in the life of Russian cities suggest that there are many more small businesses now than there used to be. Economic Development Minister German Gref estimated in spring 2005 that small business accounted for 10–12 percent of Russia's gross domestic product (GDP) and 17–19 percent of the labor force.[8]

In corporate foreign operations, Russian small businesses work in a variety of spheres, including, for example, the fruit and vegetable trade in the separatist regions of Georgia bordering Russia, and forestry in Siberia and the Far East, often using corrupt ties to state officials. In some ways, these businesses can serve larger Russian goals, such as undermining the power of the legitimate Georgian central government in Tbilisi, which has poor relations with Russia. (See the discussion in Erik Scott's chapter in this book, Chapter 11.) In others ways, though, the small firms undermine Russian interests, particularly by exporting unprocessed timber, depriving Russian workers of the opportunity to use these resources in creating jobs in Russian factories. (See Josh Newell's chapter, Chapter 12.)

Foreign business is also a player in Russia, particularly in certain parts of the country and in specific sectors. Oil companies are having a major impact in the Far East's Sakhalin Island. In the biggest deal yet in Russia, in February 2003 British Petroleum agreed to pay $6.15 billion for a 50 percent stake in the Tiumen Oil Company (TNK).[9] (See Michael Bradshaw's chapter, Chapter 7.) Food processors, automobile manufacturers, and a large variety of other firms have set up shop in Russia as well, contributing in particular to regions like Novgorod and Leningrad *oblasti*. Some flight capital that left Russia has subsequently returned to the country, often disguised as "foreign investment" from such offshore zones as Cyprus.[10]

### Criminal business

In Russia, the line between legitimate business and criminal business is often blurred. Since the mid-1990s, many firms that built up their initial capital in the criminal sphere have begun entering the legitimate economy, making it difficult to classify them as legitimate or illegitimate.[11] Some firms have distanced themselves from the criminal activities of their past, while others continue to employ criminal methods to resolve their problems. At the same time, Russian firms frequently engage in operations across a variety of economic sectors, some of which are entirely legitimate while others are not. Therefore, one firm could have separate units, some engaged in legitimate work and others engaged in the underground economy. Of course, Russia is not unique in this combination of legitimate and criminal business. An analogous situation can be found in the Mexican economy, for example.

Criminal links to the authorities through corruption are extensive. According to the annual reports of Transparency International, the situation is not improving.[12] Moreover, Putin's policies of centralizing state power, minimizing public oversight, and cracking down on media freedom are only making the situation worse along the lines of Klitgaard's famous formula, according to which the level of corruption = monopoly + discretion – accountability.[13]

Large sections of the economy remain in the shadows, with estimates of the size of the black market ranging as high as 50 percent of gross domestic product, which was $582 billion in 2004.[14] One methodologically sophisticated approach put the size of the black economy at 45 percent in 2000–2001, while World Bank officials estimate the figure at somewhere between 40 and 50 percent.[15] Official Russian estimates for 2002 claimed that the shadow economy was 23 percent of GDP, though they were inclined to increase this figure.[16] Many businesses large and small do not pay their full taxes, though large companies have increased their payments since the Kremlin crackdown on Yukos began.[17] There are large profitable sectors that are entirely criminalized, including the drug trade, illegal weapons sales, illicit trade in metals, and much of the forestry sector. The authorities have made little serious effort to combat money laundering, which is performed through numerous banks, a growing number of casinos throughout the country, and even via firms ostensibly set up to provide security services. The trading sphere is also heavily criminalized, including the import of fruits and vegetables from the South Caucasus and the extensive trade in Chinese consumer goods and Japanese automobiles.

At the beginning of 2005, the Russian authorities identified 116 operational "criminal societies," each of which was essentially an umbrella organization bringing together dozens of criminal groups.[18] Such organized crime groups are active in the majority of Russia's key economic sectors, according to Minister for Internal Affairs Rashid Nurgaliev.[19] In 2004, the authorities identified more than 4,000 cases in which criminal groups took over property illegally. Usually, such statistics only reveal the tip of the iceberg, and Nurgaliev complained that this figure came nowhere near measuring the real state of affairs.[20]

While Russia garners a lot of bad press for the extent of criminalization within its economy, the processes taking place there are not entirely different from the historical evolution of the United States. Organized crime played a major role in the development of the economies of most US cities. In New York City, for example, Italian mafia crime groups had extensive influence over key sectors of the economy such as freight handling at JFK airport, waste removal, the Fulton Fish market, and a variety of other areas. Scholars are only beginning to acknowledge the extent to which organized crime penetrated US urban areas.[21]

### Transnational activities of Russian business

At the end of the 1980s, fewer than 500 Soviet enterprises operated abroad.[22] Now the situation has changed considerably. Thousands of Russian firms have begun operations in a wide variety of countries around the globe. An even greater number are involved in export operations.

The majority of the leading actors in this field are in the natural resources sector (Alrosa, Gazprom, Group Alliance, Itera, LUKoil, RusAL, UES, Yukos).

Nevertheless, firms in other industries have become active internationally in the past few years. In 2002–2003, other members of the top 15 external Russian investors included three automotive producers, a firm dealing with information and communications technology, a telecom operator, an insurance company, and a food producer.[23]

According to official United Nations Conference on Trade and Development statistics, Russia's stock of outward foreign direct investment at the end of 2003 was almost $52 billion, making Russia the world's 21st largest outward investor.[24] Russia was in 17th place for new projects started in 2003, ahead of countries like Finland, Turkey, and Denmark. Russian firms tend to be larger and more transnationalized than the typical transnational firms of Central and Eastern Europe.

These official estimates represent only a small fraction of Russia's outflows, since capital flight from the country following the collapse of the Soviet Union is variously estimated at between $150 billion and $300 billion (see William Tompson's chapter, Chapter 9).[25] Although Russian investments abroad are relatively small by international standards, the country plays a big role in the transition economies of the former Soviet Union and the former socialist bloc.

Russian crime groups began to develop a serious presence outside the borders of the then Soviet Union in 1989, when the Soviet leadership made it possible for individuals to export hard currency, lifting a previous ban on such practices.[26] This shift launched the larger flow of Russian crime into Europe and North America. The new law also opened the gates for a flood of shuttle traders, with many Russians traveling to a variety of countries to purchase cheap goods and then resell them on the Russian market for a profit. Soon thereafter, Russian prostitution appeared in Europe, usually controlled by Russian or Caucasus-based pimps. Criminalized business quickly evolved into alcohol and drugs and then to oil, aluminum, and weapons. Groups with extensive technical expertise are involved in a variety of financial crimes. In 1997, the Center for Strategic and International Studies (CSIS) Task Force Report found that there were 200 large, sophisticated Russian organized crime groups operating worldwide and that they had relations with criminal counterparts in 50 countries.[27] Key targets for the crime groups include the United States, Germany, Switzerland, Italy, Poland, Cyprus, and Israel. In 2005, the Russian Ministry of Internal Affairs (MVD) set as one of its top priorities the task of depriving organized crime groups of the influence they currently exercise in the energy complex, significant public projects, and export operations.[28]

Smuggling remains a major problem, particularly along Russia's southern and western borders. Drugs are the most important commodity, since they provide extensive revenues for crime groups; facilitate the spread of AIDS in Russia; undermine the health of Russian youth, contributing to the country's larger demographic crisis; and generate funds for terrorist financing (see the chapter by Louise Shelley and Svante Cornell, Chapter 10). While official Russia may have difficulty getting along with its Commonwealth of Independent States (CIS) neighbors, crime groups straddling the border face no such problems. In fact, there seems to be increasing interethnic cooperation among such groups. Whereas Central Asian groups in the past were often extremely closed along ethnic lines, they are now working much more tightly with ethnic Russians. Such ethnic Russian partners are particularly helpful in carrying drugs across the border because they attract less attention than the Central Asians do.[29] In sectors such as forestry, there are numerous small companies focused on cutting down trees and sending them to foreign buyers.[30] Moreover, the MVD claims that there are 60,000 Russian firms registered in international tax havens. These firms are seeking to avoid paying Russian taxes and perhaps laundering money and avoiding prosecution in Russian courts.

In his 1999 book *Capitalism Russian-Style,* Thane Gustafson suggested that the Russian crime epidemic would subside when the causes are removed, namely when "society settles into a new order, as relations between state and private sector evolve and stabilize, and as the massive transfer of rent and property is completed."[31] Unfortunately, in the wake of Beslan and Putin's subsequent decision to eliminate the direct elections of Russia's governors, the Yukos affair, and the ongoing restructuring of Russia's key industrial sectors, it is hard to see any substantial reduction in crime levels soon. At the beginning of 2005, Russian society had lost the stability it had seemed to acquire in the first years of the decade, state–business relations are equally undefined in the wake of the destruction of Yukos, and property is still an object of constant battle.

## Characteristics of Russian business

The main characteristics that make Russian business distinctive from business in typical Western countries are the nature of property rights in Russia, the lobbying process, questions of ownership, and the personalized nature of many large Russian firms. The following sections explain these differences in greater detail.

### Property rights

Knowing about the way that the Russian business sector developed is extremely important for understanding the role that business plays in Russian foreign relations.[32] What is important about the Russian process of privatization and new business creation is that the transition from a socialist economy took place in a largely lawless environment. Successful businesspeople accumulated large sums of capital using methods that may or may not have been legal.[33] Since the legality of the methods used to acquire this property was never confirmed, the owners have no security in the belief that they will be able to hold on to it. Their property rights depend entirely on the whims of state officials and whether they will simply leave the status quo as it is or decide to prosecute some of the most successful businessmen active during the first part of the 1990s. As a result, even apparently legitimate businesses exist under a cloud of uncertainty about their origins. The system works to keep people off balance because they never know whether they have clear property rights.

Not only did businessmen operate in a situation in which their property rights were called into question, they also faced questions of public legitimacy. As in other countries, powerful businessmen in Russia are extremely unpopular and there is a widespread belief that they obtained their wealth through illegitimate means. In the 2003 State Duma elections, for example, Putin was able to use his campaign against Yukos president Mikhail Khodorkovsky and other oligarchs in order to increase the popularity of his United Russia party.

In short, Russian corporations developed in a way that deprived them of a solid legal institutionalization. The lack of clear property rights makes Russian corporations vulnerable to attacks by the state and other corporations seeking to grab their assets. In compiling a list of the most powerful oligarchs in Russia at the end of 2004, the journal *Kompaniia* concluded that "the oligarchs of the Putin era are increasingly dependent on how close they are to the head of state."[34] The oligarchs have no choice but to remain in politics. Government decisions frequently impact their business interests, as do the decisions of lower-level officials.[35]

This evolutionary path predisposed Russian firms to certain kinds of behavior. Since state actions are so unpredictable, corporations necessarily seek ways to protect themselves from bureaucratic arbitrariness, as discussed in greater detail in what follows. They are also inclined to engage in aggressive behavior abroad to further bolster their position.

### The lobbying process

Russia is not unique in having the state play an important role in shaping the nature of the business community. In various Latin American countries, the accumulated actions of the state played a major role in determining whether the business community has much say in shaping a country's policies, including the negotiation of trading zones. Ben Ross Schneider's study of five Latin American countries concluded that the "state organized or disorganized business."[36] Russia fits this model well.

Though Russian business behavior abroad is shaped by its relations with the state, it is important to remember that the state in Russia is not a unified and coherent actor. As different elite groups battle for control over the institutions of the state, the victories of one or another group have a major impact on the actions of Russian companies abroad. The example of Lithuania's Mazeiku Nafta, the only oil refinery in the three Baltic republics, is a useful case in point. Lithuania originally sold the plant to Williams, an American company. However, the Americans could not make the plant work, because they could not guarantee it consistent oil supplies, which could only come from Russia. From 1999 to 2002, LUKoil sought to gain control of this refinery. It had powerful backers in Moscow who were able to cut off oil supplies to the plant nine times in order to exert pressure on Lithuania to sell it to the Russian company.[37] However, Yukos was also able to line up its own backers in Moscow and was able to acquire a controlling interest in the plant on 19 September 2002.[38] Yukos supplied oil to the refinery until it fell out of favor with Putin and the Kremlin launched its attack on the firm.[39] In the wake of the Kremlin assault on Yukos, oil supplies to the plant again came into doubt and the stock price of the refinery dropped 22.5 percent in a single week in August 2004.[40]

In the case of Yukos, the fate of the company's investment abroad clearly lies with the firm's relationship to the Russian state. Lithuanian observers wonder what will happen with companies like LUKoil and MDM, which are big investors in the country, in the post-Yukos environment. While they had good relations with the Kremlin at the beginning of 2005, it is not clear whether they will be able to maintain those relations in the future.

The blurring of business and the state is clear in the ways that businessmen have decided to gain public office as a method for protecting their business interests. At the beginning of 2005, 13 of Russia's 89 governors were businessmen.[41] Many more businessmen are incumbent in national and regional legislatures. According to the Russian-language *Finance* magazine, 22 of the 468 ruble billionaires on its 2005 list are State Duma members, ten are Federation Council members, and three are governors.[42] Businessmen take these offices because the normal process of lobbying does not work in Russia.[43] It would be too expensive for a businessman to purchase influence on individual decisions, so ultimately it is easier for them simply to become public officials themselves. As a result, the main rules that govern the lobbying process are unwritten and the overall process is very opaque.

Yukos was one of the most successful lobbyists in asserting its own interests vis-à-vis the Russian state before the Kremlin launched a crackdown on it. For example, it had enormous clout in the State Duma that served from 1999 to 2003, and could block state initiatives that harmed its interests, such as efforts to increase taxes on the oil sector. Of course, not all businessmen have the resources to gain public office as a way of promoting their business interests. Many simply try to avoid any contact with the state as a way of protecting themselves.

More recently, state bureaucrats have been moving into the business sector, taking over key industries. Presidential chief of staff Dmitry Medvedev has long headed the board of Gazprom. But in 2004, deputy presidential administration head Igor Sechin was named chairman of the board at Rosneft and deputy presidential administration head Vladislav Surkov became board chairman of Transnefteprodukt, the oil pipeline monopoly. Presidential foreign policy adviser Sergei Prikhodko became chairman of the board of directors of TVEL, the primary nuclear fuel exporter. In other sectors, Viktor Ivanov, a high-ranking member of the president's staff, was appointed to the board of Aeroflot and Almaz-Antei Air Defense, and presidential aide Igor Shuvalov was appointed to the board of Russia's railroad monopoly, which was recently converted from a ministry into a 100 percent state-owned firm.[44]

## *Ownership*

Another key issue in defining Russian corporations is ownership. Russian companies often set up very opaque ownership structures, hiding the true owners of the company through a series of shell companies. Such a complicated system makes it difficult for the state to attack the actual corporate owners. These structures also make it difficult for the real owners to play a public role, since they generally prefer to hide the true extent of their assets.

But even private companies are not totally free of state influence in Russia. LUKoil, for example, is the traditional supplier of petroleum products to the military and works hard to keep this role. Company president Vagit Alekperov stresses that "we are not trying to separate our [company] interests from national ones."[45] The company must work to stay in the state's good graces to continue to receive state contracts and avoid debilitating criminal investigations like the one that brought down Yukos. With private companies, the state may act more as a "veto player" than anything else, blocking potential actions rather than forcing companies to enter money-losing operations.[46] Moreover, the state can exert real pressure on private oil companies not only through its security/law enforcement forces (as in the case of Yukos), but through taxes and access to pipelines, which are all controlled by the Transneft monopoly; thus, it is understandable that the oil companies seek good relations.

Monopolies like Gazprom, Transneft, and UES are more clearly tools of Russian policy in the CIS countries that border Russia. Gazprom, for example, participates in money-losing ventures when it serves Russian state interests. For example, the company demonstrated a willingness to work with the Russian-speaking Transdniestria separatists from Moldova after they declared their decision to break away from Moldova-Gaz. Both Moldova proper and Transdniester have large debts to Gazprom. But in 2004, Moldova paid for 90 percent of the gas it consumed, while the breakaway republic covered only 50 percent of its bill.[47]

### *Personalized nature of the firms*

A final key feature of Russian business is the personalized nature of many Russian companies. Most of the big companies are associated with one individual businessman and therefore have a very narrow base. Many of the firms face a thorny succession problem in which it is hard to imagine a new leader taking over from the founder. The fate of the company often depends on the fate of the man at the top, as in the case with Yukos and its jailed chief, Mikhail Khodorkovsky. The Western oil majors, in contrast, are not tied to a single individual the way that the Russian companies are.

Another interesting trait in Russian business is the firms whose leaders have close ties to the Kremlin and therefore benefit extraordinarily. One example is oligarch Roman Abramovich, whose charmed life seemed to get even better when Gazprom agreed to buy a 72.7 percent stake in his firm Sibneft for $13.1 billion, with a large part of the money going to him.

## Business–state relations and foreign relations: common and diverging interests

While Russia is no longer a superpower, it remains an extremely important factor in the security environments of Europe, the Caucasus, Central Asia, and the Far East. The evolution of Russia's business community and its relationship with the state shapes how the country behaves in these areas. Business potentially could influence traditional security players in ways that reduce levels of international conflict and promote stability, particularly by increasing trade, promoting economic development, and reducing unemployment. However, legitimate business's constant pursuit of profit in a lawless environment and the rising role of crime groups often increase conflict both within Russia and along its borders. Understanding the interplay between state and business interests helps explain the role companies and crime groups play in promoting conflict or cooperation on Russia's borders.

### *Common interests*

Russian state and corporate interests overlap in that both want to expand markets for Russian business and increase the power of Russian companies to operate abroad. Putin's primary domestic objective is doubling the size of the Russian economy, and his foreign policy is directed partly at achieving that goal. A strong economic base for Russia will make it possible for the country to once again assert itself as a Great Power. In this sense, the primary assumption of realist thinkers that a country seeks power and security works in the case of Russia.[48] The Russian state has no objection to Russian companies making money abroad. As then-CIA Director George Tenet pointed out in Senate testimony, "Russian companies, primarily for commercial motives, but in line with the Kremlin's agenda, are increasing their stakes in neighboring countries, particularly in the energy sector."[49] In such pursuits, the Russian state and the business community find it easy to work together.

Gazprom and LUKoil have taken on a high-profile role in many Russian strategic ventures in countries around Russia's borders. Russia supplies 45.1 percent of Europe's energy, just slightly less than the 46.1 percent that the OPEC countries deliver.[50] In the future, Russia hopes to increase the amount of energy it is delivering to Asian countries. US markets are on the horizon as well, and LUKoil has already purchased a chain of gas stations in the United States.

Russian energy can also be used in developing closer ties with foreign countries. Russia improved its relations with Tajikistan and Uzbekistan in June 2004 through energy deals. Gazprom and LUKoil will play a prominent role in new projects in the area. In one deal, LUKoil agreed to invest approximately $1 billion to develop Uzbekistan's Kandym, Khauzak, and Shady gas fields (see the analysis in Jeronim Perović's chapter, Chapter 5).[51]

Other analysts see Russian moves much more darkly. Gregory Gleason argues, for example, that Russia is pursuing a neomercantile strategy of expansion in Central Asia and the Caucasus.[52] He notes that the Kremlin is now coordinating the banking sector with Gazprom and the UES electricity monopoly to expand Russian influence along its southern border. UES has negotiated power supply agreements with Armenia, Azerbaijan, Georgia, and Kazakhstan on terms favorable to those countries in order to secure market share. In making these deals, the Russian government has pursued innovative new financial arrangements such as taking equity in enterprises and offering guaranteed loans and credits. The merger of the Russian state, energy companies, and the banking sector gives Russia a powerful new lever in Central Asia. However, in taking control of these enterprises, which have been passed over by commercial investors, Russia is taking a large risk and may end up paying in the future for acquiring money-losing assets in Central Asia.

The arms industry highlights mutual state and business interests, at least in the short term. During the 1990s, military production fell sharply in Russia as the Russian government could no longer afford to purchase weapons. The only factor that saved part of the industry was export sales, which also dropped, but not to the same extent as domestic purchases.[53] Export sales of Russian arms kept alive much of Russia's ability to produce such weapons (see the chapter by Robert Orttung and Boris Demidov, Chapter 8). Whether these sales will prove to be destabilizing in the longer term remains an open question.

Russian companies are going to have to expand beyond Russian borders in order to function effectively in the international economy. In November 2004, the Russian journal *Ekspert* argued that Russian resource companies would eventually have to develop sources of raw materials outside of Russian territory so that the Russian economy could focus on higher value-added activities. Noting ongoing trends, the journal pointed to Africa as a logical target for Russian expansion. If current plans remain on track, the investments of four Russian companies (Russian Aluminum, Norilsk Nikel, Alrosa, and Renova) on that continent will amount to $5 billion.[54] In contrast to the Soviet era, when the Communists sought Cold War gains in Africa, seeking to balance the military power of the West, current Russian corporate efforts are pursuing economic gains.

In the new global environment, Russia seeks to increase the dependence of other countries on its resources and corporations. This harmony of interests at home, though, does not translate to less conflict abroad. Just as Russia seeks greater power, the CIS countries along Russia's borders and European countries farther west seek to reduce their reliance on Russia, preventing it from exerting influence over them. Russia likewise seeks to keep a large and diverse number of customers for its resources in both East and West to avoid becoming dependent on the purchases of one or two customers.

### Differences

The Russian state and business do not see eye to eye in a number of areas. In the broadest terms, the Putin-era Kremlin seeks to block all forms of political opposition from gaining strength. An independent business sector represents a potential threat to the Kremlin, because it has the financial resources to fund an opposition. The Kremlin fears big business not so much for its own power, but for its potential ability to mobilize popular dissatisfaction against the government.[55] Such mobilization became a much more palpable threat after popular revolutions in Georgia and Ukraine and widespread protests against the Russian government's reform of benefits across the regions of Russia. The Kyrgyz uprising against President Askar Akayev demonstrated how different businessman were capable of mobilizing their own crowds. Although big business is not particularly popular in Russia, public opinion polls show that the public has greater antipathy toward the bureaucracy than toward the oligarchs.[56] As a result, the Kremlin can never view the business community as a benign presence, no matter how obsequious its representatives seem before state power.

The key issue of concern for the Kremlin in contemplating the opposition is that none of the existing opponents of the incumbent leadership supports the current institutions that Putin and his team are building. Any party that came to power would likely overhaul the political system and redistribute the property that Putin's associates have taken over. The overall weakness of the current Russian state, and the fact that it must operate against the background of a fragmented society, drives the Kremlin's efforts to place strict limits on the level of political competition.

Yukos was the company that went the furthest in trying to establish itself as a full-blooded political actor on the Russian stage. It funded opposition parties like Yabloko and the Communists, and supported various think tanks, such as the Institute for Applied International Research, set up in March 2002. The Russian state destroyed Yukos by arresting its key leaders in 2003 and auctioning off its most valuable assets in December 2004 to a state-owned company.

A second area of dispute between business and the state is the state's effort to maintain control of the country's infrastructure. While Russia initially privatized much of its economy, including the crucial oil sector, and is discussing moving ahead with electricity reform, key sectors of the economy, such as Gazprom's monopoly over natural gas and Transneft's monopoly over the country's oil pipeline system, remain unchanged. President Putin has made clear that he wants to maintain tight control over these sectors of the economy and will not allow private corporations to encroach on them. In fact, his government has even started to assert greater state control over the oil sector, with Rosneft's purchase of Yukos's assets and Gazprom's purchase of Sibneft.

Most likely, Putin's primary motivation in preserving the natural gas and oil pipeline monopolies is that he sees them as necessary in preventing the country from breaking apart into a number of smaller units. Additionally, the division of the natural gas and pipeline monopolies would inevitably lead to the creation of more oligarchs, another outcome that Putin seeks to avoid. Of course, state control over strategic pipelines and resources is common in many countries besides Russia.

The oil companies, in particular, come into conflict with the state on this issue because they would prefer to control the key assets required for their production cycle. Since they are beholden to the state for the right to transport oil, they are ultimately at the state's mercy. Yukos was a leader in this area because it sought to build a private pipeline that would have linked its fields in Eastern Siberia to the Chinese city of Daqing. While the company would have benefited from the deal, the Russian government feared that such a pipeline would have allowed Yukos too much independence from state control. Additionally, Russian leaders likely feared that the pipeline would make Russia too dependent on Chinese purchases of its East Siberian oil. Ultimately, Russia decided to build a pipeline to the Pacific coast so that Russia would have access to a larger number of customers, including Japan and South Korea, reducing the potential influence of such customers over the Russian state. Similarly, a consortium of five companies unsuccessfully sought to build a private pipeline to Murmansk, which sought to provide Russian oil companies more access to European and US markets. The state monopoly Transneft was ultimately able to block this effort.[57] Unfortunately for the oil companies, the Murmansk pipeline makes much more economic sense than the one to the Pacific coast.

In a third area of difference, the Russian state often has an interest in selling Russian energy resources at below market costs. On the domestic market, the state has long held down energy prices artificially, fearing that raising prices to world levels would stir political unrest among the population. Although government policy has sought to raise domestic prices slowly, Russia's leaders have not been able to move as quickly as they would have liked. Gazprom sells two-thirds of its production on the domestic market, but these sales only account for about one-quarter of the company's annual revenues.[58]

In the foreign policy sphere, Russia's main tools for exerting influence within the CIS are Gazprom and, to a lesser extent, UES. In order to gain maximal use of these tools, the Russian state has an interest in selling energy abroad at below market prices to its neighboring countries. Such sales create a dependency by these countries on Russia that serves the Russian leadership's political interests. Because CIS countries can obtain cheap energy from Russia, they have not developed alternative sources. Thus, where the Russian state has an interest in selling energy at home or within the CIS at low prices, the companies have a strong interest in selling energy elsewhere at world prices to secure the greatest returns.

The CIS countries need Russia much more than it needs them. Although the CIS countries are dependent on Russia's natural gas, Gazprom sales to the CIS make up less than a quarter of its sales and only 6 percent of its total revenue. Over 80 percent of the company's exports go to the European Union, generating nearly three-quarters of its income. Until recently, Ukraine and the Baltic countries paid $80 for 1,000 cubic meters of gas, Poland paid about $108, while West European countries paid $120–$130. The Baltic countries' preferential treatment was expected to end in 2005 and they will have to pay the same prices as Germany.[59] Russia's electricity monopoly is shifting its exports from the CIS to non-CIS countries to increase its profits. Nevertheless, its acquisition of low-performing assets and search for political control in the CIS suggest that political, rather than business, concerns dominate its expansion policy.[60]

Fourth, Russian corporations work to protect their assets and profits from the Russian state. State–business relations inside Russia have a direct impact on Russia's foreign relations. Inside Russia, as noted above, the Kremlin has carried out a policy of extending its influence over the economy and redistributing property in its favor. The Yukos affair and Kremlin moves to place officials close to Putin on the boards of key companies are prime examples of these policies. Russia's decision to increase the role of the state in its market economy gives Russian business an interest in looking for safe havens elsewhere. Specifically, Russian business seeks investments abroad, where it can park assets outside the control of Russian authorities.

One way of ensuring such protection is through simple capital flight. As noted above, an enormous amount of money has left the country since the collapse of the Soviet Union. As one would expect, given the state's crackdown on Yukos, capital flight increased in 2004 to nearly $8 billion, up from about $2 billion in 2003.[61]

However, firms are pursuing a variety of other methods. By expanding operations abroad, Russian corporations can seek to protect their assets by placing them in foreign jurisdictions, presumably outside the reach of Russian bureaucrats.[62] Establishing foreign subsidiaries is a logical extension of corporate behavior inside Russia. Since Putin came to power at the beginning of 2000, Russian companies have sought to build up their assets in the Russian regions outside of Moscow in order, among other reasons, to put greater distance between themselves and the main offices of the presidential administration.[63]

Fifth, in increasing their security, Russian corporations seek to buy up all links in their production chain. Firms that believe that they will have trouble enforcing their contracts with other firms often seek to buy out those firms, feeling it is safer to conduct transactions within the framework of one firm of which they are the owner than with outside firms they do not control.[64] Russian corporations hope to be able to control every aspect of their business, from the early production stages to delivery of the final product to the customer, reducing any potential for outside interference.

Efforts to develop this type of vertical integration are visible both domestically and internationally. Domestically, several Russian metals companies have recently purchased ports in the Far East so that they will have guaranteed access to shipping routes, allowing them to send their materials abroad.[65] Internationally, the desire to control their entire production chains leads Russian firms to invest heavily in the CIS, particularly Ukraine, Belarus, Uzbekistan, and Kazakhstan.[66] Chelyabinsk-based steel companies, for example, are buying up raw materials suppliers in Kazakhstan and Uzbekistan because they want to reduce their vulnerability to price fluctuations.[67] Severstal, through its subsidiary Severstaltrans, and other Russian companies have sought to take over parts of the Estonian railway system, which was recently liberalized. Severstaltrans has recently also purchased parts of the Latvian railroad.

Establishing vertical integration has several negative consequences. Such integration reduces the level of transparency in Russian companies. These purchases show that the Russian buyers want to maintain control over their business subsidiaries, not just act as profit-seeking investors.[68] Many Russian firms seek to establish monopolies in their spheres, taking advantage of the fact that anti-monopoly legislation is extremely ineffective. With essentially no competitors, two to three large firms can effectively control prices in their area of operations.

Of course, such vertical integration is not entirely a negative outcome for the Russian state. If the companies are so heavily concentrated, it is likely easier for the state to exert control over them. State officials have fewer problems working directly with two or three large companies than they do trying to exert influence over a large number of smaller companies.

A further way that Russian companies can protect themselves from advances by the state is through hiring foreign nationals to run key operations. The Russian government has frowned on this practice, however, pointing out that the size of Russian oil reserves is a state secret according to amendments to the federal law on secrets that went into effect in February 2004 and a 2002 government decree.[69] Just before he was jailed in October 2003, Yukos CEO Mikhail Khodorkovsky hired American Steven Theede as the COO for Yukos. After Khodorkovsky's jailing, Theede took over as CEO.[70] However, Theede's presence did not protect the company and he eventually fled Russia. On 3 August 2004, SUAL Holding chairman Viktor Vekselberg appointed Brian Gilbertson, a citizen of South Africa, as president, replacing Chris Norval, another South African.

As the above examples have shown, the difficult relations between the Russian state and Russian business have consequences for corporate actions in countries outside of Russia. In order to better understand the influence of business–state relations on Russian foreign relations, we now turn to a more fine-grained analysis of state–business relations.

## Different sectors, different relations

Observers of Russia tend to focus on what they see as either a strong or a weak Russian state. A more nuanced analysis shows instead that the strength of the state, meaning government institutions at both the federal and the regional levels, varies with the different sectors of the economy. In looking at state strength, we mean the capacity of the collected government institutions to define and implement a coherent set of rules and policies over the businesses working in a particular sector.

The strength of the business community is also variable: some sectors have a few well-defined companies while others are much more amorphous. In Russia, there is a major difference between the energy sector and the other sectors of the economy in terms of the relationship between state and business. In order to make sense of the role of business in Russian foreign relations, it is necessary to look at the two parts of the economy separately. The following section lays out these differences so that subsequent chapters can discuss them in more detail. Figure 2.1 presents these relationships in graphic form.[71] Unfortunately, we did

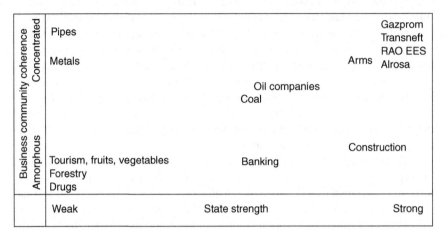

*Figure 2.1* State–business relations in various sectors of the Russian economy.

not have space in this book to discuss the metals, pipes, and construction industries; however, we placed them in the table to show their approximate positions.

### Coherent state, concentrated business

Energy is by far the most important sector of the Russian economy. Fifty-five
percent of all exports are from the oil and gas sector and 37 percent of federal
revenues come from hydrocarbons. Oil and gas make up about 20 percent of
Russia's GDP.[72] Putin has made it one of his top priorities to gain centralized
control over the energy sector. His policies reflect a belief that state control is
the only way to make the energy sector more profitable for the Russian people,
end the theft of energy resources, and rein in the oligarchs.

Accordingly, in the energy sector there is a relatively strong state and easily
identified major corporations, making for a concentrated business community.
This concentration makes it easier for the state to exert influence over the relat-
ively small number of companies working in this sphere. In countries bordering
Russia, state and business can work hand in hand to promote mutual interests.
The expansion of Russia's energy companies into Belarus, Ukraine, the South
Caucasus, and parts of Central Asia demonstrates this cooperation. Gazprom
head Alexei Miller freely admits that his company is a tool of Kremlin policy
and that its expansion goals dovetail nicely with Kremlin efforts to boost
Russian prestige abroad.[73]

However, as noted above, the Russian state does not always support the
purely commercial interests of its companies. Frequently, Russia uses its gas and
electricity monopolies (Gazprom and UES) to exert influence over its immediate
neighbors, selling energy below world prices to secure political goals, such as
keeping the countries loyal to Russia's interests.

Even in such cases, where the state owns a controlling stake, however, state officers do not necessarily do a good job of managing state assets. Accordingly, corporate officers siphon off assets for their personal benefit since there is little control from outside. Gazprom is a prime example. Through much of the 1990s, the company's leader, Rem Viakhirev, treated it as a personal fiefdom and transferred a tenth of the company's gas reserves to private companies with links to management for what experts have argued was a fraction of their value.[74] Since taking over in 2001, Miller has done little to clean up the company's practices and analysts argue that it still lacks real transparency, pointing out that despite its enormous revenues, Gazprom managers do a poor job of handling the company's expenditures, losing as much as $2 billion in miscellaneous expenses and poorly defined staff costs in 2003.[75] Conversely, international institutions have noted that UES has done a relatively better job.

Moreover, the Russian state does not always obtain political benefits for the money it spends seeking influence abroad. Russia incurs high opportunity costs by selling its energy at below world market prices. Even though many of the CIS countries are dependent on Russia for their energy supplies and markets for their goods, they do not slavishly line up to support Russian policies. The Rose and Orange revolutions in Georgia and Ukraine, which brought to power leaders who are actively more pro-Western than pro-Russian, show that these countries can assert their political independence regardless of Russian desires. Russian critics of Russian state policy point out that Russia continues to provide subsidized energy to countries such as Georgia even when such countries work to defy Russian interests.[76] Of course, the defiance is within limits, as the new leaders of Georgia and Ukraine are very careful to maintain good relations with Russia. Georgia, for example, agreed to sell much of its gas pipeline network to Gazprom. The same is true for Europe. Although European commentators frequently point out that Western Europe is growing increasingly dependent on natural gas supplies from Gazprom, Russia does not necessarily derive political benefit from this dependency. However, European leaders are careful not to deeply offend Russia as well, keeping criticism of the Chechen war, for example, to a minimum.

## Weak corrupt state, amorphous business community

In nonenergy sectors of the economy, the state often is much weaker and the business community more amorphous. While the state can establish relatively coherent relations with energy companies, large sectors of the economy are beyond its control because of the extensive corruption among state agencies. The customs agency and border guard service are often cited as among the most corrupt institutions in Russia.

Evidence of the weak state outside of the energy sphere is widespread. Russia has very little control over the growing drug trade flowing across its borders. Likewise, the state has little ability to affect the illegal export of Russian timber, where small companies simply sell logs for the personal benefit of their managers, but in violation of state interests. A similar situation exists with the food and tourism industries operating in the Caucasus.

The arms and banking sectors are somewhere in between these two extremes, with a reasonably coherent state and a more structured business environment. Of course, in all of these sectors the state retains enormous coercive powers that it can apply against individual companies: it can impose high taxes and shut down specific firms. The problem is that, while the state can deal with a handful of firms, it has lost overall control of these sectors of the economy. In effect, the state is not able to administer a coherent set of policies in areas such as forestry management or the drug trade, creating a large potential for conflict on the Russian border.

## Notes

I would like to thank Alexei Zudin, Peter Rutland, William Tompson, Andrew Jack, Andreas Wenger, and Jeronim Perović for their comments on previous drafts of this chapter. Additionally, thanks to Marc Weinstein for valuable research help. Despite their imparted wisdom, any errors and oversights in the final text are my own doing.

1  This influence is by no means unique to Russia. Recent research found that the most significant actors influencing US foreign policy were business elites. See Lawrence R. Jacobs and Benjamin I. Page, "Who Influences U.S. Foreign Policy?" *American Political Science Review* 99, no. 1, February 2005, pp. 107–123.

2  See Peter Rutland, "Business and Civil Society in Russia," in Alfred B. Evans, Laura A. Henry, and Lisa McIntosh Sundstrom, eds., *Russian Civil Society*, Armonk, NY: M. E. Sharpe, 2005.

3  For useful Russian overviews of the evolution of the Russian business sector, see Ya. Sh. Pappe, *Oligarkhi: Ekonomicheskaya khronika, 1992–2000*, Moscow: Gosu-darstvennyi universitet Vysshaya shkola ekonomiki, 2000, and *Komu prinadlezhit Rossiya: 10 let kapitalizma v Rossii*, Moscow: Vagrius & Kommersant, 2003.

4  Sergei Guriev and Andrei Rachinsky, "Russian Oligarchs: A Quantitative Assessment," *Beyond Transition* 15, no. 1, October–December 2004, pp. 4–5. Aleksandr Dynkin presents slightly different data. He claims that the top ten business groups control 38.7 percent of the country's industrial output. Aleksandr Dynkin, "Krupnyi biznes: Nashe nasledie," *Vedomosti*, 20 January 2004.

5  Guy Faulconbridge, "Putin Defends Small Business," *Moscow Times*, 15 March 2005.

6  Federico Varese, *The Russian Mafia: Private Protection in a New Market Economy*, Oxford: Oxford University Press, 2001.

7  Vladimir Kontorovich, "Small Business and Putin's Federal Reform," in Peter Reddaway and Robert W. Orttung, eds., *The Dynamics of Russian Politics: Putin's Reform of Federal–Regional Relations*, vol. 2, Lanham, MD: Rowman & Littlefield, 2005.

8  Peter Rutland, "Russian Small Business: Staying Small," *Eurasia Daily Monitor*, 15 March 2005.

9  Dmitry Zhdannikov, "Russia Backs BP–TNK Oil Merger," Reuters News, www.tnk-bp.com/press/media/2003/8/15/.

10  Elina Pelto, Peeter Vahtra, and Kari Liuhto, "Cyp–Rus Investment Flows to Central and Eastern Europe: Russia's Direct and Indirect Investments via Cyprus to CEE," Electronic Publications of Pan-European Institute, 2/2003, www.tukkk.fi/pei/verkkojulkaisut/Pelto_Vahtra_Liuhto_22003.pdf.

11 Vadim Volkov describes this process in the Tambov group in St. Petersburg, but it is common throughout Russia. See Vadim Volkov, *Violent Entrepreneurs: The Use of Force in the Making of Russian Capitalism*, Ithaca, NY: Cornell University Press, 2002, p. 112.
12 Transparency International Corruption Perceptions Index 2004, www.transparency. org/cpi/2004/cpi2004.en.html#cpi2004.
13 Robert Klitgaard, *Controlling Corruption*, Berkeley: University of California Press, 1987.
14 V. V. Luneev, "Tenevaya ekonomika: kriminologicheskii aspect," *Obshestvo i ekonomika*, 23 February 2004. For the GDP, see the *Economist* country profile for Russia, www.economist.com/countries/Russia/profile.cfm?folder=Profile-FactSheet.
15 Friedrich Schneider, "The Size and Development of the Shadow Economies of 22 Transition and 21 OECD Countries," Institute for the Study of Labor (IZA) Discussion Paper 514, June 2002, www.iza.org/index_html?lang=en&mainframe= http%3A//www.iza.org/iza/en/webcontent/personnel/photos/index_html%3Fkey%3D 206&topSelect=personnel&subSelect=fellows.
16 Ksenia Nechaeva, "Tenevaya ekonomika otrazhaet rezervy rosta," *Kommersant*, 11 November 2002.
17 "Russian Tax Revenue Totaled $45.64 Billion in First Half of 2005," RIA Novosti, en.rian.ru/business/20050805/41097750.html.
18 Speech by Minister of Internal Affairs Rashid Nurgaliev at the enlarged meeting of the MVD collegium on 16 February 2005, www.mvd.ru/index.php?newsid=5137.
19 Speech by Minister of Internal Affairs Rashid Nurgaliev to the Federation Council on 23 March 2005, www.mvdinform.ru/index.php?newsid=5345.
20 Speech by Interior Minister Rashid Nurgaliev at the enlarged meeting of the MVD collegium on 16 February 2005, www.mvd.ru/index.php?newsid=5137.
21 James B. Jacobs, Coleen Friel, and Robert Radick, *Gotham Unbound: How New York City Was Liberated from the Grip of Organized Crime*, New York: New York University Press, 2001.
22 Kari Liuhto and Jari Jumpponen, "International Activities of Russian Corporations: Where Does Russian Business Expansion Lead?" *Russian Economic Trends* 10, no. 3–4, 2001, pp. 19–29.
23 United Nations Conference on Trade and Development (UNCTAD), *World Investment Report*, 2004, p. 74, www.unctad.org/en/docs/wir2004ch2_en.pdf.
24 UNCTAD, *World Investment Report 2004*, pp. 72–74, 385.
25 For a discussion of these issues, see Willem H. Buiter and Ivan Szegvari, "Capital Flight and Capital Outflows from Russia: Symptom, Cause and Cure," European Bank for Reconstruction and Development, Working Paper 73, June 2002, www.ebrd.com/pubs/econo/wp0073.pdf.
26 A. A. Mukhin, *Rossiiskaya organizovannaya prestupnost' i vlast': Istoriya vzaimootnoshenii*, Moscow: Tsentr politicheskoi informatsii, 2003, p. 32.
27 William H. Webster *et al.*, *Russian Organized Crime*, Center for Strategic and International Studies Task Force Report, Washington: CSIS, 1997, p. 10.
28 Nurgaliev speech at the enlarged meeting of the MVD collegium.
29 Sergei Golunov, "Narkotorgovlya kak vyzov bezopastnosti v Russko-Kazakhstanskom zagranich'e," 2004, www.american.edu/traccc/overseascenters/russia. html.
30 See Anna L. Repetskaya and D. V. Sin'kovm, "Rol' nasiliya v mekhanizmakh regulirovaniya otnoshenii sobstvennosti v syr'evoi sfere regional'noi promyshlennosti," unpublished manuscript, and "Plundering Russia's Far Eastern Taiga: Illegal Logging, Corruption, and Trade," a report by Bureau for Regional Oriental Campaigns, Friends of the Earth – Japan, and Pacific Environment and Resource Center, 2000, www.pacificenvironment.org.

31 Thane Gustafson, *Capitalism Russian-Style*, Cambridge: Cambridge University Press, 1999, p. 136.
32 Stefan Hedlund makes the most elaborate argument for this approach. See his "Can They Go Back and Fix It? Reflections on Some Historical Roots of Russia's Economic Troubles," *Acta Slavica Iaponica*, Tomus XX, 2003, src-h.slav.hokudai.ac.jp/publictn/acta/20/asi20-050-hedlund.pdf. For a discussion of path dependency related specifically to Russian foreign policy, see Matthew Evangelista, "From Each According to Its Abilities: Competing Theoretical Approaches to the Post-Soviet Energy Sector," in Celeste A. Wallander, ed., *The Sources of Russian Foreign Policy after the Cold War*, Boulder, CO: Westview Press, 1996, pp. 173–205.
33 See Tatiana Popova, "Financial-Industrial Groups (FIGs) and Their Roles in the Russian Economy," *Review of Economies in Transition* 7, 30 December 1998, pp. 5–28.
34 Andrei Grigor'ev, "Biurokraticheskaia revolyutsiia," *Kompaniia*, 15 November 2004, p. 27.
35 William Tompson, "Putin and the 'Oligarchs': A Two-Sided Commitment Problem," www.bbk.ac.uk/polsoc/download/bill_tompson/Putin%20and%20the%20'oligarchs'. pdf, p. 11, and in Alex Pravda (ed.), *Leading Russia: Putin in Perspective: Essays in Honour of Archie Brown*, Oxford: Oxford University Press, 2005, pp. 179–202.
36 Ben Ross Schneider, *Business Politics and the State in Twentieth-Century Latin America*, Cambridge: Cambridge University Press, 2004, p. 5.
37 Keith C. Smith, "Russian Energy Politics in the Baltics, Poland, and Ukraine: A New Stealth Imperialism?" unpublished manuscript, p. 39.
38 www.yukos.com/RM/Mazeikiu.asp.
39 Peter Zashev, "Russian Investments in Lithuania: Politics, Business, Corporate Culture," Electronic Publication of the Pan-European Institute, October 2004, pp. 15–16, www.tukkk.fi/pei/e.
40 Vladimir Ivanov, "Lithuania Govt Not to Buy YUKOS Stocks in Baltic Refinery," ITAR-TASS, 21 December 2004.
41 Konstantin Sonin, "When Businessmen Go Governor," *Moscow Times*, 15 February 2005.
42 "Reiting rossiiskikh milliarderov 2005," www.finansmag.ru/12350/.
43 Interview with Semyon Mitelman, deputy speaker of the Chelyabinsk legislature and general director of the MIZAR group of firms, Chelyabinsk, 10 February 2005.
44 Dmitry Dokuchayev, "Kremlin Cronies Seeking Control over Big Business," *Moscow News*, 29 September–5 October 2004.
45 Roy Allison, "Central Asia and Afghanistan," in National Intelligence Council, *Old and New Drivers in Russian Foreign Policy: Conference Report, 3–5 June 2003*, Washington, DC: National Intelligence Council, May 2004, p. 63.
46 Thank you to Alexei Zudin for these insights delivered as comments on an earlier draft of this chapter.
47 Galina Bazina and Anastasiya Lokteva, "Rossiiskii gaz: Za nezavisimost' Pridnestro-v'ya," www.gazeta.ru, 5 March 2005.
48 Jeffrey W. Legro and Andrew Moravsik, "Is Anybody Still a Realist?" *International Security* 24, 1999, pp. 5–55.
49 George J. Tenet, "The Worldwide Threat 2004: Challenges in a Changing Global Context," Testimony of Director of Central Intelligence George J. Tenet before the Senate Select Committee on Intelligence, 24 February 2004.
50 "Russia to ensure 12.5% of world oil and 35% of world gas deliveries," Alexander's Oil and Gas Connections, 11 November 2004, www.gasandoil.com/goc/ history/welcome.html.
51 Alexander Zemlianichenko, "Putin Signs Historic Uzbekistan Gas Deal," *Moscow Times*, 17 June 2004.

52 Gregory Gleason, "The Politics of Integration in Eurasia" (pre-presentation draft), presented at a meeting of the Project on Systemic Change in Russia and the New States of Eurasia at the Johns Hopkins School of Advanced International Studies, 12 November 2004.
53 Antonio Sanchez-Andres, "Arms Exports and Restructuring in the Russian Defense Industry," *Europe–Asia Studies* 56, no. 5, July 2004, p. 689.
54 "Expansion of Large Russian Raw Material Companies in Africa May Serve as One of the Locomotives for Economic Development of Russia," *Ekspert*, 29 November 2004.
55 Thanks to Peter Rutland for this point.
56 Vera Sitnina, "The Rich Are Human Too," *Vremya novostei*, 24 June 2004.
57 Vasily Zubkov, "The Politics of Pipelines: Economics Takes a Back Seat in Project Decisions," *Russia Profile*, 29 November 2004, wwwrussiaprofile.org.
58 Peeter Vahtra and Kari Liuhto, "Expansion or Exodus? Foreign Operations of the Russia's Largest Corporations," Electronic Publication of the Pan-European Institute, August 2004, www.tukkk.fi/pei/e, p. 41.
59 Keith C. Smith, "Russian Energy Politics in the Baltics, Poland, and Ukraine: A New Stealth Imperialism?" unpublished manuscript, p. 13. Different sources cite different prices for the various countries. An article in the Radio Free Europe/Radio Liberty *Newsline*, citing Gazprom head Miller, claimed that Ukraine was paying $50 per 1,000 cubic meters in 2005 and $160 in 2006 (RFE/RL *Newsline*, 8 June 2005).
60 Vahtra and Liuhto, "Expansion or Exodus?" p. 49.
61 Renaissance Capital, "Capital Outflow Rises to $7.8 Billion in 2004," 17 January 2005.
62 Marshall Goldman, "Putin and the Oligarchs," *Foreign Affairs*, November–December 2004, www.foreignaffairs.org/20041101faessay83604-p20/marshall-i-goldman/putin-and-the-oligarchs.html.
63 See the discussion in Natalia Zubarevich, "Big Business in Russia's Regions and Its Role in the Federal Reform," in Peter Reddaway and Robert W. Orttung, eds., *The Dynamics of Russian Politics: Putin's Reform of Federal–Regional Relations*, vol. 2, Lanham, MD: Rowman & Littlefield, 2005, and Robert W. Orttung, "Business and Politics in the Russian Regions," *Problems of Post-communism* 51, no. 2, March–April 2004, pp. 48–60.
64 Benjamin Klein, Robert G. Crawford, and Armen A. Alchian, "Vertical Integration, Appropriable Rents, and the Competitive Contracting Process," *Journal of Law and Economics* 21, no. 2, October 1978, pp. 297–326.
65 Andrei Vin'kov, "Gavan' dlya magnata," *Ekspert*, 15 April 2002.
66 UNCTAD, World Investment Report 2004, p. 74.
67 Interview with Valerii Vaganov, head of the public relations department, Ministry of Industry and Natural Resources, Chelyabinsk *oblast*, 8 February 2005.
68 Peeter Vahtra and Kari Liuhto, "Expansion or Exodus?" p. 7.
69 Alexander Sutyagin, "British Petroleum States That Russian Oil Reserves Equal to 60 Billion Barrels," pravda.ru, 29 April 2004, http://english.pravda.ru/main/18/89/357/12652_oil.html; Alexander Sutyagin, "Classified Oil," 6 May 2004, www.bellona.no/en/international/russia/envirorights/33716.html.
70 Peter Baker, "Kansan in the Land of Kremlin Hardball: U.S. Oilman Finds Himself at Helm of Besieged Yukos Empire," *Washington Post*, 30 July 2004.
71 This figure is a modified version of a table that appears in David C. Kang, *Crony Capitalism: Corruption and Development in South Korea and the Philippines*, Cambridge: Cambridge University Press, 2002, p. 15. Kang's table looks at business–state relations as a way to explain levels of corruption, which is not the purpose here.
72 World Bank, "From Transition to Development: A Country Economic Memorandum for the Russian Federation," April 2004, pp. 8–9.
73 Gregory L. White, "Latest Move Seals Gazprom's Role as Energy Giant, but

Growing Clout, Ties to Kremlin Stir Concern," *Wall Street Journal*, 24 December 2004.

74 White, "Latest Move Seals Gazprom's Role."

75 Tat'yana Yegorova, "Gde den'gi?" *Vedomosti*, 14 July 2004; Catherine Belton, "Gazprom Leaking Billions, Report Says," *Moscow Times*, 8 June 2004.

76 See the comments of Konstantin Simonov, the director-general of the Russian Center for Political Studies, on Radio Russia, 4 March 2005, as summarized by BBC Monitoring.

# Part II

# Russian energy

Regional power and dependency

# 3 Russian energy companies and the enlarged European Union

*Heiko Pleines*

The European Union is Russia's most important partner in foreign economic activities (see Table 3.1). For both sides, the energy trade is at the core of the relationship (see Table 3.2). With the European Union's eastward enlargement of 2004, transforming the EU-15 into the EU-25, Russian energy supplies have further gained in importance. The EU-25 now purchases two-thirds of its gas imports (equal to a quarter of domestic consumption) and a third of its oil imports (equal to 15 percent of domestic consumption) from Russia.[1] Russia, on

*Table 3.1* Russia's main trading partners, 2003

|  | Russian exports ($bn) | Share (%) | Russian imports ($bn) | Share (%) |
|---|---|---|---|---|
| **EU-15** | **47.1** | **35** | **21.9** | **38** |
| Of which: Germany | 10.4 | 8 | 8.1 | 14 |
| Netherlands | 8.8 | 7 | 1.2 | 2 |
| Italy | 8.5 | 6 | 2.4 | 4 |
| Great Britain | 4.9 | 4 | 1.4 | 2 |
| Finland | 4.4 | 3 | 1.8 | 3 |
| France | 3.5 | 3 | 2.3 | 4 |
| Others | 6.6 | 5 | 4.7 | 8 |
| **New EU members** | **16.2** | **12** | **4.3** | **7** |
| Of which: Poland | 4.6 | 3 | 1.7 | 3 |
| Baltic states | 4.5 | 3 | 0.7 | 1 |
| Others | 7.1 | 5 | 1.9 | 3 |
| **CIS** | **20.5** | **15** | **13.6** | **24** |
| **Rest of the world** | **49.9** | **37** | **17.5** | **30** |
| Of which: China | 8.4 | 6 | 3.3 | 6 |
| Switzerland | 5.8 | 4 | 0.5 | 1 |
| USA | 4.2 | 3 | 2.9 | 5 |
| Japan | 2.4 | 2 | 1.9 | 3 |
| Others | 29.1 | 22 | 8.9 | 16 |
| **Total** | **133.7** | **100** | **57.4** | **100** |

Source: Goskomstat, 2004.

*Table 3.2* Russian exports to the EU-15 by product groups, 2001–2003 (accumulated)

| Product group | Billion euro | Share (%) |
|---|---|---|
| Food products | 2.4 | 2 |
| Raw materials | 7.0 | 5 |
| Energy | 80.9 | 55 |
| Chemical products | 6.1 | 4 |
| Machinery | 1.5 | 1 |
| Misc. manufactured goods | 21.2 | 14 |
| Others | 28.2 | 19 |
| **Total** | **147.3** | **100** |

Source: Eurostat 2004.

the other hand, exports more than a third of its oil production and more than a quarter of its gas production to EU countries. Russia's state budget receives a third of its income from the oil and gas industry.[2]

The energy sector dominates not only Russian exports to the European Union but also Russian foreign direct investment (FDI) in the European Union.[3] Based on data from the national banks of the target countries, the EU-15 has so far attracted a third of Russian FDI, and the new East European EU members account for another 10 percent. However, the total amount of Russian FDI, is hard to estimate. Officially registered Russian FDI (1995–2002) amounts to a mere $17 billion,[4] whereas according to United Nations Conference on Trade and Development (UNCTAD) estimates, including investments financed with flight capital, Russian FDI (1992–2003) stands at $52 billion.[5]

Given this extensive trade and investment, the oil and gas industry dominates Russian exports to the European Union and Russian foreign investment in the European Union. It could thus be expected that strong economic interests cause Russian energy companies to influence related matters of foreign policy. However, studies on the role of business interests in Russia's foreign policy making generally come to the conclusion that whereas Russia's policy toward CIS countries is heavily influenced by Russian companies, especially from the oil and gas industry, Russia's policy toward the rest of the world is in general beyond the reach of business elites. Mark A. Smith from the Conflict Studies Research Centre, for example, states, "Outside the near abroad, it is harder to argue that foreign policy is driven by business interests, or to go beyond the obvious generalization that the Russian state wishes to promote the overseas interests of Russian companies."[6]

With the assumption that Russian business does not play a significant political role in relation to the EU states, most studies on business lobbying in the sphere of Russian foreign policy have focused on the CIS countries. Accordingly, a detailed analysis of the role of Russian business interests in Russia's relations with the EU is still missing. Moreover, the European Union's eastern expansion has changed the nature of Russian business interests in some respects.

These new developments do not challenge the fact that Russian business plays a limited political role, but they demand a more detailed analysis, pointing to the exceptions from the general rule. Providing such an analysis is the aim of this chapter.

In line with some of the larger questions this book seeks to address, this chapter focuses on attempts by Russian business to influence Russian foreign relations. The focus is thus placed on Russian domestic actors shaping, or trying to shape, Russia's foreign relations and not on Russia's foreign policy as such. That is why aspects of Russia's relationship with the European Union not related to the interests of Russian energy companies are not included in this chapter.[7]

## The international environment

During the socialist era, the markets for Russian energy exports could generally be divided into the Council for Mutual Economic Assistance (CMEA) trading area, made up of countries with centrally planned economies, and the world market, which in this context meant Western Europe, because of the lack of export infrastructure to other parts of the world. Oil and gas pipelines are the most economical means for transporting oil and gas over long distances. While oil can be delivered by ship and rail, natural gas must be converted into liquid before it can be shipped, a process that the Soviet Union considered too expensive to be feasible. Accordingly, Soviet gas supplies to European customers were only possible after pipelines had been constructed, though some oil deliveries traveled via oil terminals on the Baltic and Black Seas or railway links.

### Russia's rise as an energy exporter

In the first half of the 1960s, the Soviet Union started to build an oil pipeline network intended to supply CMEA countries. After the late 1960s, the Druzhba pipeline connected Soviet oil fields with Poland, Czechoslovakia, Hungary, and the German Democratic Republic (GDR). In the second half of the 1960s, the Soviet Union also became interested in developing an extensive pipeline network for natural gas. Soviet gas deliveries to the GDR started in 1973, to Bulgaria in 1974 and to Hungary in 1976.

Soviet oil and gas exports to Western Europe were a direct consequence of the expansion of the pipeline network for deliveries to Eastern Europe and a reaction to rising world market prices for energy in the wake of the Arab oil embargo. Accordingly, Soviet oil and gas exports to Western Europe accelerated in the 1970s. Extensions to the European gas grid enabled the Soviet Union to start supplies to France in 1976.[8]

Western Europe's growing dependence on Soviet gas became a source of concern when the political conflict between the Warsaw Pact and NATO intensified following the declaration of martial law in Poland in December 1981. The United States imposed sanctions against the Soviet Union, seeking to block the deliveries of pipes and pipeline equipment in order to reduce Soviet leverage over Western Europe. However, the British, French, and Italian governments broke rank with the Americans and obliged companies located in their countries to fulfill the pipeline contracts, in violation of US legislation.[9]

In addition, the United States pressured West European governments to limit the share of the natural gas market the Soviets could supply in each country. As a result, the allies agreed that Soviet gas should not constitute more than 30–35 percent of the total gas supplies in any West European country connected to Soviet gas export pipelines.[10] Today, the European Union is still concerned about this figure, as will be discussed later in this chapter.

### Pipeline routes

The oil and gas pipelines constructed in Soviet times are still the main export routes for Russian supplies to the European market. The Soviet gas pipelines, all of which run through Ukraine, have an export capacity of 140 billion cubic meters. The Druzhba oil pipelines, with the northern branch running through Belarus and the southern branch running through Ukraine, have a total capacity of 85 million tons. In addition, Russia can export 50 million tons of oil through Baltic Sea ports and 44 million tons through Black Sea ports.

Since the end of the Soviet Union, Russia's export capacities for gas have increased through the construction of the first Yamal pipeline,[11] running from Russia through Belarus and Poland to Germany with a capacity of 33 billion cubic meters, and through the Blue Stream pipeline, running from Russia through the Black Sea to Turkey with a capacity of 16 billion cubic meters. Russia's export capacities for oil have increased with the construction of the Baltic Pipeline System, which offers an additional 42 million tons capacity for exports through Russian Baltic Sea ports.

So far, all Russian oil and gas export pipelines go to Europe (including Turkey). However, according to Russia's official energy strategy, exports to Asia and the United States will account for a third of oil exports and a quarter of gas exports by 2020. Accordingly, the majority of Russia's new pipeline projects are focused on non-European markets. Nevertheless, there are plans for an additional major gas export pipeline to the European Union. In September 2005, Russia and Germany agreed to build a Nordic pipeline through the Baltic Sea, which avoids transit countries.[12]

### The regulatory environment for the EU–Russian energy trade

Until the end of the 1980s, energy trade between the Soviet Union and the European Union was limited to specific contracts defining deliveries and payment. With the breakup of the CMEA and the liberalization of the socialist economies, the European Union tried to develop a comprehensive regulatory environment for energy trade.

A first step was the European Energy Charter, which the European Union, at that time still in the form of the European Community, initiated in 1991. The charter was meant to improve the coordination of national energy policies and to create common rules for the energy trade. Key elements of the charter were guarantees for energy transit agreements and a ban on regulations discriminating against foreign investors in the energy sector. Russia was one of 47 countries that signed the charter as a nonbinding declaration of intent.

In 1994, the signatories transformed the Energy Charter into a binding international treaty. Though 51 countries signed the European Energy Charter Treaty, many of them did not ratify it. Russia opposed the regulation of transit rights, as Russia's natural gas monopoly, Gazprom, was unwilling to offer access to its export pipelines to third parties. In December 2003, Russia refused to accept a final compromise version of the Energy Charter Transit Protocol.[13]

However, the European Union raised the same demands in negotiations over Russia's World Trade Organization (WTO) entry. As WTO entry is one of Russia's foreign economic policy priorities, the EU had a chance to put some pressure on its eastern neighbor. As a result, the Russia–EU agreement on Russia's WTO entry, signed in May 2004, for the first time made the reform of Russia's gas industry subject to international law. Russia agreed to open the gas pipeline network to third parties and to raise domestic gas prices considerably, though less than originally demanded.[14]

Another major step towards increased cooperation was the Partnership and Cooperation Agreement (PCA), which came into force in 1997. At the EU–Russia summit held in Paris in 2000 it was then decided to establish a common Energy Dialogue. As the responsible vice-president of the European Commission, Loyola de Palacio del Valle-Lersundi, put it,

> our EU–Russia Energy Dialogue is the first example of what I would call the new "practical" phase of our relationship. It addresses the fundamental building blocks for developing economic co-operation and for constructing our common European economic space. Our energy dialogue is not some kind of short-term exercise. We are engaged in building something more durable: an Energy Partnership that will achieve solid, concrete and mutually beneficial results to enhance the energy security of the entire European continent.[15]

The Energy Dialogue offers an institutionalized way of discussing the energy trade bilaterally. However, EU attempts to go beyond institutionalized negotiations and to bring Russian energy-related national regulations closer to EU rules have failed, as the WTO compromise clearly indicates. As will be described in the following section, the main reason for this failure is the interests of Russian energy companies, which the Russian state supports as being in the national interest.

## The interests of Russian energy companies toward the European Union

Russian energy companies have a wide range of interests in the European Union. They include oil and gas exports entering the domestic market of various European countries, and electricity sales.

### Oil and gas exports

Since the Russian government keeps domestic energy prices artificially low, the Russian oil and gas industry receives nearly all of its profits from exports.[16] As exports depend on available pipeline capacity, more than two-thirds of Russia's oil and gas exports go to the European Union. Most of the remaining exports go to CIS countries, which have accumulated immense debts for Russian energy supplies. Ukraine's bill for Russian gas supplies alone stood at nearly $2 billion in 2004, when it was restructured in a bilateral Russian–Ukrainian agreement.[17] As a result, exports to the European Union are the single major source of income for Russian oil and gas companies.

The same dominance of oil and gas supplies is indicated by the list of Russia's largest exporting companies. As Table 3.3 shows, half of Russia's 20 biggest exporting companies[18] belong to the oil and gas industry.

### Entering the downstream market

The commercial oil and gas companies, which took over Russian production in the first half of the 1990s, soon developed an interest in entering the EU downstream market, as the sale of oil products and the delivery of natural gas directly to the end consumer offered considerably higher profits than the sale of unrefined products at the border.

The Russian natural gas monopoly, Gazprom, was the first Russian energy company to enter the EU downstream market. Gazprom built on its strategic partnership with the German company Ruhrgas, which started in 1970, when the Soviet Union signed its first supply contract with Ruhrgas. However, Ruhrgas was reluctant to share the lucrative German domestic market with its Russian partner. As a result, Gazprom signed a cooperation agreement with Wintershall, a subsidiary of BASF and one of Ruhrgas's main competitors in the German natural gas market. The agreement included the joint marketing of Russian natural gas, as well as the joint planning and construction of gas pipelines and storage facilities in Germany and neighboring countries. The cooperation with Wintershall offered Gazprom lasting access to the West European gas supply system in the downstream sector. Ruhrgas had to accept the strategy of its main supplier and also intensified cooperation with Gazprom. In the second half of the 1990s, Ruhrgas acquired a 5 percent stake in the Russian company, thus gaining a seat on its board.[19]

In contrast to Gazprom's experience, Russian oil companies found it much

*Table 3.3* Russia's major exporting companies

| Company | Export product | Exports (in $bn) 2001 | 2000 |
|---|---|---|---|
| Gazprom | Natural gas | 16.4 | 13.9 |
| LUKoil | Oil | 6.6 | 6.2 |
| Yukos | Oil | 5.7 | 5.2 |
| Tiumen Oil Co. (TNK) | Oil | 5.6 | 3.5 |
| Surgutneftegaz | Oil | 2.4 | 1.7 |
| Russian Aluminum | Aluminum | 2.2 | 2.2 |
| Tatneft | Oil | 2.1 | 2.6 |
| Slavneft | Oil | 1.8 | 1.3 |
| Norilsk Nickel | Non-ferrous metals | 1.8 | 2.2 |
| Sibneft | Oil | 1.7 | 1.7 |
| Rosneft | Oil | 1.3 | 1.3 |
| Alrosa | Diamonds | 1.2 | 0.9 |
| Bashneft | Oil | 0.9 | 0.9 |
| Magnitogorsk Iron and Steel Works | Steel | 0.8 | 0.8 |
| Novolipetsk Metallurgical Combine | Steel | 0.7 | 0.9 |
| Sibur | Chemicals | 0.7 | 0.2 |
| Severstal | Steel | 0.7 | 1.1 |
| SUAL | Aluminum | 0.6 | 0.5 |
| TVEL | Nuclear technology | 0.5 | 0.5 |
| Evraz-Holding | Steel | 0.5 | 0.5 |
| **Total** | | **54.2** | **48.1** |
| **Share in total Russian exports** | | **54%** | **47%** |

Source: "100 krupneishikh rossiiskikh predpriiatii-eksporterov," *Ekspert* no. 23, 17 June 2002, www.expert.ru/expert/ratings/export/02–23–30/t1.htm. These data were the most recent available at the time of writing.

harder to get access to the European Union's downstream market. Two reasons largely explain this outcome. First, the EU market for oil was liberalized and dominated by multinational corporations, which were in a much stronger position than the national gas companies operating in a highly regulated environment. Second, EU-based oil companies found it much easier to diversify supplies than did EU-based gas companies, with their total dependence on pipeline deliveries. Accordingly, EU-based oil companies saw no need for strategic partnerships with Russian companies.

As the EU's eastward expansion drew closer in the late 1990s, Russian companies saw investments in postsocialist EU candidate countries as an entry ticket into the EU downstream market. As the oil and gas companies in new EU member states were being privatized, Russian oil and gas companies provided the majority of Russian foreign direct investment in the EU-25 countries. Gazprom has invested in gas transport and trading companies in nine of the EU-15 states and in seven of the ten new member states (see Table 3.4). Russia's major oil companies, particularly LUKoil and Yukos, participated in all major

*Table 3.4* Gazprom's investments in EU-25 countries

| Country | Investment | Share (%) | Activities |
|---------|-----------|-----------|------------|
| Austria | GHW | 50 | Gas trading |
| Estonia | Eesti Gaas | 37 | Gas trading and transport |
| Finland | Gasum Oy | 25 | Gas transportation and marketing |
| | North Transgas Oy | 50 | Baltic Sea Pipeline construction |
| France | FRAgaz | 50 | Gas trading |
| Germany | Ditgaz | 49 | Gas trading |
| | Verbundnetz Gas | 5.3 | Gas transportation and marketing |
| | Wingas | 35 | Gas transportation and storage |
| | Wintershall Erdgas Handelshaus | 50 | Gas trading |
| | Zarubezhgaz | 100 | Gas trading |
| Greece | Prometheus Gaz | 50 | Marketing and construction |
| Hungary | Panrusgas | 50 | Gas trading and transport |
| | Borsodchem | 25 | Petrochemicals |
| | DKG-EAST Co. Inc. | 38.1 | Oil and gas equipment manufacturing |
| | General Banking and Trust Co. | 25.5 | Banking |
| Italy | Promgaz | 50 | Gas trading and marketing |
| | Volta | 49 | Gas trading and transport |
| Latvia | Latvijas Gaze | 34 | Gas trading and transport |
| Lithuania | Stella-Vitae | 30 | Gas trading |
| | Lietuvos Dujos | 34 | Gas trading and transport |
| | Kaunas power plant | 100 | Gas fired heat and power plant |
| Netherlands | Pieter-Gaz | 51 | Gas trading |
| Poland | Gas Trading | 35 | Gas trading |
| | Evropol Gaz | 48 | Gas transport |
| Slovakia | Slovrusgaz | 50 | Gas trading and transport |
| | SPP | 16.3 | Gas transport |
| Slovenia | Tagdem | 7.6 | Gas trading |
| UK/ Belgium | Interconnector | 10 | Pipeline operator |

Source: Andreas Heinrich, "Between a Rock and a Hard Place: The Energy Sector in Central and Eastern Europe," in Kari Liuhto and Zsuzsanna Vincze, eds, *Wider Europe*, Tampere: Esa Print, 2005, pp. 457–490.

*Table 3.5* LUKoil's investments in EU-25 countries

| Country | Investment | Share (%) | Activities |
|---------|-----------|-----------|------------|
| Czech Republic | Gas stations (sold in 2003) | 100 | Retailing |
| Estonia | LUKoil gas stations | 100 | Retailing |
| Finland | Teboil[a] | 100 | Retailing |
| Hungary | LUKoil gas stations | 100 | Retailing |
| Latvia | LUKoil gas stations | 100 | Retailing |
| Lithuania | LUKoil gas stations | 100 | Retailing |
| Poland | LUKoil gas stations | 100 | Retailing |

Source: NewsBase Archive (www.newsbase.com).

Note
a  Subject to approval by the European Union.

*Table 3.6* Yukos's investments in EU-25 countries (as of 31 December 2004)

| Country | Investment | Share (%) | Activities |
| --- | --- | --- | --- |
| Austria | Joint venture with ÖMV | 50 | Pipeline construction |
| Latvia | Yukos gas stations | 100 | Retailing |
| Lithuania | Mazeikiu Nafta | 53.7 | Refining, transport, marketing |
| | Yukos gas stations | 100 | Retailing |
| Slovakia | Transpetrol | 49 | Pipeline operator |
| UK | John Brown Technology (sold in 2003) | 100 | Technological consulting |

Source: Peeter Vahtra and Kari Liuhto, "Expansion or Exodus? Foreign Operations of Russia's Largest Corporations," Electronic Publications of the Pan-European Institute (Turku, Finland), August 2004, p. 31.

privatization auctions for refineries, though with limited success, and built up a network of gas stations. Taken together, Russia's oil companies have made acquisitions in only three EU-15 states, but in all seven new EU member countries which formerly belonged to the CMEA (see Tables 3.5 and 3.6).

*Electricity exports*

Russian plans to export electricity to the liberalized EU market are another aspect of the energy partnership between Russia and the European Union. In the late 1990s, the Russian electricity monopoly, Unified Energy System (UES), developed ambitious export plans in order to boost cash earnings. However, so far Russia has achieved only very limited access to the EU market, as the electricity grids of the CIS and Central Eastern Europe never formed a unified whole. As a result, Russian electricity exports to EU-25 countries have been restricted to Finland and Latvia.

In 2000, Russia and the European Union initiated the "East–West energy bridge project," which foresees the use of high-tension cables for Russian deliveries via Belarus to Poland and Germany. In a first step, by 2003 Russia had fully synchronized the national electricity grids in the former Soviet states. Under the framework of their energy dialogue, the European Union and Russia then agreed in principle to move towards full integration of their electricity grids. Work on a detailed feasibility study started in late 2004. However, if feasible at all, the power bridge will not become operational before 2010. In order to enter the EU electricity market earlier, UES in late 2003 announced its intention to acquire power companies in Latvia, Lithuania, and Slovakia. So far, the relevant privatization auctions have not taken place.[20]

Ultimately, technical problems prevent electricity exports from taking a high spot on the political agenda of the EU–Russia energy dialogue. Only when Russian electricity supplies to the EU become a near-term option will they have the potential to significantly influence Russia's foreign policy. If Russia's attempt to reform UES has not led to a de-monopolization of the domestic electricity market by then, the situation may become similar to the EU–Russia debate about Russian gas exports and the regulation of Russia's gas monopoly.

## State interests toward the European Union and the business lobbies

Russian oil and gas exports to the European Union have not caused any major disputes between the two sides. One exception was the episode in January 2006, when Russian gas deliveries to the EU fell during a conflict with Ukraine. After the EU protested, Gazprom fully resumed supplies. With only rare and brief exceptions, both partners portray their energy trade relationship as mutually beneficial.[21] Nevertheless, neither side anticipates considerable increases in these exports, even though EU demand is expected to grow fast and Russia has declared its intention to increase exports. The European Union hopes to diversify its energy supplies to avoid excessive reliance on Russia.[22] Likewise, Russia is focusing on Asian markets, not only in order to diversify exports, but also because new oil and gas fields are geographically closer to the fast-growing Asian markets (see Michael Bradshaw's chapter in this volume, Chapter 7).[23]

However, EU demands related to the way Russia regulates its domestic energy market have led to open disagreement, highlighted by the Russian refusal to ratify the European Energy Charter. This tension indicates a fundamental problem in the EU–Russia energy partnership. Russia sees the partnership as a way to secure from the European Union a long-term commitment to purchase Russian energy and to gain financial and other support for the development of export infrastructure.

The European Union, on the other hand, seeks to integrate Russia into a Common European Economic Space, based on common liberal rules for market regulation.[24] An important condition for this system is Russia's agreement to open its gas pipeline network to third parties (including foreigners), increase prices for domestic gas consumers (thereby reducing indirect subsidies), and accept the EU antitrust trading rules, which would allow the resale of Russian gas by Russia's EU customers. According to the Russian position, the EU demands aim to discriminate against Russian companies participating in the EU energy markets and interfere with Russia's internal affairs. In particular, raising domestic prices could lead to extensive social protests by consumers used to buying cheap energy.[25]

As the European Union has concentrated its demand for Russian energy sector reform on the natural gas industry, related foreign policy issues are of direct concern for only one major Russian company – the natural gas monopoly, Gazprom.[26] Gazprom, for which the Russian state holds a majority of shares and seats on the company board, has traditionally been close to the government. As a result, the company has been able to block all attempts at reform.[27] Such corporate influence translated into Russia's refusal to ratify the energy charter. In return, Gazprom has been forced by the government to subsidize the Russian economy through low domestic gas prices.[28]

Accordingly, the WTO compromise reached with the European Union is partly in Gazprom's interest. Although the company will have to open its pipeline network, it will benefit from higher domestic gas prices. In Russia's favor, the European Union gave up many demands related to gas industry reform. There will be no major reform of the company and it will maintain its monopoly position and exclusive control over Russia's gas exports. Prohibitions remain on the construction of private gas pipelines.

In essence, the Russian government has saved the position of Gazprom against EU pressure. With the conclusion of WTO negotiations between Russia and the European Union, the European Union is no longer able to press for additional Russian energy-sector reforms. For Russian oil and gas companies, the consequence is that in order to promote their export business, they do not have to engage in foreign policy, but must fend off attempts by the Russian government to receive greater revenues by increasing customs duties.[29]

### *Promoting Russian interests in the new EU member states*

While Russian oil and gas exports have not stirred up any serious controversies, attempts by Russian energy companies to invest in the new EU member states have caused considerable friction. Many postsocialist countries oppose Russian economic dominance, which they see as a substitute for Soviet military dominance. Political resistance to Russian investors often led to year-long delays and political scandals. In Lithuania, a prime minister resigned in 1999 over a quarrel between US and Russian companies for a stake in the national oil company, Mazeikiu Nafta. It took until 2002 before a deal with Yukos was finally reached.[30] Gazprom used an EU-based subsidiary for an unfriendly takeover of Hungary's Borsodchem chemical manufacturer in 2000, a move the Hungarian government opposed and which caused numerous political protests.[31] Poland's government altered the privatization strategy for the Gdańsk refinery after assessing the political risk a successful LUKoil bid would entail. As a result, the Russian company had no chance of winning.[32] Accordingly, investment by Russian companies has by and large been restricted to natural gas pipelines and gas stations.

In this context, the oil and gas companies have lobbied the Russian state for support. Gazprom has direct access to the Russian government through state representatives on its board and, as Gazprom owns the gas export pipelines, it also has an instrument to put pressure on gas-importing countries. The relevant oil companies, however, neither have state representatives involved in management nor do they own export pipelines, as oil pipelines belong to the fully state-controlled Transneft company.

As a result, oil companies voiced their interests in foreign affairs through the system of export coordinators. Since 1995, the Russian government's interministerial commission for oil exports assigned oil companies and exporters to be coordinators of oil ports and foreign markets. The commission based its decision upon the oil companies' expressed interests.

The coordinators assist in deciding who will export oil to which destination and how much; they too must approve the quarterly schedule. The coordinators also regulate the tanker schedules and loading at pipeline sea port terminals.... Evidently, the oil companies benefit financially from their coordinating role, and it gives them the means to disadvantage their competitors or punish companies with whose actions they disagree.[33]

As a result, Russian oil companies were offered the ability to influence Russia's economic relations with countries in which they wanted to invest. Accordingly, the respective oil export coordinators, LUKoil and Yukos, have made most of the investment bids from Russian oil companies in new EU member states. Though the system of coordinators was officially abolished in 2002, informal consultations continued.[34]

However, on most occasions Russia's foreign policy was not able to promote the investment bids of Russian companies effectively, as the Russian government did not have any foreign policy instrument at hand to change the position of the countries concerned. On the contrary, Russian attempts to exert pressure on behalf of Russian companies would have been interpreted as proof that Russia, in a union of politics and business, was trying to dominate former socialist countries. As a result, Russian companies often acted without visible support from Russia's foreign policy. When they met heavy discrimination, they teamed up with Western companies or used sham firms to disguise their Russian origin. In this context, Pelto *et al.* argue that Russian flight capital is behind many Cypriot investments in new EU member states.[35]

The Baltic States are the exception to this rule. Here, Russian oil and gas companies used pressure, mainly interruptions of energy supplies, as an instrument in attempts to take over national energy companies. As Russia's oil pipelines are operated by a state-owned and state-managed company, oil supply interruptions imply the tacit agreement of the Russian government. This picture is in line with Russia's generally more aggressive foreign policy stance toward the Baltic States and with the more aggressive strategy of Russian oil and gas companies toward countries on the territory of the former Soviet Union, as the chapter by Margarita Balmaceda (Chapter 4) illustrates.[36]

As support for Russian investments in new EU member states is the main controversial issue where Russia's foreign policy has aimed to support energy companies, two case studies will be used to provide a more detailed picture. The first case is the privatization of the Gdańsk refinery in Poland and the second case is the privatization of the Lithuanian national oil company, Mazeikiu Nafta.

### Case study 1: the Gdańsk refinery

After long discussions, the Polish government agreed on a privatization plan for the country's oil industry in early 1998. According to the plan, the Gdańsk refinery, one of the first oil companies to be privatized, was to be sold to a strategic investor in the first quarter of 1999. However, as no investor was willing to pay the asking price, an alternative privatization program for the Gdańsk refinery was developed in 1999. In summer 2000, the authorities issued another tender in search of a strategic investor, bringing in 13 bids.

After lengthy negotiations, the British Rotch Group won the right to purchase a 75 percent stake in the Gdańsk refinery in August 2001. The newly elected Polish government accepted the deal in October 2001. However, Rotch proved unable to provide evidence of its ability to finance $1 billion worth of investments. In renewed negotiations, Rotch formed a consortium with Russia's LUKoil. The state oil company, Nafta Polska, agreed to the deal. However, the participation of LUKoil caused political resistance. LUKoil president Vagit Alekperov came to Warsaw in September 2002 and tried to persuade the Polish government of the advantages of moving forward. However, explicitly citing the political risks of Russian investment in the Polish oil industry, Prime Minister Leszek Miller stopped the deal.

As a result, Rotch Energy formed a new consortium with the Polish oil group PKN Orlen in November 2002. LUKoil now formed a consortium with Konsorcjum Gdańskie, which unites private owners of Polish gas stations. Though the government was opposed to the PKN Orlen offer, as it would create a monopoly in the oil sector, it was unwilling to consider the higher bid by LUKoil/Konsorcjum Gdańskie. In February 2003, the Russian prime minister, Mikhail Kasyanov, promoted LUKoil's interest during a meeting with his Polish counterpart in Warsaw. In May 2003, LUKoil renewed its offer for the Gdańsk refinery. In reaction, PKN Orlen announced that it was willing to increase its bid.

However, the government abandoned negotiations and decided to consolidate the Gdańsk refinery into the state-owned Grupa Lotus, which unites four oil refineries. Since then, both LUKoil and PKN Orlen have repeatedly voiced their interest in buying either the Gdańsk refinery or Grupa Lotus. Seeking a compromise, LUKoil also offered to rent the refinery. However, the Polish government has made no new offer.

In autumn 2004, a scandal emerged when a commission of the Polish parliament gained access to secret service documents claiming that Jan Kulczyk, a Polish businessman who holds a minority stake in PKN Orlen, had offered a Russian secret service agent political support for LUKoil's bid. Though the investigation into the case has not yet been completed, it is obvious that secret service activities could theoretically be more helpful to Russian investors in the former socialist countries than official foreign policy support. However, as the Kulczyk scandal indicates, public suspicion about Russian political involvement is likely to block any larger Russian investment in the country for a long time.[37]

### Case study 2: Lithuania's Mazeikiu Nafta

Mazeikiu Nafta, comprising the Mazeikiu refinery, the Butinge crude export terminal, and the national pipeline system, is Lithuania's major industrial enterprise, accounting for about 10 percent of the country's gross domestic product and about a quarter of tax revenues. Mazeikiu Nafta traditionally receives its crude deliveries from Russia, with Yukos, TNK, and LUKoil being the main suppliers. The latter company became Russia's oil export coordinator for the Baltics. However, Mazeikiu Nafta increasingly targeted Western markets for its products. For this purpose, a long-term marketing agreement with BP-Amoco was concluded.

Mazeikiu Nafta's integration into the Western business community was to be strengthened through a strategic investor. In 1998, the US company Williams International agreed to buy a 33 percent stake in Mazeikiu Nafta. When the Lithuanian State Property Fund announced in January 1999 that a further 33 percent would be sold that year, Williams International declared its interest to own a majority stake in the refinery.

This move was opposed by LUKoil, which was itself interested in obtaining a stake in the refinery. In January and again in May 1999, LUKoil stopped oil supplies to Lithuania, forcing the refinery to shut down operations. However, in June the Williams board and the Lithuanian government confirmed their intention to move forward with the earlier agreement on the sale of a 33 percent stake. In the same month, the Lithuanian parliament approved Williams's plan to increase its stake to 66 percent. Nevertheless, a final deal between Williams and the government was again delayed.

In October 1999, Lithuanian media reported that Yukos was interested in a 12 percent stake in return for long-term crude supply guarantees. LUKoil again increased pressure. A Russian oil executive threatened that crude supplies to Lithuania would be halted nearly completely, turning the refinery into "scrap metal," if LUKoil did not get a 33 percent stake in Mazeikiu Nafta. To underline that point, deliveries were halted and an increase in the price for any future supplies was announced.

Meanwhile, opposition to Williams was mounting in Lithuania. The head of Mazeikiu Nafta, who had openly criticized the transfer of a controlling stake to the American company, resigned in mid-October. The Lithuanian prime minister announced that he would not endorse the deal. After the resignation of the prime minister in late October 1999, the contract transferring a 33 percent stake in Mazeikiu Nafta to Williams International was finally signed. As a result, Williams gained operational control.

In November, the Mazeikiu Nafta refinery was again forced to halt operations after crude supplies from Russia had been stopped. After two weeks, the refinery resumed operations using North Sea oil, which had been delivered to the Butinge terminal at a considerably higher price than Russian oil. Negotiations with LUKoil on a long-term supply agreement were restarted and in May 2000 LUKoil and Mazeikiu Nafta finally signed a long-term deal.

However, in early 2001 LUKoil renounced all plans for long-term cooperation with Mazeikiu and again stopped crude supplies, forcing the refinery to operate at a loss. A report of the State Audit Office warned that Mazeikiu Nafta could go bankrupt. In response, Lithuania's president personally tried to restart negotiations with LUKoil over crude supplies to the refinery. The government declared its intention to support the sale of 33 percent in Mazeikiu Nafta to the

Russian company. However, Russian influence over management decisions was not on the agenda.

With Mazeikiu Nafta desperate for Russian crude supplies and LUKoil demanding more than Lithuania was willing to offer, Yukos gained an opportunity to join the negotiations. In June 2001, Williams and Yukos reached preliminary agreement. In exchange for a 26.85 percent stake in Mazeikiu, Yukos offered to finance modernization projects and guarantee crude supplies. As part of the deal, Williams's share fell to 26.85 percent, but the company retained its voting majority in Mazeikiu Nafta. Although the Lithuanian government and parliament endorsed the deal, the final agreement was delayed. In December, Williams announced that it was withdrawing from the agreement because Yukos wanted to be the sole crude supplier for the refinery. The Russian company nevertheless continued crude supplies.

In late January 2002, negotiations resumed. However, Williams also started discussions with LUKoil. In June, the deal between the Lithuanian government, Williams, and Yukos was finally signed. When financial problems forced Williams to sell its remaining stake in August 2002, the Lithuanian government decided not to exercise its preemptive right to repurchase the shares but to allow a deal with Yukos, which bought the additional 26.85 percent stake. As a result, the Russian oil company now owned 53.7 percent of the Lithuanian company and gained management control. The government still had a 41 percent stake in Mazeikiu Nafta and, by its own decision, became the junior partner of a Russian company in a Lithuanian enterprise.

The Russian government's campaign to bankrupt Yukos forced the company to stop crude deliveries to the Mazeikiu refinery in January 2005. The Lithuanian prime minister announced that the government would seek alternative crude supplies and wanted to buy back a part of Yukos's stake in the Lithuanian company. In February 2005, LUKoil again declared its intention to buy Mazeikiu Nafta, resuming the battle where it left off before Yukos intervened.[38]

## Conclusion: the potential for conflict and cooperation

The energy trade between Russia and the European Union is a clear example of the cooperation-promoting effects of economic relations. Russia's business interest in maximizing profits through long-term export contracts with the European Union is met by the interest of EU governments and EU companies to secure stable energy supplies. Accordingly, the energy trade is perceived to benefit both sides. The mutual dependence on the bilateral energy trade, common pipeline projects, and regular negotiations in the context of the Energy Dialogue have fostered economic as well as political cooperation.

However, there are two areas of the energy relationship where attempts to increase cooperation have led to conflicts of interest. First, Russia rejects the idea put forward by the European Union of a common value system, defined in the case of energy as a common economic space with shared market-oriented rules, as interference in its internal affairs. Second, some groups within the

European Union's member states have put up resistance to investments by Russian companies.

In order to assess the relevance of conflicts, Diez *et al.* propose a typology of conflicts in foreign relations.[39] They distinguish between conflict episodes, issue conflicts, identity conflicts, and subordination conflicts. Conflict episodes are isolated instances of disagreement on a particular issue. Issue conflicts arise when both parties insist on their position on a particular issue and are unwilling to compromise. In identity conflicts, a general suspicion about the motives of the other side replaces disagreement on a specific issue. The conflict is widened in its scope, and negotiations are hampered by a general feeling of distrust. Subordination conflicts then try to solve the conflict through subordination of the other side. Negotiations are replaced by economic sanctions and military force.

An application of this typology to Russia's energy relationship with the European Union shows that the relevant conflicts are of a low intensity. In the case of the energy trade, there are only some rare conflict episodes, as in January 2006. In the case of the energy charter and Russian investment in new EU member states, both sides have succeeded in limiting the conflict to the specific issue.

However, the European Union's proposal to establish common values and a common space has provoked an identity conflict as it sees every aspect of the bilateral relationship with Russia as related to the general principles of democracy and free markets. Accordingly, the European Union has linked the energy trade to regulation of Russia's internal energy market, a higher-level agreement on the common economic space, and a variety of other political issues.

At the same time, some new EU member states, most prominently Poland and the three Baltic States, have interpreted investment bids by Russian energy companies as being part of an identity conflict, related not only, and not even primarily, to energy policy, but to Russian power politics. In public debates in all these countries, politicians frequently claim that Russia is using the energy dependence of the former socialist countries to gain political influence and to blackmail the political leadership. This indicates fear of a future subordination conflict.

Russia's relations with CIS countries indeed offer several examples of the country's willingness to use energy dependence as an instrument of foreign policy. As Chapters 4 and 5, by Margarita Balmaceda and Jeronim Perović respectively, show, Russia has used cuts in gas supplies to Ukraine, Georgia, and Belarus, and the denial of pipeline access to Turkmenistan and Kazakhstan, to force these countries to comply with its political demands. As such measures can be interpreted as economic sanctions, the related conflicts contain some elements of subordination conflicts.

This analysis suggests that the cooperation-promoting effect of Russia's energy relationship with the EU plays an important role in bilateral relations. This effect is possible because of the great economic importance of the issue, which causes both sides to adopt a pragmatic stance. As a result, even the potential for identity conflicts given in many areas of Russia–EU relations is neutralized.

However, it should be noted that this cooperation-promoting effect is due to economic dependencies as perceived by politicians and only to a lesser degree to lobbying by energy companies. Of course, Russian and EU energy companies are involved in negotiations about the energy trade and they are the major force in negotiations about supply contracts and pipeline routes. But since political and business actors on both sides agree on the mutually beneficial role of the energy trade, Russia's energy companies do not need to engage in foreign policy-related lobbying.

When Russian energy companies lobby the government to protect their interests, as in the case of EU demands for gas industry liberalization and in the case of discrimination against Russian investors in new EU member states, Russian companies try to engage Russia's foreign policy in an issue conflict on their behalf. By doing so, they contribute to the cultivation of conflicts.

Overall, energy relations are the major cooperation-promoting factor in Russia–EU relations. Such cooperation exists because politicians on both sides see the energy trade as beneficial. Russian energy companies agree with this assessment and, as a result, do not see a need to lobby in favor of energy trade. When Russian energy companies engage in EU-related lobbying, their demands deal with issue conflicts and do not promote cooperation. However, neither the Russian government nor the energy companies are interested in an escalation of conflict. Accordingly, they have always agreed to a compromise to put an end to the issue conflict instead of widening it to an identity conflict. Thus, energy trade is a major source of cooperation in Russia–EU relations, but this is only to a minor degree the result of advocacy by Russian energy companies.

## Notes

1 For an analysis of energy trade between Russia and the European Union, see A. Belyi, "New Dimensions of Energy Security of the Enlarging EU and Their Impact on Relations with Russia," *Journal of European Integration* 25, 2003, pp. 351–369; Ian Lilly, "European Union–Russia Relations: The Oil and Gas Sector at the End of 2002," in Ian Lilly and Klaus Bosselmann, eds., *Repositioning Europe*, Christchurch, New Zealand: University Press, 2003, pp. 83–110; Roland Götz, "Rußlands Erdgas und die Energiesicherheit der EU," SWP-Studie S12/2002 (www.swp-berlin.org).

2 Thirteen percent of state budget revenues (equal to some $13 billion) are from oil and gas export duties alone. Elena Sharipova and Ivan Cherkashin, "Chto daet renta federalnomy byudzhetu? Analiz zavisimost dokhodov rossiiskogo byudzheta ot neftedollarov," *Voprosy ekonomiki* 7, 2004, pp. 51–69, here pp. 61–62.

3 For a detailed analysis of Russian FDI, see Peeter Vahtra and Kari Liuhto, "Expansion or Exodus? Foreign Operations of Russia's Largest Corporations," Electronic Publications of the Pan-European Institute (Turku) 8, 2004, www.tukkk.fi/pei; Kari Liuhto and Jari Jumpponen, "Russian Outward Foreign Direct Investment: Windows Open to the West, Doors Not Closed to the East," in Svetla Marinova and Marin Marinov, eds., *Foreign Direct Investment in Central and Eastern Europe*, Aldershot, UK: Ashgate, 2003, pp. 133–154.

4 Goskomstat, 2004, www.gks.ru.

5 *UNCTAD: World Investment Report 2004*, New York: UNCTAD, 2004, pp. 72–74, www.unctad.org. For a more elaborate version of the argument, see Elina Pelto, Peeter Vahtra, and Kari Liuhto, "Cyp–Rus Investment Flows to Central and Eastern

Europe: Russia's Direct and Indirect Investments via Cyprus to CEE," Electronic Publications of the Pan-European Institute, Turku 2, 2003, www.tukkk.fi/pei.

6  Mark A. Smith, "Russian Business and Foreign Policy," Conflict Studies Research Centre Paper F82, May 2003, p. 8. For similar assessments made over recent years, see for example Rosaria Puglisi, "The 'Normalisation' of Russian Foreign Policy: The Role of Pragmatic Nationalism and Big Business," in Graeme Herd and Jennifer Moroney, eds., *Security Dynamics in the Former Soviet Bloc*, London: RoutledgeCurzon, 2003, pp. 63–79; Robert Stowe, "Foreign Policy Preferences of the New Russian Business Elite," *Problems of Post-Communism* 48, no. 3, 2001, pp. 49–58; Andreas Heinrich, "Large Corporations as National and Global Players. The Case of Gazprom," in Klaus Segbers, ed., *Explaining Post-Soviet Patchworks*, vol. 1, Aldershot, UK: Ashgate, 2001, pp. 97–115; Hans-Henning Schröder, "Unternehmer und Finanzgruppen als Kräfte in der russischen Außenpolitik," *Osteuropa*, 51, 2001, pp. 393–407; Yakov Pappe, "Neftyanaya i gazovaya diplomatiya Rossiya," *Pro et contra* 2, no. 3, 1997, pp. 55–71; Igor Khripunov and Mary M. Matthews, "Russia's oil and gas Interest Group and Its Foreign Policy Agenda," *Problems of Post-Communism* 43, no. 3, 1996, pp. 38–48.

7  For comprehensive accounts of Russia's relations with the EU, see for example: Debra Johnson and Paul Robinson, eds., *Perspectives on EU–Russia Relations*, London: Routledge, 2005; Oksana Antonenko and Kathryn Pinnick, eds., *Russia and the European Union: Prospects for a New Relationship*, London: Routledge, 2005; Roy Allison: *Putin's Russia and The Wider Europe*, Oxford: Blackwell, 2005.

8  Leslie Dienes and Theodore Shabad, *The Soviet Energy System*, Washington, DC: John Wiley, 1979.

9  Jonathan P. Stern, "International Gas Trade in Europe: The Politics of Exporting and Importing Countries," Energy Paper 8, reprint, Aldershot, UK: Gower, 1986, p. 53.

10  On Soviet oil and gas exports, see Dienes and Theodore Shabad, *The Soviet Energy System*; Jochen Bethkenhagen and Herman Clement, *Die sowjetische Energie- und Rohstoffwirtschaft in den 80er Jahren*, Munich: Oldenbourg, 1985; Javier Estrada, Helge Ole Bergesen, Arild Moe, and Anne Kristin Sydnes, *Natural Gas in Europe: Markets, Organisation and Politics*, London: Pinter, 1988.

11  For an analysis of the political, security, and economic aspects of the Yamal project, see Astrid Sahm and Kirsten Westphal, "Power and the Yamal Pipeline," in Margarita M. Balmaceda, James I. Clem, and Lisbeth L. Tarlow, eds., *Independent Belarus*, Cambridge, MA: Harvard University Press, 2002, pp. 270–301.

12  A concise overview of pipeline routes and pipelines projects is given by Roland Götz, "Pipelinepolitik. Wege für Rußlands Erdöl und Erdgas," *Osteuropa* 54, no. 9–10, 2004, pp. 111–130.

13  A concise summary of the Energy Charter is given by James Chalker, "Der Energiecharta-Vertrag," *Osteuropa* 54, no. 9–10, 2004, pp. 55–67.

14  Rüdiger Ahrend and William Tompson, "Russia's Gas Sector: The Endless Wait for Reform?" OECD Economics Department Working Paper 402, September 2004, especially Annex 1.

15  Speech to the European Business Club conference, Moscow, May 2002 (quoted in *Dialogue. Special issue for the Russia–EU Summit*, St. Petersburg, May–June 2003, p. 1, www.mte.gov.ru/docs/3/416.html).

16  The only exception is the oil refineries. A calculation of profits from Russian oil and gas exports in the period 1995 to 2002 is presented by A. Smirnov and L. Posvyanskaya, "Effektivnost' eksporta rossiiskikh energonositelei," *Obshchestvo i ekonomika* 11, 2003, pp. 150–158. Half of Russia's oil production and a third of the country's gas production are exported.

17  "Russia Morning Comment," United Financial Group, 11 August 2004.

18  These are the companies with exports worth at least \$0.5 billion in 2001. Together they accounted for about half of all Russian exports.

19 Andreas Heinrich, "Russian Companies in Old EU Member States: The Case of Germany," *Journal of East–West Business*, forthcoming.

20 For an overview of Russian attempts to enter the EU-25 electricity market, see Alla Startseva, "History in the Making as Russia and Europe Seek to Synchronize Grids," *Energo* (NewsBase), 22 October 2003, p. 2; Alla Startseva, "Could UES Expansion Program Hinder Power Sector Reform in Russia?" *Energo* (NewsBase), 24 September 2003, pp. 3–4; Olga Trofimenko, "In Search of the New Lights: Internationalization of RAO UES," in Kari Liuhto, ed., *East Goes West: The Internationalization of Eastern Enterprises*, Lappeenranta, Finland: Lappeenranta University of Technology, 2001, pp. 114–133.

21 For an example of a brief interlude of complaints, see Philip Hanson, "Russia–EU Economic Relations: Dimensions and Issues," in Christian Meier, Heiko Pleines, and Hans-Henning Schröder, eds., *Ökonomie – Kultur – Politik. Transformationsprozesse in Osteuropa*, Bremen: Edition Temmen, 2003, pp. 185–200, here pp. 187–189.

22 This position has been explicitly formulated by the European Commission: Commission of the European Communities: Green Paper, "Towards a European Strategy for the Security of Energy Supply," COM 2000 0769 (01), Brussels 2000, p. 30, europa.eu.int/eur-lex/en/com/gpr/2000/com2000_0769en.html.

23 For details on the Russian strategy, see the official Energy Strategy 2020 of the Russian government, *Energeticheskaya strategiya Rossii na period do 2020 goda*, Moscow, 2003, pp. 40–43, www.mte.gov.ru/docs/32/103.html.

24 See, for example, Pekka Sutela, "EU, Russia and Common Economic Space," BOFIT Online 3/2005 (www.bof.fi/bofit); Carl Hamilton, "Russia's European Economic Integration: Escapism and Realities," CEPR Discussion Paper 3840, 2003, pp. 16–24, www.cepr.org; or Ivan Samson, "The Common European Economic Space between Russia and the EU: An Institutional Anchor for Accelerating Russian Reform," *Russian Economic Trends Quarterly* 3, 2002, pp. 7–15.

25 On EU attempts to liberalize Russian energy sector regulations, see Ben Aris, "Russia Has the Last Laugh in EU Talks," *FSU Oil and Gas Monitor* (NewsBase), 26 May 2004, pp. 5–6; Jan Adams, "Russia's Gas Diplomacy," *Problems of Post-Communism* 49, no. 3, 2002, pp. 14–22, esp. pp. 19–21; Roland Götz, *Rußlands Erdgas und die Energiesicherheit der EU*, SWP-Studie S12/2002, www.swp-berlin.org, esp. pp. 32–34.

26 Independent gas producers have a share of less than 10 percent in Russia's total production and have not gained access to national politics. Moreover, the most important independent producer, Itera, has developed its business in close cooperation with Gazprom.

27 For a detailed account, see Jan Adams, "Russia's Gas Diplomacy," *Problems of Post-Communism* 49, no. 3, 2002, pp. 14–22, and Heiko Pleines, *Wirtschaftseliten und Politik im Russland der Jelzin-Ära*, Münster: LIT, 2004, pp. 241–255.

28 Russian domestic gas prices are annually set by government decree.

29 Russia reintroduced tariffs for oil exports in 1999. They had been abolished in 1996 as a result of pressure from the International Monetary Fund (IMF). In addition, access to oil export pipelines is regulated by the government. The government has regularly offered preferred pipeline access to state companies (i.e. first of all Rosneft) and has repeatedly threatened to limit pipeline access for companies with overdue tax debts. See Pleines, *Wirtschaftseliten und Politik im Russland*, pp. 230–232. The gas monopoly, Gazprom, is in a better position, as it owns the gas export pipelines. However, it has been forced by the government to give preference to domestic gas demand. Gas exports, too, are subject to customs duties.

30 See the brief case study that follows.

31 Sean Milmo, "Russian Giants Push into CEE Petchem Markets," *Chemical Market Reporter*, 6 November 2000.

32 See the brief case study that follows.

33  US Embassy, Moscow, "A Primer on Pipeline Access and Its Politics in Russia," *Pipeline News*, 5 July 1997.
34  On the system of oil export coordinators, see also Pleines, *Wirtschaftseliten und Politik im Russland*, pp. 230–232, and the literature cited there.
35  Pelto *et al.*, "Cyp–Rus Investment Flows to Central and Eastern Europe."
36  See also Adams, "Russia's Gas Diplomacy"; Heinrich, "Large Corporations as National and Global Players"; Pappe, "Neftyanaya i gazovaya diplomatiya Rossiya"; and Khripunov and Matthews, "Russia's Oil and Gas Interest Group.
37  Based on news reports. For a longer account, see Bartlomiej Nowak, "Foreign Direct Investment in Petroleum Sector in Poland," in Alojzy Nowak, Jeffrey W. Steagall, and Mina N. Baliamoune, eds., *Globalization, International Business and European Integration*, Warsaw: Centre for Europe, 2004, pp. 215–233, here: pp. 223–226.
38  Based on news reports. For longer accounts, see Vaclovas Miškinis, "Atomausstieg und Abhängigkeit. Energieversorgung in Litauen," *Osteuropa* 54, no. 9–10, 2004, pp. 238–249, here pp. 239–242; Heiko Pleines, "Mazeikiu Nafta Sale Marks a Positive Trend for Russian Oil Companies," *FSU Oil and Gas Monitor* (NewsBase), 18 September 2002.
39  Thomas Diez, Stephan Stetter, and Mathias Albert, "The European Union and Border Conflicts: The Transformative Power of Integration," paper presented to the International Studies Association Annual Convention, March 2004.

# 4 Russian energy companies in the new Eastern Europe

## The cases of Ukraine and Belarus

*Margarita M. Balmaceda*

The Soviet period left a legacy of dependency in the former Soviet area, and nowhere is this dependency more clearly seen than in the case of energy. Indeed, Ukraine's and Belarus's degree of dependency on Russian oil and gas has remained very high since 1991.[1] This reliance on Russian energy is largely due to structural factors since both countries depend almost entirely on Russian energy for domestic consumption: there are no pipelines connecting these countries directly to other energy producers, and alternative supplies must be transported through Russia. Both states also depend on Russian capital and sales markets, and businesses in Ukraine and Belarus are tied to Moscow business structures and Soviet-era personal networks. Additionally, the Ukrainian and Belarusian economies retain strong links to Russia in other critical areas, such as metallurgy and heavy machine building.

Looking at energy links helps us to better understand the importance of various types of informal business ties in relation to formal institutions in the international relations of the former Soviet area. Structural economic and business ties are strong in stark contrast to those formal institutions created among former states of the Soviet Union, which have all remained very weak or exist virtually only on paper (the Commonwealth of Independent States – CIS, the Belarus–Russian Union,[2] and the Common Economic Space created in 2004). Thus, while integration attempts have failed at the level of formal institutions, integration is taking place at the level of economic and business links, overwhelmingly bilateral as opposed to multilateral in form. At the same time, looking at energy relations allows us to appreciate the role of multilateral (formal or informal) institutions and relationships. Indeed, one reason for the limits on Russia's ability to use Ukraine's economic dependency for political goals may be related to the fact that Ukraine's importance as a transport route for Russian oil and gas to Western Europe has also made Russia to some degree dependent on Ukraine; dependency is thus not a one-way street.

In order to appreciate both the conflict and the cooperation potential resulting from Russian business engagement in Ukraine and Belarus, it is necessary to understand the complex interplay of Russian business actors, the Russian state, and domestic political and economic actors in the two countries. Moreover, conflicts might arise not only from diverging interests between states and corporations, but also from various and competing interests within important economic actors themselves. In the case of important Russian energy companies such as Gazprom, for instance, we even encounter a situation where top managers of formally state-owned companies have used them to pursue personal interests, thus leading to conflicts between private and corporate interests within a single business.

Understanding the differing balances between state, corporate, and private interests in the behavior of Russian companies in Ukraine and Belarus is essential for understanding the different outcomes in these two cases. This chapter thus pays special attention to the role of domestic variables in both Ukraine and Belarus in order to obtain a better sense of the nature of conflict resulting from Russian business expansion. In energy-poor states such as Ukraine and Belarus, various domestic groups have taken advantage of their country's energy dependency to secure exclusive benefits either by accessing or distributing scarce resources, or by forging alliances with economic groups outside their borders.[3] Ukraine and Belarus present an interesting contrast in this regard because Russian business has been able to purchase significant energy assets in Ukraine but has had little success in Belarus.

Chronic payments arrears and the use of barter exchanges have contributed to a lack of transparency in both economic transactions and policy making within the former Soviet Union. The degree of transparency within a country matters, because nontransparent systems offer fertile ground for corruption and for the appropriation of significant "rents of dependency" at the expense of the state as a whole; at the same time, the lack of a transparent policy-making process fosters corruption. Actors benefiting from a lack of transparency will also tend to cooperate with each other, and will be more willing to work with countries where similarly low levels of transparency are generally accepted, but less willing to work with partners where a higher level of transparency can be expected.[4] Thus, these less than transparent links are more likely to be with Russia than with Western partners, likely pushing Ukraine and Belarus toward continued energy dependency, rather than challenging it. Accordingly, this chapter presents case study analyses of Ukraine and Belarus, looking at the interests of the Russian state, the major Russian companies working in the two countries, and their interaction with local actors. The concluding sections assess the potential for conflict and cooperation.

## The case of Ukraine

Ukraine's location, sandwiched between an expanding European Union and Russia, and the nature of the domestic political economy are critical for understanding the dynamics of conflict and cooperation resulting from Russian business engagement. The Ukrainian–Russian relationship is evolving in the context of Russian attempts to build a closer relationship with the former Soviet republics. From a Russian perspective, Ukraine is the most important of the CIS states because of its physical size, geographic location, and economic weight. At the same time, Ukraine's proximity to the European Union and the existence of strong pro-European integration currents within the country make the future of the EU–Ukrainian relationship central for the future of Ukrainian–Russian relations. While the European Union would like to support Ukraine's sovereignty, it has fallen short of offering the country an opportunity to become an EU member in the foreseeable future. Ukraine has been relatively neglected in an EU policy that clearly privileges the relationship with Russia, especially in the energy area.

The Ukrainian domestic context to the Ukrainian–Russian economic relationship is characterized by the extreme chaos and decline in the Ukrainian domestic economy in the first years after independence, and by the emergence of powerful and politically well connected business-administrative groups[5] from the mid-1990s on. The 1995–2004 Ukrainian system was, indeed, characterized by a system of informal balances between these strong groups, with President Leonid Kuchma playing an important steadying role for purposes of remaining in power. Whether or not this system will undergo significant changes under President Viktor Yushchenko remains to be seen.

### Russian state interests in Ukraine

For much of the postindependence period, Russia has lacked a comprehensive strategy toward Ukraine.[6] What has existed, rather, has been poorly coordinated, often badly conceived policies aimed at keeping Ukraine within the Russian sphere of influence. The heavy-handed Russian support for Ukrainian presidential candidate Viktor Yanukovich in 2004 was emblematic of this policy. Accordingly, while in many cases the interests of the Russian government and those of Russian businesses in Ukraine have coincided, there is little substance to the idea that Russian companies in Ukraine act as a well-organized "fifth column" supporting Russian policy needs. Russian policy has been too poorly defined to organize such a column.

Despite these difficulties, Russia clearly has three goals that shape its policies toward Ukraine. First and foremost, Russian leaders seek to include Ukraine in a variety of integration projects in the post-Soviet space (be it the CIS, the Customs Union, or a Common Economic Space). Second, they attempt to secure stable and low-priced transit of Russian oil and gas through Ukraine, while simultaneously looking for alternative routes by which Russia can send energy to Western markets without having to transit Ukrainian territory. Ukraine's importance for Russia along this energy dimension was made clear when President Putin appointed former Gazprom head Viktor Chernomyrdin as Russian ambassador to Kyiv in 2001. A third important goal of Russian state policy in Ukraine is the desire to prevent Ukraine's full integration into Western institutions and to maintain it as one of a number of "friendly, neutral units with maximum freedom in cultural, economic and social spheres, but strategically dependent upon Moscow."[7]

Although these goals are visible in Russian policy toward Ukraine, whether they coincide with Russia's long-term state interests (in both a foreign relations and a domestic sense) is the subject of debate among both Russian and Western scholars. Critics of Russia's pro-integrationist policies in the post-Soviet space, including heavy-handed policies toward Ukraine, argue that Russia's long-term interests are better served by a policy stressing membership in the World Trade Organization (WTO), closer relations with the European Union and the United States, and a deeper integration into the Western economic system more generally.[8]

### Interests of Russian energy corporations in Ukraine

Now that we have examined the Russian state's interests in Ukraine, this section will lay out the interests of Russian energy corporations there, particularly Gazprom, smaller gas suppliers, and the oil companies. The purpose is to determine how compatible Russian state and corporate interests are.

#### Gas sector

Gazprom's corporate interests in Ukraine are centered on guaranteeing the safety and volume of its natural gas shipments to West European markets, and on acquiring control over the gas transit infrastructure – including not only pipelines but also underground reservoirs, of which Ukraine's are some of the largest in Europe. At the same time, Gazprom has a variety of interests in Ukraine that go beyond the company's economic concerns. On the one hand, there is the evolving relationship between Gazprom and the Russian state, which takes place in a situation where "the boundaries of state and private property are increasingly blurred," allowing state officials to grab company assets.[9] On the other hand, within Gazprom itself the interests of top managers have at times competed with, or taken precedence over, corporate interests, leading top managers to create separate firms that are closely affiliated with Gazprom and receive preferential treatment so that they can engage in asset stripping to the detriment of the mother company.[10] Indeed, the case of Ukrainian–Russian gas relations provides rich examples of such practices, particularly in the cases of Itera, Eural Trans Gas (ETG), and Rosukrenergo.

Itera, an important intermediary in the sale of Turkmenistani gas to Ukraine until 2001, made a significant profit out of the relationship by overcharging Ukraine and underpaying Gazprom for transportation and other services. Despite increased state oversight over Gazprom after Rem Viakhirev's replacement as Gazprom's president by Aleksei Miller in June 2001, similar trends continued. However, since companies like Itera have become the focus of intense media scrutiny, Gazprom is now increasingly using new companies as intermediaries. In 2002, Gazprom replaced Itera with a small, unknown firm registered in Hungary, ETG, for the transportation of gas from Turkmenistan, losing between $130 million and $1 billion for services it could have provided itself.[11] While such deals benefit neither Ukraine nor Gazprom, they have the potential to enrich well-connected individuals working in both the government and the company.[12] Although deals such as these do not directly create instability in a traditional sense, they affect it by reducing the ability of countries such as Ukraine to control their energy situation. Thus, in the case of Gazprom there has been a coincidence between state and corporate interests in Ukraine, with the qualification that private interests within the company and in the public sector have played a very important role as well.

*Oil sector*

The oil refining sector well exemplifies the long-standing impact of Soviet legacies. Some of the largest Soviet refineries were established in Ukraine, but these refineries can only work profitably as part of a larger market guaranteeing regular crude oil supplies and access to markets throughout the former Soviet Union. As a refinery's profitability depends directly on the degree to which its production capacity is utilized, the end of stable oil supplies from Russia led to virtual paralysis of the sector in Belarus and Ukraine. By 1999, this crisis had made Ukraine especially receptive to Russian oil companies' offers to take over Ukrainian refineries in debt-for-shares deals. In the course of six months in 2000, Russian companies took over more than half of the Ukrainian petroleum market.[13] By 2002, the largest six of the eight Ukrainian refineries had come under Russian oil companies' control; by 2003, Russian companies did 90 percent of the refining. Russian management of the Ukrainian refineries is especially significant as it allows Russian oil companies in Ukraine to acquire control over the whole oil production and sales chain, covering crude oil imports, refining, and oil product sales and exports. Such extensive control allows them to create vertically integrated networks that operate on the Ukrainian market as self-sufficient actors.

Of the Russian companies involved in the Ukrainian refinery business, the most important is LUKoil, which owns the Odessa oil refinery and a large gas station network. Other important Russian players in the refinery sector are Tatneft and TNK-BP. TNK-BP also has important oil transit interests; it was the main motor behind the reversal of the Odessa–Brody pipeline through which the company converted Ukrainian infrastructure to Russian purposes.[14] TNK-BP also has strong interests in preventing Central Asian oil from competing with Russian oil in West European markets.

The massive entrance of Russian players into the Ukrainian refinery sector in 2000–2003 served the interests of individual companies and the Russian state, as control of Ukraine's refining sector by Russian companies helps maintain Ukraine's economic dependence on Russia and, most importantly, further binds the Ukrainian economy to Russia's, supporting Russia's integration projects in the former CIS.

When the Russian company TNK succeeded in reversing the direction of the Odessa-Brody pipeline, using it to transport Russian oil to the Black Sea instead of Caspian oil to Ukraine and beyond to Western Europe, the interests of Russian oil companies and the Russian state again largely coincided. From

TNK's perspective, the most important goals of the reversal were to prevent Caspian oil from competing with Russian oil in European markets, as well as to keep Ukraine – now a purchaser of Russian oil at world market prices – from switching to alternative suppliers. These efforts coincided with Russian policy vis-à-vis Ukraine: preventing the country from becoming economically independent from Russia and from building closer ties with Poland and Western Europe. Indeed, many believe that the real objective of the reversal proposal was not to increase the transit of Russian oil to the Odessa port, but to prevent the diversification of Ukraine's oil supply and block the entrance of competing Caspian oil to the West European markets independent of Russian pipelines. Indeed a reversal of Odessa–Brody was not even necessary for Russia to transport its oil to Western Europe, as the existing Transdniester pipelines could have been used for shipping those supplies at a lower price.[15] In this sense, the interests of Russian energy companies coincided with those of the Russian state.

In other areas, the interests of the Russian state and oil companies working in Ukraine turned out to be incompatible. One example was the value added tax (VAT) on oil and gas exports to Ukraine. Until 2004, Russia credited the VAT on oil and gas exports to Ukraine on an "exporting country" basis, meaning energy VAT income went to Russia, not Ukraine. Many Russian oil exporters opposed this system because it decreased their profitability and they lobbied the Russian government to change it. For a long time, the companies had no luck in rescinding the tax because it brought in $800 million for the state in tax revenue. When Russia finally decided to change the VAT system, switching to crediting it on a "receiving country" basis, the purpose was less to serve the interests of Russian companies than to try to boost Viktor Yanukovich's chances in the 2004 presidential electoral campaign by increasing Ukrainian revenue sources.[16]

Overall, in the course of Ukrainian president Kuchma's second term, Russian businesses, with the collaboration of some local business-administrative groups, were successful in steering Ukraine's energy policy in the direction of relinquishing *de facto* control over its oil and gas transit system in favor of Russian private or state companies. As a result of little-publicized agreements with oil companies,[17] as well as official agreements with Gazprom[18] and Transneft,[19] by late 2004, Russian oil and gas companies actually controlled most of Ukraine's oil and gas trade, export business, and infrastructure. This outcome was closely in line with Russia's state interest in keeping Ukraine tied to a Russia-centered economic space and limiting its contacts with the West.

### Russian business: enhancing stability or fostering conflict?

Russian businesses bolstered stability in Ukraine in a very basic way: they contributed to the revival of the Ukrainian oil refining sector, which had been paralyzed by a lack of investments and unstable supplies in the years following independence. It is hard to overestimate the importance of this development, since without stable oil and oil-product supplies many important branches of the Ukrainian economy – from transport to agriculture – simply could not function.

Russia is able to play this stabilizing role because of the infrastructure dependencies that exist between Russia and Ukraine.

Russian business has played a variety of conflict-exacerbating roles. Corporate Russia's virtually complete control over oil refining and oil and gas supplies to Ukraine has made the country especially vulnerable to the use of energy as a pressure mechanism by Russia. It would certainly be too simplistic to argue that the Russian state purposefully used energy-sector companies to pursue its interests in Ukraine. However, the Russian state did play a significant direct role in bilateral energy relations, in the framework of oil and gas negotiations, for example. This effort was most visible in the case of Russia's oil embargo against Ukraine in early 2000, when Russia sought to put pressure on Ukraine to stop the illegal pilfering of natural gas from the pipeline delivering Russian gas to Western Europe and to reduce transit fees. Similarly, during discussions between Russian fuel and energy minister Viktor Kaliuzhny and Ukrainian prime minister Anatoly Kinakh in December 1999, Kaliuzhny linked the issue of future oil supplies to Ukraine to the issue of Ukraine paying back its gas debts.[20] This demand was especially interesting because it required the oil sector, an area that had made the transition to market forces with relatively limited state intervention, to cover the cost of continued problems in the *gas* relationship with Russia.

In the case of the debates on the possible reversal of the Odessa–Brody pipeline, TNK generated conflict by exacerbating and taking advantage of previously existing disputes. Friction was present among Ukraine's state companies, within the strata of the country's political elite, and in Ukraine's foreign relations. The TNK proposal to reverse the oil flow fostered conflict between pro-reversal and anti-reversal supporters within state-owned companies such as Ukrtransnafta, where battles around the pipeline mirrored both internal struggles for control of the company and larger battles on the relative role of the company vis-à-vis other state-owned energy companies. At the level of the political elite, TNK's proposal exacerbated conflict by pitting the question of Ukraine's long-term national interest (in the form of the original use of the pipeline) against that of the expected immediate financial gain that would come from the reversal of the pipeline. At the level of Ukraine's relationship with Poland and the European Union, TNK's proposal fostered conflict by calling into question the degree of Western commitment to Ukraine and by strengthening the position of those – starting with then-President Kuchma himself – who accused the European Union and Poland of not providing enough economic support for the development of the project.

In gas transit issues, Gazprom's behavior has often promoted conflict. Most flagrant is Gazprom's handling of three issues: the building of new pipelines around Ukraine, the establishment of an international gas consortium to manage Ukraine's gas transit system, and the transit of Central Asian gas to Ukraine.

Gazprom's strategy of developing alternative gas export pipelines bypassing Ukraine in order to limit Russia's dependence on a single transit country and preventing the illegal siphoning of gas along existing transit routes was at the basis of the idea to build the Yamal pipeline through Belarus and Poland, construct a second branch of Yamal, which would take additional gas away from Ukraine, and seek control over Ukraine's (and Belarus's) gas transit system. Such initiatives – and the way they were pursued – have not contributed to increased cooperation in the area, but, instead, have led to growing competition and conflict between Ukraine and Belarus. Such conflict was evident in Ukraine's behavior during Russia's short-term suspension of gas deliveries to Belarus in February 2004: rather than acting in solidarity with Belarus, Ukraine promptly made available additional transit capacity, so that Russia could continue its gas deliveries to Western Europe regardless of the crisis.

Gazprom's behavior concerning the establishment of a "gas consortium" also demonstrated the potential to promote conflict. A 2001 high-level agreement between Ukraine, Germany, and Russia envisioned the creation of a trilateral consortium to operate Ukraine's gas transit system, an idea that promised to reduce the politicization of the Ukrainian–Russian relationship by introducing a third partner (Germany) into the equation. Nevertheless, Gazprom's behavior throughout the negotiations quashed many of these hopes: the company conducted negotiations with little transparency, and systematically eased German participants out of the consortium, since keeping the consortium a bilateral affair would strengthen the Russian side's power vis-à-vis a weaker Ukraine.[21] This behavior has clearly reduced the odds that a stable, sustainable and non-Russian-controlled gas transit system will be built in Ukraine in the near future.

### *Situation after the "Orange Revolution"*

Although Russia's support in the 2004 presidential elections for pro-establishment candidate Viktor Yanukovich misfired, structural economic ties remain important and both countries continue to have an interest in smooth relations. Indeed, the situation that emerged after Viktor Yushchenko's inauguration as president in January 2005 sheds light on the potential role of business in moderating conflict in Russian–Ukrainian relations. Russia's support for Yanukovich allowed the pro-Yushchenko opposition to use criticism of Russian-supported corruption as an important rallying cry in the elections.

Yet since the elections, a new trend has started to emerge: many Russian businessmen, alarmed at the growing encroachment by the Russian state on Russian business inside Russia, are looking toward Yushchenko's Ukraine, with its promises of transparent policy making and separation of state and business, as an opportunity to invest and continue their business on familiar terrain, but without the growing constraints imposed by the Russian state. Demonstrative of this trend is President Yushchenko's naming of Russian liberal politician Boris Nemtsov as an adviser, and LUKoil's February 2005 decision to invest an additional $300 million in Ukraine.[22] Although the ability of the new Ukrainian regime to keep "business" and "politics" separate and thus to implement fair and transparent rules of the game was called into question by the corruption scandals of September 2005, culminating in Yulia Tymoshenko's dismissal as prime minister[23] and the "nonaggression agreement" between President Yuschenko and former PM Yanukovich, many Russian businesses continue to be optimistic about their ability to do business in post-Orange Revolution Ukraine.[24]

## The case of Belarus

The evolution of the Russian–Belarusian integration process is the most important of the international factors affecting the role of Russian business in Belarus. During the Yeltsin period, Russia sought to develop its relationship with Belarus as part of a broader strategy of reviving economic ties with the former Soviet republics. In this strategy, integration with Belarus presumably served to make a "single economic space" with Russia more attractive to other post-Soviet states as well. For playing this role, Russia paid Belarus with low-price gas supplies and by disregarding Belarus's small violations of the single customs space.[25] The Russian expectation was that these "investments" would lead to increased opportunities for Russian capital and would eventually attract other post-Soviet republics to join the Russian–Belarusian Union or, at the very least, participate in the economic integration projects Russia proposed. When Putin came to power at the end of 1999 and Russia's emphasis further shifted toward establishing relations with the European Union, Belarusian president Aleksandr Lukashenko, who continued his sharp anti-Western rhetoric, started to become more of a hindrance and an obstacle to Russia's new priorities.[26] If by 2005 Lukashenko was still able to extract some concessions from Russia, his success had less to do with the attractiveness of the Russia–Belarus integration model than with his ability to speak for many conservative Russian politicians when accusing the Russian government of complacency in the face of Western, and particularly NATO, expansion and blaming the Kremlin for not doing enough to reintegrate the countries of the former Soviet Union.

For all the talk about a possible union between Russia and Belarus, since the mid-1990s the actual behavior of both partners reflects a different reality. The economic aspects of the charter of the Union of Russia and Belarus, signed in May 1997, have remained largely on paper, and serious disagreements have periodically occurred, most often over the issues of Russian energy supplies, energy investments, the negative coverage of Belarus in the Russian mass media, and the status of Belarus within a Russian–Belarusian common federative state.

That little real economic integration has taken place in practice is due partly to Russia's reluctance to further subsidize the Belarusian economy, but also to President Lukashenko's contradictory – and often clearly negative – attitudes toward closer economic relations with Russia. As early as 1997, Russia's then-deputy prime minister, Boris Nemtsov, deftly described the position of the Belarusian leadership regarding a potential union with Russia as a political game: "On the one hand, there is constant talk about economic integration; and, on the other, all possible juridical, administrative and economic obstacles are created to prevent this integration from really happening."[27]

Although Nemtsov's statement continues to be valid as of late 2005, Lukashenko's ability to continue playing an integration "game" without allowing it to acquire real content is becoming increasingly untenable, as one of its main components, the subsidization of the economy through lower than world prices for gas, will be hard to maintain as a result of Russia's expected admission to the WTO.[28] Once Russia joins the WTO, its domestic gas prices will rise, reducing its ability to provide gas subsidies for political goals, and this may force both sides to adopt a more businesslike approach to their relationship. At the same time, under the growing strain of an uncertain energy supply situation, Lukashenko may be more amenable to acquiesce to Gazprom acquiring control over the country's gas transit system.

The Belarusian domestic context, which largely revolves around President Lukashenko's personal role and interests, is also very important if we are to understand the dynamics of conflict and cooperation resulting from Russian business engagement. Lukashenko has used politically motivated cheap energy supplies from Russia not only to keep the whole economy afloat, but to directly finance his own ability to stay in office, as was seen clearly through the considerable financial support he received from Russian oil companies in the summer 2001 presidential campaign. Similarly, Lukashenko welcomes the absence of a customs border between Belarus and Russia because it provides opportunities to profit through tax evasion and smuggling. Companies close to the presidential administration have been able to gain significant revenue from this situation.[29] The "rents of dependency" accruing from the relationship with Gazprom and the Russian oil sector are also used for regime maintenance purposes: President Lukashenko has reportedly funneled the difference between gas prices paid to Gazprom and the higher prices paid by the population into a "parallel" presidential administration budget, which operates beyond public oversight.[30]

At the same time, propaganda plays an important role. Russian oil and gas are used for regime maintenance purposes not only in the sense that they are needed to keep the Belarusian economy going, but also to fulfill ideological purposes: only with ample, constant, and cheap supplies of Russian oil and gas is Lukashenko able to maintain the high rates of economic growth presented to the world as evidence of the superiority of the "Belarusian model" in the post-Soviet landscape.

But President Lukashenko also wants to keep total control of his country and, thus, is extremely reluctant to make any agreements that would chip away at his supremacy. Lukashenko's own fears about what the large-scale entrance of Russian capital to Belarus could mean for his power lie at the basis of his negative attitude to the economic aspects of closer relations with Russia. A real Russian entrance into the Belarusian economy, in which powerful Russian corporations purchased controlling stakes in important Belarusian enterprises rather than merely working as minority shareholders, would go against two of Lukashenko's methods of exercising almost absolute political control over the country. First, the entrance of Russian business would eventually result in the emergence of autonomous sources of economic power, which would be difficult to control. Currently, all major political and economic players in the country, from entrepreneurs to cabinet-level ministers, depend on favors from the president and cannot operate autonomously. Second, the arrival of outside firms would inevitably force greater transparency on the local economy and therefore would contradict Lukashenko's practice of "privatizing" the shadow economy and extracting money from this source for the purposes of his presidential administration. Nothing exemplifies these fears more clearly than Russia's interest in Belarus's energy sector. Thus, one of the few plausible answers to the puzzle of Lukashenko's contradictory relations with Russia is that he wants a close relationship insofar – and only insofar – as it allows him to maintain personal power.

The only event that could drastically alter this situation would be a sharp worsening of Belarus's economic situation, particularly one provoked by high energy prices or a cutoff in supplies. This point was almost reached in 2004 when Russia imposed a short-term, but total, suspension of gas supplies in February, and Gazprom subsequently refused to sign a gas supply agreement on Belarus's terms. Under this intense pressure, Belarus agreed to start the process of assessing the Belarusian gas transit monopolist Beltransgaz's market value, marking a first decisive step in the possible privatization of the company, with Gazprom gaining a significant stake in it. Gazprom's purchase of shares in the firm has been discussed between both countries for the past ten years.

### *Key Russian players and their interests*

This subsection provides an overview of the key Russian corporations working in Belarus. The most important by far is Gazprom. Some smaller natural gas companies also play a role, as do some of Russia's oil companies.

#### *Gas sector*

Gazprom is not only the most important Russian business player in Belarus, but also the most important Russian business player *for* the Belarusian government. The transit fees earned from Russian gas transported through Belarusian territory are an important source of tax revenue. Additionally, some of the income indirectly generated by the transit relationship with Gazprom is used by the Lukashenko government for regime-strengthening measures.[31]

Gazprom's main interest concerning Belarus goes beyond simply maintaining dependable gas transit through the country. The company also wants to support viable and economically competitive options for the transit of gas to Western Europe that allow Gazprom to reduce both its risks and its transit costs, and thus protect its nearly unblemished reputation as a reliable supplier, without having to rely exclusively on Ukraine.[32] Maintaining such flexibility in transit options is essential for Gazprom's strategy of making sure it does not become hostage to a single gatekeeper country for its gas exports. All of Gazprom's other interests stem from this one: purchasing a stake in Beltransgaz, the Belarusan natural gas pipeline owner, making sure there is a Gazprom-friendly government in Belarus, and maintaining low transit fees. Additionally, Gazprom seeks to maintain good relations with the Russian government by acting according to the government's perception of Russian state interests and Belarus's role in achieving these interests.

Gazprom's interest in protecting its right to transport natural gas through Belarus is exemplified in its desire to acquire Beltransgaz. Discussions about such a sale started in 1994, but have only proceeded in fits and starts and not produced any results. Gazprom's goals are to secure ultimate decision-making power in the company regardless of the form of ownership and, ultimately, to purchase the company at a low price. Negotiating a mutually acceptable price seems to be one of the biggest hurdles, as Belarus's official estimation of the value of the company is $5 billion, while Russian analysts claim that $600 million would be more reasonable.[33]

Russian frustration over Belarus's backpedaling on the privatization of Beltransgaz to Gazprom led Gazprom to temporarily suspend gas deliveries to Belarus in February 2004. Naturally, Gazprom closely coordinated this move with the Russian state. Indeed, it would have been impossible for Gazprom to suspend deliveries to Belarus without the official blessing of the Russian government. According to Belarusian sources, the suspension of gas deliveries to Belarus cost Gazprom a minimum of $10 million per day, in addition to endangering its until then unchallenged reputation as a reliable supplier. Assuming this figure is correct, it provides evidence that the suspension of gas deliveries was done with broader foreign policy goals, even seeking Belarus's "political and economic capitulation to Russia," as Belarusian analyst Tatiana Manenok claimed.[34]

In the case of Belarus, and in contrast to Ukraine, the interests of Gazprom as a corporation and those of the Russian state seem to play a larger role than private interests within Gazprom. To a great extent, Gazprom's interests in Belarus and those of the Russian state (and the Putin regime) are compatible: to safeguard transit and maintain political influence in Belarus. However, in practice the current situation goes beyond a simple coincidence of interests, because Gazprom can use "points" with the Russian state acquired in Belarus as bargaining chips in its broader relationship with the state. Here it is essential to keep in mind that not all the benefits received by the parties in the Belarusian–Russian relationship can be measured in monetary terms. Because of the very special role of Belarus in Russian foreign policy, the Russian government may reward companies engaged in Belarus in unusual ways, making the relationship between state and business especially important in this area.

What kind of nonmonetary benefits does Gazprom get from its relationship with Belarus? When Russian companies such as Gazprom lose money by selling gas to Belarus at preferential prices, they gain a certain amount of credit with the Russian state. The Russian state requires Gazprom to sell gas to Belarus at prices that are significantly lower than current market prices. Between 1999 and 2003,[35] Gazprom sold gas to Belarus at domestic Russian prices,[36] one-fourth or even less than those on European markets. The issue of subsidization of the Belarusian economy through the sale of gas at domestic Russian prices between 1999 and 2003 has been one of the most controversial aspects of the Belarusian–Russian relationship, and one of the most complex situations involving Russian business. Both partners engage in tense discussions each year during contract negotiations, arguing over prices, volumes supplied, and whether each partner has met the explicit or implied terms and conditions of the subsidized price arrangement. The "points" Gazprom accrues from such sales give the company some leverage over the Russian state and can be used later to obtain advantages in other areas. How these points are transferred from the foreign policy realm to a domestic arena and eventually converted into monetary benefits varies from sector to sector and case to case. In the oil sector, formal, institutionalized means are available, such as through the granting of additional export quotas, which are very important given the critical lack of export pipeline capacity available to oil companies that deliver to Belarus. In the gas sector, the conversion takes place in the areas of credits, gas prices, and privatization issues. Additionally, Gazprom receives state protection against international pressure for breaking up the gas monopoly into a number of smaller companies and for the de-monopolization of the Russian gas market.

The issue of credits well exemplifies the conversion of points. Historically, Gazprom has complained bitterly about gas payment arrears by both Ukraine and Belarus. To address this problem, the Russian government has provided many low-interest credits *ex post facto* (for example, after the February 2004 gas deliveries crisis) aimed specifically at helping Belarus pay its debt to Gazprom, something Russia has not done for Ukraine, or at least not with the largesse and liberal terms made available to Belarus. These payments are essentially subsidies, but from the Russian state budget rather than Gazprom's, and thus serve as a belated reward for Gazprom's previous support of state policy in Belarus.[37]

## Oil sector

Oil companies such as Slavneft and LUKoil, as well as the Russian oil pipeline monopoly Transneft, are active in Belarus. These companies have important interests in the Belarusian refinery sector, although their plans to take control of Belarusian refineries and related petrochemical industries have achieved only limited success, in contrast to the situation in Ukraine. In particular, Slavneft's attempts to gain control of the Mozyr refinery have not been successful, owing to repeated hurdles established by the Belarusian government.

Oil refining is an area of strong common interest between Russian companies and Belarus. Approximately half of Russia's oil exports go through Belarus, utilizing a key pipeline link. Belarus's oil refining capacity is comparable with Ukraine's: 11 million tons per year compared to Ukraine's 12–12.5 million tons.[38] Oil refined in Belarus is easier to export to the West than oil refined in Russia, and access to the European refined oil products market is especially important, as this market is more profitable than that for crude oil.[39] In 2003,

96.07 percent of Belarus's exports of oil products went to countries outside the CIS, particularly West European markets.[40] Additionally, the Russian oil companies find it advantageous to supply the nearby Russian *oblasti* with oil refined in Belarus rather than in Siberia or the Volga region, where many of the Russian refineries are located. A further advantage of refining in Belarus is that it allows Russian oil producers to circumvent both oil export limitations and high export duties imposed by the Russian state, as oil shipments to Belarus are not counted as exports. (Russian oil producers refine oil in Belarus for subsequent reexport to Western Europe in small batches.)

Because of Belarus's geographical convenience and the possibility of evading both export restrictions and growing export duties, from the mid-1990s onwards Russian oil companies LUKoil, Yukos, and Slavneft have been interested in acquiring full or partial ownership of Belarus's two refining complexes, Mozyr and Novopolotsk. Control over Belarusian refineries is especially important for LUKoil, because it has the capacity to refine domestically only about 25 percent of the crude oil that it extracts. For Belarus, which inherited from the Soviet Union a modern refining system much larger than necessary to process domestically produced crude, Russian supplies are essential to keep the industry alive. Indeed, the refining business is one of the main ways in which Belarus benefits from Russia's current oil boom, using the proceeds to maintain stability and the longevity of the current regime. Belarus derives significant benefits from these refining operations, through taxes, increased employment, and the spillover into the petrochemical and metallurgy sectors generated by these operations. This income is used not only to subsidize less profitable sectors of the Belarusian economy (agriculture, for example), but also by the president himself in the form of oil company contributions, channeled through the presidential administration as "voluntary donations" to finance politically important social welfare projects. As noted earlier, Lukashenko uses these means to stay in power.

### Russian state and business: converging or diverging interests?

In general, the interests of Russian energy companies and those of the Russian state largely coincide in the case of Belarus. Both the oil and gas companies and the Russian state are interested in safeguarding the stability of oil and gas transit through Belarus in the context of an export pipeline diversification policy. Both oil and gas companies and the Russian state are interested in gaining control over Belarus's refining sector and its gas transit infrastructure as a safeguard against political instability, and as a way of keeping transit fees low.

At the same time, their interests differ in two areas. First, while Russian oil companies benefit from the possibility of side-door exports through Belarus as a way of minimizing taxes and avoiding export quotas, it is not in the interest of the Russian government to lose the related tax income.

The second, and greater, difference between the Russian state and Russian energy companies active in Belarus concerns the issue of support for President Aleksander Lukashenko. While both Russian business and the state have supported Lukashenko as a way to maintain stability in the energy sector, the business sector's interest in supporting Lukashenko may run out much sooner than that of the Russian state. For the Russian state, Lukashenko is not only a guarantor of transit stability, but someone who fulfills an important political role. Despite Russian disagreements with Lukashenko, Belarus remains Russia's "last ally" in the post-Soviet area, and this situation has not escaped the Putin government, which is eager to show that it continues to have influence and at least one ally among not necessarily friendly neighbors and in the face of an expanding NATO. Indeed, Lukashenko's image as the greatest defender of the Belarusian–Russian Union has been central to his popularity in Russia, where he has been a hero to the many Russians fearful of "imperial decline." The value of Belarus as an ally can be seen mainly in the political and military spheres, helping Putin show the Russian public he is at the forefront of integration processes as a response to "anti-Russian" tendencies in Ukraine and Georgia. Indeed, the strategic and military aspect of the relationship should not be underestimated, given Belarus's latest steps in terms of strengthening its military forces.[41]

For those in the Russian business sector, on the other hand, Lukashenko's usefulness may be much more limited, because they see few tangible economic benefits. As discussed above, Russian businesses in Belarus reap only indirect rewards from the relationship, and the fact that many of them, particularly Gazprom, are called to sacrifice immediate profits for the sake of helping the Belarusian economy makes these benefits even less tangible.

### *Potential for conflict and cooperation*

In the case of Belarus, Gazprom's behavior has largely promoted stability (at least through 2004), but a very particular kind of stability. First, Belarus is heavily dependent on Gazprom. Gazprom's monopoly control of gas transit through its pipelines has made it more difficult for Belarus to use supplies from independent gas producers as a way to overcome Gazprom's pressure. Belarus signed short-term contracts with these suppliers after Gazprom refused to sign a long-term contract in 2004. Moreover, Russia's Federal Energy Commission limits the amount of gas independent producers can sell to Belarus, making it impossible for Belarus to find other suppliers.

Second, Gazprom's (and, through it, the Russian government's) support for President Lukashenko in the late 1990s and early 2000s was intended to safeguard transit along the Yamal pipeline, at that time seen as the main alternative to a Ukraine deemed unfriendly and unreliable. Yet such a strategy underestimated the conflict potential in Lukashenko's relationship with Gazprom and his willingness and capacity to obstruct the company's privatization plans in Belarus, as well as to use methods previously associated with Ukraine (such as taking gas from Russian pipelines and reexporting it illegally). Thus, by the February 2004 crisis, Lukashenko could no longer guarantee long-term stability in the transit of Russian gas through Belarus.

Moreover, Lukashenko has been able to turn conflict with Gazprom into a successful populist tool he can use in Belarus's broader relationship with Russia. In each of the gas supply crises in which Gazprom either reduced (November 2002) or suspended (February 2004) gas deliveries, President Lukashenko reacted by accusing Russia of abandoning allies and thus obstructing the reintegration process, which enjoys wide popular support in Russia. Moreover, Lukashenko even threatened to build closer relations with the West in response to Russian pipeline policy. These threats have usually produced favorable results and Lukashenko has been able to win concessions, as the Russian state provided new credits to compensate for the higher prices charged by Gazprom.

Finally, support for the Lukashenko regime has also had broader long-term impacts on stability. Such a strategy totally neglected the question of possible alternative leaders to Lukashenko, and, in addition, set the Belarusian opposition against Gazprom and Russia, reducing the chances that a new, post-Lukashenko leader would have a strong pro-Gazprom position though, of course, any post-Lukashenko leader will have to work within the framework of Belarus's dependence on Russia. Additionally, the very fact that Russia supported the Lukashenko regime was not sustainable from the point of view of Belarus as a whole – it simply allowed the preservation of an increasingly unworkable economic system, rather than establishing the basis for urgently needed reforms. Paradoxically, as the unreformed Belarusian system was kept in place with Russian support, Belarus and Russia started to drift increasingly apart in terms of their economic policies, as Russia made relatively greater progress enacting reforms, making their eventual unification more difficult.

## Conclusion

Although pursuing largely similar goals (maximizing transit options, gaining control over infrastructure important for the companies' domestic and international plans, keeping competitors out of important markets), Russian oil and gas companies have exhibited different relationships with the Russian state in their behavior in Belarus and Ukraine. Two factors explain these differences. First, even within the same companies the balance between state, corporate, and private interests has been different in Belarus and Ukraine, with private interests playing a much greater role in Ukraine. Second, the informal conversion of points for services provided in support of Russian state policies in Belarus and Ukraine has been different. The difference results from the Russian leadership's perception that Belarus is more part of the "domestic" Russian system than Ukraine is.

The most important energy actor in both countries is Gazprom, and that company's relationship with the state differs as between Ukraine and Belarus. In Belarus, Gazprom's behavior seems to be part of its domestic Russian calculations, a situation that does not hold in Ukraine. In Belarus, Gazprom's behavior seems to have been significantly influenced by its need to contribute toward official state policy goals; in Ukraine, private interests within Gazprom have played a larger role. Private interests have played a more prominent role in

Ukraine because the way the political system developed there post-1991 allowed for more points of access to energy and other rents, and for a larger role of corruption in the system more generally.

Russia's relations with Ukraine and Belarus are inextricably linked with the complex connections between energy dependency and integration issues in the former Soviet Union. Looking at these two cases, we see a somewhat paradoxical situation. In Ukraine, whose relationship with Russia has been markedly strained at times, Russian companies and interests have made actual inroads into the country's energy system and now own important assets. In Belarus, on the other hand, despite President Lukashenko's loud praise for unification with Russia, real economic integration in the energy sector has not taken place. In fact, energy issues were at the heart of the deteriorating relationship in 2003–2005. This difference is largely a function of the different calculations of the local leaders in Ukraine and Russia. Ukrainian president Kuchma felt it important to sell Ukrainian assets to Russian companies to ensure stable supplies of oil to Ukrainian refineries. Belarus's Lukashenko, on the other hand, sought to keep Russian companies out so that he could maintain his near-complete control over his country's political and economic systems.

Russian businesses have played a variety of roles in Ukraine and Belarus: sometimes promoting stability, sometimes fostering conflict. Yet in most cases, what we see is not a situation where Russian business single-handedly *creates* a conflict situation, but one where it works on the basis of previously existing conflicts and divisions of interests, sharpening them when it is to the advantage of corporate or private interests within a company.

As was noted in the introduction to this chapter, the energy dependency between Russia and its western neighbors is a two-way street. Although Ukraine and Belarus are heavily dependent on Russia for their energy supplies, and although Russia is investing heavily in new pipelines linking Russia directly with West European markets, Russia still needs Ukraine and Belarus for transporting its energy to the West and for political reasons. As a result, Russian leverage over the two countries is not as strong as one might expect given its energy dominance, and there are clear constraints on its power there. The leaders of both Ukraine and Belarus often behave independently of Russian desires.

Whether the actions of Russian business lead to conflict or stability also depends on the domestic conditions they encounter in each of the countries where they operate. For example, the role of domestic capital has not always been benign. In fact, various groups have sometimes rejected foreign investments exactly because they could threaten the "coziness" of a system of economic privileges based on connections with the executive branch of government. Although such groups feel most threatened by Western business methods, as they shine unwanted light on profitable but nontransparent ways of doing business, sometimes Russian capital has been perceived as a threat as well, either because it could upset the balance of power between well-connected local groups, as in the case of Ukraine,[42] or because, as in the case of Belarus, it could threaten the executive's monopoly control of the economy.

Unfortunately, the current stability in Belarus is not based on good gover-nance and therefore capable of withstanding political challenges. More likely, it is a short-term stability that will foster instability in the long term. Russian sub-sidies have allowed the unreformed and largely unviable Belarusian economy to be sheltered from real and overwhelming pressure for change, but not to prepare itself for the challenges ahead. The behavior of Gazprom and other Russian eco-nomic actors in Belarus may have contributed to stability in the short term, but has actually weakened the country's ability to develop a sustainable economic and political system in the medium term, a system capable of helping Belarus adapt successfully to the reality that the Soviet system is there no more.

## Notes

1  In 2001, Ukraine received 86.6 percent of its total oil imports from Russia, as well as 51 percent of its total gas imports, the rest coming from Turkmenistan through Russia. In the case of Belarus, nearly 100 percent of both gas and oil imports came from Russia.
2  See Yurii Drakokhrust and Dimitriy Furman, "Perepety integratsii," in D. E. Furman, ed., *Belorusia i Rossia: Obshestva i gosudarstva*, Moscow: Prava Cheloveka, 1998; Yuri Drakhakhrust and Dmitri Furman, "Belarus and Russia: The Game of 'Virtual Integration,'" in Margarita M. Balmaceda, James I. Clem, and Lisbeth L. Tarlow, eds., *Independent Belarus: Domestic Determinants, Regional Dynamics and Implica-tions for the West*, Cambridge, MA: Harvard University Press, 2002; Margarita M. Balmaceda, "Myth and Reality in the Belarusian–Russian Relationship," *Problems of Post-Communism*, May–June 1999, pp. 3–14.
3  See Margarita M. Balmaceda, "Understanding the Comparative Management of Energy Dependency in the Former Soviet World: An Introduction," unpublished manuscript, April 2004.
4  Most Russian energy companies do not follow current international business account-ing standards or make their books available to public scrutiny as most western firms do. See Keith C. Smith, "Russian Energy Politics in the Baltics, Poland and Ukraine: A New Stealth Imperialism?" Washington, DC: Center for Strategic and International Studies, 2004, p. 7.
5  The term "business-administrative group" is used to denote the fact that these groups combine both economic resources and decision-making power.
6  On this issue, see Tor Bukkvoll, "Off the Cuff Politics: Explaining Russia's Lack of a Ukraine Strategy," *Europe–Asia Studies* 53, no. 8, 2001, pp. 1141–1157.
7  Marko Mikhelson, "Russia's Policy towards Ukraine, Belarus, Moldova, and the Baltic States," in Janusz Bugajski, ed., *Toward an Understanding of Russia: New European Perspectives*, New York: Council on Foreign Relations, 2002, pp. 97–115, here p. 98.
8  For an interpretation of Russian state interests that strongly contrasts with the official narrative emphasizing post-Soviet Slavic integration, see Dmitri Trenin, *The End of Eurasia: Russia on the Border between Geopolitics and Globalization*, Washington, DC: Carnegie Endowment for International Peace, 2002.
9  See Gerner Grabher and David Stark, "Organizing Diversity: Evolutionary Theory, Network Analysis and Post-socialism," in John Pickles and Adrian Smith, eds., *Theo-rising Transition*, London: Routledge, 1998, pp. 54–75.
10  On Itera, see, for example, No author, "Energeticheskaya bezopasnost' Ukraini stala zalozhnitsei kompanii ITERA, schitaet partia 'Yabloko'," *Infobank Oil and Gas Monitor* (Lviv), 12 April 2001; Roman Olearchyk, "Gazprom, Naftogaz Ukrainy

Replace Itera with New Firm," *Kyiv Post*, 6 March 2003, p. 1; Igor Maskalevich, "Minus 'iterizatsia' vsei strany," *Zerkalo Nedeli*, 7 June 2003, p. 9.

11 Argued by *Jane's Intelligence Digest*, Radio Free Europe/Radio Liberty, and the early March 2003 Moscow press. In 2005, the company was replaced by Rosukrenergo, a Gazprom–Austrian joint venture. See also Roman Kupchinsky, "Naftohaz Ukraini: A Study in State-Sponsored Corruption," *Radio Liberty/Radio Free Europe Corruption Watch*, www.uanews.tv/archives/rferl/cct/cct037.htm. For additional sources, see "Energeticheskaya beznopasnost' Ukraini stala zalozhnitsei kompanii ITERA, schitaet partia 'Yabloko,'" *Infobank Oil and Gas Monitor* (Lviv), 12 April 2001. On 6 March 2003, the *Kyiv Post* wrote, "Itera paid Gazprom for the use of its pipelines and was paid in free gas by Ukraine. The agreement was believed to have cost Gazprom billions in lost revenue while inflating the gas cost for Ukraine" (Roman Olearchyk, "Gazprom, Naftogaz Ukrainy Replace Itera with New Firm," *Kyiv Post*, 6 March 2003, p. 1). See also Jerome Guillet, "Gazprom," *Wall Street Journal*, 8 November 2002, reprinted in Action Ukraine Report, available at www.artukraine.com/buildukraine/gazprom.htm (accessed 24 March 2006); Simon Pirani, "Ukraine Squeezed by Russian and Turkmen Gas Pricing Ambitions" (on Gazprom losing money to Rosukrenergo and previous companies for services it could have provided itself), available at www.quintessential.org.uk/SimonPirani/gm-oct05.html (accessed 24 March 2006).

12 See Kupchinsky, "Naftohaz Ukraini."

13 See Rosaria Puglisi, "Clashing Agendas? Economic Interests, Elite Coalitions and Prospects for Cooperation between Russia and Ukraine," *Europe–Asia Studies* 55, no. 6, pp. 827–845, especially p. 839.

14 The Odessa–Brody pipeline was originally planned as a way of fostering Ukraine's energy supply diversification, reducing its dependency on Russia and helping promote the country as a transit corridor for Caspian oil to Europe. However, when the Odessa–Brody segment was finally completed in 2002 it became obvious that little business planning had been done in advance, and no Caspian oil was ready to flow through it. The lack of ready oil persuaded Poland not to build the connecting segment to Plotsk. In early 2003, the Ukrainians responded to the absence of Caspian oil by temporarily "reversing" the flow of a 52-kilometer segment of the pipeline, using it to transport Russian oil through the Odessa port to Western Europe. Subsequently, the Russian Tiumen Oil Company (TNK) proposed a "full reversal" of the pipeline: that is, to transit Russian oil (also belonging to TNK) from Brody in the north to Odessa in the south (to be shipped further west by tanker), in the opposite direction from the one that was originally intended. TNK made and justified this proposal in the context of the acute lack of free export capacity in Russian pipelines at a time when the difference between domestic and export prices was especially large. In July 2004, the Ukrainian government agreed to TNK's proposal.

15 Transneft head Semion Vainshtok supported this view in late April 2004 by declaring that because "the capacity of the Baltic Pipeline system was increased, the reversing of Odessa–Brody is no longer a current issue." *Postup* (Lviv), 22 April 2004.

16 See Garik Churilov, "Yanukovich v Moskve 'pridumal,' kak napolnit nefteprovod 'Odessa–Brody,'" obkom.net.ua, 5 July 2004.

17 For example, the 2003 agreement with the offshore company Collide for operation of the Odessa oil terminal. Vitaly Kniazhanskii, "Comrade Reverse," *The Day* (Kyiv), 16 March 2004, p. 3; originally published in Ukrainian in *Den'*, 12 March 2004, p. 4.

18 As a result of the August 2004 agreements with Gazprom, Ukraine lost control over the transit of gas through its territory and the revenue flow associated with it, as well as of gas imports from Turkmenistan, putting these under the control of Gazprom and the Russian–Austrian company Rosukrenergo. See Oles' Tyschuk, "Vlast: Igra v poddavki," *Infobank Oil and Gas Monitor*, 25 August 2004; Natalia Nagornaia, "Ukraina

poteriala kontrol nad sobstvennoi gazotranzitnoi sferoi," *Delovaia Nedelia*, vol. 30–31, no. 190–191, 12–18 August 2004, p. 5.

19 As a result of the 15-year agreement on oil transit signed with Russia on 18 August 2004, Ukraine gave Transneft the right to set most terms and conditions relative to oil transit through Ukraine, including volumes.

20 *NefteRynok* (Ukrainian Oil and Gas Report) (Kyiv), 23 December 1999.

21 See the special issue of the journal *Natsionalna bezpeka i oborona* (also published in English as *National Security and Defense*) no. 1, January 2004 devoted to this topic. See also Volodimyr Saprikin, "Ukraine in the Context of Russia's Gas Expansion in the CIS," special issue on *Energiepolitik und nationale Souveränität in Gesamteuropa, Osteuropa* 54, no. 9–10, September–October 2004.

22 BBC Ukrainian service, morning program, 2 March 2005 5:00 UTC.

23 Although Tymoshenko herself was not accused of corruption at the time of the crisis, one of her closest aides, Oleksandr Zinchenko, accused Pyotr Poroshenko, Tymoshenko's main rival within the Orange coalition and Secretary of the Council of National Security and Defense, of corruption. Yushenko's answer was to, as he saw it, "end the bickering between the two factions" by dismissing both Poroshenko and Tymoshenko.

24 Indeed, concerns about a retreat in the transparency front called forth by the political agreement with Yanukovich have been at least partially offset by the more conciliatory tone of new PM Yuri Yekhanurov toward Russia.

25 See Balmaceda, "Belarus as a Transit Route: Domestic and Foreign Policy Implications," in Balmaceda *et al.*, eds., *Independent Belarus*, pp. 162–196.

26 See Leonid Zlotnikov, "V kil'vatere novoi imperii?" *Belarusskii Rynok*, 7 June 2004, p. 26.

27 Boris Nemtsov, "Rossia stroit narodni kapitalizm v soyuze s nami, no bez nas," interview in *Belorusskaya Delovaya Gazeta*, 25 September 1997, p. 7.

28 Even if Belarus could persuade Russia to return to charging it Russian domestic prices for gas (as it did between 1999 and 2003) despite the ups and downs of the relationship, these are likely to rise significantly (by 11 percent in 2006 and 8 percent in 2007) as a result of Russia's agreements with the European Union and the WTO. This would mean significantly increased prices for Belarus in a situation where the country's economy may be much less prepared than the Russian one to deal with them.

29 See interview with Egor Gaidar in *Svoboda*, 11 November 1997, p. 5.

30 See Piotr Fril on Vremia, Channel One TV, Moscow, 22 February 2004, 9:40 p.m.

31 The fact that Belarus charges Gazprom transit fees only half as large as those charged by other transit states is one of the factors that has contributed to Gazprom's charging Belarus below-market prices for its gas supplies. In turn, these lower prices represent a significant subsidization of the Belarusian economy as a whole. According to International Monetary Fund (IMF) estimates, the subsidy effect of selling Belarus gas at less than world prices amounts to 6–7 percent of the country's GDP. See IMF report "Rapid Growth in Belarus: Puzzle or Not?" (June 2005), available at www.imf.org/external/pubs/ft/scr/2005/cr05217.pdf.

32 The first time Gazprom suspended gas shipments to its West European partners – albeit for only one day – was in February 2004 as a result of the gas supply dispute with Belarus.

33 In 2004, the parties agreed to give the London office of Deloitte & Touche the task of making an independent valuation of the company.

34 Tatiana Manenok, "Poslednii argument," *Belarusskii Rynok*, no. 7, 23–29 February 2004.

35 The Russian side rescinded the agreement in September 2003, effective January 2004, after negotiations on the purchase of a controlling stake in Beltransgaz by Gazprom stalled.

36 More exactly, at the same price charged industrial consumers in Russia's "Fifth Region" (Smolensk).
37 For example, the $175 million credit provided in July 2004 so that Belarus could purchase gas from Gazprom for the remainder of 2004.
38 Natalia Grib, "Alians 'Lukoila' i 'Slavnefti,' No Comment!" *Belorusskaya Gazeta*, 18 January 1999, p. 13.
39 See interview with Belarus's Foreign Trade Minister, Mikhail Marynich, in *Vo Slavu Rodiny* (Minsk), 28 June 1997, p. 1, in FBIS-SOV-97-185.
40 See Aleksandr Alesin, "Za mesto pod solntsem nado platit," *Belarusskii Rynok*, no. 41, 18–25 October 2004. This article was based on statistics from the Belarus's Ministry of Statistics and Ministry of Industry.
41 In July 2005, President Lukashenko announced a plan for the modernization of the Belarusian military involving the investment of nearly $500 million per year.
42 See Puglisi, "Clashing Agendas," p. 837.

# 5 Russian energy companies in the Caspian and Central Eurasian region

## Expanding southward

*Jeronim Perović*

After more than ten years of disengagement, Russia set out to recapture some of its influence in the Caspian and Central Eurasian region around the turn of the century.[1] Russia increasingly flexes its muscles in this area by means of the Russian ruble and corporations, rather than by using arms or taking advantage of its military bases in the region, which Moscow has been keen to maintain. Since energy remains a crucial component of Russia's economic ties to its southern neighbors, companies from the energy sector have emerged as powerful players in Russian foreign relations.

At the forefront of Russia's southward expansion are three companies representing the key sectors of gas, oil, and electricity: *Gazprom*, Russia's giant state-controlled gas monopolist; *LUKoil*, the country's largest private oil company; and *RAO Unified Energy System* (UES), Russia's electricity monopolist. While each of these companies has implemented its own foreign agenda, taken as a whole, Russia is pursuing an increasingly assertive policy of economic engagement south of its border, including signing long-term energy partnership agreements, establishing joint ventures, participating in energy exploration and transportation projects, and acquiring energy infrastructure, usually through debt-for-equity swaps.

The first part of this chapter identifies the driving forces behind Russian policy and Russian interests toward the states of the region while tracing the major trends and changes that have taken place in the transition from Yeltsin to Putin. After an overview of the main structural dependencies in the energy sphere, this chapter then explains patterns of Russian business behavior by comparing three examples of Russian business expansion: UES's activities in the South Caucasus (particularly in Georgia); Gazprom's cooperation with the Central Asian gas-producing countries Turkmenistan, Kazakhstan, and Uzbekistan; and the involvement of LUKoil in international projects in the Caspian. Looking at the interests of these companies, the local situation, and the role of international factors makes it possible to understand the dynamics of Russian expansion and its impact on the balance of conflict and cooperation in the region.

## Geopolitics and change in Russian foreign policy

During most of the 1990s, in the wake of the collapse of the Soviet Union, Russia's chief objective in regard to its southern neighbors was damage limitation. In order to reassert itself as the dominant power in the Commonwealth of Independent States (CIS), Russia applied whatever means it had at its disposal to halt the further erosion of its fast-fading influence. In the Caspian region, Moscow long blocked any division of the Caspian Sea among the countries that bordered it. With Turkmenistan, Russia resorted to blackmail, such as when Moscow closed its pipelines for Turkmen gas deliveries to Ukraine until Ashgabat agreed to the price reduction Russia demanded. Russia also vehemently opposed the decision by the governments of Azerbaijan and Georgia to build a US-backed pipeline from Baku through Georgia to the Turkish port in Ceyhan (the Baku–Tbilisi–Ceyhan pipeline – BTC), a route designed to circumvent Russian territory. In the South Caucasus, Moscow favored a blunt "divide-and-rule" policy in the conflicts over Abkhazia, South Ossetia, and Nagorno-Karabakh.

In light of increased Western investment in Caspian oil and gas extraction and transportation projects toward the end of the 1990s, Russia began to reconsider its approach. The turning point came in early 1998, when Moscow suddenly, and to the surprise of many outside observers, reached a bilateral agreement with Kazakhstan over the delimitation of the Caspian Sea bed, thereby shifting from a policy of obstruction to cooperation. This shift came about after the policy makers in Moscow realized that Russia's approach toward the Caspian Sea was in effect encouraging Kazakhstan to look for outside assistance in extracting and transporting oil while skirting Russian territory, rather than preventing such efforts.

With the election of Vladimir Putin as Russia's president, this attitude began to evolve into general policy. In spring 2000, at his first Security Council meeting as elected president, Putin declared the Caspian region to be a zone of vital interest. He attributed increased Western and Turkish presence to Russian inactivity and urged Russian companies to be more aggressive in their activities in the region.[2] During this period, the Russian government started actively backing the international expansion of some of Russia's major energy companies and tried to achieve better coordination of Russian oil diplomacy, which was notorious for its lack of direction under Yeltsin.[3] At the same time, Moscow also softened its opposition toward Western-sponsored projects it had previously opposed, such as the BTC, and urged Russian oil companies to participate in international projects in the Caspian.[4]

The terrorist attacks of 11 September 2001 and the subsequent stationing of US troops in Central Asia were an important catalyst in prompting Russia to reinforce its proactive engagement and intervene more vigorously in areas where it still had considerable influence, milking to the full extent its advantageous set of dependency linkages (described below). In fact, the expanded foreign economic activities of Russian companies led to a marked upturn in trade and investment starting in 2002–2003. In 2004, exports to the CIS had grown by

41.8 percent against the previous year; imports from CIS countries by 30.7 percent.[5] Russia's growth in trade with the states of the Caspian and Central Eurasian region was well above the CIS average. Trade with Kyrgyzstan in 2004 grew by 65 percent, while trade with Azerbaijan, Uzbekistan, Georgia, Kazakhstan, and Tajikistan expanded by between 40 and 50 percent.[6] There was also a robust increase in Russia's overall financial involvement abroad after 2002, and the share of the CIS in the total flows of Russian outward foreign direct investment (FDI) has been growing. Of the $4.1 billion of total Russian foreign investment in 2002, $987.7 (24 percent) went to the states of the CIS (against 10 percent in 2000).[7] While the bulk of Russia's CIS investment has until recently been divided among Ukraine (52.7 percent in 2002) and Belarus (41 percent in 2002), recent years saw a remarkable change in Russia's regional priorities: in 2004, Kazakhstan absorbed 11.8 percent of Russia's CIS investments (up from 2.6 percent in 2002), and Uzbekistan received 19.4 percent (up from 0.8 percent in 2002). This shift toward the Caspian region came mostly at the expense of Ukraine, which accounted for only 27.3 percent in 2004.[8]

Although Putin and other Russian officials generally refrain from prioritizing Russian interests vis-à-vis individual CIS countries, the two areas of highest importance in the Caspian and Central Eurasian region are clearly Kazakhstan and the states of the South Caucasus (Azerbaijan, Georgia, and Armenia). Kazakhstan is Russia's main trading partner and a key component of Moscow's Caspian energy policy. Thanks to strong mutual interests, relations have developed smoothly since the mid-1990s. In security terms, Kazakhstan is important for protecting Russia's long southern border. The treatment of Russian minorities, a sensitive domestic political issue in Russia, plays a role because ethnic Russians make up 30 percent of Kazakhstan's total population. Finally, in geopolitical terms, the country is a gateway to Russian influence in Central Asia.

This mix of factors also plays an important role in Russian policy towards the South Caucasus. Economic issues are relevant in energy-rich Azerbaijan as well as Armenia and Georgia, where Russia's interests are related to trade and control over Caspian energy transportation routes. Military-security considerations play an even more important role in Russia's relationship with Georgia than in that with Kazakhstan. While relations with Armenia have been traditionally very good, and ties with Azerbaijan have markedly improved since Putin took office, Russia has yet to build a stable relationship with Georgia. The key sources of tension in the bilateral ties are that Georgia is heavily reliant on Russian energy, and therefore vulnerable to Russian influence; Russia continues to maintain military bases on Georgian territory despite Georgian objections to their presence; and Russia supports the separatist aspirations of Abkhazia and South Ossetia, undermining the integrity of the Georgian state (see the chapter by Erik Scott, Chapter 11).

Of course, Russia does not ignore the other states in the region. Today, Russian interests in Turkmenistan essentially boil down to the issue of gas production and transportation, and Moscow and Ashgabat have been struggling to find a suitable arrangement. Defining the Caspian Sea's legal status also remains a problem. Of the five Caspian littoral states (Russia, Kazakhstan, Azerbaijan, Turkmenistan, and Iran), Turkmenistan and Iran remain the only two countries that have so far refused to sign any agreement on the division of the Caspian seabed and the allocation of rights to Caspian oil and gas.

Relations with Uzbekistan were strained during much of the 1990s, but have markedly improved under Putin; both Moscow and Tashkent are now keen on expanding collaboration based on mutual economic interests.

Russia's economic interest toward the two poorest countries of the region, Kyrgyzstan and Tajikistan, have been less pronounced. However, both countries have recently become targets of Russian energy expansion. Tajikistan and Kyrgyzstan seek revenues from their hydropower sources, and have invited Russian companies (mainly UES and Gazprom) to participate in the development of this sector.

## Energy dependencies

Russia's important role in this region derives from the relative weakness of its southern neighbors, rather than its own strength. Russia is the key factor in providing stability, because its economy is more than five times as large as the combined economies of all eight states in the region. The World Bank estimates Russia's real gross domestic product (GDP) at $1.17 trillion for the year 2002, calculated on the basis of purchasing power parity (PPP).

Although Russia's overall significance as a trading partner for the countries of this region dropped substantially after the collapse of the Soviet Union, it remains important. However, the relationship is highly asymmetric. While trade with this group of states makes up a small portion of Russia's total foreign trade – the CIS accounted for 20.8 percent of Russian overall imports in 2004[9] – the Caucasus and Central Asian states depend heavily on Russia, especially for imports, as Table 5.1 shows.

Energy remains the single most important structural factor in explaining the economic dependency of these countries. The share of energy in the structure of Russian exports to the CIS was 61.2 percent in 2004 (24.9 percent in 2003). Gas represents the greatest share (27.5 percent), followed by crude oil (15.6) and black coal (13.1 percent). Refined products made up just 5 percent.[10]

Dependencies are very strong in the gas sector because all major pipelines run through Russia. Russia is the largest source of gas imports for the energy-poor among these countries and almost all exports must flow through pipelines on its territory. Russia accounts for some 80 percent of gas production and 90 percent of gas exports in the CIS. The other net gas exporters of the Caspian and Central Eurasian region are Turkmenistan and Uzbekistan. Table 5.2 lays out the proven oil and gas reserves of the exporting countries in the region.

Uzbekistan is the only country that has been able to avoid Russia's pipeline system for its gas exports. However, the two other gas-producing countries, Turkmenistan and Kazakhstan, depend on Russian pipelines to send their oil

*Table 5.1* Russia's share in CIS country trade volumes, 2004

| Country | Main export partners | Main import partners |
|---|---|---|
| Armenia | Belgium 16.8%, Israel 14.3%, **Russia 14.2%**, Germany 11.4%, Iran 9.9%, US 7.8%, Netherlands 5.8% | Belgium 10.3%, Iran 10.2%, **Russia 9.8%**, Israel 8.6%, US 7.7%, UAE 6.2%, Italy 5.4%, Germany 5%, France 4.6%, Ukraine 4.5% |
| Azerbaijan | Italy 31.1%, Czech Republic 14.5%, Germany 9.4%, Turkey 6.1%, **Russia 6%**, Georgia 5.3%, France 4.9% | UK 13.9%, **Russia 13.1%**, Turkey 11.5%, Germany 8%, Netherlands 5.3%, China 5%, US 4.7%, Italy 4.5%, Ukraine 4.3% |
| Georgia | Turkey 28.1%, **Russia 9.7%**, Spain 7.9%, Turkmenistan 7.5%, US 7.1%, Armenia 5.3%, Greece 5% | US 14.8%, Turkey 13.6%, **Russia 11%**, Germany 7.5%, UK 6.5%, Azerbaijan 6.2%, Ukraine 5.3%, Italy 4.1% |
| Kazakhstan | **Russia 13.5%**, Bermuda 13.4%, China 10.4%, Germany 9.2%, Switzerland 9.1%, France 6.7% | **Russia 33.9%**, China 13.6%, Germany 9.6%, France 6.8% |
| Kyrgyzstan | UAE 23.8%, Switzerland 16.9%, **Russia 16.9%**, Kazakhstan 10.1%, China 9.8% | **Russia 23.1%**, China 22.9%, Kazakhstan 19.3%, Turkey 7.2%, Germany 4.5%, Uzbekistan 4.4%, US 4.2% |
| Tajikistan | Latvia 13.1%, Switzerland 11.5%, Uzbekistan 11.3%, Norway 9.9%, **Russia 8.2%**, Iran 7.9%, Turkey 7.7%, Italy 6.6%, Hungary 4.4% | **Russia 17.8%**, Uzbekistan 13.4%, Kazakhstan 9.7%, Ukraine 6.3%, Azerbaijan 6.3%, US 5.8%, Turkey 4.3% |
| Turkmenistan | Ukraine 49.8%, Iran 17.2%, Italy 5.3%, Turkey 4.7% Germany 6.8%, France 4.6% | **Russia 14%**, Ukraine 13.8%, US 11.1%, UAE 8.1%, Turkey 8% |
| Uzbekistan | **Russia 21.2%**, China 14%, Ukraine 7%, Turkey 6.3%, Tajikistan 5.8%, Bangladesh 4.2% | **Russia 26.4%**, South Korea 10.8%, Germany 9.4%, China 8.3%, Kazakhstan 6%, Turkey 6% |

Source: CIA World Factbook 2005 (updated 30 August 2005).

abroad, excluding only a small-capacity pipeline for Turkmen gas deliveries to Iran. Natural gas exports for Turkmenistan made up 57 percent of total exports in 2001.[11] Central Asia's leading oil producer, Kazakhstan, is still a net natural gas importer, purchasing gas primarily from Uzbekistan and Russia. However, Kazakhstan plans to increase its own natural gas production significantly in coming years and become a net natural gas exporter. Tajikistan and Kyrgyzstan import gas mainly from Uzbekistan, but also from Kazakhstan, Russia, and Turkmenistan.

All the South Caucasus states depend heavily on Russian gas imports. Even energy-rich Azerbaijan currently imports over half of its gas from Russia despite boasting one of the world's largest natural gas field discoveries of the past

*Table 5.2* Oil and gas reserves for selected countries

| | Proven oil reserves | | Proven natural gas reserves | |
|---|---|---|---|---|
| | *bn bbls* | *Percentage of world total* | *tcf* | *Percentage of world total* |
| **Russia** | **60.0** | **4.7** | **1680.0** | **30.54** |
| Kazakhstan | 9.0 | 0.7 | 65.0 | 1.18 |
| Azerbaijan | 7.0 | 0.6 | 30.0 | 0.55 |
| Uzbekistan | 0.594 | 0.05 | 66.2 | 1.20 |
| Turkmenistan | 0.546 | 0.04 | 71.0 | 1.29 |

Source: Pennwell Corporation, *Oil and Gas Journal* 101, no. 49, 22 December 2003 (online access through the EIA website at www.eia.doe.gov/emeu/international/reserves.html; update as of 9 November 2004)

Note
bn bbls – billion barrels; tcf – trillion cubic feet. Proven reserves are estimated quantities derived from an analysis of geologic and engineering data, which demonstrate, with reasonable certainty, the quantity of oil and gas recoverable under existing economic and operating conditions.

twenty years in Shah Deniz. However, efforts are under way to secure export routes and customers for gas deliveries through the South Caucasus Pipeline project (SCP), which follows the route of the BTC and plans to open in 2006–2007. The SCP will carry gas from the Shah Deniz field to customers in Azerbaijan, Georgia, Turkey, and possibly other countries in the West.[12]

Overall, however, Gazprom, which owns Russia's gas transportation network, is likely to maintain its monopoly over exports and imports for some time, since it has a clear advantage over foreign investors. While infrastructure investment in the gas sector is considered much riskier than in the oil sector, for Gazprom, the market looks promising since much of the gas infrastructure is already in place from Soviet times, and it is thus relatively easy to extend pipelines within the existing system rather than building long new links (see Map 5.1). Even the opening of the SCP will not seriously challenge Gazprom, since Gazprom is likely to dominate the Turkish market through the Blue Stream gas pipeline which opened in December 2002 and transports gas from Russia to Turkey.

Although Russia plays the dominant role in the region's oil sector, dependencies have been decreasing because of considerably more international engagement over the past decade. Russia produces about 80 percent of the region's crude oil and accounts for a similar share of total net exports in the region. As of now, 70 percent of the oil exported by the three net oil-exporting states of the region (Azerbaijan, Turkmenistan, and Kazakhstan) passes through Russian pipelines (see Map 5.2).[13]

Azerbaijan's dependency will decrease significantly once the BTC pipeline, which opened in May 2005, operates at full capacity.[14] While most of Kazakhstan's oil is transported via Russia, there are plans to ship Kazakh oil through the BTC in the future. Also, in 2004, the Kazakhstani prime minister, Daniyal

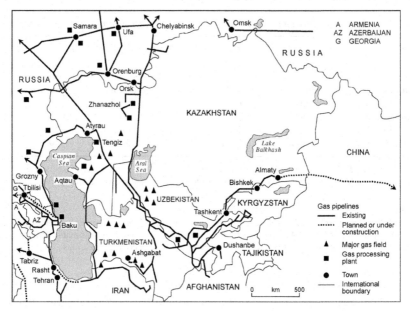

*Map 5.1* Caspian gas pipelines.

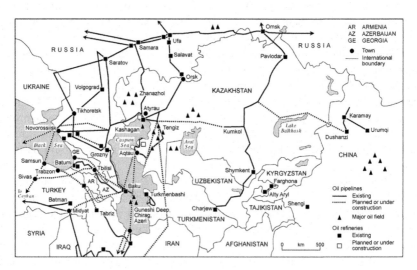

*Map 5.2* Caspian oil pipelines.

Akhmetov, gave the order for the start of construction work on a major energy export route to China.[15] Once completed, this pipeline will span almost 1,860 miles (2,990 kilometers) from its start in Atyrau to Alashankou in China. Although the pipeline is expected to have a final capacity of around 400,000 barrels per day, the quantity of crude oil supplied to China through this route will represent less than 5 percent of China's expected oil demand by the time the project reaches completion.[16] In the South Caucasus, Georgia and Armenia are dependent on Russian and Azerbaijani oil imports; in Central Asia, Kyrgyzstan and Tajikistan import oil largely from Russia. Uzbekistan is not a major oil importer, consuming most of its limited oil production. Turkmenistan's oil exports have been growing recently, but long-term prospects appear limited.[17]

Russia's monopoly on oil transportation is expected to erode further, especially since high oil prices are likely to guarantee continued international engagement in the region. The extent of this competition is reflected in foreign investment figures: Despite the enhanced activities of Russian oil companies, Russia's gross foreign direct investment in Kazakhstan, for example, amounted to only $930.5 million (or 3.1 percent of total foreign direct investment) for the period between 1993 and September 2004. The three largest foreign investors – the United States, Great Britain, and Italy – accounted for almost $15 billion (50.7 percent).[18] The high share of Western involvement in Kazakhstan, as well as in Azerbaijan (there is less foreign involvement in energy projects in Turkmenistan and Uzbekistan), reflects the fact that the major regional oil fields are currently being developed by leading Western transnational energy companies.[19]

While Gazprom seeks to maintain its monopoly and Russian oil companies are working to keep up with international competitors, in the electricity sector Russia's UES is trying to reestablish ties, which were severely disrupted after the collapse of the Soviet Union. Russia's electricity sector is the largest in Europe and the fourth largest in the world, behind only the United States, China, and Japan. The network is extensive, comprising almost 2 million miles (3.2 million kilometers) of power lines, and well integrated with neighboring countries that were part of the Soviet Union.

Although most of the states of the Caspian and Central Eurasia have significant domestic electricity resources, many have experienced severe difficulties because of aging power generating systems, inefficient distribution networks, or electricity supply problems, and thus have become net electricity importers. Only Kyrgyzstan and Tajikistan, because of their significant hydropower capacities, have remained net electricity exporters to the CIS. While Russian electricity exports beyond the states of the CIS have been maintained, or were in some cases increased throughout the 1990s, exports to the CIS were reduced significantly due to nonpayment. Only since about 2002, parallel to the growing foreign activities of UES, has there been an increase in Russian exports to the CIS and a normalization of relations in this sphere. Today, Russia exports significant quantities of electricity to the countries of the former Soviet Union, as well as to China, Poland, Turkey, and Finland. Since Central and Eastern European states were not part of the Soviet electricity grid, plans for Russian exports there have been slow to develop.[20]

To provide a better understanding of how Russian corporations work in the South Caucasus and Central Eurasia, we will now turn to three case studies focusing on the activities of individual companies. The case studies show the various ways that the Russian companies promote conflict and cooperation in this region.

## UES's activities in the South Caucasus

UES's expansion into the South Caucasus electricity market began in summer 2003 with the acquisition of shares in Georgian power companies from the US-based AES electricity corporation. By the middle of 2005, UES controlled some 20 percent of Georgia's generating capacity and 35 percent of electricity supplies to the republic's consumers. Most importantly, UES now fully controls the power supply to the Georgian capital, Tbilisi.[21] UES has made similar moves into Armenia. Through a combination of debt-for-equity swaps and buying out the American company AES, UES management controls approximately 85 percent of generating capacity in Armenia.[22] The company is also seeking to lease cross-border power transmission lines linking Armenia with Georgia, Iran, and Turkey, which will make it possible to sell excess electricity from Armenia's energy system to other countries.[23] In addition, UES acquired a 100 percent stake in Armenia's only nuclear power plant.[24] In Azerbaijan, UES secured a contract for parallel operation of the Azeri and Russian electricity systems, and has signed contracts for transmission of Azeri electricity to Turkey and Iran.[25]

Armenia and Georgia, both located at the end of the old Soviet grid, have considerable generation capacity in-country, but no significant natural resources. Azerbaijan, on the other hand, has significant fuel resources, but limited generation capacity. The breakup of the Soviet Union and subsequent conflicts in this region (Nagorno-Karabakh, Abkhazia, South Ossetia) forced these states to operate independently. However, they have been unable to rationalize their systems and have been plagued by high debts, poor transmission capabilities, gross inefficiencies in generation and transmission, and a state unable for political reasons to raise electricity prices high enough to meet costs.[26] Responding to these problems, the states of the region proposed integrating the utility network, but proved unable to accomplish this task on their own. Capitalizing on this situation, UES stepped in and took control of the South Caucasus electricity market.[27]

By buying up foreign assets, UES is following two declared corporate goals: first, it aims to improve the financial and business performance of its foreign operations; second, it seeks to expand its energy sales through transit countries into lucrative markets to obtain higher profits. In its annual report for 2003, the company explained the purchase of assets in Georgia and Armenia as being driven by a strategy aimed at expanding its presence in the Caucasus region and integrating existing businesses, ensuring the repayment of outstanding debts and timely payment of future fees, establishing the parallel operation of Armenia's energy system with those of the CIS countries, and gaining entry into the electricity markets of Turkey and Iran.[28]

In terms of the first corporate goal, UES has indeed managed to increase the profitability of its foreign energy assets. UES invested large sums in Georgia's electricity infrastructure and ensured a reliable electricity supply to consumers in the Georgian capital in the winter of 2003–2004. The payment discipline of Tbilisi's power consumers has also improved. Consumers living in the Georgian capital paid for about 80 percent of the actual cost of electricity supplied in 2004, up from 40 percent in 2003. Payment discipline has improved, not least because of the company's strict policy of delivering only the electricity that consumers actually pay for. In fact, thanks partly to very good payment collections in the CIS, UES reported profits during the past few years, a huge improvement over the 1990s, which were characterized by very poor financial performance.[29] Important in this context also is the shift away from barter, which had become the norm for payment in many post-Soviet regions, to actual monetary payment, a critical component in making the sector economically successful.[30]

As for the second corporate goal, expanding into foreign markets to boost profits, electricity exports have indeed increased to both CIS countries and other countries. Exports are a high priority for the UES management as they are seen as a major source of funds for financing domestic operations and securing badly needed investments for Russia's aging physical power infrastructure.[31] Although UES's exports stood at only 2.7 percent of total production in 2002, the company earned almost 10 percent of its revenues from the sale of electricity abroad.[32]

UES's goal of exporting energy to Turkey had been set before it started expanding into the South Caucasus electricity market in fall 2003. As early as March 2001, the company announced a contract with Turkey to supply 2.0–2.5 million kilowatt-hours (kWh) daily. According to a trilateral agreement signed at the time by UES, Georgian Energy, and Turkish TEAS, Georgia won a third of all electricity transported via its territory.[33] While UES was not able to increase exports to Turkey as initially planned, now that it has entered the South Caucasus electricity market, it expects to meet this goal. UES has now managed to link Iran and Turkey to its grids, making the Caucasus states no longer the "end of the line," but rather a linking point to potentially greater grids.[34]

Outside observers claim that UES's move into the South Caucasus had political rather than economic goals.[35] The UES explanation that it sought access to consumers in Turkey and Iran seemed too far-fetched, given the massive financial investments required to achieve these ends.[36] The oppositions in both Armenia and Georgia argued that their countries' leaders had struck deals with UES that violated their countries' interests. Moreover, in Armenia, the opposition asserted that UES operated outside international standards and gained access to too many state secrets when it took over the nuclear power plant.[37]

When Eduard Shevardnadze made a deal with UES, the Georgian opposition heavily criticized him, claiming that he was forsaking his traditional pro-West orientation in order to reach rapprochement with Russia. UES head Anatoly

Chubais and his party met a crowd of angry protesters when they disembarked in Tbilisi Airport in fall 2003 to conclude the electricity deal.[38] Domestic discontent manifested itself in other ways: for instance, when saboteurs shot at the Kavkasioni power line connecting Georgia and Russia, causing a temporary halt in Russian exports to Georgia.[39] Georgian suspicions about Russian intentions deepened when the Georgian public learned in summer 2003 about a secretly concluded deal between the Shevardnadze government and Gazprom on strategic gas cooperation over a period of 25 years.[40]

Chubais seemed to confirm these fears when he offered blunt comments on Russia's future role in Eurasia during the fall 2003 State Duma campaign. On several occasions, he stressed that Russia should strive to become a "liberal empire" in the long term, thus combining market economic practices and aggressive foreign policy expansion.[41] Although it can be assumed that Chubais was trying to win votes by appealing to the patriotic feelings of some members of the Russian electorate, his rhetoric certainly fed into local concerns over Russian foreign policy ambitions at the time.[42]

UES's penetration of the South Caucasus electricity market could prove advantageous for Russia in geopolitical terms since control over energy represents a useful lever of power. By controlling Georgia's electricity grid, for example, Russia is in a position to further strengthen its support for the breakaway republics of Abkhazia and South Ossetia.

However, although Moscow politicians and the Russian press have in general praised UES's expansion into the Caucasus, this move can hardly be considered a state-led project. In fact, relations between UES management and the Russian state were strained at the time over the dispute concerning the reform of UES. While both sides agreed on the breakup of UES's monopoly and liberalization of the market, the project favored by the government saw a much larger role for the state both as an owner of vital assets in the electricity market and with regard to control over energy delivery to the domestic and international markets.[43]

While the uncertain outcome of UES's reform could be a liability for its foreign engagement in the future, for now, UES's Caucasus expansion is a win–win situation for all parties involved. Where other foreign companies such as AES have failed to establish a common South Caucasian utility market, UES has been able to effectively rationalize the grids, so that types of power (hydro, thermal, and nuclear) are more optimally balanced, seasonal surplus is managed, peak power loads are met, and the operations of the grid remains stable. Since most of these grids were very fragile when the states tried to manage them separately, the quality of power has improved dramatically under UES's leadership.[44] In fact, while initially critical, the Georgian government of President Mikheil Saakashvili has so far shown no intention to cancel the deal with UES.

## Gazprom's penetration of Central Asia

Gazprom's cooperation with Central Asian natural gas producers started in 2001 and is largely focused on creating stable, long-term energy relationships. By mid-2005, the level of cooperation was highest with Kazakhstan. On 7 June 2002, Gazprom and KazMunaiGaz (Kazakhstan's national holding company) set up the joint venture KazRosGaz, which will transport 124 billion cubic feet (3.5 billion cubic meters) of natural gas annually through Russian pipelines in the first few years of the agreement.[45] Beyond other major projects, including the development of large energy fields, Gazprom has also agreed to upgrade Kazakhstan's natural gas pipeline network.[46]

In April 2003, Russia signed a deal with Turkmenistan on long-term energy exports, under which Turkmenistan agreed to ship gas to Russia for the next 25 years.[47] Under the agreement, Gazexport and Turkmenneftegaz signed a contract allowing Russia to purchase and sell Turkmen natural gas over the same period. During the first three years of the contract period (in 2004–2006), the payments for natural gas supplies were made through equal portions of cash and equipment deliveries aimed at the development of Turkmenistan's gas industry. The method of payment in subsequent years was to be agreed upon later.[48]

The years 2002 and 2003 were important for Russian–Uzbek energy relations. In 2002, Gazprom signed a strategic gas cooperation agreement with the Uzbek national energy company, Uzbekneftegaz. The agreement stipulated long-term natural gas purchases in Uzbekistan during the period 2003–2012, with the annual volume reaching ten billion cubic meters by 2005. Under a further agreement signed with the Uzbek government in July 2003, Gazprom is operating Uzbekistan's trunk gas pipelines. Other agreements regulate Gazprom's participation in the development of a major gas field.[49]

Gazprom's expansion into Central Asia seeks to address three major goals. *First*, assuming that the global use of gas doubles by 2030 as predicted, for instance, by the Paris-based International Energy Agency (IEA), Russia will have to invest heavily in order to meet growing demands. Some analysts estimate that upcoming expansions will require $300 billion worth of capital outlays in Russia's gas exploration, production, and transportation sectors over the next thirty years.[50] Gazprom's own estimates show that commercial plans to use Central Asian gas as a substitute for Russian gas in shipments to Europe are currently more beneficial than the capital-intensive development of new deposits inside Russia, such as the ones on the Yamal Peninsula and the shelves of the Barents and Kara seas. The company's declared goal vis-à-vis Central Asia is thus to "optimize the natural gas export resource provision system" by using the vast natural gas reserves of Central Asia.[51] While the gas bought from Turkmenistan made up for only 1 percent of Gazprom's total production in 2004, the company plans to increase this share to around 15 percent by 2009.[52]

*Second*, Gazprom's expansion into the Central Asian gas market has to be considered against the background of Russia's domestic gas market. In 2003, Gazprom made 62.5 percent of its sales on the domestic Russian market and sold the rest of its gas to foreign customers.[53] Given the extremely low domestic prices for gas set by the state, exports are essential for Gazprom to offset its huge losses from sales on the domestic market, which have led to enormous debts.[54] In 2003, revenues from foreign exports made up for over two-thirds of the company's income. Thus, in 2003, thanks to increasing sales abroad, Gazprom's foreign currency gas export earnings amounted to about \$16.5 billion (compared to \$12.8 billion in 2002).[55]

A *third* economic reason behind the creation of energy partnerships is to reduce, or ideally eliminate, potential competition between Russian and Central Asian gas on the world market. Russia understands that it will not be able simply to increase gas production on its own territory, as this would lead to a drop in world market prices and make Russian energy increasingly less competitive in comparison with the energy produced in countries with a lower cost of production. More importantly, if Central Asian gas finds direct access to world markets, Russia would come under increased pressure to raise domestic energy prices and/or reform its internal gas market in order to compete success-fully on the world market.

Accordingly, it is essential for Gazprom to seek the role of a commercial intermediary in the resale of Central Asian gas. The company's goal is to develop contracts to ensure Central Asian natural gas procurement, processing, transportation, and marketing "through an integrated export channel" controlled by Russia.[56] By 2003, Gazprom had in fact managed to sign long-term contracts not only with the three gas-producing states of the region, but has also with Kyr-gyzstan, Tajikistan, and Georgia. Moreover, Gazprom has set out to buy and/or modernize the region's transportation infrastructure. In sum, given Gazprom's importance as a critical part of Russia's long-term economic ambitions, the control of all Central Asian gas is a highly political issue and a national priority for Russia.

To be sure, Gazprom's way of tying the Central Asian states to Russia has led to a highly distorted gas market within the CIS. The company has been using access to its pipelines and heavily subsidized prices as a tool to discipline or reward countries. Gas trade among CIS countries is often based on barter and other noncash payments, which provides further incentives for corruption, non-transparency and inefficient rent seeking.[57] These practices are in stark contrast to Gazprom's energy policy vis-à-vis Europe, where links with Western com-panies are established on a fairly professional and relatively transparent basis, and Gazprom thus strives to be a reliable, nonpoliticized supplier at world prices.[58]

Despite its overwhelming dominance in the gas sector, Gazprom's position in the region is not entirely stable. In fact, the gas-producing states of Central Asia have indicated that they want to leave their options open in the future. For example, while Russia's push for a deepening of its economic engagement is mostly taking place at the bilateral level, attempts at strengthening integration at the multilateral level have had little effect so far. The Caspian states have been unwilling to commit to a formal multilateral coalition, such as Putin's "Eurasian gas alliance" (consisting of Russia, Kazakhstan, Uzbekistan, and Turkmenistan), fearing such an alliance would increase their dependency on Russia and decrease their room for maneuver regarding other possible options for exploiting and transporting their gas (and oil) in the future.[59]

Gazprom's strategy to rely heavily on Central Asian gas has in fact become a liability as it exposes the company to increasing pressure with regard to prices and export volumes. Thus, rather than applying economic sanctions as it did in the past, Gazprom has been careful to offer these states incentives to cooperate. An important incentive for Kazakhstan to agree on the establishment of the joint venture with Gazprom was the prospect that Kazakhstan would have access not only to other CIS countries for its gas sales, but to the markets of Western Europe as well.[60] A major incentive for Turkmenistan to sign the deal with Russia on gas deliveries came in Gazprom's offer to buy Turkmen gas at a price that some analysts considered too high at the time the contract was signed.[61] Another reason was political. At the time the deal was concluded, Putin gave in on the disputed issue of dual citizenship and agreed with Turkmen president Saparmurat Niyazov to abrogate an agreement of 1993 that guaranteed Russians living in Turkmenistan the right to hold dual citizenship.

As in the case of Uzbekistan, however, Turkmenistan also signed the deal with Russia partly because other foreign investors have sought to steer clear of this country. Several energy projects stalled because of Turkmenistan's prohibitive and sometimes arbitrary rules concerning the participation of foreign companies.[62]

However, the case of a dispute between Gazprom and Turkmenistan in 2004–2005 is the clearest indication that not even a long-term contract can ensure Gazprom's control over these countries. In late 2004, Turkmenistan halted its natural gas exports to Russia and Ukraine until these countries would agree to a substantial increase in prices and export volumes for Turkmen gas. Turkmenistan is especially incensed by Gazprom's practice of using Turkmen gas for deliveries to Ukraine and Russia's domestic consumption while freeing Russian gas for export to Western markets; the displaced Russian gas is then sold for approximately three times as much per thousand cubic meters.[63] While all sides quickly agreed to increase substantially the volume of Turkmen gas, only Ukraine accepted the higher prices.[64] Gazprom announced it would continue to pay the initially agreed-upon price of $44 per thousand cubic meters. Confident that Gazprom would need Turkmen gas and would thus give in to the Turkmen demands sooner or later, Turkmenistan resumed exports to Russia only in mid-April 2005, after Gazprom agreed to pay the entire amount for the purchased gas (and not only half of it) in cash.[65] This situation is in stark contrast to the mid-1990s, when it was Gazprom closing its pipelines to Turkmen gas deliveries.[66]

## LUKoil's expansion into the Caspian

The leading Russian oil company in the Caspian region is LUKoil. In fact, LUKoil in mid-2005 was the largest transnational company based in the former socialist countries, with foreign assets of an estimated $6–9 billion.[67] Even with its considerable stakes in oil fields abroad, however, LUKoil's foreign production currently accounts for only 5 percent of the company's total output in both oil and gas condensates.[68] By 2013, LUKoil plans to increase this share to 20 percent, over half of it generated through projects in the Caspian.[69] In June 2004, LUKoil president Vagit Alekperov declared that LUKoil plans to increase its investments in the Caspian by 2020 to a total of $13 billion and have projects in the Caspian account for 18 percent of LUKoil's overall hydrocarbon production.[70]

Having invested approximately $1.5 billion in Kazakhstan's economy over a period of eight years (1995–2003), LUKoil is today the single largest Russian investor in this country.[71] And LUKoil plans to expand its investment. In December 2003, the company's president stated that "LUKoil is currently implementing seven projects in the republic, and their number is sure to grow. Our planned investment in the Dostyk offshore project alone is nearly $3 billion."[72] LUKoil has been operating in Uzbekistan since 2001, but became engaged on a larger scale only in June 2004, after signing a production sharing agreement on the Kandym–Khauzak–Shady project. Investments in this project, involving LUKoil and Uzbekistan's state-owned Uzbekneftegaz, are expected to amount to $1 billion.[73] Together with Gazprom, LUKoil ranks among the leading foreign investors in this Central Asian country.[74]

While LUKoil's engagement in Kazakhstan (and now Uzbekistan) has been growing in recent years, its record in Azerbaijan has been mixed. As indicated in Table 5.3, LUKoil started four projects, but has now pulled out of two, Azeri–Chirag–Guneshli (ACG) in April 2003, and Zykh–Govsany in February 2005.

When LUKoil withdrew from the huge ACG field, most observers speculated that the company's decision reflected Moscow's opposition to the construction of the BTC, a project in which Russian companies were not actively involved. Since it was clear by 2002 that most oil developed in the ACG field would be shipped through the BTC, LUKoil's presence in the ACG consortium, it was argued, did not make sense politically.[75]

This interpretation lacks foundation beyond such speculation. The first problem is that LUKoil had always reserved the right to ship at least part of its share of production north, through the Baku–Novorossiisk pipeline.[76] Second, while there certainly was considerable opposition to the BTC on the part of some Russian agencies (particularly the Foreign Ministry) during the Yeltsin era, Putin explicitly welcomed Russian companies' more active participation in Caspian projects, even if they were Western sponsored. Third, LUKoil's withdrawal from the ACG consortium did not mean that the company would abandon Azerbaijan altogether. Notwithstanding the fact that LUKoil also terminated its participation in the Zykh–Govsany project in February 2005, the company has expanded the scale and scope of its involvement in the promising D-222 (Yamala) project.[77] Underlining its growing interest in the lucrative gas market, the company also extended its participation in the Shah Deniz natural gas project. At the same time, LUKoil acquired a 10 percent stake in the SCP project through LUKAgip.[78]

Overall, it appears that LUKoil's behavior in Azerbaijan is guided more by

*Table 5.3* LUKoil's participation in Caspian oil and gas projects (as of November 2004)

| Project name | LUKoil's share | Description |
|---|---|---|
| *Azerbaijan* | | |
| [Zykh-Govsany] | [50%] | Agreement with the State Oil Company of the Azerbaijan Republic (SOCAR) signed in January 2001 on restoration, exploration, development, and production sharing on a parity basis on the Zykh and Govsany field blocks. In February 2005, before the agreement entered into force, LUKoil pulled out of the contract. |
| [Azeri-Chirag-Gyuneshli – ACG] | [10%] | LUKoil acquired a 10 percent stake in 1994, but sold its share in April 2003 to the Inpex Southwest Caspian Sea Company (Japan) for $1.3 billion. |
| Shah-Deniz | 10% | LUKoil acquired a 5 percent share in 1996 through the LUKAgip N.V. joint venture, and in 2003 another 5 percent through acquisition of the Italian ENI Group's 50 percent share in LUKAgip NV.[a] |
| D222 (Yalama) | 80% | LUKoil bought a 60 percent share in 1998 and an additional 20 percent from SOCAR LUKoil's partner in this project in 2003. |
| *Kazakhstan* | | |
| Karachaganak share | 15% | LUKoil has participated in this project since 1997. Its production of oil and gas condensate on the field in 2003 amounted to 825,400 tons of oil and 781.1 million cubic meters of gas. |
| Kumkol | 50% | LUKoil bought its share in 1995. In 2003, output was 1.4 million tons of oil and 14.2 million cubic meters of associated gas. |
| Tengiz | 2.7% | LUKoil bought its stake in 1995. In 2003, LUKoil's share from the output of the Tengiz and Korolevskoe fields amounted to 344,200 tons of oil and 156.1 million cubic meters of associated gas. |
| Tyub-Karagan and Atashsky | 50% | In June 2004, LUKoil started marine seismic studies for the Tyub-Karagan and Atashsky projects, which are being implemented by the company on a parity basis with Kazakhstan's KazMunaiGas. Project costs are estimated at $4.2 billion. |
| *Uzbekistan* | | |
| Kandym-Khauzak-Shady | 90% | On 16 June 2004, the government of Uzbekistan, Uzbekneftegas, and LUKoil signed a PSA-agreement on the Kandym-Khauzak-Shady project, which entered into force on 24 November 2004. The investors' consortium includes LUKoil (90%) and Uzbekneftegas (10%). Duration is 35 years. Commercial gas production planned for 2007. |

Sources: www.LUKoil.com and www.LUKoil-overseas.com.

Notes
LUKoil has discontinued projects listed in brackets [].
a LUKAgip NV also owns an 8 percent share in the Azerbaijan Gas Supply Company Ltd. Additionally, LUKAgip Midstream BV owns a 10 percent interest in the South Caucasus Pipeline Company.

profitability and cost/benefit calculations than geopolitical considerations. The priority of profits over politics seems to hold true with regard to LUKoil's other Caspian projects as well. LUKoil's participation in international projects in Kazakhstan, like the one in the Karachaganak field, give the company a profit-able production-sharing scheme with favorable taxation, access to pipelines whose capacity can be increased in the future, and experience gained from working with Western partners, according to Andrey Kuzyane, president of LUKoil Overseas Holding Ltd. In fact, LUKoil's foreign-based production, while still small, accounts for a relatively larger share in total profits than those generated through domestic production.[79]

LUKoil, which was famous for its relatively independent behavior in matters of foreign engagement during the 1990s, likes to present itself today as a fully loyal Russian company and "flagship" of the Russian state in foreign economic affairs. LUKoil's relation to the state can be characterized by what Peeter Vahtra and Kari Liuhto have called the behavior of a "conformer": that is, LUKoil seeks international business opportunities, but is careful its internationalization is in line with Russian policy.[80] If LUKoil's close relationship to state authorities has caused unease among some of LUKoil's costumers, for instance in the Baltic States and Poland,[81] the Caspian states' leaders have not expressed any particular concern over LUKoil's political ties at home.

Conflict in the Caspian oil sphere is not between LUKoil and its Caspian counterparts, but relates more generally to Russia's pipeline politics, of which LUKoil is a part. Since LUKoil does not own export pipelines, it is, like other Russian and foreign oil companies, dependent on the allocation of space in Russia's existing pipeline system owned by Transneft, a fully state-owned monopoly. However, Transneft is today capable of transporting less than two-thirds of Russia's total oil production. The rest has to be shipped by rail or river routes, which are profitable only as long as oil prices remain high.[82]

The state's reluctance to expand pipeline capacities quickly is both economic and political: In a situation where the privatization of Russia's vertically integ-rated oil companies was once almost complete, the Russian government sought to assert control over them by setting crude oil export quotas and charging fees for using the Transneft pipeline system. Control over the pipes gives the Russian state the ability to cut off access to Russian companies out of favor with the government, and compels them to export via more expansive transit means. Since the Russian state strictly opposes the construction of private pipelines, LUKoil chose to give up initiatives of this kind (such as a proposed link from Western Siberia to Murmansk) and has established very close relations with Transneft in order to secure maximum access via its pipeline system. Partly because of LUKoil's close relationship to Transneft and Russian policy makers, the company was able to ship 86 percent of its oil through the state-owned pipeline system in 2003.[83]

With regard to foreign producers, Transneft follows a policy similar to that of Gazprom by using its monopolistic position as a way to discipline or reward companies (unlike in the gas sector, however, trade in oil is largely conducted on a cash basis and at market prices).[84] In order to reduce competition in the foreign oil market, Transneft usually favors Russian over foreign producers. However, this approach only works if the Caspian competitors have no export alternatives. Given the increasing diversity of pipeline options in the Caspian oil market, Transneft has come under pressure from the Kremlin to offer more space to Azerbaijan and Kazakhstan – a policy that has, of course, upset some of Russia's domestic producers. For example, Putin has pledged to supply more natural gas to Azerbaijan in exchange for more Azerbaijani oil transit via Russian pipelines. Also, it was growing international competition in the area of pipeline construction that prompted the Russian state to agree to the building of the Caspian Pipeline Consortium (CPC) link for the export of more Kazakhstani oil via Russia.

The CPC pipeline, which opened in 2001, is the only major oil pipeline running through Russia with a truly multinational ownership structure, including the Russian Federation (24 percent), the Republic of Kazakhstan (19 percent), the Sultanate of Oman (7 percent), and a consortium of private foreign investors led by the Chevron Caspian Pipeline Consortium Company. LUKoil saw the CPC as a convenient way to overcome the transportation shortage in the Caspian and also decided to participate in this project with a 12.5 percent share (through LukArco).[85]

From an economic point of view, all parties involved profit greatly from this project. During the period 1998–2003, the CPC contributed around $0.5 billion to the Russian government in taxes and fees. Once the pipeline is operating at full capacity, the CPC will be able to transport 67 million tons of crude per year (against 22.5 million in 2004), generating tariff revenues of $1.5 billion annually for the Russian government over a period of 35 years.[86]

While Transneft's management has never welcomed the CPC, seeing it as competition to its own business, the position of the Russian government has also remained somewhat ambiguous.[87] Moscow sees the CPC as a solution to meeting growing production in the Caspian and ensuring a continued flow of Kazakhstani oil via Russian territory. At the same time, Russia has not abandoned its oil pipeline balancing game, and problems over transit fees and privileges for oil exports from Kazakhstan persist. In 2003, for instance, Russia repeatedly sought to extend access to the pipeline to Russian non-shareholders at shareholder rates.[88]

Also, Russia has been unwilling to expand the capacity of the pipeline. Since transit tariffs and volumes are defined on the basis of agreement between the shareholders, rather than by state regulations, Russia cannot dictate terms, but is able to block any initiative put forward by other members. This veto power has led to conflicts with other shareholders in the past. ChevronTexaco, the operator of the CPC venture, favors a substantial increase in crude oil exports and additional investment in technical facilities required to meet the growing flow of oil.[89] This demand, which has the support of other private Western companies and Kazakhstan, was rejected by Russia on the grounds that it first wants to raise tariffs substantially in order to cut debt interest payments and channel more profits on dividends to all shareholders, and not only oil suppliers.[90]

Moscow is playing a delicate game, since its approach might eventually compel foreign investors, including Kazakhstan, to look for other ways to transport their energy westwards – for example, through the BTC, which is eager to fill remaining space capacities with Kazakhstani oil, Ukraine's Odessa–Brody pipeline, or eventually the construction of new pipelines. For LUKoil, participation within the CPC framework is seen very favorably so far. However, LUKoil also depends on pipeline space for the rising export volumes from its Kazakhstani production, and it can be assumed that the company would like to see an expansion of capacities rather than increased tariffs. At the same time, conflicts among CPC shareholders are hardly in LUKoil's interest. The company's involvement in long-term projects in the Caspian could be very negatively affected if, for instance, relations between Russia and Kazakhstan became strained.

## Observations from the three case studies

These three cases show that Russian business behavior in foreign markets varies from sector to sector. In the case of electricity, the main goal of UES is to ensure stable electricity exports to markets outside the CIS in order to increase profits for the company, since the prices it can charge on the domestic market are limited. In the case of gas, the chief interest of Gazprom is to keep neighboring countries in a state of dependency and ensure that all gas flows go through Russia's pipelines. In the oil sector, the behavior of Russian private companies depends on various factors, such as oil prices, opportunities offered by the host country (taxation policy), and accessibility to transportation infrastructure.

An important difference resulting from the goals of UES and Gazprom is that while UES's main interest is a functioning power market, Gazprom's primary objective is to own as much infrastructure as possible in order to ensure maximal control. Gazprom's goal thus largely coincides with the ambitions of the Russian state, since control is what both are interested in. UES's efforts to stabilize the electricity market are also compatible with state interest, although the political gain for Moscow is less evident, since corporate goals are relatively more important and the state does not control UES the way it does Gazprom.

In comparison to the gas market, the situation in the Caspian oil sector has become much more dynamic, with different transportation options becoming available to the Caspian states. The engagement of Western and other companies has more than anything prompted Russia to develop a flexible approach. Since Russia understands that is it no longer in a position to control all oil flows through its pipelines, Moscow sees LUKoil's participation in international oil exploration projects as a way to remain an active player in Caspian oil politics and to minimize the damage for Russia.

Business expansion is more likely to result in conflict if the primary goal is control. Gazprom's expansion into Central Asia is certainly tied to economic considerations; however, the Central Asian states are not Gazprom's primary engine for generating profit. Rather, they are merely part of Gazprom's larger strategy with regard to the lucrative European gas market. Accordingly, the gas-exporting countries of Central Asia likely will continue to look for alternative options to transport their resources west or east, unless Russia agrees to liberalize the gas market and makes prices and access to its pipelines nondiscriminatory. The dispute with Turkmenistan is likely to be the most intense. While relations between Russia and Kazakhstan exist across many sectors (but are strongest in the sphere of oil), and Uzbekistan is less dependent on Russia's pipeline system, gas export is the lifeline of Turkmenistan's economy. Given that Central Asian gas has become more important in Gazprom's long-term economic calculations, Gazprom is certainly interested in compromise rather than conflict with its gas-producing neighbor. However, as long as there are no real export alternatives for Central Asian gas other than through Russian territory, Gazprom has clear advantages in terms of its negotiating power.

As the cases of Transneft and CPC have demonstrated, the most conflictual issues in the Caspian oil sector are related not to the behavior of Russia's private companies but to Moscow's oil pipeline politics more generally. Moscow's current position is ambivalent: on the one hand, it understands that it needs to develop a more cooperative approach in order to maintain existing oil dependencies and not lose out to other foreign investors in the pipeline policy game; on the other, Moscow continues to apply a policy of pipeline scarcity through which it tries to preserve a certain level of political leverage over its neighbors.

Conflicts are less likely if the primary goal is enhancing market efficiency and increasing profit, as the case of UES has demonstrated. However, should the state decide to strengthen its control over this company, the effects for Russia's foreign relations could be profound. If the state takes full control over UES's external activities, for instance, Moscow would be able to cut power supplies and thus exert real pressure on its neighbors. The South Caucasus states are particularly at UES's mercy because, given the lack of alternatives, they have no choice but to cooperate. The situation is far different in the case of LUKoil. Since LUKoil is not even remotely in a position to control Caspian oil production, an eventual attempt by Russia to renationalize this company would not make much difference: LUKoil's withdrawal from international projects or cancellation of financial support would only open up possibilities for other foreign companies to become engaged.

## Conclusion: prospects for conflict and cooperation

Russia's relations with the states of the Caspian and Central Eurasian region are not conflict free, with continued disagreements over pipeline accessibility and energy prices. Moreover, Russia's single most critical bilateral problem in the region, its ties to Georgia, is still far from resolved. Nevertheless, in comparison to the Yeltsin era, the last few years have seen an overall improvement of relations between Russia and the states of the region. The reasons behind this improvement are manifold, but economic factors certainly play an important role. There is a genuine interest on the part of all regional leaders in a strong

Russian economy and in stable relations. Russia's enhanced economic engagement through its big energy corporations is consequently seen as an opportunity to strengthen economic ties and profit from Russia's economic revival. Thus, while many regional leaders were suspicious of Russian foreign policy intentions during the 1990s, most of them now perceive Russia's economic engagement as an overall stabilizing factor rather than a potential threat to their independence.

This conclusion is not to suggest that there will be less conflict in this region in the future. Russia and its companies will certainly try to maintain and, if possible, increase dependencies. However, while such efforts might provoke tensions in bilateral relations, the more dangerous source of potential conflict is likely to lie within the countries of the region rather than Russia. Although the Caspian and Central Eurasian region contains a significant portion of the global hydrocarbon reserves, local states remain relatively weak, and none has so far created conditions for sustainable political and economic development. The political systems in a majority of these countries are characterized by corrupt authoritarian regimes with generally weak civil societies. While there are currently no large-scale military conflicts in the region, all the violent conflicts of the past, and particularly those in the South Caucasus, are dormant rather than resolved, and continue to cause tension within or among these states. There also continue to be a number of other unresolved problems among the states of the region, including disputes over the demarcation of borders and the use of natural resources (mainly in the Caspian and in the Ferghana Valley). The weakness of the current states means that one or several of them could collapse, potentially leading to civil war that spreads violence throughout the region, creating opportunities for outside powers to intervene.

While Russian business involvement has contributed in some ways to stability in relations between Russia and the individual states of the region, it remains to be seen whether Russia's engagement helps to promote the kind of domestic stability that ensures long-term social and economic development. In fact, most of the region's authoritarian leaders understand that they gain politically from cooperating with Russia, because they obtain economic resources that help them hang on to power.

These same leaders have also shown great interest in cooperating with the United States and other Western countries; however, they do not want Western engagement to be conditioned on domestic democratic reforms. Russia's interest in cooperating with the authoritarian regimes in these countries is unlikely ever to be tied to requirements for internal reform. Also, while cooperation with Western companies may demand adherence to international business standards, Russian companies are used to working in an opaque business environment. In this way, Russia helps to undermine, rather than promote, the development of free market practices and democratization, creating conditions that impede social and economic development in the long run.

# Notes

I would like to thank Robert Orttung, Peter Rutland, Carol Saivetz, Andreas Wenger, and Oliver Möhl for their helpful comments and constructive critique of earlier drafts of this chapter. I am very grateful to Ruth Pollington from the Departments of Geography and Geology at the University of Leicester for drawing the two maps. In addition, my thanks go to Marshall Goldman for providing me with the opportunity to present my findings to the participants of the Comparative Economics Luncheon Seminar held at the Harvard Davis Center for Russian and Eurasian Studies on 13 April 2005.

1  I refer here to the three South Caucasus states Azerbaijan, Armenia, and Georgia, and the five Central Asian states Kazakhstan, Turkmenistan, Uzbekistan, Kyrgyzstan, and Tajikistan.
2  Carol R. Saivetz, "Perspectives on the Caspian Sea Dilemma: Russian Policies since the Soviet Demise," *Eurasian Geography and Economics* 44, no. 8, December 2003, pp. 588–606, here p. 595.
3  On oil policy under Yeltsin, see Peter Rutland, "Paradigms for Russian Policy in the Caspian Region," in Robert Ebel and Rajan Menon, eds., *Energy and Conflict in Central Asia and the Caucasus*, Lanham, MD: Rowman & Littlefield, 2000, pp. 163–168, here p. 163.
4  Michael Lelyveld, "Caspian: Russia Softens Opposition to Baku–Ceyhan Pipeline," *RFE/RL News and Current Affairs*, 6 March 2001, www.rferl.org (accessed 22 April 2005).
5  The Central Bank of the Russian Federation, "Social and Economic Situation in 2004 (January–December)," www.cbr.ru/eng/analytics/macro/ (accessed 16 September 2005).
6  Calculations based on Goskomstat figures: Federal'naia sluzhba gosudarstvennoi statistiki, "Rossia v tsifrakh – 2005," Moscow, May 2005, www.gks.ru/bgd/regl/brus05/IswPrx.dll/Stg/25–06.htm (accessed 16 September 2005).
7  Goskomstat figures presented by the Institute for Complex Strategic Studies, "Analytical Materials," Moscow, 9 April 2003, www.icss.ac.ru/publish/analysis/am066.html (accessed 16 September 2005).
8  Federal'naia sluzhba gosudarstvennoi statistiki, "Rossia v tsifrakh – 2005," Moscow, May 2005, www.gks.ru/bgd/regl/brus05/IswPrx.dll/Stg/23–15.htm (accessed 16 September 2005). See also United Nations Conference on Trade and Development, *World Investment Report 2004: The Shift towards Services*, New York: UNCTAD, 2004, pp. 72–74.
9  The Central Bank of the Russian Federation, "Social and Economic Situation in 2004 (January–December)," www.cbr.ru/eng/analytics/macro/ (accessed 16 September 2005).
10  Ministry of Economic Development and Trade of the Russian Federation, "On the Current Situation in the Economy of the Russian Federation (as of the End of January 2005)," Moscow, February 2005, p. 56, www.economy.gov.ru/wps/portal/english (accessed 16 September 2005).
11  *CIA World Factbook 2004* – Turkmenistan (information available as of 1 January 2004), www.cia.gov/cia/publications/factbook/ (accessed 22 April 2005).
12  Energy Information Administration (EIA), Azerbaijan Country Analysis Brief, Washington, DC, June 2003, www.eia.doe.gov/emeu/cabs/azerbjan.html; see also the South Caucasus Pipeline web site at www.caspiandevelopmentandexport.com/ASP/SCP.asp (accessed 22 April 2005).
13  Yuri Shafranik, "Neftianaia ekspansiia v SNG," *Mirovaia energicheskaia politika*, no. 5, 15 July 2002.
14  First oil began flowing in May 2005 in the Azeri section. Oil exports via BTC should reach 200,000–300,000 bbl/d by the end of 2005, with volumes climbing to 500,000

bbl/d by the end of 2006 (which is about half capacity). See EIA, Caspian Sea Country Analysis Brief, Washington, DC, December 2004, www.eia.doe.gov/emeu/cabs/caspian.html (accessed 16 September 2005).

15 Ibragim Alibekov, "While Russia Watches, Kazakhstan and Azerbaijan Explore New Ties," *Eurasia Business and Economics*, 3 March 2004, www.eurasianet.org (accessed 22 April 2005).

16 EIA, Kazakhstan Country Analysis Brief, Washington, DC, July 2005, www.eia.doe.gov/emeu/cabs/kazak.html (accessed 16 September 2005).

17 EIA, Caspian Sea Country Analysis Brief.

18 Source: National Bank of Kazakhstan; figures presented by US Department of State, 2005 Investment Climate Statement – Kazakhstan, www.state.gov/e/eb/ifd/2005/42065.htm (accessed 22 April 2005).

19 For an overview, see EIA, Caspian Sea Country Analysis Brief.

20 See Heiko Pleines's chapter in this book (Chapter 3) for more on this topic.

21 "Year Ago RAO 'UES of Russia' Acquired Energy Facilities in Georgia," UES Press Department News Release, Moscow, 1 September 2004, old.rao-ees.ru/en/news/pr_depart/; and United Energy System of Russia (UES) Annual Report 2003 (chapter 6.4.4.), old.rao-ees.ru/en/business/report2003/ (accessed 22 April 2005).

22 Presentation by Anatoly Chubais, CEO of Unified Energy System of Russia, at Brunswick UBS "Russia: Investing into Economy of Growth," 28 September 2004, old.rao-ees.ru/abc/en/show.cgi?280904bru.htm (accessed 22 April 2005).

23 "RAO 'UES of Russia' Preparing Energy Projects in NIS," UES Press Department News Release, Moscow, 17 September 2003, old.rao-ees.ru/en/news/pr_depart/ (accessed 22 April 2005).

24 "Armenian Government, ZAO 'INTER RAO UES' Sign Agreement," UES Press Department News Release, Moscow, 18 September 2003, old.rao-ees.ru/en/news/pr_depart/ (accessed 22 April 2005).

25 For an overview, see EIA, Caucasus Region Country Analysis Brief, Washington, DC, December 2004, www.eia.doe.gov/emeu/cabs/caucasus.html (accessed 22 April 2005).

26 Theresa Sabonis-Helf, "Power and Influence: Russian Energy Behavior in Its Southern 'Near Abroad,'" paper prepared for section 16, panel 4 of the conference "On the Margins of Europeanisation? Russia in the Global Political Economy," Standing Group on International Relations of the European Consortium for Political Research, The Hague, September 2004, p. 3.

27 EIA, Caucasus Region Country Analysis Brief, December 2004, at www.eia.doe.gov/emeu/cabs/caucasus.html (accessed 22 April 2005).

28 UES Annual Report 2003 (chapter 6.4.4.).

29 For an overview, see Vladislav Vucetic, "The Electricity Sector," Policy Note, The World Bank Group, Russian Federation, www.worldbank.org.ru/ECA/Russia.nsf, no date (accessed 16 September 2005).

30 Sabonis-Helf, "Power and Influence," p. 6.

31 On the state of Russia's electricity sector: *Russian Energy Survey 2003*, Paris: OECD/IEA, 2002, pp. 214–217.

32 "UES Plans Aggressive Expansion in CIS," *Alexander's Oil and Gas Connection* 8, no. 19, 2 October 2003, www.gasandoil.com/goc/company/cnr34003.htm (accessed 22 April 2005). Main export destinations in 2002 were Finland (44%), Belarus (22%), Kazakhstan (10%), Latvia (7%), Azerbaijan (7%), Moldova (3%), Poland (2%), Ukraine (1%), Georgia (1%), Turkey (1%), China (1%), and others (1%).

33 "Russia: RAO UES of Russia Exports Russian Electricity to Turkey via Georgia, Tbilisi," *PRIME-TASS*, 30 March 2001, www.rao-ees.ru/en/news/pub_uesr/show.cgi?300301turk.htm (accessed 22 April 2005).

34 Sabonis-Helf, "Power and Influence," pp. 6–7, 10.

35 Eric A. Miller, "Russian Control over Energy Raises Questions about Georgia's

Direction – Experts, Human Rights," *Eurasianet.Org Human Rights*, 28 October 2003, www.eurasianet.org; Mamuka Tsereteli, "Russian Energy Expansion in Caucasus: Risks and Mitigation Strategy," *Central Asia – Caucasus Analyst*, 27 August 2003; Igor Torbakov, "Russia Seeks to Use Energy Abundance to Increase," *Eurasia Insight*, 19 November 2003, www.eurasianet.org (accessed 22 April 2005).

36 Tatiana Kamoza, "The Silk Road for Chubais," *New Times*, October 2003, www.newtimes.ru/eng/detail.asp?art_id=940 (accessed 22 April 2005).
37 Sabonis-Helf, "Power and Influence," p. 7.
38 Tatiana Kamoza, "The Silk Road for Chubais."
39 Sabonis-Helf, "Power and Influence," p. 7.
40 This agreement was signed between Gazprom and Georgia's Energy Minister David Mirtskhulava on 1 July 2003.
41 Igor Torbakov, "Russian Policymakers Air Notion of 'Liberal Empire' in Caucasus, Central Asia," *Eurasia Insight*, 27 October 2003, www.eurasianet.org (accessed 22 April 2005); see also Erik Scott's chapter in this book (Chapter 11).
42 Tatiana Kamoza, "The Silk Road for Chubais."
43 Leon Aron, "Privatizing Russia's Electricity," *Russian Outlook*, summer 2003, www.aei.org.
44 Sabonis-Helf, "Power and Influence," p. 10.
45 EIA, Monthly Energy Chronology – June 2002, Washington, DC, www.eia.doe.gov/emeu/cabs/chrn2002.html#JUN01 (accessed 22 April 2005).
46 EIA, Kazakhstan Country Analysis Brief.
47 Igor Torbakov, "Russian–Turkmen Pacts Mark Strategic Shift for Moscow in Central Asia," *Eurasia Insight*, 15 April 2003, www.eurasianet.org (22 April 2005).
48 See the online version of the book "Gazprom in Questions and Answers," pp. 37, 40, www.gazprom.com/documents/Voprosi-i-otveti_ENG_FINAL.pdf (accessed 22 April 2005).
49 For an overview, see Stanislav Roginsky, "Restoring the Economic Ties: Russia and Uzbekistan Step Up Their Cooperation in Oil and Gas Production," *Oil for Russia*, no. 3, 2004, www.oilru.com/or/17/220/ (accessed 22 April 2005).
50 "Russian Gas Sector in Need of Investment: IEA," *Energy in East Europe*, no. 51, 12 November 2004, p. 7, www.platts.com/. The World Bank estimates that Gazprom will need to invest $80–100 billion over the next ten years simply to keep its production at current levels (of about 530 billion cubic meters per year), while ensuring that the domestic infrastructure is adequately maintained: Peter Thomson, "Reform of the Russian Gas Sector," Policy Note, The World Bank Group, Washington, DC, May 2004, p. 5, www.worldbank.org.ru/ECA/Russia.nsf (accessed 16 September 2005).
51 "Gazprom in Questions and Answers," p. 36.
52 *Neue Zürcher Zeitung*, 18 April 2005.
53 "Gazprom in Questions and Answers," p. 30.
54 Gazprom debts reached an all-time high of $15.2 billion by the end of September 2004. This is $2.69 billion more than in the previous year. Catherine Belton, "Gazprom's Debts, Costs Are Becoming a Liability," *Moscow Times*, 24 February 2005, p. 1.
55 "Gazprom in Questions and Answers," p. 28.
56 "Russian Gas Sector in Need of Investment: IEA," p. 7.
57 John R. Dodsworth, Paul H. Mathieu, and Clinton R. Shiells, "Cross-Border Issues in Energy Trade in the CIS Countries," IMF Policy Discussion Paper PDP/02/13, December 2002, pp. 7–8.
58 Sabonis-Helf, "Power and Influence," p. 20.
59 The idea of creating a "Eurasian gas alliance" was first introduced by Putin on the occasion of his meeting with Turkmen president Niyazov in January 2002.
60 Michael Lelyveld, "Kazakhstan: Deal Brings Astana Closer to Europe's Gas Markets," *RFE/RL Weekday Magazine*, 24 May 2002, www.rferl.org; "Kazakhstan:

Putin, Nazarbaev Sign Oil, Gas Agreements," *RFE/RL Weekday Magazine*, 8 June 2002, www.rferl.org (accessed 22 April 2005).
61  Sabonis-Helf, "Competition in the Caspian," p. 8.
62  For a detailed study on Turkmenistan, see Martha Brill Olcott, "International Gas Trade in Central Asia: Turkmenistan, Iran, Russia and Afghanistan," Geopolitics of Gas Working Paper Series no. 28, Program on Energy and Sustainable Development at Stanford University and the James A. Baker III Institute for Public Policy of Rice University, May 2004.
63  John Roberts, "What Role Can Eurasian Gas Play in Europe?" *Energy Economist* (London), issue 266, December 2003, p. 7.
64  In early January 2005, Ukraine agreed on a price increase from $44 to $58 per thousand cubic meters. "Turkmenistan, Ukraine Agree on Gas Price, Talks with Russia Continue," *Moscow News*, 3 January 2005, www.mosnews.com/news/2005/01/03/turkgas.shtml (accessed 22 April 2005).
65  *Neue Zürcher Zeitung*, 18 April 2005.
66  Jan S. Adams, "Russia's Gas Diplomacy," *Problems of Post-Communism* 49, no. 3, May–June 2003, pp. 14–22, here 16–17.
67  Peeter Vahtra and Kari Liuhto, "Russian Corporations Abroad – Seeking Profits, Leverage or Refuge?" Electronic Publication of the Pan-European Institute, 2004, p. 16 www.tukkk.fi/pei/NewEurope/SessionA1/Vahtra_Liuhto.pdf, (accessed 22 April 2005).
68  Oktai Movsumov, "Tackling Strategic Objectives," *Neftianie Vedomosti* (LUKoil Overseas Holding Ltd. Corporate edition) 45, no. 3, 9 February 2005, eng.neftevedomosti.ru (accessed 22 April 2005).
69  LUKOIL Overseas Holding Ltd., Corporate Report 2003, Moscow, 2004, p. 7, www.LUKoil-overseas.ru/materials/doc/reports/corpreportrus.pdf (accessed 22 April 2005).
70  "LUKoil planiruet sushchestvenno uvelichit' chislo proektov v Kaspiiskom regione," *RIA Ekonomicheskie novosti*, 5 June 2004.
71  For an overview on LUKoil's activities in Kazakhstan, see *LUKoil in Kazakhstan: Investments Bear Fruits*, Report prepared by LUKoil and presented in Aksai, Kazakhstan, 28 August 2003, www.LUKoil.com/materials/doc/presentations/2003/LUKOIL_in_Kazakhstan.pdf (accessed 22 April 2005).
72  Cited from "LUKoil President Appointed to Foreign Investment Council in Kazakhstan," *Russian Press Releases*, 4 December 2003, www.capitallinkrussia.com/press/companies/50010142/25700.html (accessed 22 April 2005).
73  "LUKoil, Uzbekistan Prepare Gas Document," *Interfax*, 19 April 2004; www.LUKoil-overseas.com (accessed 22 April 2005).
74  US Department of State, 2005 Investment Climate Statements – Uzbekistan, www.state.gov/e/eb/ifd/2005/42196.htm (accessed 22 April 2005).
75  For an overview on the different positions, see Douglas W. Blum, "Why Did LUKoil Really Pull Out of the Azeri–Chirag–Guneshli Oilfield?," *PONARS Policy Memo*, no. 286, Washington, DC: Center for Strategic and International Studies, January 2003, http://www.csis.org/ruseura/ponars/policymemos/pm_0286.pdf (accessed 22 April 2005).
76  Blum, "Why Did LUKoil. . .?"
77  For an overview, see LUKOIL Overseas Holding Ltd., Corporate Report 2003.
78  LUKoil Press Release, 22 December 2004, www.LUKoil-overseas.com (accessed 22 April 2005).
79  Pavel Bogomolov, "Policy of Cooperation," *Oil of Russia*, no. 4, 2003, www.oilru.com/or/14/137/ (accessed 22 April 2005).
80  Peeter Vahtra and Kari Liuhto, "Expansion or Exodus? Foreign Operations of Russia's Largest Corporations," Electronic Publications of the Pan-European Institute, 8/2004, pp. 94–95, www.tukkk.fi/pei/verkkojulkaisut/Vahtra_Liuhto_82004.pdf (accessed 22 April 2005).

81 See, for instance, Stefan Wagstyl, "The Pull of the West," *Financial Times*, 22 February 2005.

82 EIA, Russia Country Analysis Brief, Washington, DC, February 2005, www.eia.doe.gov/emeu/cabs/russia.html (accessed 22 April 2005).

83 LUKoil Annual Report 2003, p. 26.

84 Dodsworth *et al.*, "Cross-Border Issues in Energy Trade in the CIS Countries," p. 10.

85 For more information on the CPC, visit the project's official web site at www.cpc-ltd.com/ (accessed 22 April 2005).

86 "CPC Has Shipped 50 Million Tons of Oil," *CPC Press Release*, 12 January 2005, www.cpc.ru/portal/alias!press/lang!en-US/tabID!3460/DesktopDefault.aspx (accessed 22 April 2005).

87 Isabel Gorst, "Russian Pipeline Strategies: Business versus Politics," in *The Energy Dimension in Russian Global Strategy*, Study prepared by the James A. Baker III Institute for Public Policy of Rice University, October 2004, pp. 18–22.

88 Sabonis-Helf, "Power and Influence," p. 15.

89 Increasing capacity to 67 million tons of crude oil requires the construction of ten new pumping stations, additional storage, and a third offshore mooring facility. "CPC Has Shipped 50 Million Tons of Oil."

90 Ivan Grigoryev and Maria Yakovleva, "Alternative Routes: Exporters of Caspian Crude Look for Routes That Skirt Bosporus Straits," *WTE Russian Petroleum Investor*, www.wtexec.com/RPIAlternativeRoutes.html (accessed 22 April 2005); "Oil Exports via Caspian Pipeline Soar," *Moscow Times*, 13 January 2005, p. 7.

# 6 Russia, Iraq, and Iran

## Business, politics, or both?

*Carol R. Saivetz*

Russian relations with Iraq and Iran offer a useful opportunity to study the balance of state and corporate interests in Russia's foreign relations and its impact on conflict and cooperation, complementing the other case studies in this volume. Russian relations with these two countries are naturally different from Russian relations with the countries discussed in other chapters. In contrast to the CIS countries, Iran and Iraq are not contiguous to Russia, and while Moscow has long-standing relations with each, neither is within its immediate sphere of influence. In fact, Russia has little control over what happens in these two Middle Eastern countries. In the Caucasus and Central Asia, Russia is much more dominant, while Western countries are seeking to take a piece of the action. At the same time, the United States is obviously in a stronger position in the Middle East, and Russian policy is frequently designed to keep the Kremlin in the game.

Infrastructure – or the lack of it – also plays an important role in the Iraqi and Iranian cases. In contrast to the situation in either the European Union or the CIS, Russia did not inherit a well-developed pipeline network linking it directly to the target countries. In Europe and the CIS, these pipelines help to define the nature of the relationship between Russia and its neighbors. Since there is no similar infrastructure in the Middle East, all ties between Russia and these countries have to be built on a much less solid foundation.

The extent of mutual state and corporate interest is not nearly as clear in these two cases as well. Certainly Russia is interested in Iraq for financial reasons and seeks to assure its oil contracts. However, given that Russia has little influence over events in Iraq, the state seems content to let LUKoil make business as it can. Whereas Russia seems keen to control the actions of its energy companies in the CIS, it is more willing to let the companies operate more or less independently when they move further afield, whether it is the Middle East, North America, or Africa. When the international situation changes in the Middle East, Russia has little real choice but simply to leave its companies to fend for themselves.

In Iran, the main actor is Russia's state-controlled nuclear power industry rather than a private company like LUKoil. In this sense, the situation regarding Russia's nuclear relations with Iran is very similar to Russian arms exports to

China, discussed in a separate chapter. Russia has a strong short-term financial interest in promoting the export of its nuclear power technology, as it does in selling more arms abroad. But in the long term, it is creating a potentially unstable situation, perhaps threatening its own national security, because its exports could ultimately help Iran build nuclear weapons, an outcome that would have unpredictable consequences for the Middle East, the Central Asian states, and Moscow itself.

This chapter, with its case studies of Russian policy toward Iraq and Iran, teases out the difficulties the Russian state and Russian businesses face in working in these two volatile countries. In both cases, Russia tries to pursue both national and corporate interests, while maintaining good ties to the West and these two Gulf powers. Russia frequently tries to pursue all of its goals without taking much account of their contradictory nature: This lack of coherency leads to vague policy formulations that try to paper over important international problems, particularly Iran's acquisition of nuclear weapons.

The contributions of Russian business to conflict and cooperation differ across these cases. In Iraq, it is not clear whether Russian companies like LUKoil would be better off under a stable new Iraqi government or working in less stable, but not US-dominated, conditions. A stable Iraqi government might favor non-Russian companies, while the current chaos at least achieves the Russian state goal of constraining US unilateralism. Nevertheless, Russian oil companies, even if they have their contracts restored, cannot work effectively in current conditions, owing to safety concerns for their workers. If Russia helps the United States build stability in Iraq, it will be furthering US objectives in the Middle East with no real guarantee that LUKoil will secure its contracts. Russian goals of thwarting US unilateralism and promoting LUKoil's business are clear, but potentially contradictory. There is, thus, no obvious way to achieve these goals simultaneously.

In Iran, the situation seems more dire. Russia's economic interest in developing Iran's nuclear industry seems to be at odds with Russia's state interest of preventing the spread of nuclear weapons to Iran. Continued Russian support for the Iranian program could potentially destabilize the situation in the Middle East, and potentially in the southern regions of the former Soviet Union, and dramatically worsen Russian relations with the United States and the major European powers. The situation remains extremely volatile, again with no clear resolution.

## Iraq

It used to be said in the United States that "what's good for General Motors is good for the country!" Given the prominence of Russian big business and its proximity to the Kremlin, could we indeed say, "what's good for LUKoil is good for Russia"? Has Russian foreign policy been crafted to benefit large corporations like LUKoil? Or has LUKoil pursued policies in its business dealings abroad at the behest of the Russian government? The war in Iraq and its aftermath provide a unique case through which to examine the role of Russia's large corporations in Russia's foreign relations. The conventional wisdom in the period leading up to the US-led invasion of Iraq was that Russia objected to the war, at least in part, because it wanted guarantees that LUKoil's contract with the Iraqi government to develop the West Qurna-2 field would be honored. Indeed, as I shall discuss, Saddam Hussein attempted to use that presumed leverage in December 2002 when he annulled the agreement with LUKoil in the hopes of persuading Russia to veto future Security Council resolutions authorizing war against Baghdad. The picture, however, is far more complex. Russian president Vladimir Putin has repeatedly urged the Ministry of Foreign Affairs (MID) to promote the interests of Russian businesses. Yet certain non-business Russian foreign policy goals may actually contravene the interests of specific corporations. This section will lay out the goals of the Russian government and of LUKoil in the period leading up to and during the 2003 war. It will argue that to a great extent governmental and business goals were parallel in this period. In contrast, in the postwar period certain of the government's goals worked against those of LUKoil; additionally, some of the prewar policies on which there was agreement worked against LUKoil's longer-term interests.

## *The setting*

The long history of Soviet and then Russian involvement with the Saddam Hussein government is beyond the scope of this chapter. However, it should be noted that intensive Soviet involvement began with the July 1958 military coup that overthrew the Iraqi monarchy. Relations quickly flourished and included a broad range of economic and military ties. Relations with Saddam Hussein were never easy; nonetheless, the Soviet Union continued to count Iraq among its allies in the Middle East. During the Iran–Iraq war, the Soviet Union formally stopped deliveries of military equipment, but did allow its East European allies to provide spare parts to the Iraqi military.[1] After the 2 August 1990 Iraqi attack on Kuwait, Mikhail Gorbachev's Soviet Union worked with the United States in the attempt to force Iraq to withdraw. Simultaneously, Moscow used its long-standing contacts with the Saddam Hussein government to try to prevent the outbreak of the war in early 1991. Even after the collapse of the Soviet Union, the Russian Federation (RF) retained its ties to Baghdad, working to balance those ties with its obligations to the international community. In 1997, LUKoil won a contract from the Iraqi government to develop the West Qurna-2 field once the UN sanctions regime against Iraq was ended. It is important to note, however, that despite the contract, purported to be worth several billion dollars, Russia and LUKoil were careful not to abrogate UN sanctions.

Vladimir Putin inherited this situation when he became president of the Russian Federation. Because of his determination to restore Russia's Great Power status and to secure for the former superpower a place among the world's Great Powers, Iraq became an issue within the larger Russian–US framework. Putin began by initially reinforcing "strategic relationships" with India and with

China through the Shanghai Cooperation Organization; however, the terrorist attacks of 11 September 2001 in the United States provided Putin with an opportunity to change a policy that seemed to be going nowhere. He chose to restore Russia's status by "bandwagoning" with the United States and joining the war on terror. This move was not widely supported by the Russian foreign policy elites, who remained divided among groups supporting pro- and anti-western positions as well as several in between.[2] Many were quite skeptical toward the United States and the Bush administration. All of them were looking for the United States to reward Russia for pursuing a course that was so unpopular domestically. Within months of 11 September, though, President Bush abrogated the Anti-Ballistic Missile treaty and supported the second round of NATO expansion.

## Business and government before the war

In the context of pervasive feelings in Moscow that Putin had gained nothing for his support of US efforts in Afghanistan, including intelligence sharing and tacit support for the deployment of US/NATO troops in Uzbekistan, Russia's Iraq policy became a way to undercut US unilateralism. This desire to block American actions explains the insistence on a UN imprimatur for the war and the quasi-alliance with both Germany and France. With Duma elections in December 2003 and presidential elections scheduled for March 2004, Putin calculated that standing up to the United States would be popular among the general public.[3] Moreover, the opposition to the US-led war in Iraq was supported by at least two different groups within the foreign policy elites, those "geopoliticians" who want to counter the United States and those, presumably within the *siloviki*, who had "old school" ties to Baghdad.[4] Russia worked assiduously throughout the fall of 2002 to forestall the US-led invasion. Russian spokesmen repeatedly stated that there was no clear evidence to substantiate US claims about either weapons of mass destruction or links to Al-Qaida, and President Putin favored resolution of the Iraqi situation in line with then-existing Security Council resolutions. So in early November 2002, when the Security Council passed resolution 1441, which called for UN inspections and serious consequences if Saddam Hussein failed to meet the UN obligations, it seemed a success for Putin and Russian diplomacy. Russian officials claimed credit – along with France and Germany – for the language of the resolution, stressing that, while not ideal, it was a good compromise. Nevertheless, the determination of the Bush administration to wage war in Iraq meant that Russia's success in forestalling the invasion was short-lived.

The focus thus far has been on the geopolitical aspects of the Russian government's Iraq policy. There were, of course, financial calculations as well. As a headline in the Russian press proclaimed, "Saddam is not an enemy, but a potential buyer."[5] First, the Kremlin was clearly interested in securing repayment of the estimated $8 billion debt owed by the Saddam Hussein government. Given Iraq's weakened economic situation after years of sanctions, one could legitimately question whether or not any hopes for repayment were realistic. Nonetheless, as Kremlin spokesman Sergei Yastrzhembsky noted before the war, if the United States were to attack Iraq, Russia would stand to lose the money owed for arms supplies over the years.[6] By the same token, it is important to note that this is a government-to-government debt and not money owed to individual Russian firms. As discussed below, the debt issue was to become a major postwar negotiating point between Baghdad and Moscow and between Washington and Moscow, as well.

Second, Russian oil companies, which had the right to sell about 40 percent of Iraqi oil,[7] had a major stake in the UN-administered Oil for Food program. Then-foreign minister Igor Ivanov complained that the UN sanctions regime was "a major threat to Russian trade and economic interests."[8] Russian officials continually pushed to lengthen the list of approved goods; indeed, according to one estimate, Russian companies earned more than $2.3 billion in the Oil for Food program between 1996 and March 2003.[9]

It is of course only with the investigations into the program that we know the full extent of Russian profit. According to Russian media accounts, Russian firms bought $19.2 billion worth of Iraqi oil and exported $3.3 billion worth of food and other approved items to Saddam Hussein's regime. Zarubezhneft, a state-owned company, was the top purchaser of Iraqi oil. According to the Duelfer and Volcker commission reports, more than 280 Russian companies benefited from this UN-sanctioned trade.[10] In addition, individual Russian politicians also gained from the corruption that surrounded the program. Such high-ranking Russian officials as former presidential chief of staff Aleksandr Voloshin, former Federation Council speaker Yegor Stroyev, chairman of the board of Soyuzneftegaz, and the head of the Union of Oil and Gas Producers of the Russian Federation Yuri Shafranik, Communist Party leader Gennady Zyuganov, Liberal Democratic Party leader Vladimir Zhirinovsky and others personally benefited. Voloshin reportedly earned approximately $638,000 through the resale of 3.9 million barrels of oil between May and December 2002.[11]

Third, the Russian government and the oil companies had serious concerns about the price of oil. Russia feared that world oil prices would plunge when, in the aftermath of Saddam's ouster, Iraqi oil reentered world markets. It has been variously estimated that with each dollar increase in the price of oil, the Russian economy gains $2 billion in revenues and that the Russian budget would be in balance as long as prices did not fall below $21.50 per barrel. In the words of a postwar Russian assessment, sooner or later Iraqi oil will reach world markets and the price per barrel will fall to $12–$18.[12] It seems clear that the concern about a possible drop in the price of oil runs counter to the oft-stated prewar Russian goal of lifting sanctions. The removal of sanctions would of course open the Iraqi market; but it would also allow the free flow of Iraqi oil, thus increasing supply and lowering the price.

The final financial concern was, of course, the fate of the several contracts between Russian oil companies and the Saddam Hussein government. LUKoil alone had a $4 billion stake in the West Qurna-2 field. In the lead-up to the war, Russian diplomacy was focused at least in part on ensuring that these commitments would be honored if and when the United States overthrew the Saddam Hussein regime. In October 2002, Vagit Alekperov, the head of LUKoil, stated that he had "been hearing guarantees from the Russian government," because even if Saddam's regime were toppled, "the law is the law and the state is still there." Alekperov claimed that Putin had put oil at the top of the negotiation agenda with Washington. The oil company executive personally underscored his connections with the Russian government: "We try to understand the political situation, especially these last weeks, and we are engaged in constant dialogue with the Russian government."[13]

But Alekperov's optimism was misplaced. In mid-December, Saddam Hussein annulled the LUKoil contract, claiming that LUKoil had not fulfilled its obligations. The Iraqi authorities initially claimed that the decision was not politically motivated; however, Russian commentators clearly understood that the Iraqis were angry over negotiations between Russian oil companies and the United States to ensure that the contracts would be honored after the Saddam Hussein regime was toppled.[14] Ultimately, Iraqi deputy prime minister Tariq Aziz explained the political linkages:

> The management of LUKoil was negotiating with Washington to receive guarantees that its contracts would be valid even if the incumbent regime were overthrown. . . . This seemed outrageous to us. . . . Such behavior is not acceptable for business partners.[15]

A foreign ministry spokesman said that the Russian "side does not understand Iraq's decision at this time."[16]

It soon became apparent that the cancellation of the LUKoil contract was part of an elaborate cat-and-mouse game. Although LUKoil's participation was annulled, that of Zarubezhneft and Mashinimport (whose combined share in the project totaled 6.5 percent) was not. Vladimir Lukin, then deputy Duma speaker, accused LUKoil of naïveté, but harshly criticized the Russian government for threatening to change its policies because of the LUKoil contract. In Lukin's view, Russia's policy on Iraq should have depended on whether or not there were weapons of mass destruction. "The state policy is the policy of coordinating economic as well as geopolitical interests, thus it is wrong to say, at least in public, that if an agreement with some company is cancelled, we will automatically change our policy."[17]

If anything, the Iraqi action prompted the Kremlin to intensify the pursuit of Russian public and private economic interests in Iraq. In mid-January 2003, a high-level delegation including several oil executives traveled to Baghdad. Simultaneously, the Iraqi government was said to be dangling licenses for the Nahr Umr field in front of Zarubezhneft and Rosneft. As US policy pushed inexorably toward war with Iraq, the Russian government made what many saw as a last-ditch attempt to protect its financial stakes in Iraq. In late February, then-presidential chief of staff Voloshin traveled to Washington for meetings with then-National Security Advisor Condoleezza Rice and President Bush. The US administration used the visit to push for Russian support for a second Security Council resolution authorizing the use of force against Baghdad. However, Russian commentators stressed that Russia was prepared to cooperate with the United States under the "right conditions": that is, guarantees for Russian oil companies or compensation to those same companies for the loss of business.[18]

### The war and after

Russia could not prevent the war, but it quickly needed to decide what outcome would best serve its interests. Within weeks – especially when it appeared that things were not going well for the US-led coalition – Putin stated that Russia was not interested in a US defeat. While the Foreign Ministry continued to issue strong denunciations of the US war effort, the Russian president emphasized that Moscow would continue to cooperate with Washington. And an editorialist in *Izvestiia* wrote that "it's one matter to simply refrain from supporting the war against Iraq – and quite another to become a sworn enemy of America. Being at odds with America is just stupid."[19] Just a few days after this editorial appeared, Rice traveled to Moscow to begin to repair the damage in bilateral relations that the war had caused. Putin's backpedaling and the Rice visit seemed to indicate that Putin understood that the deterioration in US–Russian relations could not be allowed to continue.

Indeed, in the aftermath of the war there seemed to be confusion in Moscow as to exactly what Russia's interests were: On the one hand, it is clear that Russian concern about US unilateralism persisted, if not increased. But, as noted above, President Putin seemingly understood that a continuing and marked deterioration in relations with Washington was not in Moscow's best interests. (This seems to have been understood by the Bush administration as well.) On the other hand, the same economic goals as had predominated in the prewar period informed Russian policy after April 2003. So, the dilemma for the Kremlin was to balance against US unilateralism – within limits – while at the same time defending Russian economic interests in the region.

The contradiction was pronounced in the immediate postwar period. Washington pushed for a new UN Security Council resolution that would legitimize the US-appointed interim government – until an internationally recognized Iraqi government was formed – and lift the sanctions regime. Ironically, Russia at first refused. Prior to the war, Russia had looked for a UN imprimatur as a way of forestalling US unilateralism; now, it was the United States looking for UN authorization and it was Moscow blocking the Security Council deliberations. According to Deputy Foreign Minister Georgii Mamedov, Russia was seeking to ensure that previous resolutions were honored and that the role of the UN was institutionalized.[20] The Russian tactic at this time was to oppose the lifting of sanctions until inspectors returned to Iraq and declared the country free of weapons of mass destruction.

By the time Secretary of State Colin Powell visited Moscow, in mid-May 2003, there were signs that the Putin government was rethinking its position. Although Moscow was still unwilling to support the new resolution, both sides appeared eager not to disrupt the renewal of their bilateral relations. One can speculate that pragmatic considerations, both political and economic, were underpinning the incipient shift. First, France had already begun to shift its position more toward that of the United States, thus leaving Moscow in a more isolated role. This situation stood in marked contrast to the prewar negotiations when, as noted, Russia created a quasi-alliance with Germany and France to oppose the US-led intervention. Second, Putin and his advisers seemed to have realized that Russian companies stood to lose economically if the Kremlin refused to cooperate with the United States. Ilya Klebanov, Minister of Science and Industry, claimed that "having established control over Iraq, the USA may easily declare contracts signed between Russia and Iraq invalid."[21] And Yuri Fedotov, deputy foreign minister, argued that the goals of Russian policy were to "minimize [Russia's] losses from this resolution and . . . [to try] to ensure a role in the future."[22] Russian spokesmen made clear that Russia would consider backing the new UN resolution if the interim authorities in Baghdad honored both the oil contracts and the repayment of Russian debt. Powell, for his part, said that the future Iraqi government "will bear in mind its obligations to Russia."[23] Ultimately, Russia acquiesced to the US proposal and voted in favor of the resolution. Russia "sold its vote in exchange for oil," *The St. Petersburg Times* claimed.[24]

As with the question of seeking a UN imprimatur, the sanctions issue contains numerous ironies. Russia had for years prior to the war been pushing for the UN sanctions to be lifted, on the presumption that the Iraqi market would be wide open to Russian companies. Yet we now know the extent to which Russian enterprises and individuals benefited from the Oil for Food program. By the same token, Russian spokesmen defended the shift in policy by claiming that the new open environment was the best way to promote business interests. The then-foreign minister, Igor Ivanov, argued that the resolution created positive conditions for Russian business to participate in the reconstruction of Iraq, and other commentators cited the shift as an example of the foreign ministry working to defend the interests of Russian business.[25] A month later, during the three-hundredth anniversary celebrations of St. Petersburg, President Bush said that the United States would not harm the interests of Russian companies, but the fate of the oil contracts was a decision of the new Iraqi government, not the United States.

As the negotiations continued throughout the fall, the issues of debt forgiveness and the fate of the oil contracts became closely intertwined. In late December 2003, representatives of the provisional government visited Moscow. The delegation met with Vladimir Putin and the energy minister, Igor Yusufov. Putin assured his guests that Russian companies were prepared for extensive operations in Iraq; in return, the Iraqi delegation extracted a promise to write off part of the outstanding Iraqi debt. According to Russian media accounts, Putin promised to reduce Iraq's debts from $8 billion to $3.5 billion in the framework of the Paris Club. *Izvestiia* commented that "any direct linkage between the debt and permission to Russian companies was not mentioned at the meeting." But, off the record, "sources" indicated that Moscow was looking for guarantees about the LUKoil and other contracts and about the future of Russian business activities in Iraq.[26]

At a press conference, Abdul Aziz al Hakim, the head of the Iraqi delegation, confirmed that the Kremlin had attempted to link the debt issue to the interests of Russian business. He also hinted that Russian businesses would be welcome in Iraq: "Russian companies have broad opportunities for working in Iraq and for competing with other companies. We would like Russia to provide real help in the restoration of Iraq."[27] During this same trip, the Iraqi delegation met with Vagit Alekperov, who claimed that his meeting was the beginning of the realization of LUKoil's contract.[28] At the press conference mentioned above, al Hakim noted that "Iraq doesn't have a negative attitude to the participation of LUKoil in the West Qurna-2 field." One month later, Andrei Kuzyaev, the president of LUKoil Overseas, met in Baghdad with representatives of the Iraqi Oil Ministry to discuss the West Qurna-2 deal. Although no formal deal was signed, the negotiations kept the issue at the center of Russian–Iraqi negotiations.

Russian business leaders continued to express interest in working in Iraq, but recognized the difficulties inherent in the political situation. At a meeting of the Chamber of Commerce, business leaders discussed how to promote Russian business and to enter the Iraqi market before other international players. According to one *Novosti* account, a representative of the Foreign Ministry warned those at the meeting that conditions would not be easy for Russian companies: the businesses must be aggressive on their own as there would be no promises of state support. Simultaneously, a representative of the Ministry of Energy recommended that they deal solely with the United States.[29]

With the marked deterioration of the security situation in occupied Iraq, the United States and Britain looked to secure Russian support for a new UN Security Council resolution designed to end the military occupation and to transfer power to an interim government that would rule until elections scheduled for January 2005. Although both sides claimed interest in stabilizing the situation during the handover to Iraqi authorities, the Russians objected to US plans for the transfer, in particular to what they perceived as limitations Washington intended to place on Iraqi sovereignty.[30] Yet in the end, Russia voted for the resolution which turned over to the Iraqis full sovereignty and restored control over their own natural resources. Moscow supported the resolution presumably because it hoped that Russian companies would have an easier time negotiating directly with the Iraqis. In many ways, the vote represented a reversion to the earlier Russian position regarding the internationalization of the situation in Iraq and the diminution of US control.

It would seem that the carrot of renewed contracts finally persuaded the Russian government to accede to the Paris Club agreement to write off Iraqi debt. In late July 2004, Iraqi foreign minister Hoshyar Zebari visited Moscow and claimed that the two sides had reached an agreement to appoint a joint committee for the "inspection of all Russian contracts, concluded during the previous Iraqi regime, including the contracts in the framework of the Oil for Food program." He added: "The Iraqi government will respect and fulfill all contracts which are recognized valid."[31] In fact, Russia was the last of the Paris Club to agree to writing down a significant portion of the debt. In announcing the agreement, Finance Minister Aleksei Kudrin explained that Russia hoped to be involved in the reconstruction of the Iraqi economy.[32] It is important to note that earlier in the fall, the Russian government agreed to let the American oil giant ConocoPhillips purchase 7.59 percent of LUKoil. ConocoPhillips was looking for a way into the Russian oil market, and LUKoil and the Russian government seemed to understand that with the US company's stake in LUKoil the chances for reinstatement of the West Qurna-2 contract were enhanced significantly. Indeed, Iraqi prime minister Iyad Allawi met with Alekperov during his trip to Moscow at the end of 2004.

The final issue that must be considered is the price of oil. Russian official statements make clear that oil prices and the Russian share of the world market remained concerns after the war. The fact that the Russian oil contracts remain frozen – even after the agreement to write off the Iraqi debt – raised the specter of fierce competition between Russian and Western companies. Russian commentators noted that a Russian role in the Iraqi oil sector would

> reinforce the influence of Russia on the world oil market. Moreover, in this case, basic decisions by OPEC could hardly be taken without a dialogue with Moscow. Probably, for this reason, western firms are "conserving" oil sources in Iraq and not hurrying to open new fields.[33]

By the same token, this situation was not a totally negative one from Russia's perspective. As long as Iraqi oil was not flowing freely to world markets, prices would remain high. To emphasize the obvious, this situation benefits the Russian government, as Russian oil is exported to the West.

### The balance sheet

The Russian government has played an interesting game throughout the Iraq crisis. As was outlined earlier, in the prewar period geopolitical and economic considerations seemingly coincided, leading Russia to pursue a reasonably consistent policy in the prewar period and during the war itself. While on the surface the goal was to promote Russian business, it can be argued that opposition to the war did not endear the Russians to the postwar Iraqi government. As a commentator in *Vremia MN* noted before the war, the Iraqi opposition had already stated that it would not necessarily honor the Russian oil contracts; he asked rhetorically why the United States should be concerned about Russian business interests.[34] If anything, one might argue that the Russian strategy before the war has hurt Russia's economic interests in the postwar period. As many officials conceded, Russia – despite the long history of involvement in Iraq – no longer had the inside track on oil concessions or other business deals. Thus, a legacy of the prewar policy is, in effect, the fact that as of this writing the LUKoil contracts still have not been renewed. And this is despite the fact that LUKoil has given up a small percentage of the company to ConocoPhillips partially in an attempt to regain entry to the Iraqi oil fields.

In the postwar period, the coincidence between geopolitical and economic goals is less clear-cut. Russia remains inalterably opposed to US unilateralism, on the one hand, but it needs to curry favor both with the United States and with the Iraqi government if Russian companies are to have a chance of participating in Iraqi reconstruction. Thus, we find Russia acquiescing to the write-down of the Iraqi debt and supporting the series of Security Council resolutions legitimating the interim government and end of formal military occupation. But what exactly has Russia gained? Some smaller deals, including the training of Iraqi personnel in Russia, have been signed, but the large share that Russian companies hoped to have in the postwar Iraqi economy has not materialized.

In terms of geopolitics alone, Russian rhetoric regarding the Iraqi situation has not changed in the postwar period. Thus, in June 2004, Foreign Minister Sergei Lavrov stated:

> The developments in Iraq show that force must be used solely on a legal basis, with authorization by the United Nations Security Council. There had been no relationship between the problem of terrorism and the situation in Iraq before the US-led campaign began. International terrorists started coming to Iraq only after the occupation started.[35]

So what exactly does Russia want in Iraq? On the one hand, it is clear that Moscow looked upon the initial difficulties in the war and the continuing counterinsurgency struggle as constraints on US unilateralism. Yet on the other hand, neither a US defeat nor a protracted civil war, especially one in which Islamist forces might be victorious, would appear to be in the Kremlin's best interests. It would seem, therefore, that perhaps Russia was and still is looking for "managed instability": that is, a situation in which things would not go well for the United States, but one that would also not pose a serious threat to the rest of the Middle East. Lavrov has repeatedly said that his government is seeking a stable Iraq in which the United States would play the central role.

But even though the goal of "managed instability" is understandable in terms of geopolitics, it will not assist Russian business interests. In April 2004, five Russian workers were kidnapped.[36] Although these first hostages were released, the incident prompted Moscow to evacuate over 500 Russian citizens who were working in Iraq. Then, in a series of incidents in May, several Russians were killed. The dangerous security environment resulting from the "managed instability" clearly was an impediment to Russian participation in Iraqi reconstruction.

In light of the increasing difficulties in the Russian–US relationship, including the disputes over the Bushehr nuclear reactor and whether or not Putin is in the process of de-democratizing Russia, there would seem to be little or no chance that Russia's stated geopolitical goals will change. Russia refused to send peacekeepers even when pressed by the Iraqi authorities because that would have been tantamount to legitimizing the US invasion in the first place. And despite Russia's reluctant support for the new Iraqi government, Russia has still not gained what it claimed it wanted: reinstatement of the LUKoil contracts for the West Qurna-2 field and a large stake in the reconstruction of Iraq. Perhaps the final question is whether Russia gains or loses if Iraq becomes stable and the newly elected Iraqi government manages to institutionalize the political system there.

## Iran

On 24 September 2005, the International Atomic Energy Agency (IAEA) voted to refer questions regarding Iran's nuclear activities to the UN Security Council. The resolution noted that the "absence of confidence that Iran's nuclear program is exclusively for peaceful purposes ha[s] given rise to questions that are within the competence of the Security Council."[37] The vaguely worded resolution, which contained no firm date for referral, was yet another twist in international efforts to prevent Teheran from acquiring nuclear weapons. In August 2002, Iranian exile groups accused the government of hiding an enrichment facility at Natanz and a heavy-water plant at Arak. Six months later, the IAEA found traces of highly enriched uranium at Natanz, and in June 2003 it concluded that Iran had not reported imports of natural uranium and had not declared its facilities to handle the material.

Thus, within months of the end of the Iraq war, significant international attention shifted to the question of Iran's nuclear intentions. And within this atmosphere of enhanced international scrutiny of, and concern about, Iranian nuclear capabilities, the Russian Atomic Energy Agency, Rosatom (formerly Minatom), seems determined to fulfill a contract worth between $800 million and $1 billion to complete the nuclear reactor at Bushehr. Although Russian officials have stressed repeatedly that they do not want a nuclear-armed Iran, the project has been given the government's full support. Given that Russian governmental and business interests intersect in the Iranian nuclear energy sector, the Iran case provides an interesting parallel with Iraq. Both situations involve lucrative energy contracts with troublesome international allies: in Iraq the interests were those of a private company, whereas in Iran it is the stake of a Russian state agency. This case study lays out the Russian government's tightrope walk, balancing between protection of the deal for Bushehr – if not further nuclear contracts – and efforts to force Iranian compliance with the international nonproliferation regime.

## Background

There are many echoes of Russia's opposition to the US-led Iraq war in Russian objections to pressuring Iran. Post-Soviet Russia inherited the Soviet policy of pursuing multifaceted links – political, economic, and military – both with the Shah's government and with the Islamic Republic. In the 15 years since the collapse of the Soviet Union, the Russian foreign policy establishment has viewed Iran as a responsible partner in Central Asia, where it helped to negotiate an end to the Tajik civil war and worked with Russia to oppose the Taliban. In the Caspian Sea region, although Moscow and Teheran have not always agreed on Caspian demarcation,[38] they remained united in opposition to the US-supported Baku–Tbilisi–Ceyhan pipeline. More recently, Iran has backed a Russian proposal to create a Caspian rapid reaction force. Overall, as was noted above, once Vladimir Putin acceded to the presidency, larger geopolitical calculations prevailed. Thus, according to many in Moscow, ties with Iran represent a means of establishing Russia's foreign policy independence from the United States and of countering the Bush administration's unilateralism in the Middle East. One need only look at the reporting, both Russian and US, about the series of Bush–Putin summits to see that Iran is always on the agenda.

The significance of Iran in Russia's regional, if not global, policies is further enhanced by the fact that Iran is a large market for Russian arms, metals, and nuclear technology. Indeed, the Russian financial stake in ties with Iran has been generally acknowledged. According to the *New York Times*, one Western diplomat stated that the IAEA had no intention of implementing sanctions against Iran because "sanctioning Iran would hurt Russia and China."[39]

If the financial significance of the Bushehr contract was obvious at the outset, what was less clear was who benefited from the deal. Reports circulated throughout the late 1990s that Yevgenii Adamov (head of Minatom until 2001) was siphoning off at least some of the revenues from Bushehr.[40] In contrast, his successor, Aleksandr Rumyantsev, repeatedly stressed the lucrative nature of the project not only for Minatom, but also for many private companies. On a trip to Teheran in December 2002, Rumyantsev claimed that 1,200 scientists and contractors from the former Soviet Union were working in Bushehr, of whom at least 60 percent were Russian. According to an *Izvestiia* report, the Bushehr project has saved more than 300 enterprises from financial ruin,[41] while gazeta.ru estimated that Russia would lose $500 million a year if the project were not completed.[42] Thus, whether the construction of Bushehr is of public/governmental or at least partially private benefit, it would seem fair to say that Iran helped save the Russian nuclear power industry.

Given the large economic stake in the completion of the reactor, it is not surprising that the Russian government pushed to complete construction. When the deal was signed in January, 1995, the United States immediately objected: In the end, Moscow and Washington agreed that earlier contracts could be fulfilled, but that all shipments would end by 1999;[43] and the contract itself was amended to exclude gas centrifuges. Until June 2003, Rumyantsev and others could argue that completion of Bushehr did not contravene then-existing IAEA accords, that Iran was not in pursuit of a nuclear weapons capability, and the transfer of dual-use technologies was not dangerous. The June report, mentioned above, under-mined these Russian claims. Even after the IAEA report was made public, Russian foreign ministry spokesman Aleksandr Yakovenko stated that Russia was pushing Iran to sign an additional protocol renouncing a weapons acquisition policy, but that failure to do so would not hinder Russian completion of the Bushehr plant.[44]

### International negotiations, 2003–2004

With the release of the IAEA report and the "confession" from Teheran, Russia announced that it would not supply fuel for Bushehr unless the Iranians agreed to return all spent fuel rods to Russia, and that completion of the reactor would be delayed until 2005. Under pressure from Russia and from Germany, Britain, and France (the EU-3), authorities in Teheran announced, in October 2003, their intention to suspend uranium enrichment and to sign an additional protocol allowing for surprise inspections. Hasan Rowhani, secretary of the Iranian Supreme Council of National Security, made the formal announcement in Moscow. (It would seem fair to speculate that the choice of venue for the announcement was designed to emphasize the special relationship between Teheran and Moscow.) During the same meetings, the two sides continued their negotiations over the return of the spent nuclear fuel from Bushehr and the timetable for the completion of the plant. When Iran finally did sign the additional protocol on 18 December 2003, Russian relief was palpable. Deputy Foreign Minister Yury Fedotov commented that the signing "will create a favorable international atmosphere for the implementation of cooperation projects between Moscow and Teheran."[45]

Within months, new revelations about Iranian nuclear activities again placed Minatom and the Russian government in a difficult position. IAEA inspectors found previously undeclared experiments and a new type of centrifuge; and in March, traces of enriched uranium were also discovered. In this uncertain environment, the Western powers, particularly the United States, continued to pressure Russian authorities not to complete Bushehr. (What concerned the IAEA and the United States was that the dual-use technologies could be trans-ferred from Bushehr to a weapons program.) The dilemma for Russia was clear: Could Russia proceed with Bushehr, while at the same time preventing Iranian development of nuclear weapons? Could the Kremlin decide to renege on the contract and simultaneously not appear to have given in to US pressure? Russian statements, as negotiations between the EU-3 and Iran continued, were a study in purposeful ambiguity. For example, when a Rumyantsev trip to Teheran scheduled for February 2004 was delayed, Nikolai Shingariev, spokesman for Minatom, said that Russia "will never yield to US pressures to stop nuclear cooperation with Iran. Russia will continue such cooperation *as long as* there are no international decisions against it.[46]

Bilateral negotiations continued throughout the spring, and in May 2004 both Kamal Kharazi, Iranian foreign minister, and Asadollah Saburi, the deputy head of the Iranian Atomic Energy Organization, traveled to Moscow: Saburi met with Rumyantsev to discuss the often-postponed deliveries of nuclear fuel for the reactor,[47] while Kharazi met with both Vladimir Putin and Igor Ivanov, the current Security Council secretary. According to both Western and Russian press reports, Kharazi stressed the importance that Iran attached to its links to Moscow, and Putin, for his part, called Iran "our old and stable partner."[48] One can speculate that both economic and geopolitical motivations underlay Putin's statement. Iran remained a lucrative way to undermine US unilateralism, especially after the US-led war against Iraq and the toppling of the Saddam Hussein government. Moreover, with the LUKoil contracts still on hold, earning money in Iran was in all probability even more attractive. The Russian tightrope act was apparent five months later, when Foreign Minister Sergei Lavrov, in public comments in Teheran, continued negotiations about the return of spent fuel from the Bushehr reactor, but emphasized that Iran must comply with all of the IAEA's demands. Additionally, Lavrov urged the Iranian Majlis to ratify the additional IAEA protocol and stressed that completion of Bushehr should not be a cause of concern for the IAEA.[49]

Lavrov's comments came after months of Iranian foot-dragging. On 31 July 2004, Foreign Minister Kharazi announced that Iran would resume building centrifuges. For its part, the IAEA expressed serious concerns about Iran's apparent unwillingness to suspend all enrichment activities and gave Iran a November deadline to reveal all nuclear activities. Negotiations between the EU-3 and Teheran continued throughout the summer and fall, and after a meeting in Paris on 14 November, Iran announced that it would voluntarily continue and extend its suspension of enrichment activities. In return, the European Union would declare that Iran had a right to a civilian nuclear program and, in addition, agreed to provide technical assistance and to guarantee Iranian access to nuclear fuel imports. However, Iranian spokesmen also underscored that Iran would renege if Europe did not uphold its part of the agreement.

### The situation in fall 2005

The November agreement was seen in Moscow as a green light to finalize the Bushehr negotiations: what remained was the signing of the bilateral agreement guaranteeing the return of the spent nuclear fuel to Russia. Two weeks before Rumyantsev's scheduled February trip to Teheran, Rowhani traveled to Moscow. After meeting with Rowhani, Putin stated that Iran has no intention of acquiring nuclear arms and stressed that Teheran must "strictly respect all commitments it has made bilaterally with Russia and internationally."[50] In effect, Putin was telling the outside world that the deal would be completed, but in compliance with all international agreements. This intention was reinforced on 24 February, when the Russian president met with US president George Bush in Bratislava. Russian media suggested that Bush and Putin had agreed that Iran should not obtain nuclear weapons; additionally, Putin supposedly promised Bush that all nuclear cooperation with Iran would be suspended if Iran failed to return all spent fuel.[51] The agreement was to be signed on 26 February. Yet even with Rumyantsev in Teheran, the long-awaited deal was delayed for an additional day. Reports indicated that Iran demanded the immediate delivery of the fuel, but Rumyantsev insisted that the fuel would be delivered only shortly before the reactor was scheduled to go online. Ultimately the deal was finalized the next day.

Iran, however, proved to be a difficult client. While Russian authorities were focused on the specifics of Bushehr, the Europeans, the United States, and the IAEA remained concerned that Iran would move ahead with creating its own complete fuel cycle. And indeed in April, when the ongoing negotiations between Iran and the EU-3 stalled, Rowhani announced that Iran was considering a resumption of uranium conversion at Isfahan. Again in May, officials repeated the threat of restarting the facility at Isfahan, but agreed to a two-month delay. Russian spokesmen claimed that restarting "conversion will not have an impact on nuclear cooperation between Russia and Iran. . . . This does not threaten international security because this uranium will be used for peaceful ends and under the strict IAEA control."[52] Suspicions about Iranian nuclear activity were heightened in June 2005, when Iran was forced to admit previously undisclosed uranium experiments that had been conducted as late as 1998. Then in late July, Iran announced that it would resume conversion, but delay the restarting of advanced enrichment. Each Iranian announcement, delay, or threat undermined Russia's hope to complete the reactor without drawing the opprobrium of the international community, specifically Europe and the United States. Russian pundits understood the contradictions and openly questioned whether Russia could attempt to partner with both the European Union and the United States and also with Teheran.[53] When, on 9 August, Iranian officials removed the seals at Isfahan in the presence of IAEA officials, the Russian response was at first ambiguous; but within a week, the ministry of foreign affairs issued a firm statement that Iran should stop conversion activities and return to negotiations. The MID spokesman, Mikhail Kamynin, stated, "A wise decision would be to stop without delay the work that has been started on uranium conversion, and to continue Iran's close cooperation with the IAEA in removing the outstanding questions concerning the Iranian nuclear program."[54]

With the IAEA scheduled to meet in September, Iranian vice president Gholamreza Aghazadeh traveled to Moscow, where he met with Rosatom officials, Sergei Lavrov, and Igor Ivanov. In the lead-up to the IAEA meeting, commentators again noted the contradictions between Russia's Iran policy and its relations with the West, while officials attempted to persuade Iran to maintain the suspension.[55] In an ITAR-TASS interview on 20 September, Rumyantsev stated:

> Russia's position is that there are no grounds for the Iranian nuclear issue to be viewed with particular concern or for it to be referred upwards to the UN Security Council. Iran is entitled to develop civilian nuclear energy; *nonetheless, there are some issues that need to be elucidated via the IAEA.*[56]

Russia abstained in the IAEA vote, since referral to the UN Security Council is clearly something that Putin and Rosatom would like to avoid. And it is in the area of Russia's relations with the west that the Iran case is fundamentally different from that of Iraq: With the Iranian nuclear issue, Moscow lacks the "diplomatic cover" of France and Germany that it had in the lead-up to the Iraq war. As with the possibility of a second Security Council vote prior to the Iraq war, any vote to censure Iran would force Russia either to compromise its ties with Iran or to damage its standing with the Western powers. In either scenario, Rosatom presumably cannot finish the Bushehr reactor, nor can it negotiate with Iran for future construction contracts. In contrast, as long as deliberations remain within the IAEA, Russia can still hope to persuade Iran to retain its suspension of enrichment activities. Moreover, the indeterminacy of the situation also facilitates the completion of the project.

That Russia hoped, as they say, to be all things to all people is clear from Rumyantsev's statement following the 24 September IAEA resolution. The head of Rosatom noted:

> We appreciate that as a country, which has signed the non-proliferation treaty, Iran has every right to carry out its program to set up a nuclear fuel cycle. ... At the same time, we do not recommend this. ... Russia will not abandon its cooperation with Iran. If legal restrictions on such cooperation appear in international law, we will abide by them. ... There is nothing wrong in earning money in a legitimate business, and there is no reason at the moment to limit our cooperation."[57]

This statement epitomizes Russian policy and its contradictions. Can Russia continue to make money by constructing the Bushehr reactor at the same time as it wants to ensure its status as a responsible international actor? Can Russia take the risk of assisting the Islamic Republic to acquire nuclear weapons? It is definitely not in Russia's interests to have an Iran with nuclear weapons. Nor is it in Russia's interests to be ostracized by the European Union or the United States, despite the desire to be seen as a completely independent actor. It is, though, clearly in Russia's and Rosatom's interests to finish Bushehr and possibly to conclude agreements for further reactors. In February, the Kremlin and the ministry of foreign affairs undoubtedly thought they had managed the contradictions in Russian policy adroitly and also protected Rosatom's financial stake.

Iran, however, was not to be a compliant ally. Iran seems to be using its links with Russia to bolster its position as a regional superpower. This status is of course enhanced by the implicit nuclear threat represented by creating even a domestic nuclear capability. Thus, Iranian foreign policy goals create further problems for Putin's Russia. In the final analysis, if we assume that ensuring Russia's prestige as an independent, responsible, and trustworthy player on the international stage is a foreign policy goal, then what's good for Rosatom in the short to medium term may not be good for Russia's long-term standing.

# Notes

1 See Carol R. Saivetz, *The Soviet Union and the Gulf in the 1980s*, Boulder, CO: Westview, 1989.
2 See, for example, Andrei Melville, "The Achievement of Domestic Consensus on Russian Foreign Policy?" Paper delivered at the International Studies Association Meeting, New Orleans, 2002. See also A. P. Tsygankov, "Mastering Space in Eurasia: Russia's Geopolitical Thinking after the Soviet Break-up," *Communist and Post-communist Studies* 36, 2003, pp. 101–127.
3 According to the *Financial Times* and Radio Free Europe/Radio Liberty (RFE/RL), 90 percent of the Russian public opposed the US-led war in Iraq. See Robert Cotrell, "Strong Leader Strikes Cool Note in US Relationship," Special Russia supplement to the *Financial Times*, 1 April 2003 and Gregor Feifer, "Russia Must Do More than Simply Oppose US Foreign Policy," RFE/RL, 18 April 2003.
4 See, for example, "Political Rumors: Clan Power-Struggles Intensify in Russia This Spring," *What the Papers Say*, 12 March 2003.
5 Natalia Melikova, "Saddam Is Not an Enemy, but a Potential Buyer," *Nezavisimaia gazeta*, 7 October 2002.
6 Reported in "Russia worries about 'Business' with Iraq," *Zerkalo*, 16 October 2002.
7 Svetlana Babyeva and Goergy Bovt, "Deep Drilling Diplomacy," *Izvestiia*, 23 October 2002, p. 1. The 40 percent estimate comes as well from "Russian Minister Concerned by Growing US Influence in the Gulf," *Financial Times*, 8 April 2003.
8 Colum Lynch, "Russia Is Top Iraqi Exporter," *The Washington Post*, 16 January 2002, p. A8.
9 Igor Dmitriev, "Russian Companies Continue Their Work in Iraq," *Vremia novostei*, 21 November 2003.
10 Greg Walters, "Russia Profited from Iraqi Oil," *St. Petersburg Times*, 26 October 2004.
11 No author, "Russian Politicians and Companies Trading in Iraqi Oil," *Moscow News*, 13 October 2004.
12 Irina Timofeeva, "War and We. Tied as One by oil," *Novaia gazeta*, 18 March 2004.
13 Reported in Agence France Press, 4 October 2002.
14 No author, "Oil Contract Snub Erodes Russian Support for Iraq: Govt. Source," Agence France Presse, 13 December 2002.
15 *WPS-CIS Oil and Gas Report*, 20 December 2002.
16 No author, "Ministry Regrets Iraq's Scrapping of Agreement with LUKoil," Prime-TASS Newswire, 15 December 2002.
17 "Russian MP Criticizes Government's Response to Iraqi Decision on Oilfield," Ekho Moskvy, 14 December 2002, as translated by BBC Monitoring.
18 Catherine Belton, "Voloshin Trawls for Deals," *Moscow Times*, 26 February 2003.
19 *Izvestiia*, 3 April 2003, p. 2.
20 No author, "Russia Links Support for End to Iraq Sanctions to Answers on Oil Debt," Agence France Presse, 15 May 2003.
21 "Russian Minister Concerned by Growing US Influence in the Gulf," *Financial Times*, 8 April 2003.
22 Catherine Bolton, "Russia, US Inch Closer on Iraq," *Moscow Times*, 16 May 2003.
23 "Iraq: A Matter of Sanctions and Debts," *Russian Political Monitor*, 16 May 2003.
24 "Russia Sells Vote for Iraqi Oil," *St. Petersburg Times*, 27 May 2003.
25 *ITAR-TASS Weekly*, 22 May 2003. See also Sergei Kozhukhar and Vadim Lagutin, "Russia Defends its Trade/Economic Interests in Iraq," ITAR-TASS Weekly, 14 July 2003.
26 Ekaterina Grigor'eva and Evgenii Shestakov, "Russia Agreed to Write Down 2/3 of Iraqi Debt," *Izvestiia*, 23 December 2003.
27 Mikhail Petrov, "Iraq Open for Russian Business – Abdel Aziz al Hakim," ITAR-TASS, 22 December 2003.

28  Igor Fedyukin and Aleksdandr Tutshkin, "Moscow May Cut $4.5 Billion from Baghdad's Debts," *Vedmosti*, 23 December 2003, p. 2.
29  No author, "Russian Business Wants to Return to Iraq," Novosti, 28 January 2004.
30  See, for example, Dmitri Sidorov, "Rice Must Secure Moscow's Support," *Kommersant*, 14 May 2004, p. 10.
31  Aleksandr Reutov, "Baghdad's Hand Extended to Moscow with a Proposal to Exchange Debts for Contracts," *Kommersant*, 26 July 2004, p. 10.
32  Vladimir Alekseyev, "Exchanging Debts for Oil," *Trud*, 24 November 2004.
33  Aleksandr Chichkin, [no title], FK-Novosti, 5 May 2004.
34  Vladimir Skoryrev, "How to Divide the Iraqi Inheritance," *Vremia MN*, 2 October 2002.
35  Olga Levitskaya, "War in Iraq Makes Acute Question of Force in International Relations," *ITAR-TASS Weekly*, June 15, 2004.
36  In a somewhat sarcastic comment about the episode, *Vremia Novostei* entitled its report, "Business is More Important than Life." Yana Viktorova and Nikolai Gorelov, *Vremia Novostei*, 16 April 2004, p. 1.
37  IAEA Resolution entitled "Implementation of the NPT Safeguards Agreement in the Islamic Republic of Iran," dated 24 September 2005, from IAEA web site.
38  Carol R. Saivetz, "Perspectives on the Caspian Sea Dilemma: Russian Policies Since the Soviet Demise," *Eurasian Geography and Economics* 44, no. 8, December 2003, pp. 588–606.
39  Mark Landler, "Nuclear Agency Expected to Back Weaker Rebuke to Iran," *New York Times*, 24 September 2005.
40  See, for example, Andrei Zolotov Jr., "Duma Report: Adamov Corrupt," *Moscow Times*, 5 March 2001, p. 1.
41  Sergei Leskov, "Nuclear Iran," *Izvestiia*, 27 December 2002, p. 1.
42  As reported in RFE/RL Iran Report 6: 24, 9 June 2003.
43  See the summary in Robert H. Donaldson and Joseph L. Nogee, *The Foreign Policy of Russia: Changing Systems, Enduring Interests*, Armonk, NY: M. E. Sharpe, 2002.
44  As reported in RFE/RL Iran Report 6, no. 24, 9 June 2003.
45  "Russia Pledges to Continue Nuclear Cooperation with Iran," ITAR-TASS, 19 December 2003, as cited by BBC Monitoring.
46  "Russian Spokesman Says 'No Evidence' of Iran Seeking Nuclear Weapons," IRNA report, 17 February 2004, as cited by BBC Monitoring, italics added.
47  No author, "Russia, Iran discuss Bushehr Nuclear Power Station," ITAR-TASS report, 12 May 2004, 0928, GMT, BBC Monitoring.
48  For example, see RIA News Agency, "Russian Security Chief Reaffirms Importance of Relationship with Iran," 17 May 2004, 0558 GMT, and Agence France Presse report, "Russia's Putin Hails Relations with Iran during FM's Visit," 17 May 2004.
49  No author, "Moscow Urges Teheran to Sign NPT Protocol, Halt Enrichment," Agence France Presse, 17 October 2004.
50  Christopher Boian, "Iran Has No Intention of Acquiring Nuclear Arms, Putin Says," Agence France Presse, 18 February 2005.
51  Andrei Terekhov and Andrei Vaganov, "The Bushehr Nuclear Reactor Is Going into Operation with Russia's Support," *Nezavisimaia gazeta*, 28 February 2005, pp. 1, 6.
52  Agence France Presse report, 12 May 2005.
53  Anatolii Maksimov, "President of Iran: We Will Resume Enrichment of Uranium," *Novaia Izvestiia*, 29 July 2005, pp. 1–2.
54  RIA Novosti, "Russia Urges Iran to Act Prudently," 9 August 2005.
55  Mikhail Zygar and Dmitry Sidorov, "Moscow Prepares to Defend Iran," *Kommersant*, 12 September 2005, p. 9.
56  "Russian Nuclear Chief Restates Backing for Iran," ITAR-TASS, 20 September 2005, italics added.
57  "Russia Urges Iran to Extend Uranium Enrichment Moratorium," RIA Novosti, 27 September 2005.

# 7 Russian and transnational energy companies

## Conflict and cooperation in Pacific Russia

*Michael J. Bradshaw*

This chapter considers Russia's energy relations with Northeast (NE) Asia and beyond to the wider Asia-Pacific region. Japan, China, and South Korea are the key drivers in the region because they need new sources of energy and Russia could be the supplier.[1] Like the other chapters in this book, this one looks at relations between the Russian state and Russian business and the behavior of the two abroad. In addition, it adds a new player by considering the role of foreign energy companies working in Russia, looking as well at their relationship to the Russian state and Russian business.

This chapter demonstrates that state–business conflict within Russia undermines transnational energy cooperation. The Russian state has made conditions worse for its own businesses and for foreign businesses operating in Russia. The result of this state–business conflict inside Russia has been that Russia is suffering serious delays in building the capacity to meet NE Asia's energy needs. Accordingly, Russia has not been able to expand its currently minor role in the region and take advantage of obvious complementarity by supplying energy to an area that increasingly needs it. Russian state policies thus prevent the country from achieving its real possibilities.

As discussed in the introductory chapter to this volume, the notion of "business" in Russia is problematic. Such definitional issues are increasingly acute in the energy sector, where Russian state ownership of Rosneft and the recent state acquisition of a majority stake in Gazprom blur the distinction between state and business.[2] As we shall see, these two companies are playing a critical role in shaping Russia's energy relations in the region. The Kremlin is seeking to increase the role of the state in the energy sector, and the 2003 National Energy Strategy made Gazprom the coordinator of Russia's gas exports to NE Asia. But the state is no more a coherent, unitary actor in this field than it is in many others. Rather than cooperating effectively, in mid-2005 Gazprom and Rosneft seemed to be in competition to see which could control the key projects aimed at Asian export markets.

Even in the late Soviet period the possibility of increased trade and investment activity between "Pacific Russia" (the term used here to describe the south-eastern regions of the Siberian Federal District and the Far East Federal District) and NE Asia was posited on a natural complementarity between a resource-rich

Russia and a resource-poor NE Asia. During the 1970s, in the wake of the energy crisis, a number of large-scale agreements were reached between the Soviet Union and Japan to develop the resource potential of the then Soviet Far East.[3] In fact, the current development of the Sakhalin oil and gas projects dates back to that time. During the 1990s, the opening up of the Russian economy provided opportunities for transnational oil companies to participate directly in oil and gas development in Pacific Russia.

Despite this supposed complementarity, after 30 years relatively little progress has been made: most projects remain in the planning stage and Russia is not yet a major energy exporter to NE Asia. Much of the discussion regarding energy in Pacific Russia is about potential rather than actual developments. At present, Russia's energy trade with the region is limited to exports to China by railroad and from offshore Sakhalin by tanker. In 2003, China accounted for 2.0 percent of Russian oil exports and Japan a mere 0.3 percent.

Nevertheless, we might be on the verge of a substantial change in the scale of energy cooperation between Russia and NE Asia. In 2003, President Vladimir Putin described grand plans to build a giant plant for liquefying natural gas on Sakhalin and to develop massive oil and gas fields in east Siberia.[4] As these plans are realized, the new production will also change Russia's political relationship with the region.

The three major sections of this chapter address these issues. The first section examines the current pattern of energy consumption and supply in NE Asia and highlights the region's increasing reliance on the Middle East. Given the current context of ever-increasing demand for oil and gas and a heightened concern with energy security, the possibility of energy exports from Pacific Russia is seen as a very positive development in NE Asia. However, Russia's neighbors are increasingly frustrated at the length of time in turning obvious potential into reality. Increased competition, rather than cooperation, between the various NE Asian states seeking access to Russia's energy is only exacerbating tension levels. The second section reviews the current status and future prospects of the various oil and gas projects in Pacific Russia. The third section considers the impact of recent political developments in Russia's oil and gas industry and assesses their implications for the realization of the key projects in Pacific Russia. The chapter concludes by assessing the emergent opportunities for conflict and cooperation in Russia's energy relations with NE Asia.

## The energy situation in NE ASIA

Since the 1997 Asian financial crisis that dampened demand for energy, the NE Asian region has reestablished itself as one of the most dynamic regions in the global energy market. "Developing Asian countries, whose economies are booming, were the main driving force" when world energy demand grew by 2.9 percent in 2003, according to the International Energy Agency (IEA).[5] In 2003, global oil consumption increased by 2.2 percent, and China alone accounted for one-third of this growth.

Japan, China, and South Korea each face a somewhat different energy situation. Japan and South Korea have been able to develop sophisticated industrial economies without substantial domestic reserves of oil and gas. Consequently, they are almost entirely dependent upon imported energy, with the vast majority of imports coming from the Middle East. In 2003, 75.8 percent of Asia-Pacific's oil imports came from that volatile region.[6] The situation in China is somewhat different. China is well endowed with domestic energy resources, principally in the form of coal; but domestic production of oil and gas have not been able to keep up with the demand generated by China's rapid rate of economic growth. Parts of China are currently suffering energy shortages. In 1994, China became a net importer of oil and more recently it passed Japan as the second largest importer of oil, trailing only the United States. In 2003, 40.4 percent of China's oil imports came from the Middle East.[7] Only recently has China started to develop the capacity to import natural gas via the construction of liquefied natural gas (LNG)-receiving terminals at Guangdong and Fujian.[8]

Table 7.1 presents the current energy mix in NE Asia and compares it with that of the developed western countries in the Organization for Economic Co-operation and Development (OECD). Two points are noteworthy. The first is the overwhelming role that coal plays in China's energy mix; the second is that, overall, the share of natural gas in the energy mix is much lower in NE Asia than in the OECD. The relatively small share of gas has led energy specialists to conclude that there is potential to increase substantially the share of gas in NE Asia's energy consumption. The IEA predicts that natural gas consumption will grow faster in developing Asia than in any other region.[9]

This possibility raises two interrelated questions: where will that gas come from and how will it be transported to market? The answer to the first question determines the answer to the second. Compared to oil, natural gas is a more costly and difficult commodity to transport. There are two possibilities: by pipeline and as LNG. Each poses a particular set of demands in terms of the geopolitics and geoeconomics of energy security. The cheapest way to transport gas is by pipeline. In Europe, there is now a vast transcontinental pipeline network that moves huge quantities of gas from West Siberia to markets in the

*Table 7.1* The energy mix in Northeast Asia, 2003

|              | *Oil* | *Natural gas* | *Coal* | *Nuclear energy* | *Hydroelectric* |
| ------------ | ----- | ------------- | ------ | ---------------- | --------------- |
| China        | 23.4  | 2.5           | 67.9   | 0.8              | 5.4             |
| Japan        | 49.3  | 13.6          | 22.2   | 10.3             | 4.5             |
| South Korea  | 49.9  | 11.4          | 24.1   | 13.8             | 0.8             |
| OECD Average | 41.2  | 22.9          | 21.4   | 9.4              | 5.2             |

Source: Calculated from the British Petroleum Statistical Review of World Energy, 2004, www.bp.com/statistical review2004, p. 38.

Note
Percentage of energy consumption calculated on the basis of oil equivalents.

Commonwealth of Independent States (CIS), Central Europe, and the European Union (EU). However, such a pipeline network does not yet exist in NE Asia, because most of the supply comes from distant sources that make the construction of such pipelines very expensive. Instead, a complex network of LNG-based supplies has developed, initially focused on Japan, but now including South Korea and Taiwan.

Table 7.2 describes the current pattern of LNG supply in NE Asia. This LNG-based supply chain is capital-intensive, requiring substantial investments in gasification facilities in the gas-exporting countries and regasification terminals in the importing countries; furthermore, special LNG tankers are required to transport the LNG.[10] Because of the capital investments required, the LNG supply chain has traditionally been based on long-term contracts between suppliers and buyers with guaranteed volumes at fixed prices. However, this system is now breaking down as the relative cost of LNG supply is declining and as there is increasing competition from new producers. In price terms, a pipeline-based gas supply system is cheaper than an LNG-based system. In Japan, the situation is further complicated by the absence of a countrywide gas pipeline network. Thus, the LNG supply feeds a set of electricity generation companies that have regional monopolies, resulting in high domestic energy prices.

While LNG is more expensive than pipeline gas, it has one major advantage: supply source flexibility. As Table 7.1 demonstrates, Japan and South Korea have both developed a multiple-sourcing strategy that enables them to obtain LNG from a number of different sources in Asia and the Middle East. China is now just starting to develop such a strategy and is bargaining hard to drive down the price it pays for LNG, which in turn is impacting the price that Japan and South Korea are willing to pay. With an LNG system, it is possible to shift supply sources and play one supplier off another to get better terms. This flexibility is not possible with pipeline gas, but it is tempered by the tradition of LNG

*Table 7.2* Patterns of LNG supply into Northeast Asia, 2003 (million tons)

| Contracts in 2003 | Japan | S. Korea | Taiwan |
|---|---|---|---|
| USA | 1.64 | | |
| Trinidad & Tobago | 0.08 | | |
| Oman | 2.16 | 6.49 | |
| Qatar | 9.05 | 7.88 | |
| UAE | 6.87 | | |
| Algeria | | 0.23 | |
| Australia | 10.27 | 0.17 | |
| Brunei | 8.93 | 0.74 | |
| Indonesia | 24.05 | 6.93 | 4.68 |
| Malaysia | 16.72 | 3.79 | 2.80 |
| **Total** | **79.77** | **26.23** | **7.48** |

Source: Calculated from the British Petroleum Statistical Review of World Energy, 2004, www.bp.com/statistical review2004, p. 2.

being sold via long-term contracts. However, that system is gradually being eroded as consumers demand more flexibility.

The construction of transcontinental pipelines is a costly process that demands a level of commitment and trust between the supplier and the consumer. Pipelines cannot be moved, nor can alternative sources of supply be found should there be difficulties in the trade relationship. In the late 1970s and early 1980s, the United States and Western Europe debated the wisdom of developing a transcontinental pipeline network that allowed the Soviet Union to supply gas to Europe. The United States worried that the pipeline would provide the Soviet Union with leverage over Western Europe.[11] In the post-Cold War world, such concerns are less pressing, and until early 2006, Russia has shown itself to be a reliable partner. However, as North Sea oil and gas production decline, the European Union is concerned that it will become even more dependent upon Russia as a supplier of energy and wishes to limit this growing dependence (see Chapter 3, by Heiko Pleines).

Thus, from the view of the importing country, pipelines provide a cheaper means of transport, but are far less flexible than LNG. For the producing country, pipelines also pose a potential problem. In the context of Europe, Russia is supplying gas to a variety of markets, and this diversity provides a degree of protection against other countries demanding lower prices. However, Gazprom's recent experience with its Blue Stream export pipeline to Turkey shows the dangers of building a pipeline to a single market. Having built the pipeline, Turkey, as the only market for that gas, is now seeking to renegotiate the price it pays for gas deliveries. This lesson is important in an NE Asian context.

All the projections suggest that if the current rates of economic development in NE Asia, particularly in China, are maintained, energy supply security will become an even more important factor. Figures 7.1 and 7.2 present projections for oil and gas consumptions in NE Asia.[12] In absolute terms, Japan is the major market, but its economy is sluggish and its energy strategy has focused on expanding nuclear power and introducing new technologies to increase efficiency and thereby reduce demand. However, problems in the nuclear industry reduce the prospects for this strategy, and Japan will most likely have to increase gas imports to compensate for the unrealized gains in nuclear power. Japanese policy makers hope to stabilize or even reduce oil imports. South Korea has also faced economic difficulties and has put in place ambitious plans to expand nuclear and coal-based power generation. Nevertheless, it will continue to be highly reliant upon imported oil and gas.

China is in a somewhat different situation. It has substantial domestic reserves of coal, but its oil and gas industry has been unable to keep up with the demand stimulated by dramatic economic growth, in both absolute and relative terms. Growing consumerism, most importantly car ownership, promises further substantial increases in energy consumption. While coal production is unlikely to decline, future increases in energy consumption will demand increased imports of oil and gas. Already China's thirst for oil has had a major impact on global energy prices.

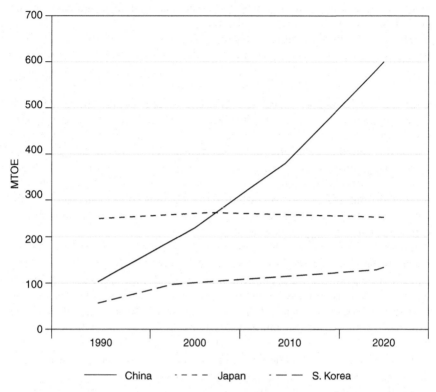

*Figure 7.1* Projected oil consumption (MTOE) to 2020 (Source: The Institute of Energy Economics, Japan, *Asia/World Energy Outlook: Burgeoning Asian Economies and the Changing Supply–Demand structure*. Toyko: IEEJ, 385th Forum on Research Works, 2004, p. 18).

Note
MTOE – Million tons of oil equivalent.

However, besides the rate of economic development, environmental concerns are having an impact. Following the ratification of the Kyoto Protocols, there is renewed pressure to reduce greenhouse emissions, favoring nuclear power and natural gas over oil and coal. While China does not have to deliver emission reductions within the Kyoto framework, the Chinese government is acutely aware of the environmental problems that have been created by its heavy reliance on coal. According to the World Health Organization, seven of the world's ten most polluted cities are in China.[13] Substantial reductions in the coal industry would be difficult for the Chinese government to sanction, especially when the current energy supply system cannot meet demand; however, there is a clear desire to meet future increases with less environmentally damaging sources of energy supply. Thus, many Chinese believe that natural gas has a major role to play in China's future energy mix. As domestic sources of supply have so far

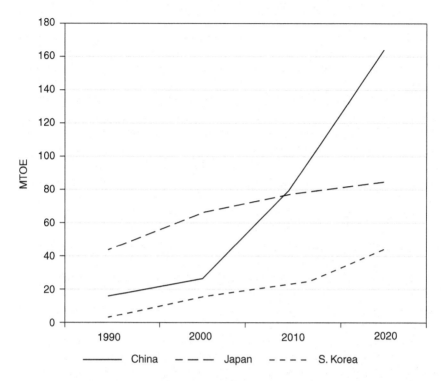

*Figure 7.2* Projected gas consumption (MTOE) to 2020 (source: The Institute of Energy Economics, Japan, *Asia/World Energy Outlook: Burgeoning Asian Economies and the Changing Supply–Demand structure*. Toyko: IEEJ, 385th Forum on Research Works, 2004, p. 20).

Note
MTOE – Million tons of oil equivalent.

proved inadequate, the question remains: where will that gas come from and how will it be delivered to market – as LNG or by pipeline, or both?

So far our discussion has not touched on Russian energy supply – deliberately so, because at present Russia is not a major supplier of energy to the region. Since 1999, there have been modest exports of oil from the Sakhalin-2 project and there have also been deliveries to China by railcar, initially by Yukos and more recently by Lukoil. However, it should already be clear that, given its geographical proximity, the current energy situation in NE Asia presents an obvious opportunity for Pacific Russia. One might well ask why it is that this opportunity has not already been seized. This question will be discussed in the third section; the next section looks at the various projects that might supply oil and gas to NE Asia.

## Energy projects in Pacific Russia

During the Soviet period, policy makers focused national energy development on the West Siberian oil and gas basin. For the most part, West Siberian output met domestic needs and provided exports to Europe. Moscow then paid little attention to regions farther east. Though geological exploration during the Soviet era had made it clear that there was oil and gas potential in the East Siberian basin and offshore of Sakhalin, these areas were neglected. In fact, the eastward oil pipeline from West Siberia still terminates at Angarsk, just to the west of Lake Baikal in Irkutsk *oblast'*. Refineries in the Far East continue to receive crude supplies by rail tanker along the Trans-Siberian Railway because their sources from deposits on Sakhalin Island are inadequate to meet regional demand.

Russian energy planners hope that this situation will change in the next five years as the anticipated expansion of oil and gas production in the waters off Sakhalin's shores will provide major new sources of energy in the Russian Far East by the end of the decade. The first signs of progress are already visible. The Sakhalin-1 project started commercial oil and gas production on 2 October 2005 and its initial production will be delivered to Khabarovsk *krai*.[14] In 2006, it will begin year-round export of oil, and managers are now discussing a possible gas pipeline to China. The Sakhalin-2 project will begin LNG and year-round oil deliveries in 2008.

Despite this optimism, the size of the deposits remains unknown and serious efforts to measure them began only in the years following the Soviet collapse. Therefore, the first uncertainty that one encounters when assessing the prospects for Russian energy exports to NE Asia is whether or not there are sufficient commercially viable reserves to justify investment in oil and gas production. Unsurprisingly, opinions vary, and the situation is further complicated by the fact that the Russian reserve classification system differs from the international system.[15]

A recent United Financial Group survey of the various potential oil and gas projects and associated reserves in the East Siberian and Far Eastern regions estimated that proven oil reserves stand at 7.3 billion barrels (bn bbl) in East Siberia and 17.5 bn bbls in the Far East.[16] Together these two regions account for 7 percent of total Russian oil reserves. Gas reserves total 3.3 trillion cubic meters (tcm) in East Siberia and a further 2 tcm in the Far East. This represents 7 percent of Russian gas reserves.[17] However, these figures undoubtedly under-estimate the true size of the reserves, since much of the area remains unexplored. Moreover, these fields are located in remote regions with little or no infrastructure and would require considerable amounts of capital investment to start producing. In East Siberia, there are four major oil and gas fields: Kovyktinskoe, Chaiandinskoe, Yurubcheno-Takhomskoe, and Sobinskoe-Paiginskoe. (See Table 7.3 for more details).

*Table 7.3* Reserves of the key East Siberian fields

| Field | Location | Oil mt | Oil m bbls | Gas bcm |
|-------|----------|--------|------------|---------|
| Kovyktinskoe | Irkutsk Oblast | 89 | 650 | 1,900 |
| Chaiandinskoe | Sakha-Yakutia | 68 | 499 | 1,241 |
| Yurubcheno-Takhomskoe | Evenk A Okrug | 466 | 3,402 | 596 |
| Sobinskoye-Paiginskoe | Evenk A Okrug | 20 | 147 | 167 |

Source: United Financial Group, Distant Horizons: Russian Energy to North-East Asia, Moscow, United Financial Group, 2004, p. 9.

Note
Oil figures include condensate; mt = million tons; m bbl = million barrels; bcm = billion cubic meters.

### East Siberian energy sources

At present, the only East Siberian field that has been the subject of extensive exploration and is at a stage where it could be developed to deliver exports to NE Asia is the Kovyktinskoe field in Irkutsk *oblast'*, just to the northwest of Lake Baikal. Rusia Petroleum has long held the license to develop this field, but the ownership of the company has changed several times. Today, the combined Tiumen Oil Company-British Petroleum (TNK-BP) owns 63 percent of Rusia, the Russian firm Interros owns 26 percent, and the Irkutsk Oblast Administration owns 11 percent. Rusia Petroleum, China National Petroleum Corporation (CNPC), and Kogas (South Korea) have completed a feasibility study to construct a pipeline to China and then on to South Korea. TNK-BP now has a three-stage development strategy in place with a first stage focusing on the gasification of Irkutsk *oblast'*. In early 2004, TNK-BP announced that it would invest $650 million in the first stage of the project to start production and supply local consumers with gas beginning in 2006.[18] The total cost of developing the field and moving the gas to market is expected to be $17 billion and includes plans to gasify regions in southern Siberia and eventually build an export pipeline to China.

The main obstacle blocking the development of the Kovyktinskoe field is that Gazprom currently has a monopoly over the construction and maintenance of gas pipelines in Russia. Gazprom wishes to join the project and TNK-BP has said that it can do so on commercial terms. However, Gazprom is more interested in using the gas to serve the domestic market, which is much less profitable than exports. Gazprom has been agitating in Moscow to get the Kovyktinskoe license removed from TNK-BP. This effort may be a ruse to lever Gazprom into the project on favorable terms, but until the issue of Gazprom's involvement is resolved, the export phase of the project is effectively stalled.

Until the fall of 2005, TNK-BP had maintained that Kovyktinskoe was the only field capable of meeting the emerging market opportunity in NE Asia in 2008–2010.[19] However, in order to circumvent Gazprom, TNK-BP appears to have decided to focus instead on the oil potential of the Verkhnechonskoe field, to the north of Kovykta, with the intention of exporting 90 percent of its production to the Asia-Pacific region, presumably via the planned export pipeline to Nakhodka.[20] The total investment could amount to $4 billion and production could begin in 2008.

In the case of the Kovyktinskoe gas project, Gazprom is willing to use its ties to the state and its monopoly position to block the project of another company for its own gain. In allowing Gazprom to set up this obstacle, the Russian state clearly favors the company in which it owns a majority stake over another where it does not. Gazprom's moves essentially block BP from investing its resources into developing the gas potential of East Siberia for export to China. TNK-BP is continuing to develop Kovyktinskoe on a stage-by-stage basis, but is now also developing other options in the region.

Another project currently in limbo is the proposed oil pipeline, connecting East Siberian sources to Asian customers (including TNK-BP's Verkhnechonskoe field). Debate has focused on the proposed construction of an oil pipeline from Angarsk to either the Chinese petrochemical center of Daqing or to an export terminal on the coast of the Russian Far East at Nakhodka. The initial project was a 2,400-kilometers pipeline from Angarsk to Daqing at an estimated cost of $2.2 billion (see Map 7.1). Yukos promoted this project and as an interim measure signed a protocol with the CNPC to deliver ten million tons per annum (mtpa) for seven years from 2006, with the deliveries being made by rail. As is

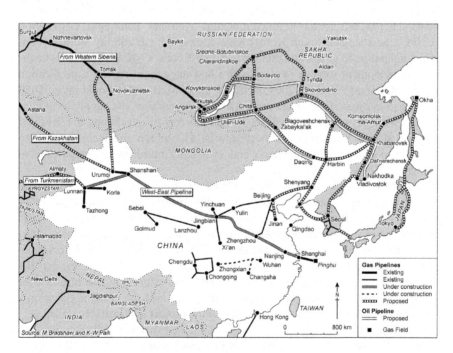

*Map 7.1* Potential oil and gas pipelines in NE Asia.

discussed in more detail below, the Kremlin did not look positively on a private oil company blazing the trail in the development of Russia's energy exports to NE Asia, and it is clear that this was one of many factors that contributed to the Kremlin's campaign against Yukos.[21]

Initially, the Russian government was in favor of the China oil pipeline; however, the Russian state-owned company Transneft, which has a monopoly on the construction and operation of oil pipelines, proposed an alternative pipeline initially from Angarsk, but now from Taishet (500 kilometers to the north of Angarsk) to Nakhodka, arguing that such a pipeline would serve a variety of markets in the Asia-Pacific region. The Transneft pipeline, routed to the north of Lake Baikal, would be over 4,000 kilometers in length and cost about $10 billion, though the price is increasing all the time. The Japanese government's offer to provide $7 billion in loans to construct the pipeline made the Transneft proposal more attractive.

The 2003–2004 debate over which of the oil pipelines to build revealed the lack of a coherent strategy in Moscow and set China and Japan against one another in a competition for Russian oil. During 2004, Moscow reconsidered the pipeline route because of the environmental sensitivity of the Lake Baikal region, and at the very end of the year Prime Minister Mikhail Fradkov announced that the Russian government had canceled the pipeline project to China in favor of the one to the Russian Far Eastern coast. Despite Fradkov's announcement, talks continued about building a spur off of the main Taishet–Far East pipeline to supply China. Despite the decision by the Russian government to build the longer pipeline, it remains unclear whether there will be sufficient oil production from East Siberia to fill the Nakhodka pipeline, let alone an additional spur to China. In spite of canceling the pipeline, Russia pledged to boost oil exports to China by rail to as much as 15 million tons by 2006. The Russian government ultimately envisages a substantial expansion of oil output in East Siberia, up to 60 million tons, and this new capacity will require some $55 billion of investments.[22] Initially, however, it may be necessary to divert production from West Siberia.

The oil pipeline saga is far from over and the Russian government may rethink its pipeline decisions. Relations between Russia and Japan have soured during 2005 as a result of continuing disagreement in the territorial dispute over the Kurile Islands. President Putin's planned spring 2005 visit to Japan was delayed until the autumn because agreement could not be reached on an agenda. Nevertheless, it is now clear that Moscow sees the construction of the oil pipeline as an anchor for the development of the East Siberian region and as the mainstay of Russia's drive to become a major energy supplier to the Asia-Pacific region (to include the West Coast of the United States); therefore, if necessary, the Russian state will fund the project. It may not be commercially viable, but it is fast becoming a strategic necessity. There is even talk of a gas pipeline following the same route supplying an LNG terminal on the coast of Primorskii *krai*.

### Sakhalin energy sources

With the battles over licensing rights and pipelines, the developers of the East Siberian fields may be missing their opportunity to supply Asian energy markets. The Sakhalin oil and gas projects represent an alternative source of Russian energy that is stealing a march on East Siberia. Table 7.4 presents a summary of the current status of the various Sakhalin projects. At any one moment in time, it is difficult to be precise about the exact structure and status of the various projects. As the projects evolve, the companies working on them change. For example, the maximum membership of the Sakhalin-2 project included the American companies McDermott and Marathon; both companies sold their shares to the remaining partners so that the current project has three partners: Shell (UK/Netherlands), Mitsui, and Mitsubishi (both Japan). The situation in Sakhalin-1 is somewhat different, because the Indian State Oil Company ONGC Videsh was able to join the project when the Russian partners, Rosneft and its Sakhalin-based affiliate Sakhalinmoreneftegaz (SMNG), sold it half of their interest to finance their continued involvement. Furthermore, the various global mergers among the leading Western oil companies have impacted the Sakhalin projects. The ExxonMobil (both US) merger brought Exxon into the Sakhalin-3 Krinskii project, and the Chevron–Texaco (both US) merger brought Chevron to Sakhalin-3. The acquisition of ARCO (US) by BP brought the UK company into the Sakhalin-4 project.

At the beginning of 2004, it was possible to identify nine different Sakhalin offshore projects at various stages of progress. At that time, I identified three distinct generations of Sakhalin project: the first generation comprised the original Sakhalin projects that dated back to a compensation agreement between Japan and the Soviet Union in the mid-1970s.[23] These have since become known as Sakhalin-1 and Sakhalin-2, and they are based on initial exploration work conducted in the 1970s and 1980s. In 1994–1995, they were two of three fields in Russia to be awarded Russia's first, and only, production sharing agreements (PSAs). The PSA is an internationally accepted mechanism for enabling high-risk resource development projects in difficult conditions. The investors shoulder the initial risk and investment costs; subsequent production is then shared between the investors and the host government (in the case of the Sakhalin PSA, the investors have first call on the production until their costs have been recovered). The investors' share of production returns their investment and provides a defined level of profit. The PSA also locks the project into the legislative framework at the time of the agreement, thus protecting the investors against subsequent fiscal and legal changes that might affect its profitability.

Somewhat confusingly, it is the Sakhalin-2 project, operated by the Sakhalin Energy Investment Company (hereafter Sakhalin Energy), that has made the most progress, achieving first oil production in 1999. It initially committed more than $10 billion to develop further offshore oil and gas production, lay oil and gas pipelines to the south of the island, and build an LNG plant and oil export terminal on Aniva Bay that will allow year-round export. In mid-2005, Sakhalin

*Table 7.4* Mid-2005 status of the Sakhalin Projects

| Project | Fields/blocks | Participants | Recoverable reserves | Project status |
|---------|---------------|--------------|----------------------|----------------|
| Sakhalin-1 | Chayvo, Odoptu, Arktun-Dagi (oil and gas) | Operator: Exxon Neftegaz Ltd (US) 30% SODECO Ltd. (Japan) 30% ONGC Videsh Ltd. (India) 20% SMNG-Shelf (Russia) 11.5% Rosneft-Astra (Russia) 8.5% | 307 mt of oil 485 bcm of gas | PSA Phase 1: early oil. First oil in 2005 |
| Sakhalin-2 | Piltun-Astokhskoe (oil), Lunskoe (gas) | Operator: Sakhalin Energy Investment Co. Royal Dutch Shell (Netherlands/UK) 55% Mitsui (Japan) 25% Mitsubishi (Japan) 20% | 600 mt of oil 700 bcm of gas | PSA Phase 1: early oil in 1999 Phase 2: Gas/LNG in 2007–08 |
| Sakhalin-3 | Krinskii Block | Operator: Pegastar ExxonMobil (US) 33.3% ChevronTexaco (US) 33.3% Rosneft (Russia) 33.3% | 453 mt of oil 700 bcm of gas | Exploration project suspended due to loss of exploration rights |
|  | Vostochno Odoptinsky, Ayashsky | ExxonMobil (US) 66.6% Rosneft (Russia) 33.3% | 167 mt of oil 67 bcm of gas | Project idle and now suspended due to loss of exploration rights |
|  | Veninsky Block | Rosneft (Russia) Sakhalin Oil Company (Russia) | 51 mt of oil 578 bcm of gas | Early exploration |
| Sakhalin-4 | Astrakhanovskaya offshore structure | Rosneft (Russia) 51% BP (UK) 49% | 89 bcm of gas | Project stopped by Rosneft |
| Sakhalin-5 | Vostochno-Shmidtovsky and Kaigan/Vasyukan (and Zapadno-Shmidtovskii) blocks | Rosneft (Russia) 51% BP (UK) 51% Joint Venture Company Elvary Neftegaz being created to develop the project | 600 mt of oil 600 bcm of gas | Exploration First well drilled in summer 2004, further exploration planned in 2005 |
|  | Lopukhovskii Block | TNK-BP (Russia-UK) 100% | 130 mt of oil 5 bcm of gas | Early exploration |
| Sakhalin-6 | Progranichnii Block | Alfa-Echo (Russia) Ronseft (Russia) | 200 mt of oil | Rosneft has withdrawn from project |

Source: Table based on oil and gas industry press and oil company websites and press releases.

Note

mt = million tons; bcm = billion cubic meters.

Energy revealed that the true cost of phase 2 was likely to be more than $20 billion. Sakhalin Energy has attributed the cost increases to errors made in the initial estimates of cost, as well as external factors such as exchange rate fluctuations and the rising cost of raw materials. All of this suggests that the true cost of developing Sakhalin's offshore potential is likely to be much greater than initially envisaged.

The second phase of the Sakhalin-2 project was officially launched on 15 May 2003. Five months later, President Putin was in Bangkok talking about a new energy configuration in the Asia and Pacific region, noting the construction of an LNG plant on Sakhalin. Although he failed to mention that it was being built by a consortium of foreign companies, it was clear that exports of Russian LNG from Sakhalin were aligned with Russia's foreign policy and commercial objectives in the region. The hard sell is working. As of June 2005, Sakhalin Energy had sold 8.0 mtpa of its 9.6 mtpa LNG capacity, and the company is confident that it will have sold all of its output by the end of 2005.[24] Table 7.5 provides information on the contracts agreed so far.

The Sakhalin-2 project was distinct in that it has no Russian participation, a characteristic that is very much at odds with the current environment of increased Russian state control over the energy sector. The Sakhalin-2 project is strategically significant for Russia because it is opening new markets in the Asia-Pacific region and the Kremlin long wanted state-owned Gazprom to be involved. The company could also advance its corporate goals by participating in the project. From Gazprom's perspective, involvement in a large LNG project would provide access to the technical expertise it needs to develop the Shtokhman field in the Barents Sea, where the aim is to export LNG to the east coast of the United States. The Sakhalin-2 project also provides valuable marketing experience for Gazprom in a new market, which can balance the company's overdependence on European export markets. For Shell and the other members of the Sakhalin-2 project, Gazprom involvement provides political support and protection for the project at the highest levels in Moscow, as well as access to other projects in Russia. For obvious reasons, Shell is very interested in accessing new reserves in Russia.

In late 2004, Shell and Gazprom started "intense discussions" about the possibility of Gazprom acquiring a significant equity stake in the Sakhalin-2 project.

*Table 7.5* Sakhalin energy's LNG deals (as of March 2005)

| Purchaser | Volume (MTPA) | Start date and duration |
|---|---|---|
| Tokyo Gas (Japan) | 1.1 | From project commencement for 24 years |
| Tokyo Electric (Japan) | 1.5 | From project commencement for 22 years |
| Kyushu Electric (Japan) | 0.5 | Commencing 2009, for 22 years |
| Toho Gas (Japan) | 0.5 | Commencing 2009, for 22 years |
| Baja Mexico (Shell Eastern Trading) | 1.6 | From project commencement for 20 years |
| Kogas (Korea) | 1.5[a] | Early 2008 for 20 years |
| Hiroshima Gas (Japan) | 0.21 | Commencing in 2008 for 20 years |
| Tohoku Electric (Japan) | 0.42 | Commencing in 2010 for 20 years |

Source: Sakhalin Energy Investment Company Ltd.

Note
a  With an option for an additional 0.5 mtpa. mtpa – million tons per annum.

As with TNK-BP and Kovyktinskoe, Shell was insistent that Gazprom should pay a fair market price for the stake that it acquires. On 7 July 2005, the two companies agreed to an asset swap whereby Gazprom would obtain a 25 percent, plus one share, interest in the Sakhalin project (leaving Shell as the operator and major shareholder with 30 percent) and in return Shell will get 50 percent of the Zapolyarnoe gas field in West Siberia. Any difference in the valuations of the assets will be compensated through a cash package and other assets agreed.[25] The Memorandum of Agreement was signed before Sakhalin Energy revealed the scale of its cost overruns. Initially, it was thought that Gazprom would have to add cash to the deal, now the Sakhalin-2 project is less valuable, and Shell may have to make a cash payment. Clearly, Shell sees the deal as a means of getting to more reserves in Russia; however, in September 2005 Shell failed to make it onto the shortlist to develop the Shtokhman field in the Barents Sea, as did ExxonMobil.[26] It would seem that the Kremlin wishes to limit the access of the foreign oil majors and is forcing them to partner with its state-owned companies, Gazprom and Rosneft. In the current context, BP-TNK is now an exception, rather than rule, in independently accessing Russian oil and gas reserves.

The Sakhalin-1 project, operated by Exxon Neftegaz Ltd. (ENL, a subsidiary of ExxonMobil), experienced a more complex development phase and only achieved first production in October 2005. Initially, the two projects planned to share their infrastructure, but they are now following quite different development strategies. Sakhalin-1 is building oil and gas pipelines to the Russian mainland and will export from the port of Dekastri in Khabarovsk *krai*. During the initial phase, gas will be consumed in Khabarovsk *krai*.[27] Sakhalin-1 has yet to commit to a second phase, but plans pipelines to either Japan or China, or perhaps even both. Gazprom has also been linked to possible involvement in the Sakhalin-1 project. Had the Gazprom–Rosneft merger been successful, Gazprom would have automatically become a shareholder in the project. Now Gazprom wishes to buy Rosneft's 20 percent share of the project and is reportedly ready to make Rosneft "an offer it can't refuse."[28] In late 2004, Gazprom, Exxon-Mobil, and CNPC were reportedly in discussions about building a pipeline from Sakhalin to China. At the ceremonies to mark first oil production from Sakhalin-1 on 2 October 2005, Steve Terni, president of ENL, confirmed that ExxonMobil is holding talks with China on the possibility of supplying it with gas from Sakhalin.[29] While the current reserve base may not be sufficient to justify such a pipeline, there are other Sakhalin fields that could be developed in the future, but so far progress has been limited.

If things had gone according to plan, there would have been a "second generation" of Sakhalin projects following behind Sakhalin-1 and Sakhalin-2, but this set of projects never materialized. Mobil and Texaco, working as the Pegastar Consortium, won exploration licenses in the mid-1990s for Sakhalin-3 acreage, including the Krinskii block, which had the most promise. Unlike the "first-generation" projects, Sakhalin-3 involved expensive exploration in deep water, and the foreign companies were unwilling to invest substantial sums without the protection of a PSA. Unfortunately, the PSA regime in Russia during the 1990s was under constant revision and was also the subject of conflict between domestic interests in both the state and the private sectors. After initial failure, the foreign partners agreed to bring in Russian companies (Rosneft and SMNG) and also agreed to carry them through the exploration phase in the hope that doing so would secure a place on the list of projects to be developed under a PSA regime.

However, in January 2004 the Russian government annulled the exploration licenses for the two Sakhalin-3 blocks, charging that the foreigners had not made enough progress.[30] Most likely, the government will hold new auctions for the site. In the conditions prevailing in late 2005, a Russian company will probably have to take the lead in the project. Minister of Natural Resources Yury Trutnev said in February 2005 that all new fields should be developed by companies with at least 51 percent Russian ownership,[31] making either Gazprom or Rosneft the likely lead partners for the Krinskii block. Additionally, Krinskii is considered a strategically significant field and, under the new Subsoil Law regulating natural resources scheduled for adoption in late 2005, foreign participation will be limited to 49 percent. Krinskii's designation would require a reconfiguration of the Pegastar consortium to give the Russian members, currently Rosneft-SMNG and the Sakhalin Oil Company, 51 percent ownership, with ExxonMobil and Chevron, the current foreign partners, sharing the remaining equity. Whether the foreign partners would be willing to finance the exploration phase remains unclear, but Rosneft now has a heavy debt burden following its purchase of Yuganskneftegaz, and likely would not be able to provide financing. The most immediate issue is that the projects that would have made up the "second generation," offshore Sakhalin have now become the "lost generation," and this has reduced the reserve base currently available offshore Sakhalin.

The "third generation" comprises the acreage now being developed as exploration projects outside of a PSA regime. The most promising project is the Rosneft (51 percent)–BP (49 percent) joint venture Elvary Neftegaz that is currently exploring the Sakhalin-5 plot. Under the terms of the alliance between Rosneft and BP, the foreign partner will carry the Russian partner through the exploration phase, which got off to a successful start in the summer of 2004.[32] In 2005, the joint venture drilled a second well and announced in September that in summer 2006 it would drill a further two wells at a cost of $200 million. Given that this project started life as an exploration program, unlike the first-generation Sakhalin projects, it is unclear how long it will take before the project can go into production. Furthermore, as the fields are 50 kilometers offshore of northeastern Sakhalin and under 100 meters of water, they present a more substantial development challenge than the first-generation projects, which are less than 10 kilometers offshore and in much shallower water.[33]

The important point here is that the effort to develop Sakhalin's offshore resources has lost momentum. The current stalemate surrounding the Krinskii block means that there is likely to be a hiatus after Sakhalin-1 and Sakhalin-2 finish their current construction phases in 2007. Whether the Sakhalin region becomes a major oil and gas province to rival the North Sea then depends on the pace at which Sakhalin-5 develops, on whether Sakhalin-1 commits to a gas phase, and on whether the Krinskii block can get back online. As is discussed below, this situation is almost entirely due to conflict in Moscow over the benefits afforded to foreign investors via the PSA and, more recently, concerns over ownership and control of the Russian natural resource base. It also means that the only short- to medium-term prospects for Sakhalin energy exports to NE Asia are Sakhalin-1 (phase 1) and Sakhalin-2 (phase 2), as these are the only projects proceeding with certainty at present. In the context of the wider themes of this volume, if increased oil and gas exports from Sakhalin to NE Asia serve the interests of Russian foreign policy, then we can conclude that the internal infighting over the PSA regime that has delayed the development of Sakhalin's offshore resources has undermined Russia's foreign policy goals in the region.

## Russian energy politics and the prospects for exports to NE Asia

When the Russian National Energy Strategy was approved in 2003, it handed Gazprom the responsibility of coordinating Russia's gas exports to NE Asia, giving it the power to block many of the agreements. At that time, Gazprom had no interests in the various projects in East Siberia and the Far East and there were no pipelines constructed. Instead, there were a handful of oil and gas projects that involved foreign oil companies and, in some cases, the state oil company Rosneft. It is noteworthy that with the exception of TNK-BP, none of the surviving major private Russian oil companies is involved in these projects. Thus, if Moscow wished to control the export of oil and gas from its eastern regions to NE Asia, it could rely partly on its control of pipeline construction via Transneft and Gazprom. However, to assert further dominance it needed to gain control over the development of new fields.

Strictly speaking, by 2005 the Russian state still had little control over the development of fields in Eastern Siberia and the Far East. However, despite the failure of the Gazprom–Rosneft merger, Gazprom is now maneuvering itself into a position whereby it can directly influence the scale and sequencing of Russian energy exports to NE Asia.

Over the past two years, four issues have brought about a deterioration in the relationship between the Russian government and the private sector (both domestic and foreign) in the oil and gas industry: the demise of the PSA, the increased politicization of the licensing process, the Yukos affair, and the changed status of Gazprom and Rosneft. The PSA and license issues have already been discussed. The point is that each of them has had a negative impact on the prospects for energy exports from Russia to NE Asia. During the 1990s, an effective PSA regime was seen as essential if foreign investors were going to invest billions of dollars in the remote regions of Siberia and the Russian Far East. The progress of the 1995 PSA legislation and subsequent amendments was slowed by constant infighting in the State Duma. The foreign oil companies and Rosneft favored the creation of an effective PSA regime, but private oil companies such as Yukos and Sibneft, which fielded a powerful army of lobbyists, felt that it gave foreign investors too many advantages.[34]

In 2000, at a conference on Sakhalin, President Putin declared that "PSAs are for Russia."[35] He transferred responsibility for PSAs from the Ministry of Natural Resources to the Ministry of Economic Development and Trade. However, this move actually made matters worse, as the PSA is highly technical and the new ministry lacked the expertise to deal with it. By late 2003, although the legislation remained in force, it was limited to a short list of fields and the PSA was effectively dead, a prognosis confirmed by the annulment of the Sakhalin-3 licenses at the beginning of 2004. The September 2003 TNK–BP deal, when BP committed $6.15 billion dollars to its Russian project, prompted a view that the investment environment in Russia was sufficiently stable that the special protection afforded by the PSA was no longer necessary and that all projects should be on a normal tax and royalty basis. However, this deal was not followed by other major agreements and the current political landscape makes it highly unlikely that there will be another TNK–BP-type deal.

The Yukos affair is not central to our current discussion, but, as noted earlier, the company's planned pipeline to China was one source of the Kremlin's irritation with the company and its leader. More generally, the Yukos affair signals that the Kremlin will be the sole determinant of the strategic direction of development in Russia's oil and gas industry, particularly in frontier regions and offshore.

This leadership role is reinforced by the state's purchase of a controlling stake in Gazprom and Rosneft's acquisition of Yukos's main production unit, Yuganskneftgaz. The result has been the creation of two state champions (which may yet merge into a single company) that will be the driving force in the domestic oil and gas industry and also provide the major vehicle for cooperation with the global oil and gas corporations. As our discussion has revealed, Gazprom may soon have interests in all of the major projects in East Siberia and Sakhalin, and the latter may be at the expense of Rosneft, which needs to raise funds to cover the cost of acquiring Yuganskneftegaz.

The dominant position of Gazprom (reinforced by its acquisition of a 72.7 percent stake in Sibneft) is a development that has been reinforced by the Russian government's political manipulation of the licensing of oil and gas fields. ExxonMobil lost the Krinskii block license because the Kremlin felt that there should have been more progress over the ten years since the license had been awarded. However, the lack of progress was entirely due to the stalemate over the PSA. ExxonMobil did respond to the changing circumstances in late 2003 when it agreed to develop the field on a tax and royalty basis, but this concession was too late.

No doubt the Russian government hopes that it will now get a much better price for the Sakhalin-3 acreage and it will align Gazprom or Rosneft with the foreign partners needed to develop the field; but this will have been at the cost of a damaging delay in the development of the Sakhalin oil and gas province. As we have already noted, the threats to TNK-BP's Kovyktinskoe license are more likely a strategy to get Gazprom into the project on favorable terms. Minister Trutnev's statement that future licenses should go to companies that are 51 percent Russian made specific mention of Sakhalin-3. Clearly, the Kremlin is privileging the position of Russian companies (principally its own companies Gazprom and Rosneft) in the future development of oil and gas in Russia. Foreign companies are still welcome, since not all fields will be subject to the 51 percent rule; but access to the most important projects will only be possible via minority ownership with a Russian partner. Of course, the Russian government has not defined what it considers a "strategic resource," thereby leaving fuzzy which fields will require majority Russian ownership.

The Rosneft-BP Elvary Neftegas joint venture in which Rosneft has 51 percent ownership may indicate the type of projects that will be able to move forward. Given that the Russian government itself estimates that $55 billion in new investment will be required to develop Pacific Siberia, it remains to be seen whether the foreign oil majors will accept the new rules of the game or whether they will go elsewhere. Clearly, the strategists in Moscow believe that Russia is sufficiently attractive as a new source of oil and gas reserves that the foreign oil majors will have to accept the new terms. Only time will tell if this is the case.

## Conclusion

Events in Russia's oil and gas industry since 2003 suggest a major change in the locus of power and control: the state has reestablished its primary position via the destruction of Russia's leading private oil company and the creation of state champions. At the same time, the terms on which foreign companies can gain entry to Russia's reserves have been tightened in favor of Moscow. This does not mean that Russia is closed to foreign investment, but it does mean that the Russian state is no longer willing to relinquish control over a key asset, its oil and gas reserves. The Kremlin points out that other oil-rich states have made similar moves and there is no reason for Russia to be different. The oil majors accept this point. It is also important to realize that a large part of Russia's oil production still remains in private hands; but when it comes to development in Pacific Russia, then with the possible exception of TNK-BP, domestic private companies are not significant actors.

The state now has strategic control over the development of energy relations with NE Asia via its controlling ownership of Gazprom and Rosneft. While the state has reasserted itself, the two-year battle for control resulted in costly delays in Pacific Russia at a critical time in terms of NE Asian energy security. Most likely, Gazprom soon will be involved in all major projects in Pacific Russia and there will be a grandiose plan to develop an integrated oil and gas pipeline network to supply both domestic and export needs (in Gazprom this is known as the "Eastern Program"). This integrated plan will demand massive investment and, in the case of gas, guaranteed access to export markets, which will require bilateral agreements between Russia and countries like China and South Korea. The lesson of the Sakhalin projects is that to make this plan a reality, Gazprom and Rosneft will need to partner with the foreign oil majors to gain access to technology, project management skills, and possibly project financing. The Russian government and its oil and gas companies may have a plan, but the key questions remain: given current conditions, will the foreign oil companies still want to work in Russia and will the market still be there by the time the plan has been realized?

At present, because the bulk of Russia's economic and population base is located west of the Urals, Russia is not seen as a serious economic player in NE Asia. However, if Russia becomes a major supplier of oil and gas, the geopolitical landscape will shift and Russia will gain real influence, a development that would ease its concerns about a Chinese invasion of its empty eastern lands and thus make it a less nervous neighbor. Such a scenario would also promote bilateral and multilateral cooperation between state and private-sector actors, reducing the potential for conflict by promoting interdependence in a region that is currently characterized by competition.

Time is pressing, as the energy-hungry economies of NE Asia will soon find alternative sources of supply. While Russia is the only potential supplier of pipeline gas, increased LNG deliveries to China and South Korea may fragment the market such that there is insufficient demand left to justify a gas pipeline from Russia to these countries. Building such pipelines is a large-scale, long-term project that needs a commitment from producers and consumers, so now is the time to decide how and from where Russia will supply pipeline gas. If the countries of NE Asia find alternative sources, the opportunity to build President Putin's "new energy configuration" will have been missed. If the opportunity is seized, it will provide Moscow with a significant resource to deploy in its future relations with NE Asia and Asia Pacific.

## Notes

*  The author would like to thank the British Academy for the award of a Small Research Grant that enabled some of the research for this chapter.

1  India is fast becoming an important factor in the Russian energy sector and also has ambitious plans for the expansion of liquefied natural gas (LNG) imports.
2  In June 2005, the Russian government purchased an additional 10.74 percent of Gazprom's stock for $7.15 billion, raising state ownership to over 50 percent.
3  Michael J. Bradshaw, "Soviet Far Eastern Trade," in A. Rodgers, ed., *The Russian Far East: Geographical Perspectives on Development*, London: Routledge, 1990, pp. 239–268.
4  Speech by President Vladimir Putin at the Asia-Pacific Economic Cooperation (APEC) Business Summit, Bangkok, 19 October 2003, available at Russian Federation Ministry of Foreign Affairs, Information and Press Department, www.mid.ru (accessed 31 August 2004).
5  International Energy Agency (IEA), *World Energy Outlook 2004*, Paris: OECD, 2004, p. 64.
6  British Petroleum (BP), *BP Statistical Review of World Energy*, 2004, p. 18, www.bp.com/statistical review2004.

7 BP *Statistical Review of World Energy*, p. 18.
8 See K. Schneider, Ye Qiang, R. Cutrotti, A. Ball, Liu Xiaoli, Wu Zhonghu, Gao Shixian, Jiang Xinmim, and Su Zhengming, *Natural Gas in Eastern China: The Role of LNG*, Canberra: ABARE Research Report 03.1, 2003 and D. Girdis, S. Tavoular-eas, and R. Tomkins, *Liquefied Natural Gas in China: Options for Markets, Institutions and Finance*, Washington, DC: World Bank Discussion Paper 414, 2000, for further discussions of China's LNG market.
9 IEA, *World Energy Outlook*, p. 161.
10 For an analysis of the global LNG market, see Energy Information Administration, *The Global Liquefied Natural Gas Market: Status and Outlook*, Washington, DC: Energy Information Administration, US Department of Energy, 2003.
11 J. Stern, "Specters and Pipe Dreams," *Foreign Policy* 48, 1982, pp. 21–36.
12 All projections are a form of educated guesswork, and at a given period of time different agencies and think tanks develop alternative scenarios and resultant projections. However, the situation in NE Asia seems relatively clear in the near term. For a thorough analysis of the energy situation in NE Asia, see I. Wybrew-Bond and J. Stern, *Natural Gas in Asia: The Challenges of Growth in China, India, Japan and Korea*, Oxford: Oxford University Press, 2002.
13 Energy Information Agency 2004 Country Analysis Brief China, www.eia.doe.gov/emeu/cabs/china.html (accessed 30 August 2004).
14 "ExxonMobil Announces Production Start-Up from Sakhalin-1 Project in Russia," www.sakhalin1.com/whatsnew/press/prs_10022005_production.asp/ (accessed 4 October 2005).
15 L. Dienes, "Observations on the Problematic Potential of Russian Oil and the Complexities of East Siberia," *Eurasian Geography and Economics* 45, 2004, pp. 319–345.
16 United Financial Group (UFG), *Distant Horizons: Russian Energy to North-East Asia*, Moscow: United Financial Group, 2004.
17 All figures from UFG, *Distant Horizons*, p. 9.
18 "BP Commits $650M to Siberian Field," *Moscow Times*, 5 March 2005.
19 S. McCormick, "East Siberia – Regional Resource Potential," in F. J. Dresen, ed., *Russia in Asia – Asia in Russia: Energy, Economics and Regional Relations*, Kennan Institute Occasional Papers 292, Washington, DC: Woodrow Wilson International Center for Scholars, 2005, pp. 23–26.
20 "$4 Billion Will Be Invested in the Development of the Verkhnechonsk Field and the 2005 Budget Will Grow to $98 million," www.tnk-bp.com/press/media/ 2005/9/1696/ (accessed 03 October 2005).
21 C. A. Kolhass, "Pipedreams: Khodorkovsky vs. Putin," *In the National Interest*, 19 November 2003, www.inthenationalinterest.com/Articles/Vol2Issue45KohlhassPFV.html (accessed 21 November 2003).
22 S. Blagov, "Russia Walks Thin Line between Japan and China," *Asia Times Online*, 2005, www.atimes.com/atimes/Central_Asia/GA05Ag01.htm (accessed 11 March 2005).
23 M. J. Bradshaw, "Sakhalin Oblast: Sectoral Globalization," in G. P. Herd and A. Aldis, eds., *Russian Regions and Regionalism: Strength through Weakness*, London: RoutledgeCurzon, 2003, pp. 141–163.
24 Andy Calitz, "Meeting Customer Energy Needs in ~~Six, Seven~~, Eight countries – Progress continued," a presentation to the Sakhalin Oil and Gas Conference, London, 16 November 2004.
25 M. Bradshaw, "The Changing 'Power Geometry' of the Sakhalin Projects," *Pacific Oil and Gas Report*, Summer 2005, pp. 3, 15, 17–22.
26 V. Korchagina, "Shtokhman Shortlist Down to 5 Bidders," *Moscow Times*, 1 September 2005.
27 Full details on the Phase 1 development can be found at www.sakhalin1.com.

28 "Gazprom Eyes a Share in Sakhalin Oil Field," Ocnus.Net, 14 June 2005, www.ocnus.net/artman/publish/printer_18620.shtml (accessed 27 June 2005).
29 A. Hurts, "Russia's Sakhalin-1 Starts Pumping Oil," *Washington Post*, 2 October 2005.
30 Valeria Korchagina, "'93 Tender Won by Exxon Annulled," *Moscow Times*, 20 January 2004.
31 Andrey Bagrov and Irina Rybalchanko, "Dig In: Russian Companies Alone Admitted to the Earth's Entrails," *Kommersant*, 11 February 2005.
32 "Rosneft–BP Joint Venture Makes Discovery in Its First Sakhalin Well," BP Press Release, 6 October 2004. http://www.bp.com/generalarticle.do?categoryID=120& contentID=7001438 (accessed 7 October 2004).
33 "BP to Spend $200 Million Drilling in Far East Russia Next Year," www. Bloomberg.com (accessed 29 September 2005).
34 S. R. Debeers, "Doomed to invest in Russian Oil," *The Moscow Times*, 10 March 2005.
35 "Report on the PSA-2000 International Conference in Yuzhno-Sakhalinsk," BISNIS, US Department of Commerce, 3 September 2000, www.bisnis.doc.gov/bisnis/country/001219rspsa.htm (accessed 8 April 2004).

# Part III

# Beyond energy

Emerging business networks and
human security

# 8  Russian business, the arms trade, and regional security

*Robert W. Orttung and Boris Demidov*

The Russian arms trade provides a useful case study of the intersection between business interests, state interests, Russian foreign relations, and the level of conflict and cooperation along Russia's borders and elsewhere in the world. This chapter lays out the overall situation in the Russian arms industry since the collapse of the Soviet Union, including the ownership structure of the major arms producers. It then examines state and business interests, highlighting where these intersect or come into conflict. Finally, it examines the potential for conflict and cooperation by investigating whether Russian arms dealers take into account who their customers are and how they might use the weapons they buy.

While state institutions formally dominate the entire process of weapons production and sales, corruption is rampant, casting considerable doubt on who actually receives the profits made from arms sales abroad and therefore who is benefiting from them. Private (nonstate) Russian business is notable mainly by its absence. Ironically, private business could probably manage this sector better than the state currently does, boosting the returns to both state and business.

## Overview of the situation

Weapons production is one of the few areas where Russia manufactures a product that is in demand abroad. Russia was the largest exporter of major conventional weapons in the period 2000–2004, accounting for 32 percent of transfers, up from second place in 1999–2003, according to the Stockholm International Peace Research Institute (SIPRI).[1] Unfortunately, Russia does not publish comprehensive data on its arms sales.

Despite its resurrection 15 years after the Soviet collapse, the size of the Russian arms industry has shrunk considerably since 1991. During the Soviet era, the government bought the majority of domestically produced arms, but once the Soviet Union ceased to exist, the Russian state no longer had the resources to keep up domestic purchases at the previous levels. The Soviet government in the late 1980s employed between seven million and 11 million workers in the defense sector of a total workforce of 100 million, with defense expenditures amounting to between 35 percent and 50 percent of gross domestic product.[2] Additionally, during the 1980s the Soviet Union exported $31 billion worth of weapons annually, but the country was not always paid for the weapons it shipped, and sometimes when payment was received, it was not in cash. In 1990, for example, arms transfers from the Soviet Union totaled more than $16 billion, while payments in cash came to only $900 million.[3]

The Russian arms industry collapsed because the post-Soviet Russian government could no longer purchase weapons for domestic security forces, nor could it afford to subsidize sales to foreign countries.[4] Starting from the early 1990s, Russian arms producers exported weapons to foreign customers who could pay for them in hard currency (or, in some cases, through barter), while the Russian military was forced to use equipment on hand that was often worn out and obsolete. The Russian air force, for example, has not bought new aircraft for more than ten years.[5] Some estimates say as much as 80 percent of Russian military equipment is past the date when it was expected to be replaced.[6] As a result, during the 1990s, exports provided the main source of income for many weapons producers, and their main customers became foreign buyers rather than the Russian government. Exports therefore came to determine what kinds of weapons Russian enterprises produced.

This state of affairs ostensibly changed after President Putin came to power and increased military purchases. During Putin's first term, state military orders increased four times over, reaching 187 billion rubles (more than $6.5 billion) in the 2005 budget.[7] In 2004, state defense orders exceeded revenue derived from exports, as Russian state purchases increased while exports began to plateau. However, as discussed below, there is extensive corruption in the state procurement process, and money allocated for weapons purchases often does not actually make it to the weapons producers.

Thus, the increased defense spending under Putin has not led to substantial changes in the defense sector.[8] Many of the workers are aging and not trained in the most recent technologies. Much of the equipment in arms factories is out of date and needs to be replaced. Often the government does not pay for the weapons that it has ordered.

As a result, foreign purchases have continued to determine the output of defense producers. Ironically, though, there is evidence that foreign payments for Russian weapons do not actually reach the actual producers. Rather, as discussed below, they disappear along a complex network of middlemen standing between the producer and ultimate purchaser.

During the five years from 2000 to 2004, Russian arms exports increased, with arms sales of $5.78 billion in 2004, the highest level of sales since the collapse of the Soviet Union.[9] In 2004, the types of weapons sold were typical of previous years. Aircraft, particularly Su-30s, represented more than 60 percent of the exports.[10] Table 8.1 lists the key Russian weapons producers, their ownership structure, their main products and customers, and their 2004 income.

At the end of 2004, China and India were the main consumers of Russian arms, purchasing 49 percent and 34 percent, respectively, of exports through the near-total monopolist arms export agency Rosoboroneksport. Most analysts anticipate that these numbers represented a high-water mark, as Russia will

*Table 8.1* Earnings of top Russian weapons producers, 2004

| Company | Ownership structure | Main products/ customers | Military product revenue |
|---|---|---|---|
| Sukhoi Aviation Holding Co. | State-owned | Su-30 fighters to China | $1.469 billion |
| Irkut | 50.53% management; 13.23% Sukhoi; institutional; private investors, 29.83%; workers 6.41% | Su-30 fighters to India | $625 million |
| Aerospace Equipment | 51% Russian federal government; 49% United Aviation Equipment Builders Consortium | Avionics equipment | $444 million |
| MiG | State-owned | MiG fighters to Yemen, several African countries | $403 million |
| Admiralteiskiye Verfi | State-owned | Submarine to China | $354 million |
| Ufa MPO | 25% Republic of Bashkortostan; Ufa Machine Building Factory, 10.25%; GTD Analitik, 5.85%; Depository-Clearing Company, 34.67%; United Finances, 12.33% | Aircraft engines | $346 million |
| Salyut | State-owned | Aircraft engines | $311 million |
| Baltiiskii zavod | 88.2% Mezhprombank (Sergei Pugachev) | Ship to India | $303 million |
| Tactical Rocket Arms | State-owned | Rocket systems | $217 million |
| Uralvagonzavod | State-owned | Tanks to India | $150 million |

Sources: Center for the Analysis of Strategies and Technologies as cited by Lyuba Pronina, "Aviation Tops '04 Arms Revenues," *Moscow Times*, 9 June 2005; and Aleksei Nikol'skii, "VPK na golodnom paike," *Vedomosti*, 9 June 2005. Ownership structure: www.sukhoi.org/company/structure/, (accessed 21 June 2005); http://www.irkut.com/ru/for_investors/structure/, (accessed 21 June 2005); www.migavia.ru/corporation/?tid=1, (accessed 21 June 2005); www.salut.ru/, (accessed 22 August 2005); www.uvz.ru/rus/index_1024.htm, (accessed 22 August 2005); www.stockmap.spb.ru/company.thtml?b=12&num=9337&p=0, (accessed 22 August 2005); Ufa MPO Quarterly Report, second quarter, 2005, www.umpo.ru/ezhekvartaln.php, (accessed 22 August 2005); www.panorama.ru/info/sprav161.html, (accessed 22 August 2005); Konstantin Lantratov, Aleksandra Gritskova, and Ivan Makarov, "Vladyka morei," *Kommersant*, 13 August 2005; Aleksandra Gritskova and Konstantin Lantratov, "Gendirektor Baltiiskogo zavoda ushel ot gosudarstva," *Kommersant*, 19 August 2005.

likely have great difficulty holding on to its current customers, particularly China and India, and expanding into new markets, thanks to the intense competition on the international market.[11]

Chinese purchases have driven the expansion of Russian arms exports. The Chinese tend to buy outdated equipment that is well tested and reliable. Chinese and Arab contracts are extremely lucrative for Russian suppliers because they can sell off-the-shelf equipment. On the other hand, the Chinese purchases do not stimulate Russian companies to improve their standards to make themselves more competitive internationally. In the future, China is likely to have more options since the European Union is discussing the possibility of lifting sanctions on arms purchases imposed after the 1989 Tiananmen massacre. However, China's belligerent moves toward Taiwan are slowing Western efforts to expand trade.[12] As discussed below, Russia may also reconsider its sales to China, fearing that China is becoming too powerful as a potential adversary on its southern border.

Indians purchase more technologically advanced equipment from Russia than China does, though naturally of lesser reliability.[13] India has also been willing to partner with Russia on some projects to develop new weapons. Indian contracts tend to yield low profits and high risk for Russian manufacturers. This situation forces Russian companies to amalgamate and seek other contracts to mitigate the risk.[14] Indian requirements for compatibility with Western and Israeli parts are forcing more innovation and creating healthy precedents for companies such as Irkut and NPOmash to be more globalized. Nevertheless, even with this pressure, Russia simply cannot compete in areas like advanced electronics. Russian companies will need to work hard to hold on to their Indian market share. In particular, Israel is aggressively seeking customers in India, which wants to diversify its sources of weapons.[15]

The combined Southeast Asian countries of Malaysia, Indonesia, and Vietnam represent an increasingly important third customer for Russia. In 2003, these countries concluded contracts for more than $1.5 billion for delivery in 2005–2007.[16] Unfortunately for Russia, though, these countries are not likely to become long-term customers and they have a tendency to pay through barter, offering things like palm oil and chicken meat, rather than cash.[17]

## Evolution of the arms sector

The state plays the main role in the defense sector, not private interests, according to the government "Program for Restructuring and Developing the Defense Industry from 2002 to 2006" adopted at the end of 2001 under the guidance of Deputy Prime Minister Ilya Klebanov. Although Klebanov lost most of his influence in 2003, the focus on the state remained a priority.

The Russian state formally exerts extensive control over the weapons industry. It determines the allocation of state orders, picking which weapons systems will be funded and which enterprises will produce them. This control also extends to exports, since 94 percent of arms exports go through the Rosoboroneksport state agency set up to handle arms sales abroad.[18]

### Rosoboroneksport

Rosoboroneksport was created on 4 November 2000 by the merger of Promeksport and Rosvooruzhenie, agencies that similarly controlled arms exports during the Yeltsin era. Rosoboroneksport has enormous power. With the exception of six enterprises that have the rights to export arms themselves, Rosoboroneksport has the exclusive right to sell Russian arms abroad.[19] Rosoboroneksport determines what equipment to recommend to a particular customer and what factory will produce it.[20] Additionally, Rosoboroneksport can control all aspects of the arms trade, including setting up transportation companies, insurance companies, banks, and industrial facilities. As a result, this agency's influence reaches throughout the entire Russian arms industry. This is the context in which all aspects of the Russian arms trade, including the extensive corruption, must be analyzed.[21]

Rosoboroneksport works under the aegis of the defense ministry.[22] The idea of the 2000 reorganization was that the export revenues earned from Russian arms should be plowed back into meeting the equipment needs of the Russian military. In particular, Rosoboroneksport would channel revenues to the enterprises considered most important in meeting Russia's defense strategy. This idea apparently was never implemented since Russian arms exports do little to support Russian military reform.

On 1 December 2000, Putin created the Committee for Military and Technical Cooperation with Foreign Countries (CMTC), also under the defense ministry. The CMTC is the federal agency responsible for regulating and monitoring defense exports. On 18 November 2003, Putin placed Rosoboroneksport under the CMTC, which in 2004 was reorganized into the Federal Military and Technical Cooperation Service, and remained subordinate to the defense ministry. The reorganization temporarily ended the plans of Rosoboroneksport managers, announced in March 2003, to turn their agency into a 100 percent state-owned corporation.[23] The managers suggested transferring 25 percent plus one share of the main defense companies to Rosoboroneksport. Clearly, such a move would have given Rosoboroneksport much greater control over the defense industry and much greater access to revenue flows.

Sergei Chemezov, appointed the manager of Rosoboroneksport in 2004, has sought to revive these plans and in late 2004 again proposed turning the agency into a corporation, which in turn would manage the state-owned stakes in Russia's key arms producers which have the right to independently export arms.[24] Rosoboroneksport would also have the right to sit on the boards of these companies. In this way, Rosoborneksport would have an absolute monopoly on the export of weapons from Russia.[25] Chemezov claims that such a monopoly would help the companies, because Rosoboroneksport has 43 offices in foreign countries and could manage sales operations there. Mikhail Dmitriev, the head of the Federal Military and Technical Cooperation Service, opposed these plans, preferring to keep the current arrangement and demonstrating that different actors within the Russian state are pursuing their own particular interests rather than those of a larger concern. The current owners of the companies also do not welcome Rosoboroneksport's advances.

### Establishing integrated holding companies

The Russian state is also seeking greater control over domestic arms manufacturers by combining many of them into large, vertically integrated holding companies. During the 1990s, there were 1,600 defense contractors.[26] On 7 July 2001, the government approved a plan to set up 74 state-controlled companies in the defense sector by 2006. In 2002, the number of companies was reduced to 42. In 2003, however, Deputy Prime Minister Boris Aleshin, Klebanov's replacement, declared that there should be no set number of companies and that they should be created as needed.[27] In 2003, officials announced that Russia would create an integrated shipbuilding company and an integrated aircraft construction corporation. Putin signed a decree ordering the creation of the aircraft firm on 22 February 2005.

Russian officials hope that putting Russia's design bureaus and production plants into giant conglomerates should help them compete on the world market and overcome the Soviet legacy in which the weapons designers were separate from the factories where their weapons were made. Additionally, the Kremlin sought to use this mechanism to eliminate unsuccessful companies. Thus, for example, the Kremlin could concentrate foreign orders in firms that make goods for the domestic market. Additionally, the state wants Russian companies to pay a larger share of research and development costs.

The main companies were formed during Putin's first term: MiG in 2000 and by 2003, Sukhoi, Irkut, Tactical Rocket Arms, Aerospace Equipment, and the united Baltic shipyards company. The state directly only played a leading role in the consolidation of Sukhoi. In the other cases, it was the heads of the enterprises, their owners, or outside players, such as Rosoboneksport, which acted through the company Oboronprom.[28]

Critics have pointed out numerous drawbacks to creating such large holding companies. Managers at the factories and design bureaus felt that the giant new companies represented sinecures for the personal benefit of high-level bureaucrats.[29] Others suggested that the creation of the holding companies, combined with the overall lack of reform and the shortage of funds for the defense sector, keeps Russian companies from innovating, condemning Russian firms to falling further behind aggressive Western companies.[30] Now, for example, there is a huge new market for pilotless aircraft, but Russia's drones are simply modified versions of planes that the Soviet Union produced in the late 1970s and early 1980s, lacking the high-tech features of their Western counterparts.[31]

The difficulty of implementing plans to create a unified aircraft company by the end of 2006 pointed up many of the problems with integrated holdings.[32] The state seeks to combine the private Irkut aircraft manufacturer and the state-owned Sukhoi, MiG, Il'yushin, and Tupolev into one giant company in which it would have a 60–70 percent share. State bureaucrats argued that the Russian state's ownership of property rights for the military aircraft designs gave it the right to push private companies into the holding company, arguing that state property rights for the aircraft trumped company owner rights. Nevertheless, regardless of the state's claims, in creating the integrated company the state is violating the property rights of the current owners of the aircraft production companies.[33] The deal is even more complicated because the European Aeronautic Defence and Space Company (EADS) in August 2005 committed to buying 10 percent of Irkut for a reported price of $55 million.[34] One major stumbling block is placing a value on the private holdings that will be included in the new company. Creating a monopoly in the field could increase costs and reduce the quality of the output. Additionally, as noted above, the lack of competition could slow the process of innovation in the company. Moreover, at least one observer sees the attempts to create a unified airplane construction company as simply an effort by bureaucrats like Federal Industry Agency head Boris Aleshin to gain control of the money in the business, despite the fact that such bureaucrats lack any sense of how to lead an effective company in market conditions.[35]

## State interests

The Russian state's interest in arms industry exports is to earn as much money as possible without upsetting the international balance of forces, especially with respect to China.[36] To the extent that export operations keep alive the Russian armaments industry, Russia benefits from them by supporting domestic weapons production with foreign countries' money. However, in some cases the goals of promoting Russian security and selling weapons abroad may come into conflict. Selling weapons to China, located on Russia's poorly protected southern border, may pose such an issue.[37] So far, Russia has resolved this conundrum by mainly selling China outdated equipment.

Russia also benefits from arms exports by the opportunities it gains to expand its influence around the globe. By grabbing international market share, Russia is able to challenge the United States in places like China, India, the Middle East, and Africa. With arms sales to Syria, Russia is able to reconnect with some of its key Soviet-era allies. By deciding which arms are made and sold, the Russian government influences the security situation in various regional hot spots. Theoretically, state control means that the state can work to minimize the possibility of unauthorized arms sales, prevent the spread of sensitive technology, and observe nonproliferation agreements to which it is a party.

In the domestic context, the Russian state benefits from arms sales by generating income that does not fill the coffers of oligarchs. Since the oligarchs have mostly been pushed out of the defense sector, in contrast to oil or metals, Kremlin leaders do not have to worry that weapons sales are funding a potential opposition. Moreover, extensive state control makes it possible to reduce tax evasion.

However, the state does not always gain the benefits that it should in the arms sector because of the extensive corruption throughout the Russian economy. The same types of corruption that exist in the regular economy are widespread in the arms sector, according to researchers at the Nizhni Novgorod think tank Rus-Ekspert-Transit. These practices include abuses in the choice of which company will gain weapons contracts, manipulations in the price of the output, vague contract terms, using funds for purposes other than those intended, and a host of other transgressions.[38]

The state sees very little of the money that comes in from the arms trade through Rosoboroneksport, according to Pavel Felgenhauer, because the agency pays very little to the state in terms of dividends. Felgenhauer also claims that the arms producers calculate their costs so that they do not make any profits. Therefore, the state cannot tax them, and the real profits are siphoned off into a corrupt system.[39] In making these assertions, Felgenhauer cites an Accounting Chamber report that came out at the end of 2001, which claimed that of the $3.7 billion Russia earned in arms exports during 2000, only $7,000 went into state coffers. A subsequent Accounting Chamber report was likewise critical, charging that in 2001 Rosborneksport transferred to the government only 4 percent of its profits: 50 million rubles instead of the 1.248 billion it owed.[40] Aleksandr Denisov, deputy chief of the Russian Government Committee on Arms Trade with Foreign Countries, told Felgenhauer that federal and regional budgets received as much as $70 million in 2000 from the arms trade, more than the Accounting Chamber estimated, but still only a tiny fraction of the actual arms sales.

The situation did not seem to change much in the first five years of the new decade. At his 9 February 2005 press conference, Rosoboroneksport head Sergei Chemezov said that the company paid $75 million in taxes in 2004 on sales of over $5 billion.[41] In 2003, Chemezov said that his firm made $210 million in commissions. Of this money, it paid $80 million in taxes and transferred $90 million to the state budget. He claimed that Rosoboroneksport's predecessor, Rosvooruzhenie, paid only taxes.[42]

The case of sales to China shows how the money disappears. To cover at least part of its purchases, China provides goods to Russia rather than paying in cash. These goods are not transferred to Russia, but sold in a third country. As a result, 50 percent of the value of the contract falls into the hands of intermediaries.[43] In other cases, Russian weapons are bought in local currency, creating additional opportunities for embezzlement and diversion of funds. Another problem is that Rosoboroneksport may have to pay intermediaries to set up deals with foreign governments.[44]

Additionally, there is extensive corruption in the state purchase of weapons. Neither the Russian parliament nor society provides any coherent oversight.[45] The numerous monitoring agencies are largely ineffective. The state order is determined at a closed meeting of the government after the parliament has already approved the budget.

The money seems to disappear without a trace. Center for the Analysis of Strategies and Technologies (CAST) deputy director Konstantin Makiyenko, an independent Russian defense analyst, said,

> The allocations for state arms procurement have been growing and this year [2004] exceeded the revenues we get from arms exports. But we don't see

any purchases for the domestic armed forces. I would like to ask the Defense Ministry where the money goes.[46]

In a similar vein, "the state defense order increased from 137 billion rubles to 180 billion rubles [approximately $6 billion], but industry does not see it," an employee of the Ministry of Industry and Energy told the newspaper *Vedomosti*.[47] Makiyenko estimates that of the approximately $6 billion state order, half goes to nuclear forces and half goes to research, most of which never produces concrete results.[48] In fact, during 2004, Russian arms production actually dropped, with part of the problem being the much higher prices for energy, according to a report by the Ministry for Economic Development and Trade.[49]

## Business interests

The Russian state is working hard to remove private business from the arms trade sector. Under these conditions, there is little room for independent private business activity.

Nevertheless, despite the dominant role of the state in the arms trade, some of the largest and most successful defense enterprises are in private hands, including Baltic Shipyards and Irkut, the aircraft manufacturer. However, these private firms are the exception rather than the rule and one of Russia's biggest players has recently left the defense sector. On 13 August 2003, Vladimir Potanin's Interros group sold its last defense asset, a 50 percent stake in the Defense-Systems Invest holding, which produced air defense equipment.[50] This company was set up in the mid-1990s and used the support of high-ranking military officers and Potanin to win rights from Rosvooruzhenie for export contracts worth $900 million.[51] Additionally, the owners of the Baltic Shipyards made clear that they planned to minimize their military production in order to focus on civilian projects.[52] In August, the IST group, which had owned the firm for much of the time since its privatization in 1992, sold it to Mezhprombank, whose leader, Sergei Pugachev, is reported to have very close ties to the Kremlin.[53]

The increasing role of the state has done little to improve the effectiveness of the defense sector. The state program for the weapons industry for the period 2002–2006 was a failure, according to an audit conducted by the Military-Industrial Complex Department of the Ministry of Industry and Energy.[54]

Moreover, increasing state control over the sector has had a negative effect on private business. In mid-February 2001, Klebanov signed an order transferring all of Rosoboroneksport's accounts to state banks. Before this transition, more than ten banks had serviced these accounts, including Alfa, Bank of Moscow, Nomos, MDM, Mosnarbank, Rosbank, and SVA Bank.[55]

Unfortunately, there are few limits on what predatory officials can do to crush private business interests in this sector. In the field of helicopter development and production, the main player is Rosoboroneksport head Chemezov, who is using the company he controls (Oboronprom) to unite all the helicopter design bureaus and production facilities.[56] At the beginning of 2004, the state made clear that it would only purchase helicopters from, and allow exports by, companies in which it has a controlling ownership stake. Thus, the Ulan Ude helicopter factory, where the state has a large stake (49 percent),[57] received orders, while the Kazan factory, where the federal government did not have a large stake, did not get orders.[58] Chemezov claims that everyone will be better off if the two plants pool their resources in one holding under his management.[59] His critics argue that such bureaucrats often do not have the ability, or even the desire, to pick successful new projects to improve the company's performance in the future.[60]

Ironically, private companies could help the state solve some of the largest problems it has with extensive corruption in the industry. Weapons production companies with private owners are more open than the state-controlled companies, according to CAST director Ruslan Pukhov.[61] A well-regulated private arms sector could ultimately provide more income for the state than the current state-regulated sector.

Assuming that the state could collect taxes on the companies' profits, the state would naturally share a mutual interest with the firms in expanding exports. However, the situation is not so straightforward, because it is not clear that the current export structure serves Russia's larger interests. Russia has not set up modern production lines to mass produce contemporary equipment, which is necessary to be profitable by cutting the per unit cost of the weapons it manufactures.[62] To set up such production lines would require a dramatic reform of the Russian defense industry.

Another major problem is that the Russian state has not been ordering large numbers of weapons, which would be necessary to support such high levels of output. According to military analyst Aleksandr Golts, "one-time export orders may be profitable for individual enterprises, but they are losing money for the national economy as a whole."[63] In this sense, assembling a few planes for China means that Russia must keep huge production capacities going in order to support a relatively small amount of output. Since the Kremlin wants Russia to be able to produce the entire range of weapons, it spreads its resources very thinly to support a wide range of producers, but only at a minimal level.

Since there is only a very limited scope for private business in the Russian arms export sector, the owners of the private firms naturally seek to protect their property rights from the state. However, there is little opportunity for the weapons producers to be independent of the state. They must rely on the Russian state to purchase weapons and gain permission to export. Although the managers control their firms, they do not have enough capital for investment. Both private and state-owned firms seek to gain as much support as possible from the state budget.

In recent years, the state has sought to solve its problems in the military production sector by bringing some businesses into the process, according to an analysis published in *Voenno-promyshlennyi kur'er*. But, again, there are limits on what the business sector can do. Unfortunately, the Russian banking sector and the poorly developed stock market lack the financial resources to develop the military production sector.[64] Moreover, an analysis of shareholders in 231 companies shows that their shares were purchased by 510 legal entities for the purpose of making a quick profit rather than investing in improving production.[65] Even if they had more resources, most businesspeople would not want to invest in defense companies, because they are characterized by unstable property rights, and could easily be nationalized. Since the Federal Agency for Industry determines who gets state orders, all of the weapons producers are at its mercy.

## Potential for conflict and cooperation

As the previous section shows, the state decides what weapons Russia sells and to whom. Private business has very few opportunities to get around the state monopoly to sell weapons independently on the foreign market. Moreover, the Russian state is pushing to eliminate what few opportunities there are for private companies to work independently in the arms export sector.

While formally the state has extensive control over arms exports, in practice its influence is limited because of the extensive corruption in the process. Russia sells weapons to foreign countries but neither the state nor the weapons producers seem to benefit from the sales. Rather, many of the profits are swallowed by middlemen or lost through various manipulations.

In practice, Russia sells whatever weapons it can, within some limits, without putting into place a long-term strategy to maintain current market share. Most of Russia's weapons sales are *ad hoc* and driven by a desire to take advantage of opportunities as they appear.

Reviewing Russian sales on a country-by-country basis suggests that many sales have the potential to increase conflict. At the same time, opportunities from sales or projects that promote greater cooperation are not fully utilized, as is the case with sales to India.

### China

Russian arms sales to China are considered high risk because China could eventually pose a threat to Russia's security. In the early 1990s, Russia tried to prevent China from acquiring its high-tech weapons. But just ten years later, Russia was selling China weapons that it had earlier been reluctant to discuss.[66] In the case of the Su-30MMK2 and Su-30MKK3, Russia has sold China planes that are more advanced than those used by the Russian military. Moreover, China is using Russian technology to develop its own capacities for weapons production much more quickly than had been expected. Perhaps Russia could sell China more high-tech weapons. But the growing gap between Russian and Chinese financial power may force Russia to limit the scale and quality of such sales.[67]

Despite the dire warnings of some Russian nationalists, China is extremely unlikely to present a military threat to Russia. In fact, Chinese purchases of planes made in the Far Eastern city of Amur help boost the economy of the Far East, one of the most economically depressed regions in Russia.[68] Russia's military-industrial complex survives mainly because of Chinese purchases. Thus, blocking sales would be more painful to Russia than to China.

Russian sales to China could do more to upset the balance between US and Chinese forces than between Russian and Chinese forces. In the future, China could use weapons it buys from Russia as a way of pressuring Taiwan to return to China. In particular, China might use Russian strategic bombers to neutralize the US Seventh Fleet, which currently enjoys military superiority in the region.[69]

In sum, Russian arms sales to China seem to be promoting mutual cooperation between the two countries, as witnessed by the joint military exercises the two countries held in August 2005. However, these relations could go sour if China decides to seek other sources of weapons besides Russia. Russia's off-the-shelf sales of obsolete weapons to China provide temporary support for Russian manufacturers, but they do not provide long-term development for the Russian industry, meaning that the current relationship cannot last long. Another source of tension could arise if China uses the weapons it buys from Russia to threaten US efforts to protect Taiwan's independence.

## India

In contrast to China, India is more interested in joint development projects with Russia. One example is the Brahmos antiship missile, a project that forces Russia to invest in its capacity to produce more modern weapons that have a better chance of competing on the world market.[70]

While these deals seem to have the potential to help Russia develop its economy and cooperative relations with India, Russia's current policy prevents it from fully exploiting these opportunities. The Russian navy by law cannot deploy the Brahmos missiles manufactured by the joint venture because it is required to purchase the less advanced Yakhont domestic equivalent.[71] Because of such shortsighted policies, Russia is missing out on the full potential of its relationship with India.

## Venezuela

On 18 May 2005, Venezuela formalized a deal to buy 100,000 Kalashnikov assault rifles worth $54 million from Russia. The US government objected to this deal because it sees Venezuelan president Hugo Chávez as destabilizing the situation in South America. Since coming to power in 1998, Chávez has built strong ties to Cuban leader Fidel Castro and has supported Marxist guerrillas in neighboring Colombia.[72] The American authorities fear that the Russian weapons could ultimately fall into the hands of the rebels in Colombia, a view supported by Colombian president Álvaro Uribe. Venezuela's Chávez has claimed that the weapons are supposed to improve border security and would not end up in the hands of Colombian rebels. However, US ambassador to Venezuela William Brownfield expressed concerns that the purchase of the new weapons would allow Chavez to transfer the old weapons they replaced to Colombia.

Overall, Russia annually sells about $300 million worth of arms to Latin American countries.[73] Its customers include Argentina, Brazil, Colombia, Ecuador, Mexico, Nicaragua, Peru, and Venezuela. Among its projects, Russia is cooperating with Brazil in the manufacture of small arms. Russian exporters see the Latin American market as a lucrative place to expand that does not entail the political risks of working in the Middle East.[74] The Russian foreign ministry pointed out that it has the right to sell weapons to any country that is not under international sanctions.[75] A 2003 study of Russian small arms exports found that there were no large-scale violations of international arms embargoes in recent years.[76]

### Syria

In spring 2005, Russia announced that it would sell an Igla (SA-18) antiaircraft missile system to Syria, despite objections from both the United States and Israel. Israel warned that Hezbollah could use the system against the Jewish state, and the United States feared that the weapons would wind up in Iraq, where they could be used against American forces. Putin agreed with Israel that Syria will not get shoulder-launched weapons, but stressed that the Igla sale to Syria would go ahead.

Syria has been on the US State Department's list of state sponsors of terrorism since the list was created in 1979.[77] Because Syria supports terrorism, US legislation forbids the country from purchasing US weapons. The United States has imposed sanctions on the state-owned KBP Tula enterprise for selling weapons to Syria and Iraq.[78]

### Sudan

The state-owned MiG jet producer delivered 12 MiG-29 planes to Sudan in July 2004. Critics like Amnesty International fear that the planes could be used by the Sudanese government, which backed militias that have attacked indigenous tribes in the Darfur region, leaving thousands dead and forcing millions to flee.[79] As in the case with Syria, the US has classified Sudan as a state sponsor of terrorism.[80]

Overall, the sales to China are the most important since they are the largest income generators for Russia and could have the largest impact on its security. Indian sales are also important, but more because of the missed opportunities they represent. The other sales are worrying, but ultimately not likely to have a major impact.

## Conclusion

The Russian state plays the main role in the arms export sector since it owns most of the arms producers and has a near-monopoly on export sales. Where private firms do exist, such as the case of Irkut, the state is working to bring them under greater, though still vaguely defined, state control as part of a large holding company. The state's expansion at the expense of private owners is already causing conflict within Russia as property owners seek to protect their rights. Such state expansion is unlikely to improve the sector's performance, because it will block private interests from becoming involved in this sector of the economy.

The extensive state control means that there is massive corruption in the arms export sector. Although the state decides which weapons to export to which customers, neither the state nor the producers receive the benefits of such exports, since middlemen are usurping potential profits. Money is siphoned off in payments to arrange the foreign deals, currency exchange schemes, and barter arrangements. In particular, the state has not met its goal of using profits from the arms export sector to fund other aspects of military reform. Five years after Putin's rise to power, military reform has made little progress. Unhappiness over the failure of Russia to do a better job with exports is only one of a much broader set of problems with the military.

Greater use of private companies would provide more transparent operations and likely reduce the level of corruption in the arms export sector, but the Russian state has decided to crush, rather than encourage, private-sector participation in weapons production.

The current success of the Russian arms industry could be short-lived because Russia has probably saturated the international markets that are available to it. Unfortunately, Russia does not have a mechanism to develop new weapons that would be competitive with those of Western suppliers. Beyond combining many of the existing companies into large holdings, the state has not articulated a way for Russian companies to innovate new technologies. Likewise, the state has not given much autonomy to market forces so that private firms could innovate on their own.

The main danger in Russian weapon sales abroad ironically is to Russia itself since it is arming China, a potential rival on its southern border. At the moment, though, the chance of conflict between the two countries is remote, since they have just successfully demarcated their mutual border, removing one of the most important causes of friction. However, if Russia does not develop higher-quality weapons, it will lose China as one of its main customers, particularly as Europeans seek to return to this market.

Russia has recently supplied weapons to such hot spots as Syria, Venezuela, and Sudan, provoking the ire of the United States in particular. However, such sales are unlikely to change the balance of power in these areas.

Russia has failed to take advantage of the opportunities that its relationship with India provides, choosing not to deploy the missile it is producing in conjunction with Indian partners. As the Indian experience shows, Russia could gain considerably more benefits from its existing relationship than it is currently receiving.

An arms industry that suffers from widespread corruption and a failure to innovate, existing largely beyond state control and doing little to speed up the country's painstakingly slow military reform, limits the Russian state's capacity to address the security risks on its borders. While ostensibly expanding the role of the state in the arms sector, Russia seems to be getting little in return. The weakness of state capacity in this area, combined with Russia's inability to deal with its drug problem or successfully manage the conflict on its southern border, as discussed elsewhere in this volume, means that Russia will have little ability to face the challenges of the coming years.

## Notes

1 Siemon T. Wezeman and Mark Bromley, "International Arms Transfers," in *SIPRI Yearbook 2005: Armaments, Disarmament and International Security*, yearbook2005.sipri.org/ch10/.
2 John Berryman, "Russia and the Illicit Arms Trade," *Crime, Law and Social Change* 33, no. 1–2, 2000, p. 85.
3 Berryman, "Russia and the Illicit Arms Trade," p. 94.
4 Pavel Fegenhauer, "Arms Exports and the Russian Military," *Perspective* 12, no. 4, March–April 2002, www.bu.edu/iscip/vol12/felgenhauer2.html.
5 "Putin khochet znat', kak tratiatsia den'gi, vydelyaemye na vooruzhenie," *Vedomosti*, 21 September 2004. In September 2004, air force general Yury Morozov, in charge of the weapons administration, was fired for financial abuses uncovered by the military procurator and his inability to explain the lack of progress in buying and modernizing aircraft equipment.
6 Tekhnokompleks president Givi Dzhandzhgav, "Ustarelo 80% oborudovaniya rossiiskoi oboronki," Interfaks, 26 September 2002.
7 Viktor Myasnikov, "Oboronnye raskhody rastut, a postavki vooruzhennii probuksovyvayut," *Nezavisimoe voennoe obozrenie*, 26 August 2005; Konstantin Lantratov, "Military-Industrial Complex 2000–2004," *Kommersant Vlast*, 24 May 2004. In English, see kommersant.com/tree.asp?rubric=3&node=36&doc_id=476700.
8 Myasnikov, "Oboronnye raskhody rastut, a postavki vooruzhennii probuksovyvayut."
9 Konstantin Makienko, "Financial Results of Russian Arms Trade with Foreign States in 2004," Moscow Defense Brief 1, 2005, http://mdb.cast.ru/mdb/1–2005/at/ financial_results/.
10 Lyuba Pronina, "Aviation Tops '04 Arms Revenues," *Moscow Times*, 9 June 2005. This trend changed in 2005 as shipbuilders were likely to outperform the aircraft manufacturers in terms of foreign sales, according to CAST analysis. But aviation will likely again dominate in 2006.
11 Aleksei Nikol'skii, "BPK teryaet klientov," *Vedomosti*, 16 June 2005.
12 "EU May Delay China Arms Move," BBC News, 22 March 2005, news.bbc.co.uk/2/hi/asia-pacific/4371361.stm.
13 Konstantin Makiyenko, "The Russian–Chinese Arms Trade: An Attempt at Qualitative Analysis," Russian Defense Brief 2, 2004, mdb.cast.ru/mdb/2–2004/ at/rcat/.
14 Konstantin Makienko, "Russian-Indian MTC: An Attempt at a Qualitative Analysis," Moscow Defense Brief 1, 2004, http://mdb.cast.ru/mdb/1–2004/at/rima/.
15 Makienko, "The Russian–Chinese Arms Trade."
16 Dmitry Vasiliev, "Russian Arms Trade with Southeast Asia and the Republic of Korea," Russian Defense Brief 1, 2005, mdb.cast.ru/mdb/1–2005/at/ russian_arms.
17 "Thailand Offers Chickens for Russian Arms," *The Russia Journal*, 1 September 2004, www.russiajournal.com/news/cnews-article.shtml?nd=45266.
18 Lantratov, "Military-Industrial Complex 2000–2004."

19 The exceptions are MiG Russian Aircraft Corporation, Sukhoi Aviation Holding Company, Tula-based Instrument-Making Design Bureau (KBP), Kolomna-based Machinery Design Bureau (KBM), Salyut Moscow Machine-Building Production Enterprise, and Machine Building Scientific Production Association. Aleksandr Golts, "Russia's Arms Exports: Hitting the Ceiling?" *Moscow News* no. 7, 2005, 18 February 2005, english.mn.ru/english/issue.php?2005-7-20.

20 Il'ya Bulavinov, "Military-Industrial Complex 1991–2000," *Kommersant Vlast*, 4 December 2001. In English see kommersant.com/tree.asp?rubric=3&node=36& doc_id=300257.

21 Ian Anthony, "Corruption in Russia's Arms Export Trade," in Transparency International (UK), *Report on the Conference Corruption in the Official Arms Trade*, Cambridge, UK, 5–7 April 2001, 29, www.transparency.org/integrity_pact/dnld/report_coat.uk-swe.pdf.

22 Anthony, "Corruption," p. 37.

23 Lantratov, "Military-Industrial Complex 2000–2004."

24 Konstantin Lantratov and Ivan Safronov, "President RF oznakomilsia s planami torgovli oruzhiem," *Kommersant*, 18 September 2004 and "'Otryzhka perestrechnogo khozrascheta' ('Rosoboroneksport' meniaet formu sobstvennosti')," *Gazeta*, 20 September 2004.

25 "Sergei Chemezov: Gosposrednik v eksporte oruzhiya dolzhen byt' odin," *Izvestiia*, 19 July 2004.

26 Bulavinov, "Military-Industrial Complex 1991–2000."

27 Lantratov, "Military-Industrial Complex 2000–2004."

28 Ruslan Pukhov, "Vyzhivaet sil'neishii," *Russkii fokus*, 28 June 2004, www.cast.ru/publications/?id=68.

29 Lev Makarevich, "Padenie oboronki," *Ekonomicheskaia gazeta*, 16 August 2005.

30 Dzhandzhgav, "Ustarelo 80% oborudovaniya rossiiskoi oboronki."

31 Nikolai Poroskov, "Tovar stvolom," *Vremya novostei*, 10 February 2005, www.vremya.ru/2005/22/4/118012.html.

32 Aleksei Nikol'skii, "Russkii EADS ne srastaetsia," *Vedomosti*, 2 June 2005.

33 Aleksandr Rozhkov and Dmitrii Kostin, "Minimizatsiya riskov: Godudarstvennyi kontrol' nad avaiapromom dolzhen byt' sokhranen," *Voenno-promyshlennyi kur'er*, 6–12 April 2005, www.vpk-news.ru/article.asp?pr_sign=archive.2005.79.articles.company_02.

34 No author, "MAKS 2005 Breaks Records in Number of Visitors, Deals," *The Moscow Times*, 22 August 2005.

35 Letter to *Nezavisimoe voennoe obozrenie* from Vladimir Krasnov, "Ob'edinennaia aviatsionnaia korporatsiia ne nuzhna," *Nezavisimoe voennoe obozrenie*, 26 November 2004, nvo.ng.ru/notes/2004-11-26/8_letter.html.

36 See, for example, no author indicated, "Gonka za vooruzheniem," *Delovie lyudi*, September 2004, www.dl.mk.ru/article.asp?artid=38131.

37 See Robert H. Donaldson and John A. Donaldson, "The Arms Trade in Russian–Chinese Relations: Identity, Domestic Politics, and Geopolitical Positioning," *International Studies Quarterly* 47, 2003, pp. 709–732.

38 See V. N. Valuev *et al.*, *Regional'nye struktury oborony i bezopastnosti: Korruptsionnie i antikorruptsionnie praktiki*, Nizhnii Novgorod: Nizhnii Novgorod State University, 2004, chapter 2.

39 Felgenhauer, "Arms Exports and the Russian Military."

40 Vadim Solov'ev, "Oboroneksport obnosit goskaznu," *Nezavisimoe voennoe obozrenie*, 25 April 2003, nvo.ng.ru/printed/concepts/2003-04-25/1_vpk.html.

41 www.rosoboronexport.ru/p_frame/main.htm (accessed 24 August 2005).

42 "FGUP "Rosoboroneksport," *Forbes* (Russian edition) no. 7, October 2004.

43 Solov'ev, "Oboroneksport obnosit goskaznu."

44 Aleksandr Golts, "Russia's Arms Exports: Hitting the Ceiling?" *Moscow News* no. 7, 2005, 18 February 2005, english.mn.ru/english/issue.php?2005-7-20.

45 Aleksandr Golts, "Dorogie tovarishchi generaly!" *Moskovskie novosti*, 26 February 2004, www.mn.ru/issue.php?2004-6-18.
46 Pronina, "Aviation Tops '04 Arms Revenues"; Aleksei Nikol'skii, "VPK na golod-nom paike," *Vedomosti*, 9 June 2005.
47 Nikol'skii, "VPK na golodnom paike."
48 Nikolai Poroskov, "Nikakoe real'noe voennoe stroitel'stvo v Rossii ne vedetsya," *Vremya novostei*, 9 August 2005.
49 "Oborononesposobnost'," *Profil*, 14 March 2005. Another part of the reason why the Russian military does not get new planes, ships, and tanks is that Russia spends a lot of its weapons procurement money on intercontinental ballistic missiles, such as the new Topol-M, and submarines. Additionally, much of the procurement money goes into repairing existing aircraft in facilities controlled by the defense ministry. Much of this money is abused, as demonstrated in the scandal surrounding the firing of air force general Dmitrii Morozov in the fall of 2004. Aron Tsypin, "Na chto budet israskhodovan gosudarstvennyi oboronnyi zakaz," polit.ru, 21 September 2004, www.polit.ru/economy/2004/09/21/opk.html.
50 Lantratov, "Military-Industrial Complex 2000–2004."
51 Bulavinov, "Military-Industrial Complex 1991–2000."
52 Lyuba Pronina, "St. Pete Shipbuilder Sold to Old Rival," *Moscow Times*, 15 August 2005.
53 Konstantin Lantratov, Aleksandra Gritskova, and Ivan Makarov, "Vladyka morei," *Kommersant*, 13 August 2005.
54 Vadim Solov'ev and Vladimir Ivanov, "Gosprogramma vooruzhenii na 2002–2006 gody provalena," *Nezavisimoe voennoe obozrenie*, 29 July 2005.
55 Lantratov, "Military-Industrial Complex 2000–2004."
56 Pukhov, "Vyzhivaet sil'neishii."
57 A. Khazbiev, "Okhota na vertushki," *Ekspert*, 19 April 2004.
58 V. Seregin, "Gosudarstvo poigraet s VPK v rynok," RBC Daily, 18 June 2004, www.rbcdaily.ru/news/company/index.shtml?2004/06/18/56169.
59 Nikolai Poroskov, "Sergei Chemezov: Na salone vlyublyayubsia, a svad'ba i deti potom," *Vremya novostei*, 21 June 2005, www.vremya.ru/2005/108/4/127958.html.
60 Poroskov, "Nikakoe real'noe voennoe stroitel'stvo."
61 Ruslan Pukhov, "Korabli potesnili samoleti," *Russkii fokus*, 28 June 2004.
62 Golts, "Russia's Arms Exports."
63 Goltz, "Russia's Arms Exports."
64 Rozhkov and Kostin, "Minimizatsiia riskov."
65 No author, "Gonka za vooruzheniem," *Delovie lyudi*, September 2004, www.dl.mk.ru/article.asp?artid=38131.
66 Wezeman, *SIPRI Yearbook 2005*, pp. 422–423.
67 Makienko, "The Russian–Chinese Arms Trade."
68 Makienko, "The Russian-Chinese Arms Trade."
69 Golts, "Russia's Arms Exports."
70 Wezeman, *SIPRI Yearbook 2005*, p. 425.
71 Makarevich, "Padenie oboronki."
72 Carmen Gentile, "Venezuela Formalizes Russian Arms Deal," *ISN Security Watch*, 20 May 2005.
73 Roger N. McDermott, "Russian Defense Industries Expand Foreign Sales," *Eurasia Daily Monitor*, 3 May 2005.
74 McDermott, "Russian Defense Industries."
75 Viktor Yasmann, "U.S., Russia Continue to Spar over Venezuela Arms Deal," *Radio Free Europe/Radio Liberty Newsline*, 24 March 2005.
76 Maxim Pyadushkin with Maria Haug and Anna Matveeva, "Beyond the Kalashnikov: Small Arms Production, Exports, and Stockpiles in the Russian Federation," Small Arms Survey, August 2003, p. vii, www.smallarmssurvey.org/OPs/OP10Russian Federation.pdf.

77 "State Sponsors of Terrorism," www.state.gov/s/ct/c14151.htm (accessed 17 June 2005).
78 Pavel Felgenhauer, "No Stopping Russian Arms," *Moscow Times*, 27 July 2004.
79 Felgenhauer, "No Stopping Russian Arms."
80 "State Sponsors of Terrorism."

# 9 Russian banks and Russian diplomacy

## Occasionally rather embarrassing

*William Tompson*

The Russian banking sector is in some respects a rather odd sector for inclusion in the present volume. To be sure, the sector's development and the interactions between financial-sector business interests and the state have had implications for Russian foreign relations. However, despite the overseas ambitions of a few banks, the banking sector remains overwhelmingly focused on the domestic market. It has been neither the source of serious transnational conflict nor an important instrument for advancing Russia's foreign policy agenda. It has, however, complicated Russia's external relations from time to time. Usually, this has been a product of problems that afflict the banking system, such as corruption and money laundering, or with the authorities' manipulation of the system in ways that have subsequently proved embarrassing. The story of the banks' role in Russian diplomacy is thus a story about the banks' weakness rather than their strength.

### Structure and interests of the system

This is not the place for a detailed assessment of the structure and development of Russia's banking sector.[1] However, it is necessary to highlight certain characteristics of the system before considering its actual and potential role in high politics and policy. First, the Russian banking sector, though growing rapidly since 1999, remains small and fragmented (see Table 9.1). Russia still has a very large population of very small banks, a legacy of the administrative chaos of the last years of the Soviet Union and the extremely liberal licensing regime of the immediate post-Soviet period.[2] The average Russian bank at the end of 2004 had total assets of around 5.4 billion rubles ($197 million); the aggregate assets of the smallest 1,100 amounted to under $30.8 billion, ($27.9 million per bank). Many of these "dwarf banks" are banks in name only and are used by the owners for other purposes, such as tax "optimization" or money laundering. Even the largest Russian banks are quite small by international standards. In 2004, Russia's largest bank, the state-owned Sberbank, ranked 152nd in the world by tier-1 capital. The largest private bank, Mezhprombank, was 392nd.[3]

The small size of banks is particularly striking when contrasted with the size

*Table 9.1* Selected balance-sheet indicators for the Russian banking sector

|  | 1998 | 1999 | 2000 | 2001 | 2002 | 2003 | 2004 |
|---|---|---|---|---|---|---|---|
| Number of operating credit institutions | 1,476 | 1,349 | 1,311 | 1,319 | 1,329 | 1,329 | 1,299 |
| Assets | 39.8 | 32.9 | 32.3 | 35.3 | 38.3 | 42.4 | 42.5 |
| Capital (own funds) | 2.9 | 3.5 | 3.9 | 5.1 | 5.4 | 6.2 | 5.6 |
| Funds attracted from physical persons | 7.6 | 6.2 | 6.1 | 7.6 | 9.5 | 11.5 | 11.7 |
| Funds attracted from enterprises and organizations | 10.7 | 9.7 | 9.9 | 10.1 | 10.1 | 10.5 | 11.8 |
| Credits extended to nonfinancial enterprises and organizations | 11.4 | 9.2 | 10.4 | 13.2 | 14.7 | 17.2 | 18.8 |
| *(as percentage of total assets)* | *(28.5)* | *(28.0)* | *(32.1)* | *(37.2)* | *(38.4)* | *(40.5)* | *(44.1)* |

Source: Central Bank of Russia.

Note
Number of operating credit institutions is absolute number. Other figures are percentage of gross domestic product (GDP), end of period.

of Russia's major industrial corporations, many of which are very large by any standards. As a result, Russia's banks, unable to meet the financing needs of the country's biggest borrowers, are losing many of their best clients to foreign rivals and to bond markets. Russia's blue-chip firms increasingly find that they are able to borrow larger sums, for longer periods and on better terms, from foreign banks and capital markets.

Second, the banking system tends to be segmented along regional, sectoral, and "group" lines. A large proportion of Russian banks (the great majority, according to some observers) are "pocket banks" controlled by a single large shareholder or a small group of related shareholders, who operate the bank for their own convenience. As noted above, this sometimes involves running banks for legally dubious purposes, but in other cases such pocket banks merely function as external "corporate treasuries," reflecting above all the desire of their owners to retain tight control over their own financial flows. Thus, most pocket banks are best understood as tools of business groupings or state institutions rather than independent, profit-oriented businesses, although some pocket banks have gradually developed into more substantial financial institutions. Even they, however, generally retain their links to their founder-owners.

Whether pocket banks or not, Russian banks are often closely affiliated with specific financial-industrial groupings – be they middle-sized regional groupings or the "oligarchic" groups that loom so large on the national political scene. Such banks are chiefly oriented to serving the needs of group members. This tendency is reinforced by factors such as poor creditor protection and lack of transparency, which make intragroup operations less risky than arm's-length transactions. In general, therefore, the banking sector remains highly segmented, with little trust among banks. The interbank market, though growing, is underdeveloped, and there is still very little of the sort of interaction among banks typically found in a well-functioning network of financial intermediaries – i.e. there is little pooling, trading, or sharing of risk.[4]

Third, despite the efforts of the Central Bank of Russia (CBR) to promote transparency in the sector, both the formal ownership structures of Russian banks and many of their activities tend to be opaque. Banks' connections to their beneficial owners are often concealed behind complex webs of nominee share-holders, trusts, and offshore companies, even when the identities of the true owners are well known. This is generally legal. In an International Finance Corporation (IFC) survey conducted in 2003, half of the banks responding admitted that they did not disclose the names of their real owners.[5] Opacity of ownership reduces both transparency and confidence in a system where lack of trust is already a problem. It also impedes efforts to implement new criteria concerning who is "fit" to own and/or manage Russian banks and undermines efforts to control related-party transactions.[6] Moreover, the lack of transparency surrounding ownership is closely linked to the lack of transparency surrounding much of what banks *do*: although the pace of banking reform has accelerated markedly since the appointment of Sergei Ignat'ev as CBR chairman in 2002, the sector remains undergoverned, and a great many banks are actively engaged in activities that are – at best – legally questionable, and in many cases clearly criminal.[7]

A fourth important characteristic of the sector is the extent to which it continues to be dominated by the state. At the beginning of 2004, there were 20 banks in which the state (federal or regional authorities) held majority stakes.[8] Such banks accounted for 68 percent of retail deposits, 29 percent of capital, 36 percent of assets and 38 percent of credit outstanding to the non-financial private sector. They also accounted for 80 percent of Russian government bonds in the portfolios of Russian banks. In addition, regional authorities held minority stakes in many banks, and a large number of state unitary enterprises were part-owners of banks. The most important state-owned banks are the savings monopolist Sberbank and the former foreign trade bank Vneshtorgbank (VTB); they are also the largest banks in Russia in terms of both capital and assets. While ownership of VTB has been transferred to the government, the CBR continues to hold the state's controlling stake in Sberbank. This presents a number of conflicts of interest: the CBR is at once the sector's regulator, its largest single creditor and the owner of its biggest bank. It also has considerable control over most aspects of insolvency proceedings in the sector. Finally, many private commercial banks have developed on the basis of close links to state institutions, relying on political connections to secure various benefits. Many regional banks have established near-monopoly positions on local markets thanks to official backing.[9]

There are good reasons for seeing state dominance as a problem. State ownership and state intervention in credit allocation tend to distort competition, to aggravate moral hazard by encouraging the expectation of a bailout, and to undermine the efficiency of intermediation, as banks often pursue policies that reflect the noncommercial requirements of the authorities rather than good commercial sense.[10] The short history of Russia's banking sector exemplifies many of these problems, particularly with respect to competition and the imposition of hard budget constraints on banks. State-owned banks (both federal and regional) have continued to derive substantial competitive advantages from state ownership, especially Sberbank.[11] In addition to the explicit state guarantee backing their retail deposits, which was scrapped only at the end of 2003, state-owned banks have enjoyed privileged access to state funds, *de facto* exemption from some regulatory norms, and, on occasion, financial support from the state. Their cost of capital is reduced by the perception that the state will stand behind them, an implicit guarantee that is little affected by recent legal changes. Sberbank, moreover, is the only Russian bank with a fully developed (indeed, over-developed) branch network. This extensive reach in the Russian regions gives it a near-monopoly in handling things like pension and utilities payments, which bring with them large volumes of low-cost funds. At the same time, state-owned banks have at times been required to perform unprofitable "social functions" on behalf of the state or to adopt policies that reflect the requirements of macroeconomic management rather than profitability.

Many of the problems outlined above were evident in the banking "mini-crisis" of May–July 2004, when the CBR's intervention in the case of a bank accused of money laundering triggered several weeks of turbulence and placed a number of banks under strain.[12] The CBR's attempt to impose a temporary administration on the bank in question, Sodbiznesbank, was bound to be unsettling; it was, after all, the first time such an intervention had occurred *before* a bank had actually defaulted on its obligations. However, the situation was exacerbated by the uncertainty about Sodbiznesbank's ownership, which led to pressure on banks thought to be linked to it via common owners, and by rumors of a "blacklist" of banks slated for closure by the authorities, which led to runs on several banks. A number of players in the sector appear to have fueled the rumors and speculation in an effort to undermine rivals. Lack of trust among banks, as well as the awareness that almost any bank might be found to have shady deals on its books (and thus to be vulnerable to such intervention) led to a drying up of liquidity on the interbank market, putting pressure on the hundreds of smaller banks that are highly dependent on it. At the same time, rumors concerning blacklists and political vendettas were widely accepted as true, partly because neither the banks nor the general public had much faith in the authorities' impartiality and partly because, in the case of Guta-bank at least, political factors do seem to have underlain the bank's troubles. While the turbulence eventually abated, the whole episode highlighted problems of opacity and lack of trust, as well as the widespread (and well-founded) belief that many banks were engaged in legally dubious activities.

Finally, it is important to note that there is still relatively little foreign involvement in the sector. At the beginning of 2004, nonresidents owned stakes in only 128 Russian credit institutions, of which 32 were wholly foreign owned. The foreign share of the sector's total capital in early 2005 was estimated at 5.2 percent, down from 10.7 percent at the beginning of 2000, and majority foreign-owned banks accounted for 7.6 percent of sector assets. This picture contrasts starkly with Central Europe, where local banking systems are now largely foreign owned. Russia does not necessarily need or want a banking sector dominated by foreign players, but it does need a higher level of foreign involvement in the sector, if only to reap the benefits foreign banks can bring in terms of skills, technology, and credibility. The lack of foreign involvement is partly a product of protectionist policies, but the significance of bank protectionism should not be exaggerated.

While there was, for almost a decade, a 12 percent ceiling on the foreign capital share in the sector, the cap had never actually had legal force, and foreign banks never came close to breaching it anyway, except for a brief period immediately after the 1998 financial crisis.[13] Its real importance was not legal but symbolic: the existence of the ceiling sent a strong signal to foreign investors about the CBR's attitude toward foreign entry. Formally, it was scrapped in 2002, after Sergei Ignat'ev replaced Viktor Gerashchenko as CBR chairman. A number of lesser restrictions on foreign involvement remain, including the requirement that the Central Bank approve any acquisition of shares in a Russian bank by nonresidents, but the CBR under Ignat'ev has adopted a much more positive attitude toward foreign banks and is working to relax many of the remaining restrictions.[14] The most contentious issue remains the Russian authorities' insistence that foreign banks entering the Russian market establish fully capitalized Russian subsidiaries rather than simply opening local branches. That said, the real deterrents to foreign entry are generally reckoned to be informal rather than formal: the weak contracting environment, the attitude of officialdom, and the difficulties of operating in Russia's opaque and sometimes unstable financial system all constitute much more serious obstacles to entry than the formal rules administered by the CBR.

## The evolving political role of Russian banks

The above overview already suggests a number of important points about the political role of Russia's banking sector. First, the banks are not – and, contrary to popular belief, rarely have been – a particularly powerful sectoral lobby. Second, their lobbying weakness is at least in part a function of the sector's fragmented structure, which is reflected in its politics. Rarely has it ever acted as a unified force, even when lobbying the authorities with respect to very sector-specific issues – a reality highlighted by the rivalry that exists between the two major banking organizations, the Association of Russian Banks and the "Rossiya" Association of Regional Banks. Banks' lobbying activities tend to be highly particularistic: individual banks or bankers tend to lobby specific politicians and officials to secure their interests. In this, of course, the banks' behavior is perfectly typical of business lobbying in Russia more generally. Third, major banks identify far more closely with the regions, industrial sectors, and business groupings to which they are linked than with any broader sectoral lobby. While groups of banks do sometimes join together in an effort to influence policy, bank lobbying is generally most effective when supported by the large industrial companies and groupings to which so many banks are allied.[15] Finally, a great deal of policy still reflects the entrenched power of the big state banks, particularly Sberbank and VTB, and the authorities' reluctance to restructure them in order to level the competitive playing field between state and private banks.

### Banks and the state in the 1990s

A look at the political history of Russian banks illustrates these points and quickly makes clear that Russia's commercial banks have generally been less powerful than they sometimes appear. Banks in the early 1990s were not an especially powerful lobby at the federal level. At that time, industrial lobbies came to dominate the government. Such lobbies grew steadily more influential in the cabinet from June 1992, as growing resistance to the "market Bolshevism" of the Gaidar government led to the promotion of "industrialists" like Viktor Chernomyrdin, Oleg Soskovets, and Oleg Lobov. The banks did not have much of a role in policy making at this time, nor did they really need one in order to do well. They were making easy profits from trade finance, foreign exchange speculation, and the handling of state accounts, soft credits, and other official financial flows. As Timothy Frye observes, the banks profited handsomely from the lax financial policies of the time, but these policies were adopted under pressure from industrial and regional lobbies and supported by a CBR chief – Gerashchenko – who regarded support for the real sector as a key priority for the Central Bank, even at the expense of price stability. In short, the banks were well positioned to appropriate a share of the rents being generated by and for other actors.[16]

The banks did not evince much interest in using their rapidly growing wealth for political ends during this period, beyond ensuring that the state did not curtail the speculative opportunities they were exploiting. The government's remaining liberal reformers, such as Anatoly Chubais, who were later identified very closely with the leading banks, viewed them with suspicion at this stage, for at least three reasons. First, many banks were obviously shaky (and shady) institutions. Second, the banks were closely tied to the CBR, then headed by the liberals' *bête noire*, Gerashchenko. Third, the banks were perceived as enemies of stabilization. It was thus no accident that the liberal architects of Russia's early privatization policies worked to limit the banks' participation in that process. Banks were barred from acquiring equity stakes in enterprises undergoing privatization, and their shareholdings were limited to 10 percent of the shares of any given company and 5 percent of the banks' own assets.[17]

These restrictions did not appear to have upset the banks much at the time. In any case, the earliest attempts to organize some sort of real sectoral lobby were encountering limited success, at best, even with respect to issues of direct concern to the sector. The Association of Russian Banks (ARB) purported to speak for the sector, but many of the largest banks refused to join. The organization came to be seen by many as a vehicle for small and medium-sized banks only, although critics argued that its agenda was largely determined by a small number of larger banks.[18]

Tensions within the sector manifested themselves in the battles surrounding the passage of the 1995 banking law. On issues where the sector was united, it generally prevailed: the banks preserved a degree of protection from foreign entry in the banking law and gained the right to deal in shares and securities for which no special license was required under federal law. On other issues, however, the banking lobby split. On the issue of charter capital increases, the great mass of small and medium banks, backed by powerful regional elites, secured an important victory over their larger Moscow- and St. Petersburg-based rivals. Article 11 of the law stated flatly that the CBR could not apply increases in the minimum charter capital requirement to existing banks. This effectively closed off one strategy for forcing the consolidation of the sector, something smaller banks had feared and some larger banks had seen as a welcome opportunity to extend their reach into the regions. For similar reasons, the big banks based in the capitals pressed for liberal rules on the opening of new branches, which their smaller rivals opposed. That round went to the "federals," but the big banks soon discovered the limits of their victory, as regional authorities continued in many cases to pursue protectionist policies designed to keep the big metropolitan banks at bay.[19] Tensions within the sector continued to grow in 1995, chiefly as a result of the authorities' renewed push for macroeconomic stabilization. In August 1995, tightening liquidity conditions triggered a crisis on the interbank market. Once again, the banking lobby split, as financially stronger banks failed to back the ARB's calls for state support, tacitly favoring the bankruptcy of their weaker rivals instead.

The tightening of monetary conditions in conjunction with the stabilization policies of 1995–1998 aggravated both the real sector's problems with access to finance and the government's fiscal problems. The banks, too, felt the strain of stabilization, but, with a near-monopoly on ruble liquidity in an increasingly liquidity-starved economy, they found it easy to exploit the situation. As Clifford Gaddy and Barry W. Ickes observed, "in the land of the cashless, the man with pocket change is king, or at least an oligarch. . . . It is the Russian tycoons' relatively cash-rich status in a cashless economy that gives them so much power."[20] Real-sector enterprises needing access to finance thus had every incentive to develop their own pocket banks or to draw closer to friendly banks. At the same time, the government itself came to depend increasingly on the banks for short-term financing – despite the fact that the banks themselves were in some cases actively pursuing strategies that aggravated the government's fiscal headaches. Other factors strengthened the banks further. The beleaguered position of President Boris Yeltsin in 1995–1996 left the Kremlin particularly vulnerable to bank lobbying, while the government's remaining liberal reformers searched for allies to help them shore up their positions in a cabinet dominated increasingly by people like Chernomyrdin and Soskovets. Corruption, too, may have played a role: the instability and uncertainty of 1995–1996 do appear to have fueled it, particularly at the highest levels. In late 1995, officials in the government apparatus claimed that the main problem they faced in dealing with the Kremlin was that their colleagues in the presidential administration believed that the Yeltsin era would soon end and were consequently preoccupied with arranging jobs for themselves outside the Kremlin and establishing contacts in the business community.[21] Such officials would have made far easier targets for the banks' lobbying efforts. These circumstances formed the backdrop for the infamous loans-for-shares deals of 1995–1997.

It would, nevertheless, be a mistake to view loans-for-shares and other give-away privatizations of 1995–1997 solely in terms of the banks' political muscle.[22] While the banking lobby was at its most powerful during 1995–1997, such deals generally took place when the banks had managed to forge alliances with key industrial companies. Hostile acquisitions were rare and were fiercely contested. Even prior to the loans-for-shares auctions, banks had generally pre-ferred acquiring stakes in enterprises with whose managers they had close rela-tionships.[23] Despite their enormous financial problems, the industrialists' position was far from weak. In the absence of a credible bankruptcy threat, they did not need to surrender control to outsiders simply because their finances were a mess, nor were they inclined to do so. In the end, the vast majority of enter-prises originally slated for inclusion in the infamous loans-for-shares auctions were able to lobby their way out.[24] Only nine of the original list of 64 actually ended up on the auction block. Three of these had the funds to secure control of their own shares, albeit in auctions that effectively excluded other participants, and five were acquired by banks to which they were already closely linked. The only major exception was the nonferrous metals giant Norilsk Nickel. Oneksim-bank acquired a controlling stake in this concern against its managers' wishes and had to fight a protracted legal, commercial, and political battle to secure real control. In short, the bank-driven loans-for-shares privatizations are in reality best understood as simply a further stage in the process of privatization to insid-ers that began with the asset stripping of the late Soviet period and continued during the voucher phase of 1992–1994.

Even at the peak of their political influence, in the mid-1990s, Russian banks were small and often unstable. Their survival depended chiefly on the patronage of the state, to which they were closely linked in every sphere of activity.[25] Indeed, although the banking sector in the mid-1990s was regarded by some as the sector "most advanced as far as the progress of market reforms is con-cerned,"[26] it actually had a strong claim to being the most *subsidized* in the Russian economy.[27] The subsidies it received persisted even as state support for other sectors dried up, in large measure because they were usually implicit rather than explicit subsidies. The reputed power of Russia's banks in the mid-1990s must thus be viewed alongside this very dependent position vis-à-vis the state. The image of hugely powerful banks dominating a weak state tended to obscure the reality that *both* were weak. The state's reliance on the banks reflected its inability to perform a number of basic functions, while the banks' reliance on the state reflected their limited ability to survive without easy access to state funds. What the scandals of 1996–1998 highlighted most of all was the extent to which the banks' futures depended on this access. The so-called banking wars of 1997 thus reflected banks' vulnerability more than their strength. Tighter monetary policies, exchange rate stabilization, falling yields on government securities, and lower inflation put the banks under enormous pressure. Central bank credit became more expensive, reserve requirements grew tougher, and access to budgetary funds was curtailed. With so many sources of state subsidy drying up, the battle for the subsidies that remained, and especially for control of state assets still to be privatized, could not but escalate.

### Banks and the state under Vladimir Putin

The foregoing analysis suggests why the banks have been less politically prominent since the 1998 crisis than they were before it. The most important factor of all was clearly the passing of the extreme illiquidity that afflicted the economy during 1995–1998. Indeed, the main problem afflicting the financial system during 2000–2004 was *excess* liquidity. The remonetization of the real sector and the related dramatic transformation of state finances greatly reduced the banks' political leverage. The corporate balance of forces also changed. In the postdevaluation recovery that began in 1999, money was made chiefly from the economic rents associated with the exploitation of natural resources. Control over oil, gas, and metals, rather than mere liquidity (no longer such a scarce commodity), represented the keys to real wealth and economic power. This evolution coincided with changes in the structure of the more dynamic business groupings such as Rosprom and Interros. The center of gravity within these groupings shifted from the banks to the parent holdings or the core resource-exporting companies.

This shift in the internal balance of power within the business groupings also reflects the shift in the sources of their profits. In the mid-1990s, superprofits were earned in the government securities markets, where real yields on short-term GKOs (government short-term bonds) reached triple-digit annual rates. The incentives to strip industrial assets and accumulate payment arrears in order to play the GKO market were enormous, and this is precisely what many managers did. In the postcrisis recovery, however, it was exports, particularly oil exports, that generated huge profits. Even many of Russia's processing industries returned to profit. The banks' role as profit generators was dramatically reduced. The "banking wars" of the 1990s gave way to "oligarch hunting" and conflicts among powerful groupings in various industrial sectors. Battles among oil companies, metals producers, and other industrial concerns – not bankers – now tend to dominate the headlines where commerce meets politics. The politically prominent bankers of the 1990s who remained major players after the financial crisis were those with strong positions in other sectors. Those like SBS-Agro's Aleksandr Smolenskii and Inkombank's Vladimir Vinogradov, who failed to establish themselves as dominant players in other sectors, proved far more vulnerable – politically and financially – after the crisis. Thus, Vladimir Potanin is now more closely involved with Interros and, in particular, Norilsk Nickel, than with Oneksimbank's successor, Rosbank. Even before the financial crisis,

Mikhail Khodorkovsky left Bank Menatep to head the Rosprom Financial-Industrial Group. The official assault on Khodorkovsky launched in mid-2003 led to the dismemberment of Yukos, while Menatep's successor banks hardly figured in the affair.

One area in which there is all too much continuity with the past is the treatment of state-owned banks. Official policy is that state-owned banks should exist – if at all – to correct market failures. Their activities should be concentrated in sectoral and other niches which the market will not address on its own.[28] In practice, however, the major state-owned banks tend to operate as universal banks, with Sberbank, in particular, exploiting its protected retail monopoly to extend its business in other directions. It is now the dominant bank in a number of market segments, not only retail. Sberbank's size and status thus distort competition in many segments of the banking market. The same might be said, albeit to a lesser degree, of VTB. The inconsistency of policy with respect to state banks was particularly evident during the minicrisis of the summer of 2004. The CBR, having refused to extend a stabilization credit to the pressured Guta-bank, instead lent $100 million to VTB, enabling it to buy Guta and thus to nationalize one of the country's larger private banks. There is some reason to believe that the CBR extended this loan under strong pressure from individual members of the presidential administration. At the same time, the CBR appears to have encouraged Sberbank to step up its activities on the interbank market in order to ease the liquidity problems of smaller banks. Since Sberbank traditionally does around 90 percent of its interbank lending to foreign banks, this amounted to asking the savings monopolist to undertake a major change in its commercial practices, at very short notice, in order to suit the needs of the monetary authorities. In short, the CBR once again succumbed to the temptation to use Sberbank as a policy instrument.

## The banks and foreign policy: the potential for conflict – and embarrassment

Much of what can be said about the role (or lack thereof) of Russia's banks in shaping its foreign policy follows directly from the above analysis of the banking sector and its politics. Rarely do the interests of specific banks or the banking lobby as a whole appear to have been important in determining the course of Russian foreign policy. This is hardly surprising. Russian banks remain overwhelmingly focused on the rapidly growing domestic market; few are seriously interested in overseas expansion (particularly outside the Commonwealth of Independent States – CIS) and fewer still in a position to pursue that interest. The most active Russian banks abroad tend to be those closely affiliated with Gazprom and Unified Energy System in the CIS or major financial-industrial groups.[29] Such banks often move abroad in the footsteps of the other members of their respective groups (an exception is the state-owned Vneshtorgbank). Nor have banks served as important instruments of foreign policy in the way that, for example, Gazprom has sometimes done.

Where the banks' interests and activities do seem to have had a significant impact on Russia's foreign relations, it has been the sector's weakness and its specific pathologies, rather than its lobby power, that have tended to be at issue. The frequent crises, large and small, that have rocked the Russian banking system at intervals since 1991 have sometimes done the country's image considerable, albeit usually temporary, damage. In addition to highlighting Russia's financial fragility, banking crises and scandals have often drawn attention to the seedier side of Russia's often very dirty business environment. A brief analysis of two specific issues – protectionism and money laundering – will serve to illustrate the ways in which banking-sector weakness sometimes complicates Russia's foreign relations.

### Protectionism

Since the early 1990s, Russia's banks have been protected from foreign competition by a variety of formal and informal mechanisms. The issue of foreign access to the banking sector has loomed large in discussions of Russia's World Trade Organization (WTO) accession. As noted earlier, for roughly a decade until 2002 there was widely perceived to be a 12 percent limit on the foreign capital share in the sector. In fact, the quota was never legally enforceable. No method for calculating this quota was ever officially approved and official statements on the subject were contradictory.[30] Since neither the size of the quota nor the formula for applying it was ever agreed upon, it was simply assumed that the 12 percent ceiling announced by the CBR in 1993 remained in force. Its formal removal in 2002 thus had little or no legal significance, although it sent a powerful signal to foreign banks about the authorities' attitude toward foreign entry.

There is little doubt that the protectionist measures adopted in the early 1990s were in large measure a product of bank lobbying. A number of local banks actively lobbied for protection, deploying an "infant industry" argument. In addition to the capital ceiling, the authorities imposed a moratorium on foreign banks' servicing of Russian clients, and a range of other regulations, such as those restricting the employment of expatriate staff and governing the appointment of foreigners as top managers or board members of Russian banks. The practical significance of these rules depended to a great extent upon the judgments of the CBR.[31]

By 1996–1997, the domestic political pressure for protection was waning. Thus, the moratorium on foreign banks' handling of Russian clients was allowed to lapse as scheduled, on 1 January 1996, and other restrictions on foreign banks' activities were gradually eased. Later on, the minimum charter capital for establishing a foreign bank was reduced from €10 million to the €5 million required of new local banks. By 1996–1997, the banking lobby had split over the issue of protection, as over so many other issues. The largest and most ambitious banks were starting to think (prematurely, as it turned out in most cases) in terms of overseas expansion. They understood that opening the sector up somewhat would be necessary if they were to enter foreign markets. In any case, it had become clear by the mid-1990s that the threat of foreign competition was exaggerated. Russian banks operating on their home turf enjoyed significant competitive advantages vis-à-vis their foreign rivals.[32] Russian firms found local banks quicker to take decisions and less demanding when it came to their requirements for financial information. Many Russian businesses were unable or unwilling to provide information that would meet Western standards. While their professional and technological sophistication grew rapidly in the mid-1990s, Russian banks continued to levy much lower fees for their services. They were also – and this was, for many businesses, a crucial consideration – far more willing than their foreign rivals to participate in "gray" tax-evasion and capital-export schemes, which were legally dubious but were nonetheless standard operating procedures for many Russian corporations.

There was and is, to be sure, some danger that foreign banks entering Russia on favorable terms might be able to "cherry-pick" the most promising of the Russian banks' clients – chiefly, the country's large resource exporters, plus a few prominent companies oriented toward the domestic market, such as Wimm-Bill-Dann. However, such companies have hitherto tended to retain Russian banks for local services, while successfully tapping foreign capital markets and banks abroad. Access to external markets means that the remaining protections in force do little to prevent large Russian corporations from raising foreign capital.

As the foregoing implies, many of the most important barriers to foreign entry arguably had little to do with the sort of explicitly protectionist measures adopted in 1993–1996. The undergoverned, often corrupt nature of the financial system itself was a deterrent to many foreign banks, as was the recognition of the fact that the attitudes of officials – federal or local, in the CBR or in other state institutions – mattered at least as much as the formal rules in determining what kind of welcome a foreign bank might receive on entering any given market. The elaborate system of foreign exchange controls constituted another impediment to foreign entry. Gradually relaxed before 1998, the currency control regime was tightened up again after the crisis, and the lifting of those controls is still not complete. Currency controls – which were viewed as a nuisance by Russian as well as foreign banks – were adopted as tools of macroeconomic management but their effect was undoubtedly to discriminate against foreign banks.

Nevertheless, while the domestic political pressure for protection waned after the mid-1990s, numerous restrictions on foreign involvement have remained in force. Even now, the CBR must approve any acquisition of shares in a Russian bank by nonresidents. The CBR is pressing for the removal of many of these restrictions, but it continues to stand firm on what has become the most contentious issue of all: Russia's insistence that foreign banks wishing to enter the sector must form fully capitalized subsidiaries, registered in the Russian Federation, rather than simply opening local branches of their overseas parent banks. As will be discussed, this requirement means that the foreign banks are subject to Russian regulation rather than the regulation of their home country.

How then might we account for continued protectionism, if not in terms of the power of the banking lobby? The first point to make is that declining pressure for protection should not be equated with mounting pressure for liberalization. There was no strong domestic lobby *in favor* of opening up the banking sector, and a substantial part of the banking community, as well as many nationalist politicians, did remain opposed. The role of the latter in maintaining some protections should not be underestimated, as the fear of a foreign-dominated financial system runs deep among elements of Russia's political elite. Moreover, the access regime in place after 1993–1995 effectively left the CBR as the gate-keeper to the sector, a role that some in the CBR, including Viktor Gerashchenko, appear to have been determined to retain. Their preferred model for foreign entry, particularly after the 1998 crisis, was for foreign investors to buy – with CBR approval, of course – stakes in Russian banks.[33] In any case, since there was little evidence that liberalization would trigger a flood of foreign investment into the sector, the Russian authorities had little incentive to liberalize autonomously; many policy makers clearly preferred waiting until there was a quid pro quo on offer, which is why the issue came to be so important in the context of Russia's WTO negotiations.

This brings us to the issue of branching versus subsidiaries, which remains one of the most problematic WTO accession issues. Here, the principal source of opposition is the CBR rather than the banking lobby, although the commercial banks generally seem to support the CBR position. Allowing foreign branches to operate freely within Russia really would create a competitive situation that could threaten the interests of Russian commercial banks. Nevertheless, it is the Central Bank's position that is somewhat puzzling and that requires some consideration. The CBR is broadly in favor of greater foreign access and, under its current leadership, it has done much to facilitate such access. Yet it rejects foreign branching. For the CBR, the key issue is: who regulates? A fully capitalized, locally registered subsidiary is effectively a local bank, albeit a foreign-owned local bank, and is regulated by the host country regulator – in this case, the CBR. A branch, by contrast, is not a legal entity independent of its parent and it thus falls under the prudential supervision of the parent bank's home-country regulator.

Concerns about branching are focused on this distinction. First, the CBR is not happy with the idea that banks operating in Russia will not all be subject to the same oversight. Second, it is concerned about the quality of supervision that can be expected from some foreign central banks, including some in offshore jurisdictions from which banks could well be expected to try to branch into Russia. Third, it is not clear that even the most competent developed-country regulators have an adequate understanding of Russian realities.[34] Fourth, some Russian officials fear that branching would make it easier for foreign banks to withdraw from the Russian market in the event of a crisis; in their eyes, a fully capitalized subsidiary represents more of a commitment to the market.[35] Finally, even if the quality of supervision is good in both Russia and the home jurisdiction, the different regulatory regimes associated with the two forms of representation can generate very different regulatory responses to the same information. While both arrangements have their drawbacks, the model devised by Giacomo Calzolari and Gyöngyi Lóránth suggests that branching is more likely to be problematic, as it is likely to lead, *ceteris paribus*, to softer regulation of the home unit, while the home country regulator's behavior toward the foreign unit will vary depending on its assessment of the home unit's prospects and may be softer or tougher than it ought to be.[36]

It is worth noting that central banks and banking regulators in many developed countries also dislike the presence of foreign branches in their jurisdictions and often restrict the range of activities in which they may engage. This may be one reason why, to date, Russia appears to have been able to avoid yielding on the branch–subsidiary distinction in its bilateral WTO accession talks. Its May 2004 agreement with the European Union reportedly allows Russia to continue to insist on the creation of subsidiaries rather than branches and to retain a limit, rumored to be of the order of 50 percent, on foreign participation.[37] The crucial test here will be the negotiations with the United States.

### *"Dirty laundry"*

Although the issue of bank protectionism has been much discussed in recent years in the context of WTO accession, it has most often been the banking-sector pathologies, rather than the sector's desire for protection, that have made it a source of international conflict, or at least embarrassment, for Russia. This problem was highlighted most spectacularly in 1999–2000 with the eruption of the so-called "BONY case," which centered on the illegal movement of an estimated $7–10 billion of Russian money through the Bank of New York (BONY) over a period of just four years.[38] Of course, problems such as money laundering, tax evasion, and illegal capital flight from Russia were hardly unknown prior to the summer of 1999: there had already been widespread discussion of these issues in the West, not least in conjunction with investigations into claims that IMF funds had been spirited out of the country just prior to the August 1998 financial collapse. Nevertheless, the *New York Times* investigation of BONY, which found that $4.2 billion had moved through a single account in more than 10,000 transactions over a six-month period, highlighted the scale of the problem and drew attention to the involvement of an apparently "respectable" Western bank.

It is not possible to assess with any precision the role of Russian banks in capital flight. Estimates of total capital flight from the country vary widely, depending on the definition and methodology used.[39] There is, however, little doubt that the sums involved are enormous: even the lowest estimates suggest a figure of at least $10 billion per annum since 1992, and some of the higher but still plausible estimates run to $20 billion. These are staggering sums for an economy the size of Russia's. While a large part of this money has left Russia via mechanisms that avoid the Russian banking system altogether (such as the failure to repatriate foreign exchange earnings from export operations in the first place), the Russian banks were probably directly involved in the illegal export of at least $5 billion a year from 1992 on – and probably substantially more than that. The Russian authorities in the 1990s estimated that up to one-third of the funds leaving the country illegally were themselves the proceeds of criminal activity, which suggests that money-laundering operations amounted to between $3 billion and almost $7 billion per year.[40] This estimate, it should be noted, appears to include contraband trade in otherwise legal goods (in order to avoid customs duties), as well as more serious forms of organized crime, such as narcotics trafficking.

In focusing attention on the problem, the BONY scandal prompted Western banks to undertake widespread checks of accounts held by Russian physical and legal persons, and caused considerable embarrassment to Russia. Politicians across the Russian political spectrum denounced the affair as a deliberate attempt to smear Russia for political or commercial reasons – a claim rendered all the more plausible in Russian eyes by the speed with which Western press coverage of the story went well beyond the known facts. Within Russia, after all, such stories would likely have received wide circulation only if influential interests were promoting them. While Western headlines focused attention on large-scale money laundering by the "Russian mafia," most of the suspicious transactions appear to have been attempts to evade taxes, tariffs, or currency controls, rather than money laundering by organized criminal groups. While tax evasion and capital flight were, of course, illegal, most Russian observers saw them in entirely different terms from laundering the proceeds of organized criminal activities.

Nevertheless, the money-laundering issue would not go away, and the BONY scandal did prompt the CBR to begin scrutinizing offshore transactions more closely. This effort was not enough, however, to satisfy the OECD-based Financial Action Task Force (FATF), formed by the G7 to coordinate efforts to combat money laundering. The FATF placed Russia on its "blacklist" of non-cooperative jurisdictions in 2000, when the list was created. Being fingered as an offender was not merely an embarrassment to Russia; the prospect of sanctions against states on the FATF list threatened to complicate Russia's integration into the world economy. In mid-2001, therefore, Russia at last adopted a new law on the prevention of money laundering and the establishment of a new Financial Monitoring Committee to which banks and other organizations report on certain types of financial and property transactions.[41] (The committee became the Federal Service for Financial Monitoring during the March 2004 reorganization of federal executive bodies.) Further amendments were adopted in October 2002, providing for banks to act if they have reason to believe that an account or transaction is being used to finance terrorist activities. The amendments also extended the remit of the original statute to cover a wider range of entities, including investment funds, casinos, private pension funds, lottery operators, bookmakers, and dealers in precious metals and stones.[42] The amendments were adopted at the request of the FATF, which in October 2002 finally removed Russia from its list of states that fail to fight money laundering. The FATF decision entailed the removal of some restrictions on Western banks' links to their Russian counterparts. In June 2003, the FATF went further, inviting Russia to become a full member of the task force.

The impact of these steps is difficult to assess. While they clearly have not come anywhere close to putting an end to money laundering in Russia, they should not be dismissed as meaningless. Within six months of the adoption of the 1999 regulations, wire transfers from Russian banks to offshore centers had dropped significantly, and the CBR also succeeded in imposing stricter requirements concerning the establishment of correspondent relations with offshore banks.[43] In 2004, the CBR withdrew the licenses of 28 banks for failure to comply with anti-money-laundering rules, accusing two of those banks (Sodbiznesbank and Novocherkassk City Bank) of involvement in money laundering. In March 2005, the Federal Service for Financial Monitoring announced that it would be pressing the CBR to act against a further ten banks it believed to be involved in money-laundering activities. Nevertheless, as of April 2005, enforcement activities have focused entirely on small banks. Moreover, some observers have suggested that, as regulation in Russia has been tightened, Russian banks' illegal activities have been increasingly conducted via their subsidiaries and affiliates in less well-regulated CIS states, particularly in unrecognized statelets such as Abkhazia, where they are beyond the effective reach of any regulator. At the same time, the high level of corruption in Russia, the porousness of its borders and the vast international financial flows into and out of the country all mean that it remains a relatively attractive jurisdiction for individuals and groups interested in laundering the proceeds of criminal activities.

If the BONY scandal centered on the activities of private agents, its state-centered counterpart was arguably the FIMACO affair, which likewise blew up in the months following the financial crisis. In February 1999, less than half a year after the August meltdown, it emerged that the CBR had for a numbers of years in the 1990s secretly used the Jersey-registered Financial Management Company (FIMACO) to manage a portion of its foreign exchange reserves. Formed in 1990 with a charter capital of just $1,000, FIMACO was a subsidiary of the Paris-based Eurobank, which was wholly owned by the CBR. FIMACO began to manage CBR funds in July 1993. While it is not unknown for central banks to rely on private companies to manage a portion of their funds, this idea was extremely unpopular in Russia, and the case of FIMACO aroused serious concerns in both Russia and the West, for a number of reasons. First, FIMACO's activities were wholly opaque: its transactions, profits and losses did not show up anywhere in the published CBR accounts, and the International Monetary Fund (IMF) was unaware of its existence until early 1999. Ordinarily, international "best practice" requires that a central bank's reserves be invested by and in the name of the central bank. Indeed, in the brouhaha that followed the initial revelations about FIMACO, it also emerged that the CBR had at times – apparently deliberately – misstated the level of its reserves. Second, the whole point of using private managers for central bank reserves is to draw on superior expertise and experience. Yet instead of employing an experienced and prestigious international firm, the CBR used an unknown subsidiary. Finally, Gerashchenko openly admitted that one purpose of FIMACO was to keep the CBR's reserves hidden at a time when there was a risk they might be seized by foreign creditors. Technically, at least, this argument may have had some validity up to the mid-1990s: until the CBR's independent status was enshrined in law, the funds it held technically belonged to the government and could in theory have been seized. After 1994, however, this was no longer the case.[44]

Unlike the BONY case, the FIMACO affair did not result in criminal convictions, nor did any leading Russian officials even lose their jobs over it; Gerashchenko weathered the crisis, despite the fact that he had been chairman in 1993 when the CBR first started to use FIMACO as a secret offshore vehicle. The IMF did, however, insist that the CBR undergo an audit by PricewaterhouseCoopers, the results of which were (briefly) posted on the IMF website, over the protests of the CBR.[45] The Fund also required the CBR to revise its method of reporting foreign exchange reserves to the public, excluding such assets as loans to its foreign subsidiaries, and to adopt International Accounting Standards in its reporting. In the end, the repercussions of the FIMACO affair were less dramatic than they might have been, because Russia was, in any case, coming to the end of its dependence on IMF credit. Relations with the Fund were strained on many counts – not just over FIMACO – and the combination of oil price rises abroad and postdevaluation recovery at home was reducing the Fund's leverage on the Russian authorities. Thus, the IMF's demand that the CBR withdraw from its participation in the five state-owned banks abroad (the so-called *Roszagranbanki*) was never fully implemented.

## Conclusion

I have chosen to conclude the above discussion with the FIMACO case, as it illustrates two important points that remain relevant today, not least in connection with such issues as the still mysterious financing of Rosneft's purchase of Yuganskneftegaz, which effectively allowed the nationalization of Yukos's key asset. First, the Russian authorities have been as prone to exploit and manipulate the weaknesses of the country's financial system as have private entrepreneurs. While such action is most often linked to rent seeking and corruption on the part of officials, at times it is also done in order to facilitate the implementation of specific policies. Second, as noted at the outset, most Russian banks have tended to be, first and foremost, tools of their owners rather than independent, profit-oriented financial intermediaries. The banks' subordinate status applies to both the state and the private sectors. In many cases, these tools have been – or are – used for purposes that are often nakedly opportunistic and sometimes simply criminal. Many of these activities spill across Russia's borders daily, especially when it comes to tax evasion and money laundering, and from time to time they cause Russia international embarrassment and even economic loss.

The state of the banking system – and, indeed, of the financial sector as a whole – undoubtedly continues to complicate Russia's efforts to pursue integration into the international economy. However, the current, unreformed state of the Russian banking system suits many powerful domestic actors, and the international costs of such a system are frankly limited, at least as far as those actors are concerned. After all, Russia's most powerful companies now face little difficulty in raising capital abroad. In any case, the diplomatic costs of banking weakness are dwarfed by the price Russia pays for its weak financial system in terms of slower growth. The evidence linking financial development to growth is now extremely strong, and there are good reasons to believe that Russia, in particular, needs a sound and efficient banking system in order to sustain the kind of growth rates it requires over the longer term.[46] Recent progress with respect to banking reform suggests that the situation may be changing, but progress is slow, and efforts to improve transparency and strengthen prudential supervision continue to meet fierce resistance from entrenched vested interests. Unless and until Russia's governing elite is prepared to give up the easy, short-term rents that can be gained by manipulating an opaque and undergoverned financial system, Russia's banking sector is likely to remain a drag on growth at home and a source of periodic embarrassment abroad.

## Notes

The opinions expressed in this chapter are those of the author and do not necessarily reflect the views of the Organisation for Economic Co-operation and Development or its member states.

1 For such an analysis, see William Tompson, "Banking Reform in Russia: Problems and Prospects," OECD Economics Department Working Paper 410 ECO/WKP(2004)33, 9 November 2004.
2 Hundreds of banks emerged in the last years of the Soviet era under the very permissive provisions of the Law on Cooperatives. Politicians challenging the power of the center used the lax entry regime then in force to undermine the financial power of the all-Union authorities, while managers and bureaucrats quickly discovered the rents that could be derived from running a bank. This rapid growth continued into the post-Soviet period, as high inflation made it easy for would-be bankers to meet minimum capital requirements. As late as 1994, a new bank needed only $65,000 in charter capital.
3 "Top 1000," *The Banker*, July 2004, pp. 167ff. Gazprombank was ranked 352nd, but I have opted not to treat Gazprombank as a private bank, as it is an arm of the state-controlled Gazprom.
4 R. Hainsworth, O. Yeremenko, and S. Tubin, "Rossiiskie banki: Sektor ili sistema?" *Rynok tsennykh bumag*, May 2001.
5 In fact, probably rather fewer than half actually did so.
6 OECD, *Related Party Transactions and Beneficial Ownership and Control: Issues Paper for Discussion*, Paris: Organisation for Economic Co-operation and Development, March 2004.
7 See OECD, *Economic Surveys: Russian Federation*, Paris: Organisation for Economic Co-operation and Development, 2004, chapter 5.
8 These figures exclude the former Soviet trade banks abroad and banks under the tutelage of the Agency for Restructuring Credit Organizations. State ownership is confined to federal and regional executive organs, the Bank of Russia, and state unitary

enterprises. The data do not include numerous stakes held by state-owned joint stock companies.

9 See OECD, *Economic Surveys: Russian Federation*, Paris: Organisation for Economic Co-operation and Development, 1997, pp. 100–102; William Tompson, "Old Habits Die Hard: Fiscal Imperatives, State Regulation and the Role of Russia's Banks," *Europe–Asia Studies* 49, no. 7, November 1997, pp. 1159–1185; and William Tompson, "The Present and Future of Banking Reform," in David Lane, ed., *Russian Banking: Evolution, Problems and Prospects*, Cheltenham, UK: Edward Elgar, 2002. Competition for political favors is, of course, competition of a sort, but it is unlikely to produce more efficient intermediation.

10 J. R. Barth, G. Caprio Jr. and R. Levine, "Bank Regulation and Supervision: What Works Best?" NBER Working Paper 9323, November 2002; S. Djankov, R. LaPorta, F. Lopez de Silanes and A. Shleifer, "The Regulation of Entry," *Quarterly Journal of Economics* 117, no. 1, 2002, pp. 1–37; and K. Sherif, M. Borish, and A. Gross, *State-Owned Banks in the Transition: Origins, Evolution and Policy Responses*, Washington, DC: World Bank, 2002.

11 Sberbank's position is examined in detail in William Tompson, "Russia's 'Ministry of Cash': Sberbank in Transition," *Communist Economies and Economic Transformation* 10, no. 2, June 1998, pp. 133–155.

12 See Richard Hainsworth, "No Echo of 1998 in Current 'Banking Crisis,'" *Moscow Times*, 23 June 2004; A. Boulgakov and P. Westin, "About Storms and Teacups," *Aton Capital Flash Note*, 10 June 2004; S. Moiseev, "Kak lechili krizis," *Vedomosti*, 12 August 2004; and V. Kudinov, "Sami vinovaty," *Vedomosti*, 16 August 2004.

13 According to CBR officials, the foreign capital share breached the 12 percent limit after the August crisis simply because so many local banks suffered severe damage during the crisis. However, CBR chief Gerashchenko took no action, and, indeed, no figures for the foreign capital share in late 1998 or early 1999 have been published. At the start of 2000, the foreign share was about 10.6 percent and falling.

14 See OECD, *OECD Investment Policy Reviews: Russian Federation: Progress and Reform Challenges*, Paris: Organisation for Economic Co-operation and Development, 2004, pp. 71–73 for further detail on these and other restrictions on foreign banks. There has been pressure from the banking lobby to establish a 25 percent ceiling on the foreign capital share, but the authorities have so far resisted such proposals, which run counter to their overall policy of seeking to encourage greater foreign participation in the sector.

15 As I have argued at length, the role of industrial lobbies was at least as important as the influence of the banks in pushing the notorious "loans-for-shares" scheme of the mid-1990s.

16 Timothy Frye, "Governing the Banking Sector in Russia" (mimeo: Ohio State University, October 2003); see also Tompson, "Present and Future."

17 *Sobranie aktov Prezidenta i Pravitel'stva Rossiiskoi Federatsii* 1, st. 2, January 1994.

18 Later, as more of the large banks became active in the ARB, a rival association, the Rossiya Association of Regional Banks, began to grow rapidly.

19 On the passage of the 1995 banking law, see "Banking Sector," *Oxford Analytica Daily Brief*, 8 February 1995; and "Banking Laws," *Oxford Analytica Daily Brief*, 11 April 1995.

20 Clifford Gaddy and Barry W. Ickes, "Russia's Virtual Economy," *Foreign Affairs* 77, no. 8, September–October 1998, p. 73.

21 Private information.

22 For one of the best available accounts of the collateral auctions, see Duncan Allan, "The Banks and Loans-for-Shares," in David Lane (ed.), *Russian Banking: Evolution, Problems and Prospects*, Cheltenham, UK: Edward Elgar, 2002.

23 Lev Freinkman, "Financial-Industrial Groups: Emergence of Large Diversified

Private Companies," *Communist Economies and Economic Transformation* 7, no. 1, March 1995, p. 61.

24 The initial bank proposal for the scheme involved a list of 64 enterprises. Yeltsin's 31 August decree included a list of 44, but within a fortnight this was reduced to 29, then 26, and, finally, by mid-October, just 16 (mainly in oil, metallurgy, and river transport). For an excellent analysis of the collateral auctions, focusing on their dubious legality, see *Nezavisimaya gazeta*, 27 January 1998.

25 See Pekka Sutela, "The Role of Banks in Financing Russian Economic Growth," *Post-Soviet Geography and Economics* 39, no. 2, 1998; William Tompson, "The Future of the Russian Banking System: Liquidation or Mergers?" in Graeme Herd, ed., *Russia in Crisis*, Sandhurst, UK: Conflict Studies Research Centre, 1998, pp. 7–25; and Tompson, "Old Habits," pp. 1170–1178.

26 Elena Zhuravskaya, "The First Stage of Banking Reform in Russia Is Completed: What Lies Ahead?" in Jacek Rostowski, ed., *Banking Reform in Central Europe and the Former Soviet Union*, Budapest: CEU Press, 1995, p. 167.

27 For details, see Tompson, "Old Habits."

28 See "Kontseptual'nye voprosy razvitiya bankovskoi sistemy Rossiiskoi Federatsii," *Vestnik Banka Rossii* 12, February 2001; and "Strategiya razvitiya bankovskogo sektora Rossiiskoi Federatsii: prilozhenie k zayavleniyu Pravitel'stva Rossiiskoi Federatsii i Tsentral'nogo banka Rossiiskoi Federatsii 30 dekabrya 2001 goda," *Vestnik Banka Rossii* 5, January 2002.

29 See Gregory Gleason, "Financing Russia's Central Asia Expansion," *Central Asia–Caucasus Institute Analyst*, 3 November 2004, www.cacianalyst.org/view_article.php?articleid=2796.

30 CBR documents on the issue stated that it applied only to the share of charter capital of 100 percent foreign-owned banks in the charter capital of the sector as a whole. Calculated on this basis, the foreign share would never have approached 12 percent, even after the financial crisis. The banking law, by contrast, stated that the indicator should be calculated on the basis of *all* foreign participation in the charter capital of banks in Russia, but the law nowhere specified the size of the quota, which was to be agreed upon by the CBR and the cabinet, along with the formula for calculating it.

31 There has been pressure from the banking lobby to establish a 25 percent ceiling on the foreign capital share, but the authorities have so far resisted such proposals, which run counter to their overall policy of seeking to encourage greater foreign participation in the sector.

32 See "Foreign Banks," *Oxford Analytica Daily Brief*, 17 January 1997.

33 See Tompson, "Present and Future." See also CBR First Deputy Chairman Oleg V''yugin's comments in *Vremya novostei*, 19 August 2003.

34 The author discussed this issue with CBR officials and with the representatives of the Association of Russian Banks at some length in 2003.

35 *Nezavisimaya gazeta*, 22 August 2003. Up to a point, this view may be correct. However, the liability of the parent is far more easily limited in the case of a separate subsidiary: as the Argentine case shows, multinational banks can and sometimes will simply abandon local subsidiaries to their fate.

36 Giacomo Calzolari and Gyöngyi Lóránth, "Regulation of Multinational Banks: A Theoretical Inquiry," CEPR Discussion Paper 4232, February 2004.

37 This summary reflects press coverage of the agreement, the text of which remains confidential.

38 For a summary of the BONY case, see "Russian Money Laundering Operation," in *Money Laundering and Financial Crimes*, Washington, DC: US Department of State, 2000.

39 For assessments of the scale of capital flight from Russia in the 1990s, see Prakash Loungani and Paolo Mauro, "Capital Flight from Russia," mimeo: International Monetary Fund, April 2000; Willem H. Buiter and Ivan Szegvari, "Capital Flight and

Capital Outflows from Russia: Symptoms, Cause and Cure," EBRD Working Paper 73, June 2002.

40 See William H. Cooper and John P. Hardt, *Russian Capital Flight, Economic Reforms, and U.S. Interests: An Analysis*, RL30394 CRS Report to Congress, Washington, DC, March 2000. See also the comments of then-First Deputy Finance Minister Oleg V"yugin quoted in Chase Bank, *Next Week*, 1 October 1999, p. 20.

41 "Federal'nyi zakon RF ot 07.08.2001 No. 115-FZ 'O protivodeistvii legalizatsii (otmyvaniyu) dokhodov poluchennykh prestupnym putem.'"

42 "Federal'nyi zakon RF ot 30.10.2002 No. 131-FZ 'O vnesenii izmenenii i dopolnenii v federal'nyi zakon o protivodeistvii legalizatsii (otmyvaniyu) dokhodov poluchennykh prestupnym putem.'"

43 For details, see the Russia country note in *International Narcotics Control Strategy Report 2005* (Washington, DC: US Department of State, 2005).

44 Gerashchenko appears to have had in mind the Geneva-based Nessim Gaon, whose companies sued Russia for $600 million. Gaon succeeded in freezing Russian accounts in Switzerland and Luxembourg in 1993.

45 The audit report was posted on the IMF web site on 5 August 1999 and withdrawn by 4 September of the same year, at the request of PricewaterhouseCoopers.

46 See Tompson, "Banking Reform in Russia," for an extended discussion of the importance of banking reform for growth and the prospects for its success.

# 10　The drug trade in Russia

*Louise I. Shelley and Svante E. Cornell*

The drug trade has become one of Russia's most significant problems at the beginning of the twenty-first century, affecting many regions of the country and generating large profits for drug traffickers. Even though drug traders operated illicitly in the Soviet Union as early as the 1960s, the rapid rise of narcotics trafficking marks a significant evolution in the workings of Russian crime. In the early 1990s, organized crime groups focused primarily on extracting profits from the legal economy, making Russian crime patterns relatively distinctive from those of other regions in the world. In recent years, Russian organized crime activities have begun to more closely resemble typical global patterns, in which drugs make up a central part of crime group profits.

The globally increasing problem of drug trafficking and consumption has disproportionately affected the countries of the former Soviet Union, because of their weak state institutions, ineffective law enforcement and border controls, high levels of corruption, and unfortunate geographic location near Afghanistan. Further enhancing Russia's vulnerability to the drug trade has been the opening of borders, the collapse of economies in neighboring countries, and the rise of regional conflicts in the 1990s.

As a consequence, millions of illegal immigrants from the Caucasus and Central Asia have poured into Russia. Many of them are unable to support themselves in the legitimate economy and therefore turn to the drug trade as a means of survival. Russian prejudice against peoples from these regions has further marginalized them within the Russian economy.

The civil war in Tajikistan (1992–1997) and the US-led invasion of Afghanistan (starting in 2001) have resulted in an enormous rise of drug trafficking. In Afghanistan, US forces concentrated on routing the Taliban and devoted relatively little attention to developing an alternative economy to replace the traditional poppy harvest. In the past decade, the so-called Northern route of heroin smuggling has linked Afghanistan via Central Asia to Russia and Europe. Perhaps Russia was first intended as a transshipment country, but its main importance in the global heroin industry nevertheless has been as a major consumer, with several million heroin users. Many of these consumers are young people and military personnel formerly deployed on the borders in Central Asia and in the Chechen conflict.

The actors in this illicit economy include Russian military personnel, law enforcement agents, ordinary criminals, ethnic-based crime groups, and illegal immigrants from Asian and Caucasus countries. The corrupt relationships that exist between the drug traffickers and local and regional officials allow these crime groups to operate throughout Russia, even in its capital. Furthermore, crime groups from many other countries are active in Russia, including those based in the neighboring states of the former Soviet Union, Eastern Europe, Japan, China, Korea, Vietnam, and even Latin America and Africa.[1]

The profits from the Russian drug trade fund a variety of activities in Russia and abroad. Some drug proceeds exit Russia, mainly to West European countries, through the complex money-laundering operations used by Russian organized crime. Inside Russia, drug profits enter the legitimate economy after being laundered through restaurants, bars, and casinos – sectors typically controlled by organized crime. Drug profits partially support the illegal immigrant communities within Russia from both Central Asia and the Caucasus, but also from Afghanistan and Pakistan. Some of the proceeds are used to fund the conflict in Chechnya. Other profits are used to fund insurgencies in adjoining regions and possibly to provide funding for terrorist activities supported by remnants of the Taliban.

This chapter analyzes the drug trade as a form of business within Russia and beyond its borders. The strength of these trading networks demonstrates the weakness of the central state in Moscow in its inability to address this problem. State efforts to crack down on the drug trade have had little effect, and even the state's own agents, such as soldiers and policemen, are heavily involved in this business. The expansion of the Russian drug trade will only undermine state capacity further by providing funding for separatist and terrorist groups inside Russia, spreading AIDS among the population and weakening the young generation through addiction and other health problems.

The growing reach of drug traffickers along Russia's borders and within the country is expanding the basis for conflict in Russia's relations with the outside world. Drug trafficking is providing the wherewithal for Russia's enemies to arm themselves. By not dealing with domestic drug addiction and the complicity of state agents in the trade more effectively, the Russian state is undermining its own security.

The following discussion examines this problem by tracing the evolution of the drug trade in and around Russia. It lays out the transportation routes and describes the key actors in the trade. Then it looks at the role of Russian crime groups operating abroad and the contribution of drugs to higher levels of conflict along the Russian border.

## Trajectory of the drug trade

Russian law enforcement sources report an enormous and rapid rise in the drug trade within Russia. The number of users, the geographical reach of the problem, and the variety of drugs consumed have all increased. Currently, 2.1

percent of the Russian population abuses drugs, whereas the comparable figure in West European countries is between 0.1 and 0.9 percent, according to UN data.[2] As the market grows, ever larger and more powerful organized crime groups are involved in the trade, although no group has yet managed to monopolize the market.

The past decade witnessed a 15-fold jump in the number of drug-related crimes and a tenfold increase in the number of drug users, according to the head of the Federal Service for the Control of Narcotics.[3] Although these statistics are unreliable and may not accurately reflect the situation on the ground, they suggest an alarming trend in the increasing size and reach of the drug trade. For example, in 1985 the Ministry of Internal Affairs had identified only four regions in Russia with over 10,000 serious drug addicts. By the beginning of the twenty-first century, that figure had climbed to over 30. Five years later, in 2005, there was hardly a city in Russia free from drug addicts.[4]

Drug abuse is not evenly spread. While 310 addicts were registered per 100,000 people in Russia as a whole in January 2004, the figure in the Russian Far East was significantly higher at 542.[5] The Far East has a much more severe drug problem than the rest of the country because of its proximity to Asian organized crime operating in its ports, the highly criminogenic situation in the region overall, and the criminalization of the local and regional government.[6]

Russia has truly entered the international drug trade. If in the early 1990s, 30 percent of the drugs in Russia came from abroad, including the Commonwealth of Independent States (CIS), the comparable figure at the beginning of the twenty-first century is twice as large. In several regions of Russia, including Moscow, St. Petersburg, and Khabarovsk, 80 percent of the confiscated drugs are of foreign production. Countries supplying drugs to Russia are not limited to one geographical area and include Peru, Colombia, the Netherlands, several countries in Eastern Europe, Afghanistan, and several Central Asian states. Russia is also increasingly a transit country for drugs from Afghanistan, Pakistan, and Iran into European markets.[7] At present, there are no reliable statistics on the share of drugs transported to Europe via Russia. Estimates from research on drug trafficking in Eurasia at the Central Asia-Caucasus Institute and Silk Road Studies Program suggest that between a quarter and a third of heroin consumed in the European Union is transported through Russia.

The drug business appears to employ an ever larger number of Russian citizens annually. Not only are crime groups more actively engaged in the drug trade, but many impoverished Russians serve as drug couriers. Russian governmental sources estimate that the number of organized criminal groups involved in the drug trade has increased by 85 percent since 1993,[8] reaching 950 groups by 2004.[9]

With the expanding drug trade, corruption issues have become more acute, as drug traffickers find protection within Russian law enforcement structures and local and regional governments.[10] The active role of the Russian military in the drug trade is further undermining the integrity of this central Russian institution.[11]

With approximately 450,000 registered users in Russia and an estimated four to five million users overall, narcotics now comprise a large share of the $9 billion to $10 billion Russian shadow economy.[12] Mark Galeotti describes an even more severe problem, estimating over six million users, of whom two million are addicts.[13] Russia, in a very short period, has developed one of the world's most serious drug abuse problems.

## Russian drug use

The Russian drug trade consists of a variety of commodities. Although Russia only acknowledged its drug problem in the late 1980s under Gorbachev, drug abuse dates back to the Khrushchev years.[14] The most frequently abused drugs in the Soviet period were various opium derivatives such as heroin and hashish, as well as addictive pharmaceuticals.[15] In addition, the use of nonstandard narcotics, such as glue and cleaning fluids, was also a serious problem, but did not require the establishment of an extensive drug trading network.

In the Soviet period, in contrast to today, most Russian addicts used drugs grown in the Caucasus and Central Asia, where vast poppy fields were cultivated. Drug addiction was a serious problem even before the Soviet invasion in Afghanistan, but worsened significantly after the protracted war. The 1979–1989 conflict exposed large numbers of military personnel to drugs, driving up usage among soldiers during the war and among demobilized personnel once they left the battlefield. Without drug treatment programs, returning veterans continued their drug habits and became drug traffickers in their home communities.[16] Serious problems of drug abuse continue to plague the Russian military today.[17] Data from the Russian Ministry of Defense in spring 2000 reveal that 10 percent of conscripts in the ground forces and navy are drug addicts, and many of the crimes committed in the army are related to drugs or drug trafficking.[18]

Since the collapse of the Soviet Union, Russian organized crime has evolved by establishing connections with other international organized crime groups. As a result, new types of drugs have entered Russian markets, though the poppy-based drugs that flow from Central Asia and the Caucasus remain the most widespread. Synthetic drugs flow into Russia from the West and East alike, be it ephedrine from China and North Korea or ready-made synthetic drugs from Poland and the Netherlands.[19] Cocaine smuggled from Latin America, usually through Spain and the Baltic countries, is the most recent arrival, becoming a problem by 2005. Domestic production of synthetic drugs is also on the rise.[20]

Drug abuse trends in Russia have changed over the past decade: users are increasingly using intravenous drugs and starting at younger ages.[21] Six percent of 15- and 16-year-olds in Moscow are reported to have used heroin at least once. In Western Europe, the figure was never over 2 percent.[22]

Seventy thousand Russians were reported to have died as a result of drug use in 2003 alone.[23] The situation is only getting worse, because in Russia the spread of HIV/AIDS is closely connected to the drug problem. In fact, one can measure drug use in part by tracking rates of HIV/AIDS infection. Three-quarters of the people infected with HIV are intravenous drug users in the 17 to 30 age bracket.[24] A quarter-million HIV cases have been registered, but the real number is much higher. UNAIDS estimated the number of cases at one million in December 2003.[26] In 2002, the US National Intelligence Council estimated one to two million cases.[26] The epidemic has yet to reach its apogee, and, depending on its development, demographers predict that between five and nine million people will contract HIV in Russia by 2010. Nick Eberstadt estimates that if only two million people were affected, any anticipated improvement in life expectancy between 2000 and 2025 would be erased. Even in the case of a mild epidemic, the working-age population would be reduced by 15 percent, since the disease primarily affects young people.[27] Forty percent of recruits to military service are already sent home due to poor health, of whom 20 percent are drug users.[28]

## Transporting the drugs

Trains move most passengers and freight within Russia, and drug flows mainly follow these routes.[29] The highest concentrations of drug abuse are in the major cities along the Trans-Siberian Railroad: Vladivostok, Irkutsk, Yekaterinburg, and Moscow.[30] Additionally, St. Petersburg, a major city and transportation hub, is a center of drug abuse.

The railroad line that runs from Dagestan to Moscow transports large quantities of drugs that have arrived in Russia from the Caspian Sea. In using this line, the drug traffickers are exploiting the same routes used by the sturgeon and caviar traders who supply the lucrative markets of the capital.

The presence of drug addiction in remote regions of Russia indicates that there is a network within Russia that has developed the capacity to move drugs even to areas that are far from transportation hubs. Central to the spread of drugs nationwide are two different groups. Representatives of ethnic groups based in the Caucasus and Central Asia are heavily involved in the drug trade because they are linked to sources of supply through their home regions. Their crime networks help them distribute drugs throughout Russia. Also important are military personnel who serve on bases across Russia and are seeking additional sources of income to compensate for their meager salaries. Military transport planes are ideal for smuggling, since they take off from Russian military bases in the Caucasus and Central Asia without customs controls or passenger records. Likewise, they arrive in Russia without having to pass through the normal customs control system.

### Opiates

Afghanistan is the major source of heroin entering Russia, with Tajikistan serving as the major launching pad for smuggling toward Russia.[31] Afghan heroin is smuggled through Kyrgyzstan, Uzbekistan, and Kazakhstan, and the vast Russian–Kazakh border, with its limited border controls, is increasingly becoming an entry point for drugs into Russia.[32]

The most frequent initial route for Afghan heroin coming into Russia is through Tajikistan. When Russian troops were helping the Northern Alliance resist the Taliban in Afghanistan before the US-led invasion in 2001, Russia admitted the large-scale involvement of its troops in the drug trade.[33] The subsequent flow of drugs from Tajikistan to Russia proceeds with the complicity of very high-level officials in Tajikistan who have profited enormously from this trade.[34] The UN assistance program in the late 1990s to curtail the drug trade from Tajikistan may actually have exacerbated the problem by providing millions of dollars worth of sophisticated telecommunications equipment to these corrupt officials.[35]

Tajik paramilitary forces and high-level government officials forged links to the drug trade during Tajikistan's civil war of 1992–1997. Profits from the drug trade have built palaces for government officials in this poor country, both in the capital, Dushanbe, and in regional centers. Parliament speaker Mahmadsaid Ubaydollayev and former Drug Control Agency and President's Guard head Ghafor Mirzoyev (arrested in August 2004) are two of the most prominent officials accused of being involved in the drug trade.[36] Additionally, Kazakhstani authorities detained two Tajik diplomats, including the ambassador, with dozens of kilograms of heroin in 2000.[37]

Individual couriers and Russian military aircraft transport the bulk of the heroin from Tajikistan to Russia. Ethnic Tajik drug couriers carry small-scale shipments to Russia. Poorly paid Russian soldiers serving on the Russian–Tajik border use their planes to bring in much larger shipments.

From Tajikistan, many drugs flow through Kyrgyzstan's Osh region, which has become a major point for drug trafficking in Central Asia. In the late 1990s, the highway from Khorog, on Tajikistan's border with Afghanistan, to Osh was a major trafficking route. The interdiction efforts along this route led traffickers to transfer their operations to the so-called Batken route, linking northern Tajikistan through southwestern Kyrgyzstan to Osh. The Islamic Movement of Uzbekistan (IMU) helped open this route in the late 1990s, though it is unclear who has replaced the IMU after it was decimated in the 2001 war in Afghanistan.[38] From Osh, it seems that other actors move the drugs north through Uzbekistan's Ferghana Valley or through northern Kyrgyzstan toward Kazakhstan and Russia. These actors include Russian crime groups and local couriers, an increasing number of whom are women.[39]

Russia shares a 6,846-kilometer border with Kazakhstan, and in 1998 alone 80 percent of heroin, 84 percent of hashish, and 53 percent of marijuana intercepted coming into Russia was caught on the Russian–Kazakh border.[40] Most of the drugs enter Russia from Kazakhstan through 60 road crossings.[41] From Kazakhstan, opiates are trafficked through the Kurgan region to the Sverdlovsk, Chelyabinsk, and Tiumen regions, among others.[42] Research in Volgograd sponsored by the Transnational Crime and Corruption Center (TraCCC) revealed that this region adjoining Kazakhstan is increasingly a route for drug trafficking from Central Asia into Russia.[43]

Additionally, the Caspian Sea port of Astrakhan and the Black Sea port of

Novorossiisk are major transit points for Turkish and Afghan heroin into Russia.[44] Sea routes are important for trade even though land transport predominates.

It is an open question to what extent Turkmenistan is involved as a transshipment point to Russia. The isolationist policy of the country and its lack of regional and international cooperation in antinarcotics efforts make information from Turkmenistan scarce and unreliable. Turkmenistan's heroin seizures peaked at nearly 2 metric tons in 1997, by far the largest amount seized in Central Asia at the time. Similarly, 4.6 tons of opium was seized in 1999.[45] During 1995–2000, more than 198 tons of precursor chemicals were seized in the country, mostly acetic anhydride, used in the manufacture of heroin.[46] Since 2000, Turkmenistan has not provided data on drug seizures. The evidence at hand suggests that smuggling networks were built up in the country and that a substantial quantity of Afghan heroin did transit Turkmenistan.

Evidence from police cases in Western Europe has uncovered links to Turkmenistan in cases of heroin smuggling via Ukraine.[47] Numerous allegations from exiled former government officials point to high-level collusion with the drug trade.[48] A recent International Crisis Group report cites numerous eyewitnesses reporting government involvement in the drug trade from the lowest to the highest levels.[49]

The South Caucasus plays a less important role as a trafficking route of opiates today than it did in the past, according to analyses done in 2004–2005 by the Georgian border patrol.[50] The declining importance of this route is a significant change from earlier years when the Pankisi Gorge was an uncontrolled territory and was used as a transshipment point for drugs, and even contained laboratories for drug production staffed by foreign experts.[51] With military assistance from the US government, the Georgian government now has much greater control of this area. Nevertheless, Abkhazia, outside the control of the Georgian central government, is a transit point for cocaine and hashish arriving by sea intended for Russian markets.[523]

### Synthetic drugs and cocaine

There are two major sources of synthetic drugs (amphetamines and ecstasy) in Russia. German, Polish, and Dutch producers smuggle drugs into Russia from the west. Major entry points include the Polish–Russian border and through the enclave of Kaliningrad on the Baltic Sea. Russia is also integrated into the synthetic drug markets of the Far East, which are dominated by Chinese and Japanese crime groups and crime networks connected to the North Korean government.[53] The increase in synthetic drug flows from North Korea has coincided with reduced barriers to travel between the Russian Far East and North Korea.[54] LSD has also appeared in Russia, having been sent from the United States and European states.[55]

Cocaine is not consumed in significant quantities in Russia even though Russians serve as money launderers and aid in the cocaine trade out of Latin

America. Russian drug users generally prefer the relatively cheap narcotics from Central Asia to the more expensive white powder. [56] The market for cocaine is basically limited to affluent consumers in Moscow, who receive their supplies by air routes.

## Participants in the Russian drug trade

A diverse range of actors operate the drug trade within Russia, ranging from large-scale crime groups down to small groups of individuals.[57] The range of actors in the drug trade is similar to those involved in human smuggling in that there are both large and small groups.[58] This finding that a variety of group sizes were involved contradicts the work of Letizia Paoli, who found that there were no large-scale crime groups involved in the drug trade, only smaller network structures.[59]

The key actors in the Russian drug trade are non-Russian ethnic groups, particularly those from Central Asia and the Caucasus; ethnic Russian crime groups; and representatives of state agencies. We will discuss each of these actors in greater detail.

### *Ethnic communities*

Representatives of ethnic communities have been important actors in organized crime since Soviet times. In Russia, as in other parts of the world, diaspora communities that are cohesive and speak a common language generally incomprehensible to the residents of the host country are ideal bases for organized crime, since the ability of law enforcement to infiltrate such networks is highly limited. Moreover, the presence of co-ethnics across the entire former Soviet Union gives these groups an infrastructure that is particularly well suited for smuggling. Many representatives of the ethnic groups now involved in the drug trade have a long history of participating in the Soviet Union's underground economy and in organized crime activity.[60] In the period before the collapse of the Soviet Union, 40 percent of the thieves-in-law, the elite of the criminal underworld, were of Georgian origin, and the preponderance of this criminal elite were non-Slavic.[61] It is only natural that these groups, with such deep criminal traditions, continue to assume a major role in the Russian drug trade.

The ethnic-based organized crime groups involved in the drug trade include, but are not limited to, representatives from the Armenian, Azeri, Assyrian, Chechen, Georgian, Tajik, and Tatar communities. Obviously, such a clear segregation does not exist in reality, but is a useful aid in classifying the major crime groups. Members of these groups frequently cooperate across ethnic lines even when there are conflictual relations between the groups in general. For example, in food markets, which are often used as outlets for drug distribution, Armenian and Azeri criminals can cooperate, or at least work out a *modus vivendi*, even though these two ethnic groups are fighting over disputed territory.

Members of ethnic organized crime groups operate throughout Russia. Their links connecting drug-producing regions to distribution centers are essential for the operation of the drug trade. For example, Chechen crime groups in Khabarovsk purchased drugs in Central Asia and then marketed them to crime groups in the Far East, according to the US Drug Enforcement Agency.[62] Tajik illegal immigrants working in numerous Russian regions in the construction industry and other menial sectors of the economy often serve as couriers to supplement their incomes. Their role is reminiscent of the Mexicans who carry drugs while illegally crossing the US–Mexican border seeking work.[63]

### Russian organized crime groups

The Slavic-dominated crime groups, such as those working in Moscow, Yekaterinburg, and Siberia, are international actors. Their criminal activity is not confined to just the former Soviet states or Eastern Europe, but extends to Western Europe and links even into Latin America. Members of the organized crime groups residing abroad are key facilitators in the international movement of drugs.

Major Russian organized crime groups such as the Solntsevo group in Moscow and the Uralmash group in Yekaterinburg are known to be involved in the drug trade.[64] According to reliable American law enforcement sources, the Siberian crime group linked to Vyacheslav Kirillovich Ivankov, better known as "Yaponchik," had a base in Spain where he linked with Colombian crime groups. Semyon Mogilevich, a key Russian organized crime figure, operated out of Budapest and ran a diversified criminal operation that trafficked arms, drugs, and women in the mid-1990s.[65] The dimensions of his business became public knowledge as a result of the money-laundering investigations concerning the Bank of New York (see William Tompson's chapter, Chapter 9). Criminal investigators then tracked the money trail of his illicit operations.[66]

Of course, not all crime groups are involved in the drug trade. In the mid-1990s, the original crime groups that benefited from the privatizations of the early post-Soviet period began to pursue different activities. In the latter half of the 1990s, some of the crime groups preferred to concentrate their businesses in the legitimate sectors of the economy, whereas others moved progressively into the most criminal aspects of organized crime: drug trafficking and trafficking in women.

Moreover, the ethnic Russian and non-Russian groups do not always cooperate with each other. Whereas the Solntsevo group is ethnically mixed, the members of the Uralmash group are overwhelmingly Russian. The 2005 prison death of a major Uralmash crime figure in Yekaterinburg indicates that an enormous conflict is presently under way between the domestic Russian crime groups and non-Russian groups from the Caucasus and Central Asia which are trying to achieve dominance over the domestic Russian drug markets.[66]

Today, Russian and CIS groups no longer have the field to themselves. Increasingly, Russia is being integrated into the global drug market. Both Colombian and Nigerian groups are operating within Russia, providing drugs to local consumers.[67] Moreover, Nigerian trafficking organizations were recruiting Russian women as couriers by the late 1990s, according to analyses of the National Drug Intelligence Center. The women's nationality and gender made them less suspicious than African couriers.[68]

### State actors

The drug trade in Central Asia and Russia could not have reached its current proportions without the active participation of individuals in high bureaucratic and political posts. The problem is not simply individual corrupt soldiers or border guards willing to look the other way as drugs flow across the border, but entire bureaucratic subunits, implying the criminalization of parts of the state bureaucracy. Several parts of the Russian state are involved. The participation of military personnel is crucial. Moreover, the police, the border guards, and the customs service, possibly the most corrupted part of the Russian law enforcement community, are all deeply implicated in the burgeoning drug trade. When arrests are made, they are almost always limited to the lowest links of the drug chain, and few efforts have been made to target those involved in higher-level operations.

Even though Russian military and law enforcement personnel are involved, they do not participate in such an organized fashion as in Mexico, where key government officials are on the payroll of drug-trafficking organizations. Nevertheless, while Moscow officials have gathered detailed information on the drug operations of Afghan and Tajik immigrants in the Russian capital, including identifying centers for drug distribution, the authorities have made no efforts to stop this drug trade.

In Russia's case, the most deeply implicated in the drug trade are the members of the Russian military stationed on the Tajik border and in the area of the Chechen conflict.[69] Many soldiers are serious drug abusers because they serve under very difficult conditions in an environment in which drugs are widely available. These active duty personnel suffer from low wages, widespread demoralization, and extensive corruption. Since the soldiers are stationed throughout Russia, they have an enormous logistical advantage in selling drugs to customers located across the country. Because they can travel and transport goods without being subjected to customs or border controls, they are ideally suited to narcotics trafficking.

Apart from the Russian military, Russian border guards in Tajikistan are heavily involved in the drug trade. In 2004, several Russian border guards stationed in Tajikistan were arrested on charges of drug trafficking. In 2003, a warrant officer from the border guard service of the Russian Federal Security Service was caught with 12 kilograms of heroin, and later that year another warrant officer from the same service was caught with eight kilograms of heroin.[70]

Specialized units designated to fight organized crime and the drug trade have also engaged in trafficking. In January 2004, a former head of the antidrug unit was apprehended for the second time for heroin sales in Yekaterinburg. He had first been caught in spring 2001 and charged with participating in the heroin trade.[71] Also in January 2004, the Federal Security Service (FSB) arrested a police colonel serving as head of the unit combating organized crime in Vladivostok for attempting to sell 100 grams of heroin. The colonel was head of the department responsible for the infiltration of agents into crime groups trading in drugs.[72] In December 2003, FSB agents found 12 kilograms of heroin in the home of a police lieutenant-colonel they had just arrested.[73]

### Russian crime actors internationally

Drug traffickers are active throughout the CIS. For example, Chechens with ties across Russia have formed links with other Chechens who have lived in Central Asia since Stalin deported them there during World War II. Chechen crime groups in Kyrgyzstan and Kazakhstan, specifically the local Chechen group under Aziz Batukaev in Bishkek, are allegedly involved in drug trafficking to Russia.[74] In Kazakhstan, Chechen groups are particularly active in the areas adjoining the Russian border.[75] Unlike in Kyrgyzstan, they do not appear to clash with Kazakh gangs, but rather coexist peacefully. Russian crime groups work in tandem with corrupt law enforcement and security personnel from the neighboring countries of Kazakhstan and Uzbekistan. The presence of current and former law enforcement personnel from these countries in the drug rings makes it impossible to capture any members of the group, according to an FSB official.[76]

Russian crime figures also facilitate the international drug trade far beyond the former Soviet space. In addition to setting up their own supply lines, Russian criminals residing abroad use their knowledge and connections to provide services to other drug organizations, including skills that would not otherwise be available within that organization. An example of the Russian crime diaspora serving the Latin American drug organizations is the famous case of Ludwig Fainberg, aka "Tarzan." Fainberg, a known Russian crime figure according to Robert I. Friedman, opened a strip joint near the Miami International Airport. At this locale, frequented by Colombian drug traffickers, Fainberg discussed how he could help the Colombians purchase Russian military equipment.[77] One of the authors of this chapter interviewed the prosecutor working on this case, and was shown photographs that Fainberg provided to the prosecutors. These photographs, assembled during Fainberg's visits to military sites, revealed the range of sophisticated military equipment that he was attempting to buy for the Colombians. Fainberg's photographs reveal a man of thuggish appearance. There is little possibility from these photographs that the Russian admirals negotiating with Fainberg thought they were dealing with an honest businessman. Yet these top officials clearly meant to keep the proceeds for themselves, thereby accruing significant personal profits. Only the intervention of American law enforcers, with no help from their Russian counterparts, foiled the plot.

In another case, Colombian authorities found a submarine under construction in a remote location in Colombia. The instructions were in Russian, indicating that Russian technicians were helping the Colombians assembling it. The Colombian drug runners may have tried to build their own submarine after Fainberg was arrested before he could purchase the submarines from the Russian navy.[78]

Investigations by Colombian authorities and the US Drug Enforcement Administration (DEA) have revealed other important links between Russian and the Latin American drug traffickers. In the late 1980s, the DEA seized a villa in the south of France and a multimillion-dollar apartment in Paris that belonged to a Russian who laundered money for Colombian traffickers.[79] Other Russians have been implicated in laundering money for the Colombian drug cartels as well.

Around 2000, over a dozen Russians and Ukrainians were arrested on the Pacific Ocean while transporting cocaine for Latin American dealers to the United States. DEA investigations could not establish whether these were freelance criminals hired by the Colombians or whether this incident represented a more direct linkage with Russian organized crime groups.[80]

Russian crime groups also link with Chinese and Japanese groups to provide drugs to lucrative Asian markets. This trade may also go on in tandem with human trafficking.

## Drug trade and conflict: Chechnya and Tajikistan

In Russia, as in many other parts of the world, the drug trade is not only part of the illicit economy, but also linked to prolonging conflict and to terrorism. Narcotics are one of the major funding source for terrorism internationally.[81] Despite the centrality of drugs to the conflicts of greatest concern to Russia, the country has done little to address the narcotics trade as a source of terrorist funding. For example, the Chechen conflict gains support from a variety of funds, including international aid money, diversion of oil, kidnapping, and diaspora funding. Drugs are just one component of the funding for this conflict.[82] Nevertheless, Russia prefers to use its military force to handle the conflicts in Chechnya and in Tajikistan rather than to go after the financial resources that help fuel these conflicts.

Central to Russia's failure to address drugs as a funding source for terrorism is the corruption that permeates all levels of Russian society. Over the years of the Chechen conflict, Russian authorities have done little to crack down on Chechen involvement in the drug trade despite the fact that Russian law enforcement was aware that Chechen organized crime groups were providing funds to purchase arms and maintain insurgents. Russia's failure to address this major source of terrorist funding may make the country vulnerable to future attacks by Islamic fundamentalists who are operating in the CIS, and may find more support among Chechens after the killing of secular separatist president Aslan Maskhadov in March 2005.

Over the course of the 1990s, Chechnya became one of the largest suppliers of drugs to Russia, according to the Russian newspaper *Kommersant*.[83] Russian soldiers have played a big role in this trafficking.[84] In fact, Russian units have cooperated with Chechen separatist units in smuggling operations. Indeed, beyond drug trafficking, Russian forces have been involved in abducting civilians for ransom, selling arms to Chechen rebels, and smuggling oil and petroleum products produced in, or transiting through, the North Caucasus.[85] In some ways, the Chechen conflict has gradually been transformed from a military confrontation pitting two sides against each other into a criminal operation with cooperation across enemy lines. Russian troops under different commands (the Federal Security Service, Military Intelligence, the Army, or the Ministry of the Interior) fight some Chechen rebel groups while appearing to engage in smuggling operations with other groups.

This state of affairs may constitute part of the explanation why President Vladimir Putin is not altering the manifestly failing Chechnya policy: he is afraid to upset the ongoing profit-generating activities dear to the military leadership. The status quo endangers continued civilian control of the military in Russia as well as regional security.

The Russians in the late 1990s turned a blind eye to the drug dealing of the Northern Alliance, seeking to gain its support for the ouster of the Taliban, a tactic the Americans repeated after their 2001 invasion. Russian officials then tolerated the drug trade along the Afghan–Tajik border. The Northern Alliance relied on smuggling heroin for a large percentage of its income, and this trade was apparently deemed necessary in the greater strategic aim of preventing the Taliban militia from acquiring control over all of Afghanistan's territory. Moreover, Russian military aid to the Northern Alliance traversed the Afghan–Tajik border, allowing drugs to be transported along the same roads as the military assistance.

This trade allegedly not only benefited the local commanders of the Russian military, but enriched numerous high-ranking Russian officers. President Putin, upon coming to power in 2000, reportedly purged some of the general staff, as some generals were deeply implicated in this trade, which was spiraling out of control.[86] In spite of Tajikistan's distance from Russia and the difficult conditions for Russian troops there, it is reportedly the only posting that Russian officers compete for, indicating the potential for significant material gain.[87] An International Crisis Group report, analyzing the implications of the planned withdrawal of Russian border troops from the Tajik–Afghan border, states that Afghan narcotics traders are worried, as they fear they will lose their point of contact across the border.[88]

Russians are increasingly analyzing their drug problem, perceiving that it is affecting their national security by undermining military capacity, their labor force, and their national health, and contributing to a growing illicit economy. Although they blame the Chechen or Central Asian drug trade for funding terrorism, they have failed to address the complicity of Russian officials' role in this illicit business. The Russian authorities have so far failed to acknowledge that drug funding of conflicts is not just a problem in which others are working against Russian interests, but is sustained on Russian territory and abroad only with the active participation of Russian military and law enforcement, and with protection provided by government officials at all levels. The failure to address the link between terrorist funding and drugs within Russia will provide a growing source of funding for conflicts in the region and terrorist attacks against Russia.

## Conclusion

The Russian drug trade is a large and rapidly growing part of the illicit economy. Its consumers represent 2 to 4 percent of the Russian population, a large percentage of a national population in both absolute and comparative terms. The drug trade in Russia does not resemble the Mexican model, where several significant drug organizations control all the market.[89] Rather, the situation in Russia is more reminiscent of that in Colombia, where the assaults against the major drug cartels have left an enormous opening for a variety of both domestic and international drug traffickers.

The Russian situation also recalls the Colombian situation in that drug trafficking in many cases is used to finance violent nonstate actors, including separatist and terrorist movements.[90] Although the connections between insurgencies and the drug trade are not as strong in Russia as in Colombia, there is an important link in both areas between drugs and violent conflict. Organized crime, including drug trafficking, has been a factor prolonging the war in Chechnya, providing income and the motivation to continue fighting on both sides of the conflict.

The emergence of the enormous Russian drug market has been rapid. Furthermore, Russian drug users are no longer consuming cheap, local products, but imported drugs that are much more expensive. The enormous increase in revenues associated with the drug trade has been insufficiently analyzed within Russia. Little is known about the disposition of drug trade profits. We are only beginning to study how much is transferred overseas, how much is invested in the local economy, and what are the major means of laundering the increasing profits of the drug traffickers.

Much of Russian business survives only through strong and often highly corrupt links with the state. The same is true for the drug trade. Although corruption associated with major industrial sectors in Russia is at the ministerial level, corruption associated with the drug trade is linked more to corruption at lower levels of the bureaucracy in law enforcement, the military, and municipal and regional government. The impunity of corrupt officials has impeded the disruption of ties to the criminal community. The Russian legal response to the growing drug trade has been weak. Criminal prosecutions have targeted mainly the lowest level of the drug-trafficking chain. But in the absence of a large network analysis of the crime groups, their assets and organizations stay largely intact. Low-level ethnic drug couriers who cannot afford to pay bribes are convicted, while more important traffickers often evade sanctions.

Huge quantities of drugs cross the border without detection. Putin has acknowledged that the drug trade and widespread abuse are threats to national security. But drugs have not been integrated into the national security debate as has occurred in the United States and, to a lesser extent, in Europe. Narcotics flows have only recently been integrated into Russian–Kazakh talks, but are not a central part of Russia's foreign policy agenda.

The Russian state is weak vis-à-vis the drug trade. While it is trying to reestablish control over the Russian energy sector, it is failing to take a strong initiative in this area that poses such a serious and rapidly growing threat to its useful population. The corruption of the law enforcement system and even the newly created organs to combat the drug trade make it ever more difficult for the state to exert control over this growing share of the illegitimate economy. The collusion of politicians, bureaucrats, and organized crime in the drug arena further threatens the legitimacy of the state and the attractiveness of the business environment.

The drug trade intersects with the legitimate economy in many different ways. Drugs are transported through commercial flights, railroads, and civilian trucks. The profits of the drug trade enter the legitimate economy through the restaurants, nightclubs, and casinos operated by the crime groups. Some of its profits enter into the global economy as they are laundered through banks in Russia, the CIS, and international financial centers. Other money flows through the underground banking system and is integrated into the legitimate economies of other countries, particularly in Asia.

The rise of the Russian drug trade has had an enormous negative impact on legitimate business in Russia. The drug trade threatens the labor force because it disproportionately affects the young and the working-age population. The rise of HIV/AIDS, tuberculosis, and other diseases associated with the spread of drug use is having a significant demographic impact on a Russian population that is shrinking. The health costs to businesses and the loss of labor force capacity are an enormous drain on Russian competitiveness not sufficiently recognized by the state or the Russian business community.

## Notes

The authors would like to thank the Swedish Drug Policy Coordinator's Office for making this research possible and Maral Madi for research assistance.

1 Letizia Paoli, *Illegal Drug Trade in Russia*, Freiburg: Max-Planck-Institut für ausländisches und internationales Strafrecht, 2001, p. 83.
2 United National Office on Drugs and Crime, *United Nations World Drug Report 2005*, www.unodc.org/pdf/WDR_2005/volume_2_chap8_drugabuse.pdf, p. 365.
3 V. Cherkesov, "Otvechaet na voprosi glavnovo redaktora almankha 'Organizovannaya prestupnost', terrorizm, i korruptsiya', Professor V. V. Luneev," *Organizovannaia prestupnost', terrorizm, i korruptsiya*, no. 4, 2003, p. 8.
4 B. Tselinsky, "Sovremennaya narkosituatsiya v Rossii: Tendentsii i perspektivii," *Organizovannaia prestupnost, terrorizm, i korruptsiya* 4, 2003, p.21.
5 Based on the analysis of the Vladivostok branch of the Transnational Crime and Corruption Center, www.crime.vl.ru/docs/obzor/1104.htm, accessed 20 February 2005.

6 M. Iu. Semeniuk, "Problemy protivodeistviia nezakonnomu oborotu narkotikov v Primorskom krae," www.crime.vl.ru/docs, accessed 1 March 2005.
7 Tselinsky, "Sovremennaya narkotsituatsiya v Rossii," p. 23; Kairat Osmonaliev, *Developing Counter-narcotics Policy in Central Asia*, Washington, DC, and Uppsala: Silk Road Paper, Central Asia–Caucasus Institute and Silk Road Studies Program, 2005.
8 "Narkobiznes – ugroza natsional'noi bezopasnosti", press release, Federal Narcotics Control Service, 15 July 2003.
9 Vladimir Vorsobin, "Putin prizval bortsov s narkotikami rabotat' 'na polnuyu katushku,'" *Komsomol'skaya Pravda*, 31 March 2004.
10 V. Ignatov, "Korruptsiya – Osnova nezakonnovo oborota narkotikov," *Organizovannaia prestupnost, terrorizm, i korruptsiya* 4, 2003, p. 25.
11 Graham H. Turbiville Jr., *Mafia in Uniform: The Criminalization of the Russian Armed Forces*, Fort Leavenworth, KS: Foreign Military Studies Office, 1995; Scott P. Boylan, "Organized Crime and Corruption in Russia: Implications for U.S. and International Law," *Fordham International Law Journal* 19, 1999; Vladimir N. Brovkin, "Corruption in 20th Century Russia," *Crime, Law and Social Change* 40: 2, 2003, pp. 195–230; Peter Kneen, "Political Corruption in Russia and the Soviet Legacy," *Crime, Law and Social Change* 34: 4, 2000, pp. 349–367.
12 Cherkesov, "Otvechaet na voprosi ..." pp. 8–9. See also *The Economic Consequences of HIV in Russia*, Report for the World Bank Group, 15 May 2002; United States Department of State Bureau for International Narcotics and Law Enforcement Affairs, *International Narcotics Control Strategy Report 2005*, March 2005, www.state.gov/p/inl/rls/nrcrpt/2005/vol1/html/42368.htm, accessed March 16, 2005.
13 Mark Galeotti, "Russia's Drug Crisis," *Jane's Intelligence Review*, October 2003.
14 V. Nekrasov, "Vadim Tikunov," *Sovetskaiia Militsiia* 8, 1990, p. 22.
15 The homemade mixture of narcotics rose from 2 percent of all drug seizures in the early 1980s to 30 percent in the late 1990s. See interview with a Moscow police officer, "Esche raz o narkomanii," *Izvestiia*, 23 November 1987.
16 See Louise I. Shelley, *Policing Soviet Society: The Evolution of State Control*, London: Routledge, 1996, pp. 145–146.
17 K. Kharabet, "Narkotsituatsiya v vooruzhennikh silakh Rossii (sostayaniya, tendentsii izmeneniia, prichinii, i problemii effektivnosti borbi)," *Organizovannaia prestupnost, terrorizm, i korruptsiya* 4, 2003, pp. 70–82.
18 Frank Umbach, "Future Military Reform: Russia's Nuclear and Conventional Forces," Conflict Studies Research Centre/Defence Academy of the United Kingdom, D65, August 2002, pp. 7–8.
19 "Masshtaby ugrozy," press release, Federal Narcotics Control Service, 19 January 2004; A. V. Fedorov, "Narkomania v Rossii: Ugroza natsii," analytic report, working group in the Council on Foreign and Defense Policy, 2000, p. 6; Paoli, *Illegal Drug Trade*, p. 83.
20 United States Department of State Bureau for International Narcotics and Law Enforcement Affairs, *International Narcotics Control Strategy Report 2005*, March 2005, www.state.gov/p/inl/rls/nrcrpt/2005/vol1/html/42368.htm, (accessed 10 March 2005.
21 John Kramer, "Drug Abuse in Russia: Emerging Pandemic or Overhyped Diversion?" *Problems of Post-communism*, November/December 2003, pp. 12–27; Fedorov, "Narkomania v Rossii," p. 1.
22 Letizia Paoli, "The Development of an Illegal Market: Drug Consumption and Trade in Post-Soviet Russia," *British Journal of Criminology* 42, 2002, p. 23.
23 "FSN: V Rossii ot upotrebleniia narkotikov v minuvshem godu pogibli okolo 70 tysiach chelovek," ITAR-TASS, 3 June 2004.
24 William E. Butler, "Injecting Drug Use and HIV," in William Alex Pridemore, ed.,

*Ruling Russia: Law, Crime and Justice in a Changing Society*, Lanham, MD: Rowman & Littlefield, 2005, p. 208.

25  UNAIDS, "AIDS Epidemic Update 2003," December 2003, www.unaids.org/wad/ 2003/Epiupdate2003_en/Epi03_05_en.htm#P118_26729, (accessed July 2004).

26  U.S. National Intelligence Council, "The Next Wave of HIV/AIDS: Nigeria, Ethiopia, Russia, India, and China," September 2002, www.odci.gov/nic/ other_nextwaveHIV.html, accessed July 2004.

27  Nicholas Eberstadt, "The Future of AIDS," *Foreign Affairs* 81, no. 6, 2002, pp. 22–45; U.S.–Russia Working Group against HIV/AIDS, *On the Frontline of an Epidemic: The Need for Urgency in Russia's Fight against Aids*, New York: Transatlantic Partners Against Aids, 2003, p. 6.

28  Murray Feshbach, *Russia's Health and Demographic Crisis: Policy Implications and Consequences*, Washington, DC: Chemical and Biological Arms Control Institute, 2003.

29  Forty-eight percent of seizures occurred on trains; Paoli, *Illegal Drug Trade*, p. 77.

30  The Siberian city of Irkutsk has a particularly acute drug problem, according to the analyses of the TraCCC center there: T. M. Sudakova, "Narkoticheskaia prestupnost' nesovershennoletnykh kak chast' obshei problemy narkotizma," www.irkcenter. isea.ru/salt, (accessed 14 March 2005).

31  United States Department of State Bureau for International Narcotics and Law Enforcement Affairs, *International Narcotics Control Strategy Report 2005*, March 2005, www.state.gov/p/inl/rls/nrcrpt/2005/vol1/html/42368.htm.

32  S. Golunov, ed., *Narkotorgovlya cherez rossiisko-kazakhstanskuyu granitsu: Vyzov i problemii protivodestviya*, no. 1, 2004; Osmonaliev, *Developing Counter-narcotics Policy in Central Asia.*

33  Personal communication to authors, international drug control official.

34  Johan Engvall, *Stability and Security in Tajikistan: Drug Trafficking as a Threat to National Security*, Uppsala: Working Paper 86, Department of East European Studies, January 2005.

35  United States Department of State Bureau for International Narcotics and Law Enforcement Affairs, *1998 International Narcotics Control Strategy Report*, 26 February 1999, www.hri.org/docs/USSD-INCSR/1998/Europe/Tajikistan.html, accessed 15 March 2005.

36  Sanobar Shermatova, "Kto zakazal arest Atovulloeva," *Moscow News*, no. 29, 2001; "Tajikistan Capital's Mayor Involved in Drug Business," *Pravda*, 30 July 2001, english.pravda.ru/main/2001/07/30/11317.html, accessed July 2004; Maureen Orth, "Afghanistan's Deadly Habit," *Vanity Fair,* 1 March 2002; "Tajik President Reappoints Former Head of Drug Control Agency," *BBC Global Newswire*, 9 August 2004.

37  "Tajik Ambassador's Car Used in Drug Smuggling," *Agence France Presse*, 22 May 2000.

38  The IMU is an Uzbek-origin extremist Islamic group, tracing its roots back to an Islamic uprising in the Ferghana Valley in 1991. After being evicted from Uzbekistan in 1992, its members joined the Tajik civil war on the side of the Islamic opposition, but left Tajikistan for Afghanistan after the Tajik peace treaty in 1997. In Afghanistan, IMU leaders developed close ties to Al-Qaida and later joined forces with Osama Bin Laden's troops in the last stand at Kunduz against coalition forces. Subsequently, the IMU has disintegrated into smaller groups that have conducted several terrorist attacks on the territory of Uzbekistan. The IMU was responsible for car bombings in the city of Tashkent and has been active in the Ferghana Valley (see Center for Defense Information, "In the Spotlight: Islamic Movement of Uzbekistan," 25 March 2002, www.cdi.org/terrorism/imu.cfm).

39  Osmonaliev, *Developing Counter-narcotics Policy in Central Asia*, pp. 16–23.

40  A. V. Fedorov, "Narkomania v Rossii," p. 5.

41 "Territoriya URFO – Perevalochnaya baza dlya dostavki narkotikov," press release of FSN, 12 November 2003, p. 2.
42 "Territoria URFO – perevalochnaya baza dlya dostavki narkotikov," press release of FSN, 12 November 2003.
43 Golunov, Narkotorgovlya cherez rossiisko-kazakhstanskuyu granitsu.
44 United States Department of State Bureau for International Narcotics and Law Enforcement Affairs, *International Narcotics Control Strategy Report 2003,* www.state.gov/g/inl/rls/nrcrpt/2003/vol1/html/29838.htm, accessed 20 November 2003, p. 2.
45 *The Drug and Crime Situation in Central Asia: Compendium Analysis,* Regional Office for Central Asia United Nations Office on Drugs and Crime, 2003.
46 United Nations Office of Drug Control and Crime Prevention (ODCCP), *Illicit Drugs Situation in the Region Neighboring Afghanistan and the Response of ODCCP,* New York, November 2002, p. 13, www.unodc.org/pdf/afg/afg_drug-situation_2002-10-01_1.pdf. Some Central Asian countries have their own large chemical industries, which makes it possible to divert chemicals required for manufacturing heroin. During 1995–1998, 77.6 tons of precursor chemicals were seized in Uzbekistan.
47 Personal communication to authors.
48 Rustem Safronov, "Turkmenistan's Niyazov Implicated in Drug Smuggling," *Eurasianet,* 29 March 2002; Alec Appelbaum, "Turkmen Dissident Accuses Niyazov of Crimes," *Eurasianet,* 26 April 2002; "Russia Turns its Back on Turkmenbashi," *Gazeta.ru,* 27 May 2003.
49 International Crisis Group, *Cracks in the Marble: Turkmenistan's Failing Dictatorship,* January 2003; Safronov, "Turkmenistan's Niyazov."
50 The Caucasus has been affected by the drug trade primarily because of the weakness of the states of the region, and their location along both major smuggling routes from Afghanistan to Europe: the so-called Iranian/Balkan and Northern routes. The Caucasus is where the two main routes meet, and the chief area where smuggling on these two routes intersects. Some of the drugs transiting the South Caucasus head from the Iranian border across Azerbaijan to Dagestan for transport farther into Russia, whereas some are trafficked to Georgia and on to Central Europe. The drugs being trafficked are both heroin and raw opium, the latter being significant since it likely originated from Iran whereas drugs coming from Central Asia are typically in the form of heroin. (*Yeni Musavat* (Baku), 13 May 2003, p. 2.) A second point of entry appears to be the border between Iran and the Armenian-occupied territories of Azerbaijan, from where drugs transit Armenia toward Georgia, or possibly into Russia by airplane. Azerbaijani sources have increasingly accused the separatist Nagorno-Karabakh government of complicity in the drug trade (see, for example, *Zerkalo,* 20 July 2002, p. 11), and have even submitted a motion to the Parliamentary Assembly of the Council of Europe on this matter (stars.coe.fr/documents/workingdocs/doc02/edoc9444.htm, January 2004). Finally, the Azerbaijani exclave of Nakhichevan has long been cited as a major transit point for drugs. From Iran, opiates enter Nakhichevan headed primarily for Turkey and the traditional Balkan route.
 The main known artery of the Northern route through Tajikistan does not involve the Caucasus. The Caucasus nevertheless does factor into smuggling from Turkmenistan. Most of the heroin that transits Georgia, and a substantial part of that transiting Azerbaijan, comes to the Caucasus from across the Caspian Sea, meaning from Turkmenistan and, in some cases, from Uzbekistan through Kazakhstan. Shipments reach the ports of Derbent, Kaspiysk, and Makhachkala in Dagestan, from where a portion veers north toward other parts of the Russian Federation and Eastern Europe. The remainder transits Dagestan, Chechnya, or South Ossetia into Georgia and then on to the ports of Poti, Batumi in Ajaria, or Sukhumi in Abkhazia, headed to Central Europe. Drug shipments from Turkmenistan also enter the South Caucasus directly at the Azerbaijani port of Sumgait, north of Baku. The high quality of the drugs

apprehended occasionally in Sumgait contrasts with the lower quality of those cross-ing over from Iran at Astara. These seizures provide further evidence that the drugs crossing through Sumgait are produced in Afghanistan itself, and could reflect that criminal groups involved in this segment of the trade are likely more sophisticated (especially in terms of the political–criminal nexus) than those groups that engage in complex cross-country trafficking. (See, for example, *BBC Monitoring*, 4 August 2001, quoting ANS TV, Baku, 1600 GMT, 3 August 2001 regarding the seizure of over 1 kilogram of high-quality heroin.)

51  Statement by Georgian police specialist on police records at TraCCC–Georgia confer-ence, 8 March 2005.

52  Alexandre Kukhianidze, Alexandre Kupatadze, and Roman Gotsirdize, *Smuggling through Abkhazia and Tskhinvali Region of Georgia*, Tbilisi: TraCCC GO, 2004, p. 34.

53  A. I. Rolik, "O sostoianii narkotsituatsii v Primorskom krae i perspektivakh mezh-dunarodnogo nauchno-prakticheskogo sotrudnichestvo so stranami ATR i severo-vostochnoi Azii v bor'be s organizovannoi narkoprestupnostiu," www.crime.vl.ru/docs/stats/tseminar2003/t_9.htm, (accessed 21 February 2005).

54  Semeniuk, "Problemy protivodeistviia nezakonnomu oborotu narkotikov..."

55  Fedorov, "Narkomania v Rossii," p. 6.

56  United States Department of State Bureau for International Narcotics and Law Enforcement Affairs, *International Narcotics Control Strategy Report 2005*, March 2005, http://www.state.gov/p/inl/rls/nrcrpt/2005/vol1/html/42368.htm, (accessed March 16, 2005).

57  See, for example, Guy Dunn, "Major Mafia Gangs in Russia," in Phil Williams, ed., *Russian Organized Crime: The New Threat?* London: Frank Cass, 1997, pp. 63–87; Dimitri de Kochko and Alexandre Datsekitch, *L'Empire de la drogue*, Paris: Hachette, 1994; and Observatoire Géopolitique des Drogues, *Géopolitique des Drogues 1995*, Paris: La Découverte, 1995.

58  Robert Orttung and Louise Shelley, "Russia's Efforts to Combat Human Trafficking: Efficient Crime Groups versus Irresolute Societies and Uncoordinated States," in William Alex Pridemore, ed., *Ruling Russia: Law, Crime and Justice in a Changing Society*, Lanham, MD: Rowman & Littlefield, 2005.

59  Paoli, Illegal Drug Trade in Russia.

60  Arkadii Vaksberg, *The Soviet Mafia*, New York: St. Martin's Press, 1991.

61  Giorgi Glonti and Givi Lobzhanidze, *Vory v zakone*, www.traccc.cdn.ge/ publica-tions/index.html, (accessed 10 March 2005).

62  Interview with Drug Enforcement Administration analyst specializing in post-Soviet crime groups in the drug area, January 2005.

63  Based on research presently being supported by TraCCC in Moscow and Irkutsk.

64  Dunn, "Major Mafia Gangs in Russia," and interviews with TraCCC researchers in Yekaterinburg.

65  Louise Shelley, "Transnational Crime: The Case of Russian Organized Crime and the Role of International Cooperation in Law Enforcement," *Demokratizatsiya*, Winter 2002, pp.49–67.

66  No author, "Ural'skii bespredel," *Argumenty i Fakty* no. 6, 2005.

67  A. N. Sukharenko, "Transnatsionalizatsiia narkobiznesa v Rossii," in V. A. Nomokonov, ed., *Problemy borb'by s proiavleniami kriminal'nogo rynka*, Vladivos-tok: Far Eastern State University Press, 2005, pp. 242–247.

68  Louise Shelley was shown network charts based on seizures of passports and arrests of personnel for Nigerian organizations on a visit to the National Drug Intelligence Center in the late 1990s.

70  Turbiville, *Mafia in Uniform*; also Dale R. Herspring, "The Continuing Disintegration of the Russian Military," in Michael H. Crutcher, ed., *The Russian Armed Forces at the Dawn of the Millennium*, Carlisle Barracks, PA: Center for Strategic Leadership,

2000, pp. 133–146, www.carlisle.army.mil/usacsl/new_site/publications/RW. pdf; Orth, "Afghanistan's Deadly Habit"; Jean-Christophe Peuch, "Central Asia: Charges Link Russian Military to Drug Trade," *RFE/RL Weekday Magazine*, 8 June 2001; *Moskovskiie Novosti*, 29 May 2001; Martha Olcott and Natalia Udalova, *Drug Trafficking on the Great Silk Road*: The Security Environment in Central Asia, Working Paper 11, Washington, DC: Carnegie Endowment for International Peace, 2000.

70  "V Tajikistane zaderzhan rossiyskiy pogranichnik s 12 kg geroina," *Interfax*, 5 May 2004.

71  "Za torgovlyu narkotikami zaderzhan byvshiy nachal'nik," *Noviy Region*, 27 January 2004.

72  "Polkovnika militsii poimali na torgovle geroinom," cry.ru, 9 January 2004 (accessed 20 October 2004).

73  "V Ekaterenburge zaderzhan podpolkovnik militsii," cry.ru, 29 December 2003 (accessed 20 October 2004).

74  See Gulnoza Saidazimova, "Kyrgyzstan: Criminal Kingpins Thriving in Prisons," *Eurasia Insight*, 4 November 2004.

75  Communication to authors from Central Asian drug control officials, Bishkek, May 2005.

76  "Nizhegorodskaya oblast prevratilas' iz tranzitnoi v potreblyayushyuyu," cry.ru, 31 March 2004.

77  Robert I. Friedman, *Red Mafiya: How the Russian Mob Has Invaded America*, Boston, MA: Little, Brown, 2000.

78  Robert I. Friedman, "Land of the Stupid: When You Need a Used Russian Submarine, Call Tarzan," *The New Yorker*, 10 April 2000.

79  An author of this chapter interviewed an officer of the US Marshal Service who was responsible for the seizure of these assets and their placement for sale with Sotheby's realty division.

80  Interview by one of the chapter's authors in 2002.

81  Rachel Ehrenfeld, *Evil Money: Encounters along the Money Trail*, New York: Harpers Business, 1992.

82  Paul Murphy, *The Wolves of Islam: Russia and the Faces of Chechen Terror*, Washington, DC: Brassey, 2004, pp. 134–156; and Yuri Andrienko and Louise Shelley, "Crime, Violence and Political Conflict in Russia," in Paul Collier and Nicholas Sambanis, eds., *Understanding Civil War: Evidence and Analysis*, vol. 2: *Europe, Central Asia, and Other Regions*, Washington, DC: World Bank, 2005, pp. 93–95.

83  Olga Allenova and Pavel Roshchen, "Shamil Basayev byl direktorom shkoly," Kommersant, 4 March 2000.

84  For a discussion of their activities, see Murphy, *The Wolves of Islam*, pp. 69–70, 136–137.

85  Stephen Shenfield, "Chechnya at a Turning Point," *Brown Journal of World Affairs* 8, no. 1, Winter–Spring 2001, pp. 63–71; "Russian Journalist Accuses Federal Troops of Exploiting Chechen Oil Plants," *BBC Monitoring*, 29 June 2001.

86  Western intelligence source, communication to author, 2003.

87  Orth, "Afghanistan's Deadly Habit."

88  International Crisis Group, *Tajikistan's Politics: Confrontation or Consolidation*, Dushanbe and Brussels: International Crisis Group Asia Briefing, 19 May 2004, p. 17.

89  "Prison Killings Spur City's Crisis," www.eluniversal.com.mx/pls/impreso/noctica. html?id_nota+96198&tabla=miami, 16 March 2005, (accessed 16 March 2005).

90  Tamara Makarenko, "Terrorism and Transnational Organised Crime: the Emerging Nexus," *Transnational Violence and Seams of Lawlessness in the Asia-Pacific: Linkages to Global Terrorism*, Honolulu: Asia-Pacific Center for Strategic Studies, 2004; Kimberley Thachuk, "Transnational Threats: Falling through the Cracks?" *Low Intensity Conflict and Law Enforcement* 10, no. 1, 2001; Sabrina Adamoli, Andrea Di Nicola, Ernesto Sarona, and Paula Zoffi, *Organized Crime around the World*,

Helsinki: HEUNI, 1998; Barbara Harris-White, *Globalization and Insecurity: Political, Economic and Physical Challenges,* Basingstoke, UK: Palgrave, 2002; Ivelaw L. Griffith, "From Cold War geopolitics to post-Cold War Geonarcotics," *International Journal* 30, no. 2, 1993–1994, pp. 1–36; R. Matthew and G. Shambaugh, "Sex, Drugs, and Heavy Metal: Transnational Threats and National Vulnerabilities," *Security Dialogue* 29, 1998, pp. 163–175.

# 11 Uncharted territory

## Russian business activity in Abkhazia and South Ossetia

*Erik R. Scott*

While the Soviet Union, one of the most highly militarized states in world history, may have met a relatively peaceful end, the violence and profound instability generated by its demise continues to afflict residents of the South Caucasus. Each of the three nations composing the South Caucasus – Armenia, Azerbaijan, and Georgia – faces entrenched, low-intensity conflicts that threaten its territorial integrity, sap national resources, and contribute to the criminalization of the region's economy by fostering widespread contraband trade. These conflicts have also resulted in the displacement of large numbers of persons, straining these newly independent nations and making their position all the more precarious.

Perhaps most notably, these conflicts have led to situations of *de facto* sovereignty for ethnic groups that sought separation from the socialist republics to which they once officially belonged. After a string of military victories in the early 1990s, Nagorno-Karabakh, which has an ethnic Armenian majority, gained *de facto* independence from Azerbaijan. At the same time, Abkhazia and South Ossetia effectively seceded from Georgia. In an effort to consolidate power and gain legitimacy, secessionist leaders established parliaments, issued passports and visas, and printed postage stamps. Yet while these "statelets"[1] acquired many of the trappings of sovereignty, they continued to lack international recognition and, on most maps, are included as part of the countries they hoped to leave. Most of these areas have instituted cease-fire agreements, though sporadic bursts of violence test the residents. The situation is one neither of full-scale war, nor of stable and lasting peace.[2]

The unresolved nature of these conflicts has broad implications for stability in the area, particularly in the regional context of low state capacity, economic impoverishment, high rates of organized crime and corruption, and continued conflict in nearby Chechnya. Although *de facto* governments have established authority in these statelets, their unofficial status makes them legal "gray zones" that effectively exist in uncharted territory beyond the jurisdiction of recognized governmental bodies. The distinction between these statelets and the recognized states of the region has economic implications as well. The statelets' murky status means that they are not only uncontrolled politically, but unregulated by the global financial system as well.

The authorities of these statelets depend on largely unregulated economic activity for their survival.[3] While Nagorno-Karabkah needs economic contacts with Armenia and donations from diaspora Armenians, Abkhazia and South Ossetia rely on economic ties to Russia and revenue from unregulated trade with Georgia.[4]

The continued economic involvement of Russian businesses in Abkhazia and South Ossetia constitutes the main source of economic sustenance and political legitimacy for the regimes in place there. The interests of the economic actors involved in this activity – ranging from petty traders to politically connected investors to organized crime groups – must be taken into account when considering efforts at conflict resolution. Russia's inability, or unwillingness, to crack down on unregulated economic activity with the statelets along its borders occurs in the context of tacit political support for the secessionists, despite Russia's claim to be a neutral mediator in these conflicts.

This examination of the activity of Russian businesses in Abkhazia and South Ossetia helps illuminate the themes of this book in several ways. First, the theoretical question of whether Russian businesses promote cooperation or foster conflict has very real consequences in the context of these unresolved conflicts, which occasionally become violent. Second, this study will allow us to look comparatively at licit and illicit business activity in relatively detailed terms. Finally, an analysis of Russian business activity in these statelets provides valuable insight for understanding Russian business behavior in a largely unregulated environment where it is free to behave as it pleases.

This chapter proceeds by first examining Russian state interests in the South Caucasus. It then examines how Russian business and state interact in the context of Abkhazia and South Ossetia. Next, the chapter provides a detailed study of the various goods being smuggled through the separatist regions and their links to Russian business. The analysis makes a distinction between licit (fruits, nuts, etc.) and illicit (weapons, drugs) goods. The concluding section examines the role of Russian business in conflict and cooperation, arguing that the legalization of trade in licit goods could provide a basis for future cooperation, while continued smuggling of illicit goods would undermine stability in the region.

## Economic empire building in the South Caucasus

In contemporary Georgia, as in the rest of the South Caucasus, Russia's foreign policy goals are multifaceted. Russia strives to maintain a military foothold in the region, cooperating closely with Armenia, seeking stronger ties with Azerbaijan, and, until recently, stalling on the removal of its military bases from Georgia.[5] Russia also seeks to minimize outside involvement in the region. Efforts by the United States and European countries to expand their influence in the South Caucasus and the growing political and economic influence of Turkey, one of Russia's traditional rivals in the region, creates feelings of insecurity for Russian policy makers. Russia has been particularly concerned with the construction of major oil and gas pipelines running through Georgia from east to west (and thus avoiding Russian territory), as well as by the recent US efforts to train and equip Georgian soldiers.

In this context, Russian licit and illicit businesses seek to maintain and expand their presence in the South Caucasus, sometimes with the tacit support of the Russian state. As will be discussed, these businesses not only seek profit, but can be mobilized as an instrument of Russian foreign policy.

The economies of Georgia and Russia – both formal and informal – are closely linked, thanks largely to Soviet-era trade and transport networks. Russia is Georgia's largest trade partner, a trend that is likely to continue in the near future despite the expansion of Turkish economic activity in the region. Even though Russia requires Georgians to obtain visas when it does not make this demand of other Commonwealth of Independent States (CIS) citizens, an estimated 500,000–700,000 Georgians work in Russia, and many Georgian families depend on the monetary remittances sent from relatives employed in the north. It has been estimated that these remittances could total $1.5 billion annually, almost one-quarter of Georgia's GDP.[6] Russia's economic clout in Abkhazia and South Ossetia is greater still. Although internationally Russia's economy is relatively small, it towers over the struggling South Caucasus markets. Russian economic activity is further facilitated by Soviet-era contacts and first-hand knowledge of the region among Russian businesspeople.

Although Russia was slow to relinquish its bases in Georgia, it increasingly relies on economic, rather than military, leverage to achieve its foreign policy objectives in the post-Soviet space. In September 2003, Anatoly Chubais, an influential figure in Russian politics and head of the massive electric monopoly Unified Energy System (UES), outlined a platform for Russia's "liberal empire." In an opinion piece published in Russia's *Nezavisimaia gazeta,* Chubais wrote that Russia is a "natural and unique leader" in the region, and that only by combining liberal values with a program to reestablish its empire can Russia "occupy its natural place alongside the United States, the European Union, and Japan, the place designated for it by history."[7] The announcement was particularly interesting because it followed UES's acquisition of Tbilisi's electricity grid and discussion by the company of a Caucasus-wide energy network.[8] Despite frequently being described as Russia's "most unpopular man," Chubais managed to remain a powerful player throughout the Yeltsin era and under Putin as well. His call for empire was supported by Russia's Eurasianists, a group led by Aleksandr Dugin that seeks the development of pan-Eurasian political, cultural, and economic structures.

In some ways, Chubais's proposal is reminiscent of the model of "informal empire" perfected by the British in the nineteenth and twentieth centuries, famously described as "trade with informal control if possible; trade with rule if necessary."[9] Seen in the global context, Russia's shift makes sense. While the international community views military intervention as destabilizing and dangerous, it considers economic influence exerted through the private sector as a more appropriate means of achieving foreign policy goals.

## Russian businesses' tangled ties to the state

Although Georgian president Mikheil Saakashvili has had a rocky relationship with Moscow, Russian economic involvement in Georgia has expanded during his tenure. In April 2005, Georgian prime minister Zurab Nogaideli announced that trade turnover between Russia and Georgia had increased by 90 percent since 2003.[10] While Saakashvili and his allies once criticized former president Eduard Shevardnadze's economic deals with Russia, upon coming to power they have pushed for increased Russian investment and Russian participation in Georgian privatization efforts, albeit on terms more favorable to the Georgian state. Saakashvili's appointment of Russian-based tycoon Kakha Bendukidze to the post of State Minister for Economic Reforms was a sign to many that Tbilisi hoped to facilitate closer ties with Russian investors.

Although Georgia is in desperate need of investment, there are inherent risks that accompany such a strategy stemming from the complex relationship between Russian businesses and the Russian state. It is impossible to completely disaggregate the interests of these businesses from those of the state, owing to what Peter Rutland has referred to as the "interpenetration of state and economy."[11] Under Putin, Russian businesses have increasingly come to operate in an atmosphere that encourages close alignment with both the official and the tacit goals of the state. In the case of the South Caucasus, Russian businesses and the Russian state see a mutual interest in projecting their influence in what Russian policy makers often refer to as the "near abroad." The blending of public and private interests in Russia does not make it fruitful to ask whether the state drives business interests, or the other way around. Instead, it is more useful to look at the interdependent relationship between the state and business in determining and implementing policy.

In his chapter (Chapter 2), Robert Orttung suggests that we can best understand business–state relations by looking at the degree of business community coherence and state strength. In the case of Russian business involvement in Abkhazia and South Ossetia, we are speaking of an amorphous business community with multiple actors who do not have a high degree of coordination. This trend is apparent in the sectoral discussion of Russian business activity below. As for the state, it can be described as weak, with a few important qualifications.

The first qualification is that, while the Russian federal government does not play a major role in regulating cross-border economic activity with these statelets, Russian business activity in Abkhazia and South Ossetia includes economic actors who are connected to strong political actors at the regional level in Moscow City and the Krasnodar region.[12] Despite Putin's efforts to centralize power away from the regions into the Kremlin, regional governments still have lots of autonomy, and even pursue their own policies in violation of the country's laws. One example is Moscow mayor Yury Luzhkov, whose rule is based on an estimated 150 extrabudgetary funds that according to federal law are supposed to be used for charity, but are in fact often used as capital for investments in private companies, banks, and other economic enterprises.[13] To a large extent, the city of Moscow also conducts its own foreign economic relations which seem to escape the Kremlin's oversight. The city of Moscow's partners abroad include ten members of the CIS and Lithuania, as well as unrecognized political entities including Abkhazia and Transdniestria.[14] Other Russian regions, particularly the Krasnodar region, have economic relations with Georgia's separatist statelets. The existence of these foreign economic relations at the regional level makes direct control by the Kremlin an elusive goal.

Second, while it is questionable whether the Russian state has the capacity to regulate economic activity with Georgia's separatist regions over the long term, Russia's effective enforcement of the blockade of Abkhazia for several days in December 2004, following disputed elections in the statelet, leads one to wonder whether Russia is perhaps unwilling – rather than unable – to regulate economic exchange effectively.

It is important to recall that the scale of Russian economic activity in Abkhazia and South Ossetia is extremely small relative to the size of the Russian economy. Most of the Russian businesses involved would be classified as small and medium-sized enterprises, and, as Orttung has shown, it is more difficult to analyze how the Russian state relates to businesses of this size. Thus, Russian economic involvement in these areas is characterized by a fundamental asymmetry in which a few Russian rogue actors have a major economic impact, even though these actors do not always represent large business interests. However, the Russian government's inability or unwillingness to stop them negatively affects the situation in Georgia. The Russian central government is likely aware of much of the economic activity at the regional level, but has largely not responded. If one assumes that Russia pursues a tacit policy of support for these statelets, then there might be political advantages in selectively maintaining low state capacity along the country's southern borders. According to this line of reasoning, it would seem that the Russian state lowers or raises the barrier to unregulated economic activity with these statelets on the basis of its own political self-interest, managing instability for its own benefit.

Russia essentially has it both ways, claiming officially to back Georgian territorial integrity while allowing some Russian small businesses to support separatist regimes, asserting, when necessary, that the businesses have no ties to the state or Russia's political leadership. The main advantage of using these economic agents to achieve foreign policy goals is that the small businesses, though linked to the state, are not as easily held accountable by the international community. The lack of transparency, corruption, and the presence of organized crime that characterize much of the Russian economy make international regulation of these economic actors even more difficult.

## Sustaining unrecognized statelets: political and economic support from Moscow

Russian economic and political support is essential to the sustenance of the *de facto* authorities in Abkhazia and South Ossetia. The fact that the economies of both entities are based on the Russian ruble is indicative of their reliance on tacit economic and political support from Russia. Without access to Russia's markets and the tourist industry, Abkhazia's economy would face imminent collapse. Russian military bases in the territory also do much to keep the economy afloat by providing thousands of jobs for the surrounding population. Similarly, the Roksky tunnel, which links breakaway South Ossetia with North Ossetia and the Russian market, provides vital business to the south. Russian border guards at the North Ossetian checkpoint in Nizhnii Zaramag estimate that 700–800 vehicles pass in both directions through the tunnel every day. According to estimates, trucks carry millions of dollars worth of contraband goods across the Russian–South Ossetian border each year.[15] The post already contends with twice as much traffic than it is equipped to handle, which may partly explain why some goods enter South Ossetia undetected. From a purely technical standpoint, however, the tunnel would be fairly easy to control if Russian authorities in North Ossetia were willing to allocate the resources to do so. Thus, it seems more a problem of political will than of law enforcement capacity.

Russian economic support of the separatist statelets is greatly facilitated by links between the separatist leadership and Moscow's business and political elite. Through former Abkhazia president Vladislav Ardzinba, who was closely tied to key figures within the Soviet, and later Russian, military establishment, Abkhazia's ruling circles had a direct connection to members of the Russian leadership in Moscow. During his tenure as deputy in the USSR's Supreme Soviet, Ardzinba was a close associate of Anatoly Lukianov, then the parliamentary chairman and reportedly the ideologue behind the hardliners' coup that sought to remove Gorbachev from power in August 1991.[16] Through Lukianov, Ardzinba forged ties with conservative members of Russia's military and political elite.

When Abkhazia held elections in 2004 to determine Ardzinba's successor and opposition figure Sergei Bagapsh unexpectedly gained a majority of the votes, Moscow intervened, cutting off all economic links with the breakaway statelet until a Russian-sponsored power-sharing deal was brokered to include former prime minister Raul Khajimba, the candidate favored by Ardzinba and Moscow, into the government. Russia's actions clearly revealed its economic clout in the breakaway republic and its willingness to use economic measures as a tool of foreign policy.[17]

The current *de facto* leader of South Ossetia holds a Russian passport and is referred to as either Eduard Kokoev or Eduard Kokoity (the former being a Russified variant of an Ossetian family name). In the past, Kokoity was heavily involved in Russia's business community, living in Moscow until returning home to head the breakaway republic in 2001. Under Kokoity's rule, an estimated 90 percent of South Ossetia's residents have received Russian citizenship, stoking fears in Tbilisi that Russia might have a case for future intervention in the statelet on behalf of its new citizens. The figure is likely similar for Abkhazia, where the majority of residents have chosen to accept Russia's offer of citizenship. Kokoity has repeatedly called for the incorporation of South Ossetia into the Russian Federation, and has discussed this issue with members of the

Russian Duma. Kokoity is also a major supporter of the pro-Putin United Russia party. In the March 2004 Russian presidential elections, it was reported that 99 percent of South Ossetia's residents voted for Putin, obviously a heavily inflated figure generated no doubt thanks to Kokoity's enthusiastic support for the Russian president.[18] In the lead-up to the elections, huge portraits of Putin hung from the major public buildings in Tskhinvali, South Ossetia's capital, bearing the slogan "Putin is our president."[19] It is difficult, however, to tell how much real popular support Putin has in either South Ossetia or Abkhazia. In sporadic fighting still prevalent along the cease-fire lines between Georgia and the separatist statelet, Russian political figures lend rhetorical support to the *de facto* authorities. It has been alleged that such rhetorical support may be complemented by military support for the *de facto* regime in the form of weaponry and possibly Cossack mercenaries.[20]

The leaders of breakaway Abkhazia and South Ossetia hold frequent meetings with Russia's leadership in Moscow. Since Shevardnadze's ouster as Georgian president in 2003, they have increasingly sought to enhance ties with Russia, fearing that Tbilisi will attempt to reassert its control in the statelets. Shortly after Shevardnadze left office, South Ossetian leader Kokoity, Abkhazian former prime minister Khajimba, and former Adjarian[21] leader Aslan Abashidze held talks with Igor Ivanov, then serving as Russian foreign minister, behind closed doors. Asked about the meeting, held in late November 2003, Kokoity said that "economic issues" were discussed.[22]

Finally, ties between the separatist leaders and Moscow are evidenced by the fact that they could likely seek refuge in the Russian capital if forced from power. Abashidze's ouster as head of Adjaria, another region that sought to leave Georgia, appeared to have been partially negotiated by Igor Ivanov, acting in his new position as head of Russia's National Security Council. Following his downfall, Abashidze relocated to Moscow, where he reportedly owns real estate worth millions of dollars.[23]

### Licit and illicit Russian business activity in postconflict economies[24]

The economies of Abkhazia and South Ossetia represent more institutionalized, postconflict versions of what Mary Kaldor characterized as globalized war economies.[25] In Abkhazia and South Ossetia, armed groups with various degrees of international legitimacy, including the armed forces of the *de facto* statelets, as well as paramilitary and guerrilla groups linked to the warring sides, have sporadically engaged in low-level violence directed at establishing and maintaining control of contraband trade networks to fund further operations and enrich individual leaders. Since the cooling of active conflict in these areas, institutions have developed that regulate this trade on the statelets' side, while guerrilla activity on the Georgian side has tapered off dramatically in recent years. Thus, the situation is not as chaotic or violent as that described by Kaldor, but still remains fundamentally unstable.

*Map 11.1* Major contraband trade routes in Georgia. (source: Aleksandre Kukhianidze, Aleksandre Kupatadze, and Roman Gotsiridze, *Smuggling through Abkhazia and Tskhinvali Region of Georgia*, Tbilisi: Polygraph, 2004. Used with the permission of American University's Transnational Crime and Corruption Center (TraCCC) Georgia Office).

Economic impoverishment and lack of legitimacy make contraband trade the main source of revenue for the statelets. Such trade is facilitated by corruption on the Russian and Georgian sides, particularly corrupt members of Georgian military and security forces and members of the CIS peacekeeping force in Abkhazia. Map 11.1 shows the main contraband routes in and out of Georgia.

In the atmosphere of state collapse that pervades these areas, it remains difficult to disaggregate the business and political goals of these armed groups. Contraband trade to and from Russia through the statelets is a valuable resource that such groups seek to control. Russian business activity in the statelets is highly diversified and includes a vast range of actors. Although of great importance for the statelets, much of it is relatively insignificant in terms of the Russian economy, allowing it to pass under the radar of the Russian authorities without always necessitating high-level political support from Moscow or the regional leadership.

Contraband trade continues to represent the most commonplace and economically significant form of Russian business activity for the statelets. Much of the contraband trade that takes place is in goods, such as tangerines, nuts, alcohol, and cigarettes, that, if it were not for their means of transport, would be considered licit. For the purposes of the following discussion of contraband trade, *licit* goods will refer to goods otherwise legal except for their means of transport, according to Georgian law, while *illicit* goods will refer to goods that are illegal under Georgian law.

This distinction between licit and illicit is important because the trade in licit goods has different implications for conflict resolution than the trade in illicit goods. The future legalization of trade in licit goods could be considered as part of a conflict settlement, whereas any conflict settlement leading to the reestablishment of legal control over the separatist statelets might lead to a crackdown on the trade in illicit goods. Those involved in the illicit goods trade have a definite interest in maintaining the status quo. Thus, the trade in illicit goods is a greater hindrance to conflict settlement. Of course, because of the blockade imposed on the statelet as part of the cease-fire in 1993, all goods flowing into or out of Abkhazia, with the exception of international humanitarian aid, are technically illegal. Similarly, neither Georgia nor Russia has formal economic relations with the *de facto* government of South Ossetia, so all goods that pass through the separatist statelet could be considered contraband.

In Abkhazia and South Ossetia, smuggling in contraband goods is the main livelihood for local inhabitants and the major source of income for the *de facto* regimes. The following section describes prevalent contraband trade activity, organized by sector. Licit and illicit goods often follow the same routes, and some organized crime groups control the trafficking of both licit and illicit goods.

### *"Licit" economic activity and the role of Russia*[26]

#### *Citrus and hazelnut smuggling*

Abkhaz farmers take their tangerines and nuts to sell in Russian markets, as they did during the Soviet era. This economic activity, once considered routine, now constitutes a criminal act. The traditional trade routes used to bring tangerines and nuts to the Russian market currently cross cease-fire lines and international borders. However, the demand for these goods in southern Russia remains.

Trade in tangerines is loosely organized, but many residents of Abkhazia rely on it as their sole source of income. In the absence of any legitimate economic activity, smuggling is vital to the livelihood of ordinary residents in the statelet. However, traders must still bribe Russian peacekeepers and border guards, and organized crime groups sometimes establish protection rackets, forcing small-scale tangerine merchants to pay tribute.

The hazelnut trade is considerably more organized, and features higher stakes. The head of Abkhazia's regional administration in the predominantly Georgian Gali district, Ruslan Kishmaria, reported that the Russian confectionery company Babaevskii has hazelnut plantations in the Ochamchire district.[27] Babaevskii is the third largest confectionery company in Russia, and won a contract in 2003 to supply confectionery foodstuffs to the Russian armed forces.[28] The political connections necessary to win such a concession could conceivably have facilitated the expansion of its operations into the unrecognized statelet, which is not under Russian jurisdiction but where there is a significant Russian military presence.

Organized crime protection rackets also prey on small-scale hazelnut farmers.

One report shows that a Moscow-based crime boss has organized an extensive racket in the Gali region for hazelnut farmers bringing their goods into Russia from Abkhazia. Reportedly, this organization has streamlined the process of hazelnut smuggling, and "rationalized" the process of extortion, since only one payment is required for the entire trip from Gali into Russia.[29] Russian companies may soon have to compete with their Turkish counterparts in Abkhazia, since Turkish companies have expressed interest in the statelet's hazelnut crops.

### Cigarette and alcohol smuggling

Other contraband activity includes smuggling untaxed cigarettes and alcohol into Georgian-controlled territory. Such goods can readily be seen for sale alongside many major Georgian roads, as nearby law enforcers extract a profit by turning a blind eye. According to a study from Georgia's ministry of tax revenues, approximately 4.5 million packages of smuggled cigarettes entered Georgia via Abkhazia each month.[30] The same study estimated that almost 75 percent of the cigarette market in Georgia was filled with contraband goods.[31] Although the level of smuggling appears to have declined somewhat, owing to law enforcement operations conducted by the Saakashvili administration, trade in contraband goods, particularly cigarettes, still appears to constitute a major source of economic activity in Georgia.

Cigarettes and alcohol enter Georgia from both Abkhazia and South Ossetia. Smuggling these goods from Russia involves close coordination among the sides ordinarily engaged in conflict. Russian exporters and Abkhaz, Ossetian, and Georgian contraband traders work together to bring these goods across international borders and cease-fire lines. Dealers sell smuggled cigarettes and alcohol in particularly large amounts through Ergneti, a vast informal market that straddles the cease-fire line between South Ossetia and Georgian-controlled territory, occasionally shifting northwards into South Ossetian-controlled territory in order to elude Georgian law enforcers.

There are also several cigarette-producing factories operating in Abkhazia. The factory in Sukhumi is closely controlled by the separatist government, since the former owner and manager, Levan Ardzinba, is a cousin of Vladislav Ardzinba, Abkhazia's former *de facto* leader. By placing top relatives in such key economic positions, Abkhazia's leadership created a tightly knit, clan-based ruling group that continues to seek economic domination. The Sukhumi factory is reportedly a joint venture with the Russian company Geogravionik.[32] Cigarettes produced at the factory in Sukhumi are sold in both Georgia and Russia.

### Gasoline smuggling

Owing to corruption in Georgia's customs agency and poor border control, a significant amount of gasoline is smuggled into Georgia, the majority of it from Azerbaijan. However, gasoline smuggling through Abkhazia and South Ossetia is notable because it provides needed income for the *de facto* regimes there. Research by the Georgian ministry of finance estimated the volume of oil products smuggled from Ergneti to be approximately 5,000 tons per month, or about 7.7 percent of all of the fuel consumed in Georgia.[33] Gasoline smuggling hinders legitimate economic development in Georgia and costs the state budget much-needed tax revenue.

### Wheat and flour smuggling

Large-scale smuggling in wheat and flour products through Ergneti market has seriously negative implications for the Georgian economy. Bread is a basic staple of nutrition in the average Georgian household, which according to one study spends as much as one-fourth of its income on bread products.[34] In 2000, bread products made up an estimated 41.9 percent of the total daily caloric intake of a Georgian citizen.[35] Bread consumption is likely higher among the poorest members of the Georgian population.

According to the Georgian National Security Council, 70 percent of the flour consumed in Georgia is of foreign origin and 35–40 percent of it is smuggled into the country.[36] The Ergneti market in South Ossetia serves as the major supplier of smuggled wheat and flour to Georgia. Illegally imported wheat and flour products coming from Russia via the Roksky Tunnel are unloaded at special terminals located outside of the city of Tskhinvali. At the terminals, shippers load the goods into other vehicles and transport them to the Ergneti market, where they are sold both to legal entities and to individuals who bypass customs and bring the goods to internal Georgian markets. Georgian law enforcement officials are sometimes bribed to accompany smugglers safely to their destination.

Smuggling in wheat and flour from Russia drastically undermines Georgia's agricultural sector. According to the research of the Transnational Crime and Corruption Center, 16 Russian companies from Russia's Krasnodar and Stavropol regions import flour through the market into Georgia. If the Kremlin were able to control the activities of these companies, it could conceivably use the price of bread and bread products as a lever to influence Georgia, much in the way that Russian energy companies have used oil and gas influence as a Russian foreign policy instrument in the CIS.

While high bread prices might prove an obvious threat to the livelihood of the Georgian population, paradoxically a more worrying long-term trend is the extremely low cost of smuggled flour. Georgia's indigenous flour industry, which was relatively well developed in the Soviet period, has been unable to compete with the low price of smuggled flour and, as a result, has drastically decreased production. In this sense, the smuggling of flour from Russia functions as a form of dumping, increasing the Georgian economy's dependence on the Russian market for flour.

*Timber trade*

The contraband timber trade provides one of the main sources of revenue for the Abkhaz government. Abkhaz officials have estimated that the local timber industry brings in $1.7 million per year, a figure the local authorities would like to increase.[37] The Abkhaz economy minister has declared that developing the timber-processing industry in Abkhazia "is of paramount importance."[38] He complained that while wood is exported from Abkhazia, products like parquet, tables, chairs, and furniture are not available there. The Abkhaz government will likely seek Russian investment for such a move.

*Russian investment*

Russian investment is vital to the economic development of Abkhazia and South Ossetia. While Russian investment brings much-needed jobs to the statelets, it also lends legitimacy to the separatist regimes and could prove a hindrance to conflict resolution. Certainly a resolution of the conflicts would bring significantly more Russian investment to the region. However, numerous Russian companies, sometimes with tacit support from the Russian government, have already made their investments. For example, in Abkhazia Russian investors have purchased numerous hotels and resorts, and Russian companies are engaged in lucrative joint ventures to process granite and rehabilitate factories.[39] Russian investors would be wary of any change in the status quo, since the deals they have concluded with the existing authorities would come under review if regime change were to occur.

Russian investment is most often coordinated by Russia's regional leaders or by business leaders in Moscow. The Abkhaz government has set up six working groups focused on establishing trade agreements with the neighboring Krasnodar region. These groups deal with minerals, electricity, fuel and gas, agriculture, railways, and fishing.[40] The Abkhaz government is eager to attract outside investment, and its statute on foreign investments includes provisions for the participation of foreign investors in the privatization process and the creation of free economic zones for investors. Investments are sometimes backed by key figures among Russia's political elite. For example, a winery in Sukhumi was purchased by Russian businesspeople who allegedly are connected to the former Russian prime minister Sergei Kirienko.[41]

Sometimes Russian government structures themselves direct investment. As already mentioned, the Moscow City government maintains economic relations with Abkhazia and reportedly has several investments in the statelet. Russian government structures are directly involved in the tourist sector, leasing resorts in Abkhazia inexpensively over long periods of time. Among the key players are the defense ministry, the ministry of atomic energy, the Institute of Metallurgy, the State University of Kabardino-Balkaria, as well as leading Russian companies, including Lukoil and Gazprom. Leases generally run for 25–30 years, and are most often concluded with Madina Ardzinba, daughter of the former *de facto* Abkhaz president.[42] Ms. Ardzinba runs a travel agency in Moscow, Rusal Tour. In the long term, Russian participation in the *de facto* government's privatization effort could lead to the acquisition of vital strategic assets by Russian investors with close links to the Russian state.

Although Russia still officially upholds the blockade on Abkhazia, Russian politicians have pushed legislative measures to get around this obstacle. Most measures fly in the face of the spirit, if not the word, of the agreements that led to the cease-fire. In November 1997, Russian prime minister Viktor Chernomyrdin signed a decree allowing the import of citrus products and other agricultural products. In 1997 and 1998, the Russian Duma attempted to lift sanctions against Abkhazia. In December 2002, Russian authorities turned a blind eye when the rail service between Sochi, in Russia, and Sukhumi was resumed despite the terms of the conflict settlement, which prohibit such measures. The Russian coast guard is also lax in enforcing the blockade of maritime vessels between Russia and the statelet. And, as was noted earlier, Russia's ability to enforce the blockade of Abkhazia following the apparent victory of opposition candidate Sergei Bagapsh demonstrated that a lack of political will is a significant factor in Russia's lax enforcement.

### *"Illicit" economic activity*

Not all smuggled goods are benign: narcotics, arms, stolen cars, and scrap metal stolen from state enterprises are regularly smuggled via Abkhazia and South Ossetia. In such cases, the presence of conflict shapes the dynamic of the illicit shadow economy. As Svetlana Glinkina and Dorothy Rosenberg point out, conflict provides a *market* for items such as illegal arms, an *opportunity* due to lack of state control for activities like drug trafficking and kidnapping, and a *justification* for criminal activities, since many resistance groups engage in illicit activities to finance their operations.[43]

Because of the lucrative nature of smuggling in illicit goods, organized crime groups inevitably seek to control such trade. According to some observers, Abkhazia is divided into zones of influence and areas of activity controlled by criminal groups. One analysis shows something closely resembling an ethnic division of criminal labor, with Abkhazia split up along the following lines: a group in western Abkhazia has control over oil, food, and tobacco shipments, and is partially engaged in smuggling illicit drugs into Russia; a group based in Gagra, made up mainly of Armenians, is involved in the production of drugs; another group in Gudauta, mainly composed of ethnic Abkhaz, effectively controls the export of drugs; and a Chechen organized crime group controls the eastern part of the republic, the Sukhumi railway station, major transportation routes, and cargo movement on the Georgian–Abkhazian border.[44] This last group allegedly has maintained contacts with Georgian guerrilla groups, which in the past have financed their operations through smuggling, though the prominence of guerrilla groups has since subsided.

Criminal groups seek to control smuggling routes used to transport agricultural products like fruit and nuts, as well as illicit goods, such as small arms, stolen cars, and narcotics. Soviet economic planners developed a major rail and road transport corridor in the South Caucasus that ran from Baku, Azerbaijan to the northwest, through Georgia and out to the Black Sea along the coast of Abkhazia. During the Soviet period, this corridor was a major route for the transport of goods from Central Asia, oil and gas from the Caspian basin, and tea, fruits, and nuts from Georgia to Russia and the rest of the Soviet Union. In addition, the main link between Armenia and Russia ran through Georgia and Abkhazia. Similarly, South Ossetia is located on the main route between the North and South Caucasus, with goods passing through the Roksky Tunnel from North Ossetia into South Ossetia and the rest of Georgia. The collapse of Soviet authority left control of these routes up for grabs. Thus, when one is looking at the outbreak and continuation of conflict in these areas, geographical factors should also be considered.[45]

For the most part, however, there is close cooperation among the various groups involved in contraband trade. Surprisingly, this cooperation cuts across ethnic divisions. Georgian and Abkhaz criminal groups routinely cooperate to smuggle contraband goods into Georgia for sale on the Georgian market.[46] In contrast, because of political differences and a lack of logistical coordination, Georgian and Abkhaz law enforcement personnel rarely cooperate on joint investigations into smuggling operations.

Many law enforcement personnel are themselves involved in smuggling operations. Those charged with upholding the law are paid such low wages that in many cases even subsistence on the basis of their salary is impossible. Smuggling operations offer lucrative opportunities for law enforcers by paying them simply to remain inactive and to ignore contraband activity. CIS peacekeepers – most of them Russian citizens – who have access to desired goods, such as arms and other military equipment, are also allegedly involved in the criminal economy.[47] Officials who try to take on organized crime groups can be threatened, kidnapped, or killed, as likely happened in the case of the murder of Zugdidi police officer Valery Morgoshina.[48] In many cases, renewed conflict in breakaway statelets can often be linked to business disputes rather than the renewal of interethnic strife.[49]

## Drug trafficking

Heroin and cocaine are smuggled through the breakaway statelets, while marijuana and hashish are cultivated and processed there for sale in local markets, according to the research of the Transnational Crime and Corruption Center.[50] It is, however, difficult to measure the level of such trade. Drugs are apparently smuggled from Abkhazia to Russia in vehicles or carried by ordinary contraband traders. In one case, employees of Sochi's customs post seized one kilogram of narcotics transported by a woman going to Sochi to sell citrus products. The woman allegedly agreed to transport the drugs for $70.[51]

The governments of Abkhazia and South Ossetia have made several statements indicating the need to crack down on drug trafficking. However, with few alternative sources of revenue, it is likely that some members of the *de facto* governments simply seek to reduce and control drug trafficking, rather than to eradicate it altogether. If they do not succeed in gaining control of drug trafficking, organized crime figures profiting from the drug trade could mount a serious challenge to the authority of the *de facto* regimes, and the level of drug trafficking could increase further.

## Money laundering

A real threat exists that the statelets' unregulated banking systems could be used by Russian businesses to launder illegally gained assets. As Russian banks face tighter regulation at home, there is an increasing possibility that money-laundering operations may increasingly occur in less regulated areas of the CIS. The fact that Abkhazia and South Ossetia base their economies on the Russian ruble and are unregulated by the global financial system and by international agreements on money laundering makes them ideal offshore zones for Russian businesses engaged in illicit activity.

## Arms trafficking and the role of Russian peacekeepers

Trafficking in small arms throughout the conflict area makes the outbreak of violent conflict more likely while dimming prospects for any future disarmament. In most cases, the trade seems to be in small arms, although Georgian authorities are concerned that radiological materials used to make a "dirty bomb" could easily be smuggled through the statelets.[52] Organized crime groups reportedly control the trade in arms moving between Georgia and Russia. Despite the fact that these weapons could be used to arm the conflicting sides, those groups still at war with one another apparently cooperate to facilitate the arms trade. In 2002, a Russian organized crime figure, Artur Liudkov (better known by his pseudonym, Yasha Astrakhansky), and Major Mchelidze of Georgia's Ministry of State Security, were arrested outside of Tbilisi for transporting rocket launchers and other weapons, which they claimed to have bought in South Ossetia from Russian peacekeepers. They were convicted and served time in Georgia for these crimes. Liudkov was gunned down outside a hospital in Moscow in April 2003 in what appeared to be an organized crime-related killing shortly after returning to Russia following the completion of his prison sentence.[53]

These peacekeepers, sent to mitigate the conflicts in Abkhazia and South Ossetia, face similar challenges to those confronting other members of Russia's armed forces. They are underpaid and sometimes poorly supervised. In such situations, they must rely on their own entrepreneurial activities, licit or illicit, to earn a living. It is thus not surprising that arms are reportedly sold from Russian peacekeeping posts.

However, the role of Russian peacekeepers in supplying arms for these conflicts should not be overestimated. Georgia itself has many surplus weapons from the Soviet period that may be too obsolete to be used in conventional warfare but might be valued on the black market. Russian peacekeepers do play another economic role. Russian bases in Abkhazia and South Ossetia support local economies that have come to depend on them. A similar situation holds for Russian bases in other parts of Georgia, most notably in Akhalkalaki. Very often, economic transactions in these areas use Russian rubles rather than local currency.[54]

Russian peacekeepers reportedly receive bribes in exchange for turning a blind eye to contraband trade. Some may also cooperate with organized crime groups to assist in drug and human trafficking. The corruption of peacekeepers threatens the integrity of the peacekeeping mission and, thus, is a hindrance to conflict resolution.

## Russian business and the prospects for conflict resolution in Abkhazia and South Ossetia

How harmful is illegal business activity for the region? In the short term, the informal economy that has grown up in the absence of formal economic institutions has proven to be a stabilizing force. Families living in the region rely upon contraband trade for their very livelihood. Contraband trade remains the only point of contact among many Georgians, Abkhaz, and Ossetes, bringing members of these otherwise contentious ethnic groups into close interaction in the interests of profitable exchange. In the long term, however, continued criminalization of the economy in the conflict zones could be more harmful than beneficial. Informal networks exclude those without access to them, often society's most vulnerable. In addition, some scholars claim that reliance on family networks serves to reinforce traditional gender hierarchies and increase inequality along ethnic or confessional lines.[55] In the absence of overriding state authority, individuals, families, and population subgroups can be completely excluded from access to any economic, social, or political benefits because they do not have access to select kinship networks. Thus, a situation where institutions remain poorly developed and social networks are the sole source of support tends to reinforce social divisions and can also lay the grounds for future conflict.[56]

The unresolved nature of these conflicts also destabilizes the political situation in the rest of Georgia. Spillover effects of the Abkhaz conflict are especially great in the neighboring region of Samegrelo. In Samegrelo's capital, Zugdidi, the influx of refugees and the operation of criminal groups associated with the conflict have led to such an increase in crime that many of the city's inhabitants fear to leave their homes at night.

Refugees from the conflicts in Abkhazia and South Ossetia further strain Georgia's collapsed economy. In the absence of an adequate state-sponsored social safety net, many refugees do not have proper access to health care or education. The collapse of state services has led to a lack of care for the elderly and growing illiteracy among the youth, most of whom have parents who received a university education. Awaiting decisive conflict settlement, refugees exist in a sort of limbo. The desperation of their situation could make them prone to supporting radical political movements within Georgia. Numbering over 250,000 in a nation of less than 5 million, they are certainly a force to be reckoned with.

Finally, the criminalization of these entrenched conflicts undermines the legitimacy of the grievances the Abkhaz and the Ossetes had at the conflict's outset. Few Georgians now recognize that either group had any grievances at all. Instead, most perceive the conflict to be nothing more than a manipulation of these populations masterminded by Russia and sustained by criminal interests.

Perpetuating the current situation is undesirable to all but the few who benefit from it. Ultimately the contraband trade cannot be effectively eradicated until Georgian borders are secured. Currently, Georgian authority is demarcated by cease-fire lines. These lines are not official borders but show the current limits of Georgian control. Obviously, Georgia is hesitant to set up checkpoints and fences along these cease-fire lines, since doing so would be an implicit recognition of the sovereignty of the separatist statelets. On the other hand, Abkhazia and South Ossetia have little incentive to join Georgia. Russia, which is more developed economically, is a much more lucrative source of patronage and security than Georgia. Few Abkhaz and Ossetes are fluent in the Georgian language, further complicating integration. If ethnic Georgian refugees returned to Abkhazia, they would outnumber the ethnic Abkhaz, who would fear both acts of retribution and the establishment of a pro-Georgian or anti-Abkhaz regime in Sukhumi. So, while the status quo is undesirable, many of the proposed solutions on the table that involve integration with Georgia may be politically unfeasible.

For there to be any chance for conflict resolution, the economic interests of Russian business elites active in the statelets must first be addressed. The interest of these elites in prolonging the conflict is a major impediment to any lasting peace agreement. Russian investors representing diverse economic interests may fear a loss of the near-monopoly they enjoy in the economies of these statelets, and the possibility of increased competition, should Georgian authority be reestablished and Abkhazia and South Ossetia opened for international investment. Russian investors could form a potent lobbying force to oppose plans for conflict resolution that would threaten the assets to which they lay claim. Organized crime groups, which operate freely in the region, could also prove to be a stumbling block to peace, as they might seek to undermine any conflict resolution plan that would pave the way for the establishment of the rule of law in the statelets. Russian business activity has provided a lifeline for the de facto authorities in Abkhazia and South Ossetia and has created Russian stakeholders in the status quo. Unless the economic interests of these stakeholders are addressed, Moscow would have difficulty brokering a peace agreement, even if there were the political will at the top to do so.

Although destined to be politically unpopular on the Georgian side, legitimizing some contraband trade may be a first step in providing incentives for transparency on the part of the groups now involved in smuggling. Recent political developments in Georgia indicate that limited economic cooperation and confidence-building measures might be accepted by the leadership in Tbilisi. Trade in cigarettes, alcohol, fruits, and nuts could conceivably be regulated by a joint Georgian–Abkhazian or Georgian–Ossetian authority. With the legalization of trade in licit goods, authorities could focus their efforts on cracking down on the trade in small arms, stolen cars, and narcotics. Some groups involved in contraband trade might then have the incentive to shift their activities away from trade in illicit goods, and could ideally begin establishing legitimate trading businesses. Once legitimate, these businesses would likely ally with authorities in their attempt to squash illegal enterprises threatening their legitimate interests. Furthermore, a reopening of transit routes through Abkhazia and South Ossetia would provide economic benefits for both Russia and Georgia derived from the increased flow of goods. Until the economic incentives facilitating contraband trade are addressed, such trade is bound to persist in some form, regardless of the law enforcement operations pursued by the authorities in Tbilisi.

Recent attempts by Georgian law enforcement to suppress smuggling without addressing the economic incentives of those involved have proved risky. In early 2005, ethnic Azeris in southern Georgia claimed that their region was being unfairly targeted in a Georgian antismuggling operation that for many threatened their sole source of income.[57] Unless evenly applied, such efforts could alienate ethnic minority communities within Georgia. Similarly, the Georgian government's posting of customs officials along the cease-fire lines with South Ossetia in the summer of 2004 as a means of curbing contraband trade led to increased tension between Georgian and South Ossetian forces. The conflict escalated when Georgian troops were sent to the cease-fire zone as reinforcements, leading to the outbreak of armed conflict and a number of combat deaths. Thus, the possibility of increased conflict exists if operations to curtail smuggling from the statelets are not pursued cautiously.[58]

On the other hand, outright legalization is politically complicated. While there is a chance that conflict resolution can be achieved through the legitimization of some types of contraband trade, it is difficult to predict what such a plan would mean for Abkhazia's and South Ossetia's future status. Legitimization of contraband trade inevitably raises questions regarding its control and regulation. It seems unlikely that Georgian forces would be permitted to control trade at Abkhazia's or South Ossetia's border with Russia. Likewise, Georgian control of contraband trade along the cease-fire lines would be a tacit recognition of the sovereignty of the separatist statelets.

Any political solution must inevitably address the region as a whole. More than any other area of the former Soviet Union, the Caucasus has been plagued with conflict since the collapse of Soviet authority. Although impeded by concentrated groups seeking to prolong conflict, development of the South Caucasus into a tourist destination and a stable transit hub serves the interests of the vast majority of the region's inhabitants. While cooperation among diverse ethnic groups is difficult, the future economic development of the area depends on it. Only by achieving peace and stability will these small nations be able to attract outside investment. Ideally, development would include a resurrection of the legitimate economic networks that once spread across the region.

## Notes

1  I use "statelets" for lack of a better term to describe these internationally unrecognized quasi-states.
2  To loosely paraphrase the title of the article by Edward Walker, "No Peace, No War in the Caucasus: Secessionist Conflicts in Chechnya, Abkhazia, and Nagorno-Karabakh," Occasional Paper, Strengthening Democratic Institutions Project, John F. Kennedy School of Government, Harvard University, February 1998, bcsia.ksg.harvard.edu/publication.cfm?program=CORE&ctype=paper&item_id=244.
3  The situation in these Caucasian statelets closely resembles that in Transdniestria, which has an unrecognized de facto government and a thriving black market economy. Transdniestria, which proclaimed independence from Moldova, reportedly has a flourishing illicit arms trade.
4  Borders with Russia and relative autonomy during the Soviet period may have played a role in the strategic decision making by local elites in Abkhazia and South Ossetia in their separation from Tbilisi. When Georgia first gained independence, Abkhazia had the status of autonomous republic, and South Ossetia the status of autonomous region (*oblast'*). *De facto* governments in Sukhumi (Abkhazia) and Tskhinvali (South Ossetia) now seek full independence. Tbilisi has recently made overtures to both separatist statelets, proposing the establishment of a loose, federative framework. However, under most of the proposals under consideration, Abkhazia would retain greater autonomy than South Ossetia, much as it had during the Soviet period.
5  Despite agreeing in principle to remove its troops from Georgia at the Organization for Economic Security and Co-operation in Europe (OSCE) Summit in Istanbul in 1999, Russia was slow to negotiate a concrete deadline for the removal of its forces from Batumi and Akhalkalaki, finally agreeing to a 2008 withdrawal deadline in May 2005. As part of the move, some of Russia's military hardware will be relocated from Georgia to neighboring Armenia.
6  Michael Emerson and Sergiu Celac, "How to Cool the Caucasus," *Financial Times*, 5 January 2001.
7  Igor Torbakov, "Russian Policymakers Air Notion of 'Liberal Empire' in Caucasus, Central Asia" *International Eurasian Institute for Economic and Political Research*, iicas.org/2003en/28_10_an_en.htm.
8  For a more detailed analysis of UES's activities in the South Caucasus, see Jeronim Perović's chapter in this volume (Chapter 5).
9  Raymond E. Dummett, *Gentlemanly Capitalism and British Imperialism: The New Debate on Empire*, London: Longman, 1999, p. 8.
10  "PM: Georgia Welcomes Russian Investments," civil.ge, 26 April 2005, www.civil.ge/eng/article.php?id=9713.
11  Peter Rutland, "Business and the State in Russia," in Peter Rutland, ed., *Business and the State in Contemporary Russia*, Boulder, CO: Westview Press, 2001, p. 19.
12  In Russia's federal system, the cities of Moscow and St. Petersburg have the same status as regions because of their importance to the country's political and economic systems.
13  Virginie Coulloudon, "Moscow City Management: Russian Capitalism?" in Rutland, ed., *Business and the State in Contemporary Russia*, p. 93.
14  Donald N. Jensen, "The Boss: How Yury Luzhkov Runs Moscow," Conflict Studies Research Centre, Defence Academy of the United Kingdom, E105, 1999, p. 3. See also Oleg Alexandrov, "The City of Moscow in Russia's Foreign and Security Policy:

Role, Aims and Motivations," Working Paper 7, Zurich: Center for Security Policy, April 2001.

15 See Erik R. Scott, "Corruption, Uncertainty Fuel Illegal Russia–Georgia Trade," *Russian Regional Report* 7, no. 29, 18 November 2002.

16 Svante Cornell, *Autonomy and Conflict: Ethnoterritorialism and Separatism in the South Caucasus: Cases in Georgia*, Uppsala: Department of Peace and Conflict Research, 2002, p. 182.

17 Vladimir Socor, "Moscow Enforces Blockade of Abkhazia, Invalidates Bagapsh's Election," *Eurasia Daily Monitor* 1:140, 6 December 2004.

18 Dina Gassieva, "South Ossetia Voted for Putin," *Brosse Street Journal*, 17 March 2004.

19 Margarita Antidze, "Georgia's Breakaway Region Ossetia Votes, Defiant," Reuters, 23 May 2004.

20 In an interview with *Nezavisimaia gazeta*, Don Cossack leader (*Ataman*) Nikolai Kozitsyn admitted that his troops were operating in South Ossetia as mercenaries. Somehow these fighters were able to pass through – or were let through – the Roksky Tunnel from Russia into South Ossetia. See Jean-Christophe Peuch, "Russia Weighs In as Fighting Worsens in South Ossetia," Radio Free Europe/Radio Liberty Newsline, 19 August 2004.

21 Adjaria was another region in Georgia with separatist tendencies, but Saakashvili was able to remove its leader and return the region to centralized Georgian rule.

22 Simon Saradzhyan, "Georgian Hopefuls Eye Moscow," *The St. Petersburg Times*, 28 November 2003.

23 See "Direct Presidential Rule Introduced in Adjara," Rosbalt News Agency, 7 May 2004, eng.globalization.ru/live/news.asp?id=5681, and "U Abashidze kvartira s vidom na Moskvu-reku: Stoimost' kvatratnogo zhil'ia v etom dome sostavliaet \$4,5 tysiachi," *Rossiiskaia gazeta*, 6 July 2004.

24 The following section on "licit" and "illicit" economic activity in Abkhazia and South Ossetia is heavily indebted to research on this subject by Transnational Crime and Corruption scholars Aleksandre Kukhianidze, Aleksandre Kupatadze, and Roman Gotsiridze. This research group, working in close coordination with the Transnational Crime and Corruption Center's headquarters in Washington, DC, was able to obtain extensive information on contraband trade. The major findings of this group are contained in Kukhianidze, Kupatadze, and Gotsiridze, *Smuggling through Abkhazia and Tskhinvali Region of Georgia*, Tbilisi: Polygraph, 2004. The group's report is also available online on the website of the Transnational Crime and Corruption Center's Georgia Office: www.traccc.cdn.ge/publications/index.html.

25 Such economies, which differ from earlier war economies in their relatively low level of violence, combined with local predation and external support, are described by Mary Kaldor in *New and Old Wars: Organized Violence in a Global Era*, Stanford, CA: Stanford University Press, 1999. While some have called into question the distinction made by Kaldor between old and new types of conflict, her model of the globalized war economy is a useful conceptual tool for approaching the economies of these breakaway republics. For a critique of Kaldor, see Stathis N. Kalyvas, "'New' and 'Old' Civil Wars: A Valid Distinction?" *World Politics* 54, no. 1, 2001, pp. 99–118.

26 This overview of licit economic activity, like the description of illicit economic activity that follows it, is based largely on field research conducted by Transnational Crime and Corruption Center scholars in 2002–2003. The situation on the ground is in constant flux, and the information provided here can at best provide a "snapshot" of economic activity in a given period and explore some of the general dynamics and trends of contraband trade and unregulated Russian investment, which are essential to the continued existence of these statelets.

27 Interview with R. Kishmaria by Z. Tsivizhba, *Respublica Abkhazia*, 8 August 2003.

28 From the company web site "Pressa o Babaevskom" at www.babaev.ru/about/pressa17.html.
29 From T. Shonia's report "Abkhazia: Lucrative Farms Attract Mafia," Institute of War and Peace Reporting's Caucasus Reporting Service, no. 192, 21 August 2003.
30 Roman Gotsiridze, *Economic and Social Consequences of Internal Conflicts in Georgia*, Tbilisi: Parliamentary Budget Office, 2003, p. 8.
31 Gotsiridze, *Economic and Social Consequences*, p. 12.
32 Transnational Crime and Corruption Center interview with the Government of Abkhazia in Exile Ministry of State Security, 2003.
33 Gotsiridze, *Economic and Social Consequences*, p. 10.
34 Report "Bread Production in Tbilisi," State Department for Statistics of Georgia, 2001, p. 3. Cited in B. Lezhava and G. Chumburidze, "Economic Crime and Money Laundering in the Flour and Baking Industry: Solutions for Overcoming these Problems," Unpublished report by the Transnational Crime and Corruption Center's Georgia Money Laundering Project, 2004.
35 "Georgian Agriculture" Report, State Department for Statistics of Georgia, 2001, p. 11. Cited in Lezhava and Chumburidze, *"Economic Crime and Money Laundering."*
36 Report by the National Security Council of Georgia on Anti-Smuggling Measures, p. 9. Cited in Lezhava and Chumburidze, "Economic Crime and Money Laundering."
37 Cited in Kukhianidze, Kupatadze, and Gotsiridze, *Smuggling through Abkhazia*, p. 42.
38 Minister of Economy Konstantin Tuzhba, quoted in *Aspnypress* no. 96, 20 May 2003, http://aspnypress.narod.ru.
39 François Gremy, "Tender Offer for Abkhazia." Marie Anderson, trans. *Caucaz Europenews*, 28 February 2005, www.caucaz.com/home_eng/breve_contenu.php?id=133 (accessed 8 October 2005).
40 *Bor'ba klanov vykhodit iz pod kovra* (Summary of Abkhaz Press), www.marinews.ru/allnews/103877/, 26 March–6 April 2003.
41 Based upon interviews conducted by Transnational Crime and Corruption Center Staff with the Government of Abkhazia in Exile Ministry of State Security, 2003.
42 From a 2002 report by Valery Khaburdzania, minister of state security of Georgia, cited in Kukhianidze, Kupatadze, and Gotsiridze, *Smuggling through Abkhazia*, p. 48.
43 Svetlana P. Glinkina and Dorothy J. Rosenberg, "Social and Economic Decline as Factors in Conflict in the Caucasus," WIDER Discussion Paper 2003/18, Helsinki, 2003, p. 6.
44 Gotsiridze, *Economic and Social Consequences*, p. 18.
45 For a persuasive analysis of conflict that takes geographical factors into account, see Philippe Le Billon, "The Political Ecology of War: Natural Resources and Armed Conflicts," *Political Geography* 20, 2001, pp. 561–584.
46 T. Shonia and G. Mindzhoria, "Kriminal'nii oazis tsvetaet v zone gruzino-abakhazkogo konflikta," *Panorama*, March 2003, p. 5.
47 See David Darchiashvili, "Georgia: A Hostage to Arms," in *The Caucasus: Armed and Divided – Small Arms and Light Weapons Proliferation and Humanitarian Consequences in the Caucasus*, collective monograph, London: Saferworld, 2003, pp. 20–21.
48 Shonia and Mindzhoria, "Kriminal'nii oazis tsvetaet," p. 5.
49 This is often true for many of the conflicts in the Caucasus, including Chechnya. For more on this issue, see the excellent study by Uwe Halbach, "Erdöl und Identität im Kaukasus," *Internationale Politik und Gesellschaft*, 2003, pp. 140–166.
50 Kukhianidze, Kupatadze, and Gotsiridze, *Smuggling through Abkhazia*, pp. 34–36.
51 *"V Abkhazia vyrashivaiut narkotiki. Mnogo,"* www.abkhazeti.ru, 13 March 2003.
52 See Joby Warrick, "Smugglers Enticed by Dirty Bomb Components," *Washington Post*, 29 November 2003.
53 "Gangstera rasstreliali za sviaz' s'lesnymi brat'iami'"? *Moskovskii komsomolets* April 22, 2003 (www.mk.ru/numbers/295/artlicle9788.htm), accessed May 19, 2006.
54 The *de facto* governments of Abkhazia and South Ossetia do not have their own

currencies and rely on the ruble. Thus, the impact of conducting economic transactions related to Russian military bases in rubles is less in these areas. The impact of using the ruble is greater in other parts of Georgia, like Akhalkalaki, where separatist tendencies have been a concern.

55　Glinkina and Rosenberg, "Social and Economic Decline," p. 7.

56　In a thought-provoking piece entitled "The Tale of Two Resorts: Abkhazia and Ajaria before and since the Soviet Collapse," Georgi M. Derluguian emphasizes that the inability of Abkhazia's patrons in Moscow to provide support for its elite following the Soviet collapse – in this case through official institutions that were often inextricably bound to personalistic networks – was a key factor in the Abkhaz elite's decision to "play the ethnic card" and engage in direct conflict with the Georgian state. The chapter appears in Beverly Crawford and Ronnie D. Lipschutz, eds., *The Myth of "Ethnic" Conflict: Politics, Economics, and "Cultural" Violence*, Berkeley: University of California Press, 1998, pp. 261–292.

57　Ramilya Alieva, "Georgia: Smuggling Crackdown Hurts Azeris," *Institute for War and Peace Reporting's Caucasus Reporting Service* no. 274, 17 February 2005.

58　For further evidence that violent reactions can ensue when the entrenched interests of those involved in contraband trade are threatened by antismuggling operations, one might also consider the explosion of a car bomb in the Georgian city of Gori on 1 February 2005 that left three police officers dead, an event that many in the Georgian media speculated was connected to the antismuggling operations of the region's authorities. See "Saakashvili: Gori Blast is a Terrorist Act," *Eurasia Insight*, 2 February 2005, www.eurasianet.org/departments/insight/articles/eav020205.shtml. One might also include the repeated assassination attempts against Abkhaz prime minister Alexander Ankvab. The lead Abkhaz prosecutor investigating these events has suggested that Ankvab's actions against "entrepreneurs who were actively engaged in corrupt deals with the authorities over the past 10 years and whose interests were undermined as a result of increased control over the economy" may have been a motive. See "Official Speaks of Reasons behind Attack on Abkhaz PM," Civil Georgia website, 8 April 2005, www.civil.ge/eng/article.php?id=9553.

# 12 Timber in the Russian Far East and potential transborder conflict

*Josh Newell*

Economic globalization, the rise of Asian markets, and unstable center–periphery power relations stemming from post-Soviet reform inside Russia are fundamentally reshaping the economic structure of the Russian Far East (RFE), the vast eastern third of the Russian Federation (see Map 12.1). A great shift is taking place for the RFE – away from its traditional role as raw materials supplier to Russia's European core toward becoming a resource periphery for Northeast Asia. The RFE's links to the Chinese, Japanese, and South Korean markets already eclipse the region's economic ties to European Russia, and their importance will continue to grow.[1]

Moscow's declining economic influence in a region long known for its maverick governors and unruly organized crime poses significant development, foreign policy, and security dilemmas for the Russian state.[2] In addition to being a rich resource base, the Far East remains a vital military outpost securing Russia's borders and reaffirming the country's presence in Northeast Asia.[3] A stable RFE is therefore crucial to counteract rising Chinese influence. Russian fears of China primarily center on immigration.[4] But there is also growing concern, at least among regional leaders and local citizens, over China's economic dominance in the region.

The Putin administration's primary economic strategy to restitch the region to European Russia appears to involve an extensive series of oil and gas pipelines.[5] The decision to route the East Siberian oil pipeline to the Sea of Japan rather than to China is undoubtedly an effort to gain access to multiple markets (as discussed in Michael Bradshaw's chapter, Chapter 7), but it is also part of a broader geopolitical strategy to counteract Chinese influence. Despite optimistic official statements, this project will take decades to complete, assuming it is realized at all.

Unlike in other parts of Russia, the oil and gas sector at present plays a relatively minor role in the RFE economy. Fishing, mining, and forestry employ many more people and generate much more revenue.[6] These industries are particularly important in the administrative regions that form the Russian side of the 4,300-kilometer border with China (Primorskii and Khabarovskii *kraia*, Amur and Chita *oblasti*).

Dealing with fishing, mining, and forestry in the Far East presents a difficult

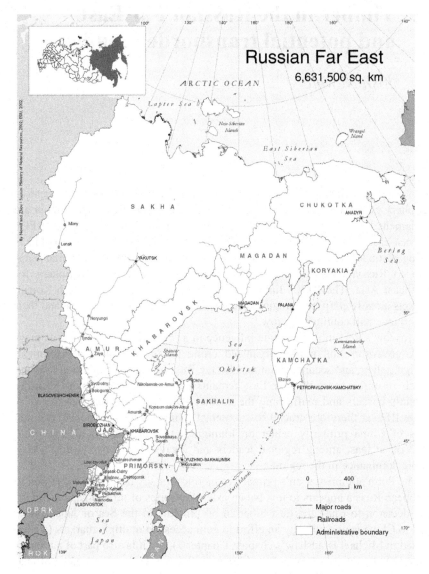

*Map 12.1* Administrative regions of the Russian Far East (source: Adapted from J. Newell, *The Russian Far East: A Reference Guide for Conservation and Development* (McKinleyville, CA: Daniel & Daniel, 2004).

challenge to Moscow because, in contrast to the energy sector, small and medium-sized companies are the primary economic actors in these industries. State control varies within these sectors, with mining the most centralized among the three and timber the least. Benefiting from weak federal control over forests, regional governments have long been vested with considerable administrative powers, including the all-important ability to allocate, and take back, rights to exploit forestry resources.[7]

This chapter focuses on the Russian Far East timber sector and is divided into three sections. The first shows how, through privatization and radical decentralization, the timber sector has devolved into a complex network of state actors, businesses, and criminal interests. The second considers where business and state interests converge and diverge, teasing out the consequences for regional economic growth, internal stability, and foreign relations. The final section discusses how development in the timber sector will shape regional stability and Russia's prospects for conflict and cooperation with China. Overall, the chapter argues that if the Russian state does not take measures against corrupt public officials and criminal businesses to increase Russia's ability to exploit its own natural resources, the possibility for conflict with China will grow.

## Key actors in the Russian Far East timber industry

Russia has the world's largest forestry resources. The forests of the Russian Federation comprise 22 percent of the earth's total forest cover and more than 57 percent of its coniferous forest cover.[8] In economic terms, this represents 21 percent (82 billion cubic meters – bcm) of the world's standing timber volume, with a quarter of that total (20.4 bcm) in the Russian Far East alone.[9] During the Soviet era, Moscow held tight control over the country's forests. After the Soviet Union fell, radical privatization and decentralization of state functions fragmented Rosleskhoz, the once highly centralized Russian forestry agency responsible for both forest management and timber production. As regional governments grabbed more power, the federal agency fell into disarray, owing to a lack of financing and internal corruption.[10]

With regional bureaucrats and businessmen seeking to grab as much as they could, privatization in the early 1990s spawned thousands of small and medium-sized timber companies throughout the RFE. Many of the Soviet-era regional timber elite prospered during the transition by setting up their own companies, but new, smaller players were also able to establish their own businesses.

Of necessity, all these firms developed alliances with the state gatekeepers who control timber resources. Among the gatekeepers are powerful officials and entities within regional governments and the impoverished federal forest service. Other gatekeepers include individuals within the state security apparatus, such as policemen, border guards, customs officers, and immigration officials, who regulate the transport of timber along its many stages from harvest site to wholesale yards and, eventually, over the border, and who help (or hinder) Chinese operators in the purchase and transfer of timber. Entwined within these relationships is the strong presence of organized crime, some participants in which also work in the state or business sectors. These complex relationships, combined with inadequate legislation and an often dependent judiciary, block any efforts to reform the timber industry.

Rather than attempting to untangle the multitude of state–business–criminal arrangements, this section summarizes the major actors and, where possible, notes their connections to each other. The last part of the discussion briefly addresses illegal logging and trade to give the reader some concrete examples of how these actors collaborate.

### Rise of the private sector: old elites and the explosion of new operators

The Soviet-era Russian Forestry Ministry (Rosleskhoz) consisted of two main branches: one for forest management, Minleskhoz (the Federal Forest Service), and one for timber production, Minlesprom.[11] Minleskhoz had 81 regional forest services – roughly corresponding to Russia's 89 administrative units. Each regional service managed the *leskhozy* (forest service units). These *leskhozy*, in turn, regulated the activities of the *lespromkhozy*, or state-owned timber harvest companies that formed the core of Minlesprom. Another division of Minlesprom, Exportles, tightly controlled timber exports by setting prices and regulating supply. Exportles had an extensive network of offices in major importing countries.

In 1993–1994, privatization of the state-owned timber harvest companies (*lespromkhozy*) began, and by 1996 their conversion into joint stock companies was essentially complete.[12] This process, like the privatization of many other sectors in Russia, was far from transparent, involving a bewildering, often shady, array of state–private sector arrangements. One common strategy was to divide a *lespromkhoz* up into separate units, strip the assets of the undesirable ones, let their debts mount, and then declare them bankrupt. New companies were built on the assets from the previous structures. The abolition of state export controls made it possible to ship forest products to China. Small new players could easily enter the business because some of the largest and most valuable timber grows in easily accessible areas near roads or, in winter, along the banks of frozen rivers.

The changes transforming the industry were quick and far-reaching. In 1991, just prior to the introduction of economic and administrative reform, 82 *lespromkhozy*, 14 sawmills, and ten pulp and paper plants were operating in the entire Russian Far East.[13] By 1995, 316 timber companies had registered officially in Khabarovskii *krai* alone, and by 2001 this figure had mushroomed to 550.[14] In 1998, approximately 700 entities were registered as exporters to China. By 2002, the number of exporters had increased to more than 2,300 (see Figure 12.1).[15]

To some degree, the presence of so many operators makes the forestry industry amorphous. However, a couple dozen sizeable timber companies emerged out of the ashes of the huge *lespromkhozy*. Together they produce the majority of reported timber output in the RFE.[16] Their connection to the smaller firms in the industry is not entirely clear. Sometimes larger companies create smaller ones to avoid taxation; others may simply buy timber from them, and still others

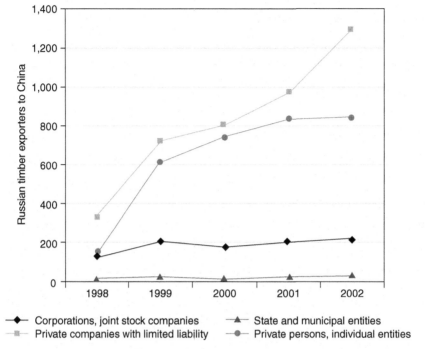

*Figure 12.1* Russian timber exporters to China, 1998-2002, by category and number
(source: Original source cited as "Database of electronic customs declarations of Russian Federation forest products exports in 1998–2003," distributed by M-INFO Consulting Company: Moscow, 2004. Adapted, with
permission, from Alexei Lankin, *Forest Product Exports from the Russian
Far East and Eastern Siberia to China: Status and Trends*, Washington,
DC: Forest Trends, 2005, p. 26).

have no connection at all. In many instances, the same managers who ran the
industry during Soviet times are still in control of the largest companies.

### Regional administrations

Other industries have certainly involved questionable privatization schemes, but
the timber sector is distinctive because the federal government delegated to
Russia's 89 regional governments control over the allocation of forest
resources.[17] Accordingly, the way each *krai* and *oblast'* administers these
resources varies considerably. Of prime importance is the power vested to
regional administrations to allocate and cancel timber leases, the primary means
by which timber companies gain access to the trees they harvest. In
Khabarovskii *krai*, the largest timber-producing region in the RFE, Governor
Viktor Ishaev firmly controls this power. His first vice-governor heads the all-
important Commission on Forest Resource Use, which considers applications
from local firms, makes decisions on competitions for leasing rights, has the

power to cancel leasing agreements, and collects industry taxes.[18] In Primorskii *krai*, the power structure is similar.

These arrangements can be highly fluid. Rights and responsibilities often shift between the various commissions, committees, agencies, and other governmental bodies, as each jockeys for control over the resources. Timber companies – to maximize income, avoid taxation, and increase access to untapped resources – also continually lobby for more favorable arrangements.

### *The regional* siloviki

Broadly understood as officials within the Ministry of Internal Affairs, Federal Security Service (FSB), Border Guard, Customs, military, police, and other agencies involved in security and defense, the *siloviki* regulate the transport and export of logs to Northeast Asia. Corrupt officials within these institutions benefit financially from these cross-border activities. Loggers must bribe policemen who operate road checkpoints. Wholesalers and traders pay protection to police captains to ensure their business is safe from police raids and criminals.[19] Detailed data on the extent of this corruption are difficult to obtain, but one survey of 100 Chinese migrant traders in Primorskii *krai* revealed corruption at all levels. When asked, "Whom do you pay for your security?" 80 percent named the police, 62 percent identified government officials, 60 percent cited transportation providers, and 55 percent, border guards.[20]

### *The Federal Forest Service: oversight agency or logging company?*

In contrast to Minlesprom, the basic structure of the Minleskhoz (Federal Forest Service) has remained essentially intact. The Forest Service is the primary government agency responsible for the sustainable use, protection, and management of the country's publicly held forests. But the Forest Service has been rendered largely ineffective as a result of inadequate funding and internal corruption. The federal budget is supposed to provide 80–90 per cent of the funding for the *leskhozy*, with the rest coming from the *leskhozy* themselves. In most cases, they receive far less. In 2003, for example, the federal budget covered only 20 percent of the *leskhozy* budget in Khabarovskii *krai*.[21]

To augment these meager resources or, in some cases, where unscrupulous *leskhoz* officials seek to enrich themselves, many *leskhozy* regularly abuse the practice of salvage logging. Also frequently referred to as "sanitary" or "maintenance" logging, salvage logging is intended to remove old and unhealthy trees and trees posing fire threats. This kind of logging, allowed within protected territories, is usually exempt from lease payments and stumpage fees. *Leskhozy* themselves log or give salvage logging licenses to companies to do so. The focus is usually on species that command a premium price in Northeast Asian markets, such as Korean pine (*Pinus koraensis*) and Manchurian ash (*Fraxinus mandshurica*). Such extensive disregard for the law by the *leskhozy* has fostered widespread indifference toward logging regulations among timber companies.

*Foreign companies*

Unclear property rights, a weak legal system, crime, corruption, and a general Russian mistrust of foreign involvement have dissuaded many foreign companies from investing in the RFE timber sector. At one point in the early 1990s, the US company Weyerhaeuser considered investing in the region but decided not to proceed when company managers realized, according to one analyst, that "basic parameters, such as the rights to a forest site and the right to export could evaporate at the whim of the authorities."[22]

Nevertheless, the RFE's extensive timber reserves remain highly attractive, and foreign companies continually try to penetrate the market. Hyundai Corporation made the first major investment by forming the Svetlaia Timber Venture with two Primorskii *krai*-based timber companies in 1991. Named after the coastal settlement of Svetlaia, the venture managed to secure a 30-year lease from the regional government to log on a plateau just above the settlement. The venture operated, in fits and starts, until 1997, when logging was abruptly scaled back and the operations were declared bankrupt. From the outset, the venture had trouble securing access to the resources, partially due to concerns about the environmental and social impacts of logging in the upper watershed of the Bikin River. Others speculate that the Russian partners sought to bleed the venture into bankruptcy so they could seize the timber harvesters and other equipment it owned and use the renovated port facilities.[23]

The handful of foreign investment projects that have been successful share a common feature: either strong and steady support by a powerful state entity or support by a large timber company that enjoys close ties with the state. The former is the case with the Malaysian transnational corporation, Rimbunan Hijau, which managed to secure two 48-year timber concessions in Khabarovskii *krai*. The first concession, with an annual allowable cut (AAC) of 550,000 cubic meters, encompasses most of the upper Sukpai River basin, about 150 kilometers from the city of Khabarovsk. The second concession, with an AAC of 495,000 cubic meters, is in the Bitchi River basin in Ulchskii *raion* in the central part of the *krai*.[24] Rimbunan is now the second-largest timber producer in the *krai* and exports logs to China and Japan. Governor Ishaev, who as mentioned before has strong control over the industry, personally courted Rimbunan during a visit to Kuala Lumpur.[25]

The other foreign venture – and the only major one in the entire RFE that produces processed timber – is Technowood. Sumitomo (Japan) and Terneiles, the largest and most economically sound Russian-owned timber company operating in Primorskii *krai*, joined forces to form this venture. Terneiles operates out the coastal town of Plastun and, like other large forestry companies in the southern RFE, supplies most local jobs and revenue for the town and *raion* budget. The firm even provides the wood chips used to fuel the boiler that generates the town's electricity. By providing these social services, Terneiles enjoys enormous influence with the *raion* and *krai* administrations. The company holds more Primorskii *krai* forest land in long-term lease than any other, giving

Technowood a stable supply of raw material, as well as comparably smooth relations with state entities.

According to government statistics, Chinese timber enterprises operating on Russian territory produce a minute portion (less than 2 percent) of total timber exported by Russia to China.[26] Even this figure seems high given that, officially at least, Chinese investment in all sectors of the RFE totaled just $13.2 million for 2003.[27] Russian nongovernmental organizations and industry representatives, however, paint a different picture. According to Anatoly Lebedev, director of a Vladivostok-based nongovernmental organziation specializing in forestry issues, Chinese money is financing numerous small Russian timber enterprises. He also claims that Chinese operators control wholesale timber yards in the Primorskii *krai* cities of Luchegorsk, Dalnerechensk, Lesozavodsk, Ussurisk, Nakhodka, and Dalnegorsk.[28]

Illicit Chinese financing has been a hot-button issue in the local Russian media for some time. While there is clearly illegal investment, the strong reaction can be partially attributed to phobias about Chinese commercial activity on Russian soil. The presence of purchasing agents representing trading companies, usually operating in Russia with a tourist visa, can be misconstrued as investment when they are simply buying timber.

### Organized crime and the emergence of illegal logging and trade

Criminal elements have infiltrated, or enjoy tight relations with, state entities and private enterprises, making it a challenge to identify where organized crime begins and where it ends. Few would dispute its influence in the industry, however. Local RFE papers regularly report on contract killings, intimidation, and other forms of violence in the industry.[29] One of the highest-profile assassinations in recent years was the murder of Bogdan Kovaliuk, then general director of Khabarovskglavles, a major timber enterprise in Khabarovskii *krai*.[30]

Weak regulation, corruption, and the explosion in the number of companies operating in the industry have led to a sharp rise in illegal logging. After years of trying to minimize public attention to the problem, the Russian government finally admitted in 2003 that it is an issue of concern.[31] Internationally, the Russian Federation is recognized as a major center for illegal logging, along with Indonesia, Cambodia, and a handful of other countries.

The *extent* of illegal logging depends on how it is defined. If defined purely in terms of adhering to all Russian forestry regulations, then virtually all logging operations, large and small, would technically be illegal.[32] However, illegal logging is usually more narrowly defined by excluding basic forestry violations such as failure to clean up a harvest site or logging on steep slopes. World Wildlife Fund-Russia (WWF) defines it by limiting it to five major violations: "harvesting more than permitted volumes, harvesting outside the permitted area, logging banned species or those not allowed for logging in a given area, commercial logging under the guise of salvage logging, and logging without a license or forged papers."[33]

*Table 12.1* Disparities in trade statistics for logs, 2002–2003 ($)

|  | *2002* | *2003* |
| --- | --- | --- |
| Exports reported by Russia | 735,941,000 | 718,868,188 |
| Imports reported by China | 975,270,140 | 969,024,232 |

Source: *World Trade Atlas*, Washington, DC: Global Trade Information Services, Inc., 2004 and Ivan Eastin, *Testimony before the U.S.–China Economic and Security Review Commission*, 13 January 2005, Center for International Trade in Timber Products (CINTRAFOR), www.uscc.gov/hearings/2005hearings/written_testimonies/05_01_04wrts/eastin_ivan_ wrts.htm (accessed 1 June 2005).

Using this definition as the basis for analysis, WWF estimates that roughly 50 percent of the logging in Primorskii *krai* is illegal.[34] For the country as a whole, WWF estimates losses at $1 billion, with total turnover of the industry at $6 billion. These losses include taxes that would have been paid to the state if illegal timber harvest were included, as well as timber that is sold underpriced. How much of this illegally logged timber is exported is difficult to gauge. One can get a rough idea by comparing Russian export statistics with Chinese import statistics, as in Table 12.1. The numbers indicate that Russia is significantly underreporting export volumes.

Both large and small companies are involved in illegal logging, as are the numerous regional and federal state entities (e.g. border guard, forest service, police) described earlier. Smaller companies, in particular, rely on individuals within these institutions to help ensure that illegally logged timber is "legalized" before it is exported, as they often do not have the necessary logging or export documents.[35] Such legalization can be secured at virtually every stage of the chain by bribing the officials responsible for that particular segment. It is most advantageous to start at the beginning by getting logging permits (usually for salvage logging) from the Forest Service. My field research, conducted in 1999–2000 in Roschino village in Primorskii *krai*, revealed that logging and transport certificates, complete with the embossed seal of the Forest Service, could be bought for $300.[36] These licenses and certificates make it much easier to pass through police checkpoints. If such papers are not available, then police at checkpoints must somehow be coerced, bribed, or avoided. Logs are then sold to a wholesaler who acquires or forges customs export documents.

Although larger companies may indirectly control smaller logging companies or "launder" timber for them, larger companies can more easily acquire forest-land through a lease or salvage license. Nevertheless, they also engage in illegal logging. Large numbers of high-quality Korean pine logs ready for export to Japan can be seen in the port of Plastun (where Terneiles operates), even though Russian regulations forbid commercial logging of the species. Korean pine may be logged only under certain circumstances, such as for building roads or during salvage logging. This timber may then be exported legally. The Forest Service participates by issuing bogus logging licenses, granting permission to build roads through Korean pine stands, and agreeing to expand the size of leased plots to include Korean pine areas – all of which facilitate the commercial logging of the species. Many larger companies are also exporters and have been known to use fraudulent shipment declarations that list inaccurate prices, grades, species, and timber volume. One specific strategy is to mislabel high-quality timber as pulp logs to lower tax payments.

## Business and corrupt officials versus larger state interests

It should now be evident that there exist myriad ways in which elements within state structures have formed murky, but mutually beneficial, alliances with timber companies, traders, and organized crime. In some respects, for all the illegality and corruption involved, these alliances have enabled the RFE forestry sector to maintain some stability during a period of tremendous social, economic, and political upheaval. Revenues generated by salvage logging have enabled the Forest Service to fulfill at least some of its regulatory functions. Soviet industrial development patterns meant that entire towns and villages were built around one industry, and the example of Terneiles maintaining road infrastructure and providing heating and other social services is a business–state model seen throughout the RFE. Timber companies such as Terneiles provide services that the state can no longer, or is unwilling to, provide.[37] Individuals within the state security apparatus, such as border guards and customs officials, have created *de facto* stability along the Russian–Chinese border region, as the continued flow of economic benefits depends on the continued functioning of the timber trade and holding ethnic conflict to a minimum.[38]

Unfortunately, what should have been, at best, temporary state–business alliances have endured and solidified. Corruption and cronyism have evolved into what Judith Thornton has identified as "stable institutionalized norms."[39] Ultimately, these alliances undermine the broader, long-term interests of the state. Loss of tax revenue, due to sheltering of profits and illegal logging, impoverishes state institutions administratively, financially, and morally. Unstable property rights and ownership regimes prove hostile to long-term private-sector stability and investment, both domestic and foreign. Links between Russian organized crime and its Japanese *yakuza* counterpart have been strengthening for some time, fueled by the timber trade as well as the lucrative trade in fish and used Japanese automobiles. This extensive black market has negatively affected Russia's relations with its Northeast Asian neighbors, which regularly voice concerns about Russian corruption and crime. Corruption within customs, the border service, and other security agencies responsible for regulating cross-border flows of people and resources has led to a vigorous trade in illicit goods at trading points along Russia's porous borders.

This section demonstrates that the collaboration of small and medium-sized logging businesses with corrupt state officials is working against the larger interests of the Russian state. Many of the Far Eastern timber companies and their crooked collaborators are making large profits by exporting raw logs to China. Such sales deprive Russia of much-needed jobs and tax revenue. Federal efforts to improve the situation have failed because they have not been able to over-come the resistance of entrenched interests.

### *Prolonged collapse in Russian processing capacity*

The short-term collaboration between individual state officials and business interests is setting up steep obstacles to timber-sector reform. Nowhere is the situation more evident than in the prolonged collapse of the wood processing industry. The RFE has never been known as a manufacturing center, but in 1989 processed timber (lumber and panel products) accounted for 20 percent of the region's total timber production. The Sakhalin and Khabarovsk pulp and paper mills produced much of the paper and paperboard used in the region (see Figure 12.2). Almost half of all timber production was consumed regionally, 25 percent was sent to other parts of the former Soviet Union, and 30 percent was exported.[40] Today, virtually all of the pulp mills are closed; processed or "value added" timber comprises just 7 percent of total production; and the region exports more than 70 percent of its total harvest, primarily in the form of raw logs. If higher transport and energy costs, combined with outdated machinery, started a downward spiral in the processing sector, then crime and corruption

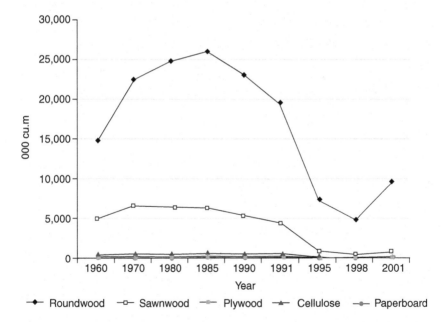

*Figure 12.2* Timber production in the Russian Far East, 1960–2001. (source: Original source cited as database of the Economic Research Institute, Far Eastern Branch of the Russian Academy of Sciences, 2004. Adapted, with permission, from Alexander Shein-gauz, *Overview of the Forest Sector in the Russian Far East: Production, Industry, and the Problem of Illegal Logging*, Washington, DC: Forest Trends, 2005, pp. 54–55).

have certainly speeded its demise and repeatedly blocked efforts to rebuild the industry. Like foreign investors, most Russian timber companies have chosen not to reinvest in processing capacity, but instead reap immediate returns on log exports while sheltering profits abroad.

### Booming Chinese wood demand and increased manufacturing capacity

Weak processing capacity has meant that Russia has remained almost entirely a raw log exporter, despite a decade-long boom in demand in Northeast Asia (see Map 12.2).[41] In just ten years, Russian timber exports to China, Japan, and South Korea have more than quadrupled, from 6.9 million cubic meters in 1993 to 26.6 million cubic meters in 2002 (see Figure 12.3).[42] China is the driver behind the dramatic rise, although Korea and Japan have both steadily increased imports.

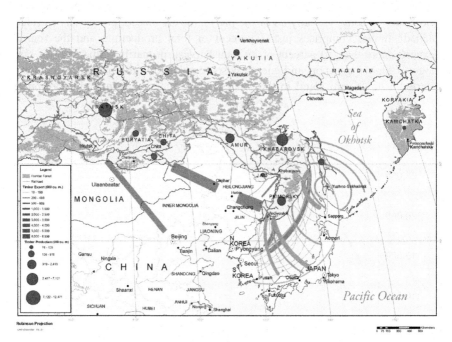

*Map 12.2* Russian timber export to Northeast Asia, 2002 (source: Frontier forest data provided as a digital file courtesy of the Biodiversity Conservation Center, Moscow, www.biodiversity.ru, 2004. Timber production data from Alexander Sheingauz, *Overview of the Forest Sector in the Russian Far East: Production, Industry, and the Problem of Illegal Logging*, Washington, DC: Forest Trends, 2005, pp. 54–55. Original source data for timber exports are from the "Database of electronic customs declarations of Russian Federation forest products exports in 1998–2003," distributed by M-INFO Consulting Company, Moscow, 2004. For the more readily accessible statistics on timber exports by administrative region of the Russian Federation, as well as by specific customs export point, see Alexei Lankin, *Forest Product Exports from the Russian Far East and Eastern Siberia to China: Status and Trends*, Washington, DC: Forest Trends, 2005).

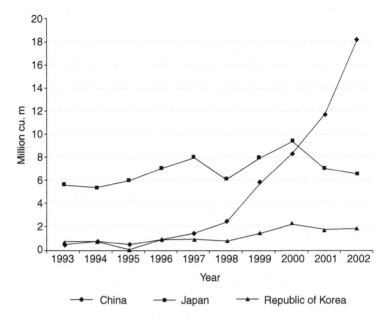

*Figure 12.3* Russian timber exports to Northeast Asia, 1993-2002 (source: Online trade database, European Forestry Information and Data Analysis System, European Forestry Institute, www.efi.fi/efidas/ (accessed on 5 June 2005)).

Following flooding in China in 1998, attributed to the deforestation of upper-river watersheds, the Chinese government passed the National Forest Protection Plan. To protect the few remaining natural forests, control water levels, and prevent soil erosion, this plan has strictly limited timber harvests in China. These restrictions, combined with rapid economic growth, have led to the sky-rocketing imports. Overall, Chinese wood product imports have almost tripled since 1998, from 12 million cubic meters to 36 million cubic meters in 2003, catapulting China past Japan to become the world's second largest importer of forest products. Russia now provides about 45 percent of this total – including 61 percent of all Chinese log imports, up from 21 percent in 1997 – making it by far the most important source.[43]

Chinese wood deficits are projected to expand rapidly. By 2025, according to the Center for International Trade in Forest Products, China may face a deficit of 200 million cubic meters of wood per year. At 2003 rates (45 percent of China's total imports), Russia may therefore be expected to provide China with 90 million cubic meters of timber by 2025. This figure is more than three times the total reported yearly harvest in both the RFE and Eastern Siberia.

China has been expanding wood-manufacturing capacity throughout Northeast China (Heilongjiang, Jilin, and Inner Mongolia provinces), one of the country's major timber centers. Because of the region's proximity to the RFE and Eastern Siberia and the similarity between tree species in these parts of Russia and China, Russian logs have proven eminently suitable for the hundreds of new sawmills and processing facilities in the region. Although the Chinese central government has not publicly formulated a development model whereby Russia supplies the logs and then China processes them into semifinished and finished goods for domestic use and export, this is how the development scenario is playing out. The provincial governments and Chinese forestry agencies have been instrumental in setting up modern timber processing mills along the Russian–Chinese border. And the Chinese government has adopted an ambitious new state program to modernize existing large pulp and paper factories throughout the region. These efforts are designed to take advantage of the inexpensive (and seemingly plentiful) Russian roundwood.

### *Russian efforts to develop domestic processing capacity*

Many Far East governors recognize that Russia's future stability and prosperity depend on the jobs and tax revenues derived from processing more of the region's rich natural resources. Local factories would reduce external dependence on processed products, such as furniture and paper. A strong value added sector is likely to have the environmental benefit of stemming the steady decline in the quality of the timber resource base, because processing would increase demand for woodchips, branches, and smaller-diameter trees. In addition to being tremendously wasteful, this unwanted timber, currently left at the harvest site, is fuel for forest fires. Expanding Russian processing capabilities is likely to reduce illegal logging. Closure of wood-processing enterprises has led to high unemployment in forest communities, leading some to log illegally simply to survive.

Khabarovsk governor Ishaev has long promoted wood processing but, despite the *krai* administration's relatively strong control over the timber sector, he has made little headway. In spring 2000, he issued a decree that by 2003 all Khabarovsk-based timber companies should export only processed and structural lumber. This decree proved too ambitious, given the dilapidated state of the processing industry, and was not enforced. Resistance from entrenched interests, who have profited from exporting logs, and the lack of federal support no doubt contributed to its demise. Ishaev subsequently issued a more modest directive requiring that at least 20 percent of the *krai*'s timber harvest be processed locally, a requirement that was even written into the lease agreement with Rimbunan Hijau. But in the case of Rimbunan, as well as with other operators, this regulation has also proven virtually impossible to enforce.

Previous attempts to modernize the processing sector focused almost exclusively on Japanese investors. But, as discussed earlier, key Japanese investors are no longer working in the region. As a result, Ishaev and other regional leaders have started to target Chinese investors, and there have been some positive signs of interest. In 2003, three Chinese enterprises tentatively agreed to invest $278 million in wood-processing projects in the Eastern Siberian region of Chita, which if completed would produce 300,000 cubic meters of wood and 400,000 tons of pulp annually.[44] In 2004, the city of Khabarovsk hosted the first ever

China–Russia Conference for Investment Promotion.[45] Subsequently, presidential envoy Konstantin Pulikovsky led a delegation to the annual International Trade Fair in Harbin, China, in June 2004. Evidently, a number of agreements were signed, including a joint venture agreement between one of Khabarovsk's largest timber companies, Flora, and Shenyang Heavy Machinery Corporation to build a $300 million plant capable of producing 80,000 cubic meters of engineered wood products annually.[46] These agreements were quickly followed by an announcement of plans to build a quasi-free trade zone on both sides of the border at the Suifenhe–Pogranichny railroad junction. The zone will reportedly enjoy favorable tariffs and be free from visa requirements.[47]

But it remains to be seen whether foreign investment, Chinese or otherwise, and the proposed free trade zone will indeed improve the timber export mix in Russia's favor. Japanese investment in wood processing quickly dried up and did little to enhance the region's wood-processing capacity. Given China's rapid expansion of capacity in Manchuria, the window of opportunity for the RFE to build its own plants is closing quickly.

### *Moscow seeks increased investment through recentralization*

The federal government is seeking to encourage the private-sector investment necessary for constructing a competitive wood-processing sector. Aside from coordinating support through presidential envoy Pulikovsky's office, the Putin administration's forest sector development strategy has focused on legislative and administrative reform. In 2003, after years of piecemeal attempts, the administration proposed a complete overhaul of the 1997 Russian Forest Code in hopes of finally providing transparent and stable rules for the management and use of forest resources. Establishing a clear division of responsibilities between the center and regions – a relationship that has oscillated back and forth since early *perestroika* reforms – is a primary objective of this revision. With these responsibilities sorted out, federal officials hope a legal framework will finally be in place that provides secure and long-term access to forest resources. Such a stable environment should attract more investment.

Under the Putin plan, regional governments would retain some control, but the proposed changes are designed to recentralize power. Restructuring the timber leasing process is one of the primary means to achieve this goal. The 1997 Code predominantly favors discretionary and short-term allocation of forest leases by regional administrations.[48] This crony-friendly system would be replaced with a federally controlled, open price-based auction system. Long-term leases would be extended to 99 years (from the current 50) and regional governments would no longer be able to allocate leases for short-term use (five years or less). They would retain the right to administer auctions, but only through special delegation agreements. In addition to increasing federal control, these changes clearly favor large companies by making it even more difficult for small companies to gain access to timber resources. To address the problem of weak law enforcement, a new Federal Service for Oversight in Natural

Resources, which would not be able to charge fees, would oversee forest users, the leasing process, and the Federal Forest service, which will remain the primary agency responsible for forest management and use.

Yet four years after efforts to revise the Forest Code began, revisions remain in draft form, stymied by continual, but fruitless, debates between stakeholders. To illustrate the problem, in one case the Putin administration wanted to give lessees in good standing the right to buy (privatize) their leased forest parcel 15 years into their lease, but after vociferous debate this plan was temporarily shelved. Those who benefit from the current arrangements, including regional administration officials, are clearly resisting reform. In the case of the timber sector, Yeltsin-era reforms delegated so much power to the regions, and there are so many vested interests benefiting from the status quo, that even a very strong central government will have difficulty regaining control. As Thornton notes, policy makers will try to "block or distort changes in the rules of the game that threaten to reduce the value of their existing control rights."[49]

Moscow's neglect becomes apparent when one considers the perverse nature of Russian export tariffs for timber. Currently, tariffs are higher for processed wood products than for raw logs. The export tariff for particleboard is 10 percent of the production cost (but not less than $4 for each cubic meter) versus 6.5 percent for logs (not less than $2.50 per cubic meter). Fortunately, there are signs that the Russian government has finally started to address this situation. The government has adopted resolutions abolishing tariffs for laminated forest products and newspaper in sheets or rolls, and a recent proposal recommends a gradual increase in export duties on logs.[50]

The federal government may elect to follow in Indonesia's footsteps and take the more drastic measure of banning all log exports. Such bans have been shown to increase domestic value added processing. But they are highly controversial, because some believe such protections prop up an industry that would otherwise be uncompetitive internationally. Others criticize them because the countries that institute them are generally inefficient at milling their own timber and would, therefore, be better off by specializing in log export. It is hard to imagine how a ban would exacerbate resource waste, given the already enormous levels of waste at Russian logging sites. The more pertinent issues with respect to Russia are whether such a ban would temporarily debilitate the entire industry, whether the sector would attract foreign and domestic investment, and whether the Russian government would be willing to risk retaliatory trade measures by the Chinese government. These concerns aside, it is curious that export bans have been noticeably absent in federal-level debate about how to reform the timber sector.

## Conclusion: prospects for conflict and cooperation

An array of corrupt state–business alliances emerged out of the chaotic post-Soviet era to provide a certain stability in the Russian Far East timber sector. Today, there is little chance of a complete breakdown of law and order, such as in the Congo, where rebel-occupied territories are financed by illegal logging and trade.[51] Individual officials inside the Russian government who profit from the status quo ensure order within the industry and keep the peace along the Russian–Chinese border so that the trade can continue. But these alliances provide benefits only for a select few and undermine the broader, long-term interests of the state, such as increased domestic and foreign investment, higher tax revenue, improved forest management and use, and an internationally competitive wood-processing sector.

If Russia does not take action soon, the rife corruption in the Far Eastern forestry sector could provoke conflict with China, which has benefited from the situation. Public resentment about the export of jobs and lost profits across the border could undermine the current stability.

Regional leaders realize the need to reform the timber sector and increase Russia's ability to profit more from its natural resources. But reform efforts have been sporadic. Regional administrations are crippled by internal corruption and generally lack the necessary financial and administrative resources necessary to impose change. Only a federal government committed to fundamental and comprehensive reform will be able to wrest control of the timber sector from current power brokers, though such efforts ultimately may only move corruption from the regional to the federal level. For the Putin administration, the timber sector remains a low priority, efforts to rewrite the Forest Code and public announcements about the need for foreign investment in the processing sector notwithstanding.

Whatever measures the Putin administration decides upon, it would be well advised to find a solution to the RFE's weak manufacturing capacity soon. Public resentment in the RFE over perceived Chinese economic dominance appears to be steadily increasing, if regional newspapers like *Tikhookeanskaia Zvezda*, *Vladivostok*, *Dal'nevostochnyi Federal'nyi Okrug*, and *Priamurskie Vedomosti* are any indication.[52] Of course, the Far East's governors have long manipulated public sentiment toward China for their personal political purposes, and the region's newspapers reflect the interests of their corporate and state owners, but their discussion of the forestry sector touches on issues of real concern and cannot be dismissed as mere propaganda.

"China has the clear intention of turning the RFE into a raw materials appendage of its northern provinces," writes *Tikhookeanskaya Zvezda* journalist Raisa Eldashova.[53] Russian leaders frequently express similar views. After an October 2003 meeting between regional Russian and Chinese leaders, presidential envoy Pulikovsky commented that when presented with investment projects, "the Chinese party always returned to the idea of simple trade as the most beneficial to China."[54] This is emblematic of the contrast between Russian development visions for the RFE with those of the Chinese decision makers: Russians want investment, Chinese want timber without any strings attached.

Local papers are also littered with reports of illegal resource harvesting by Chinese on Russian territory. Russian resources are being "shamelessly plundered by the Chinese," writes *Priamurskie Vedomosti* journalist Pavel

Bondarevskii.[55] The numerous reports of logging and timber smuggling, and collection of pine nuts, endangered ginseng, fur pelts, and the like undoubtedly have merit, but so do the countless incidents of illegal harvesting by Russian nationals. "What Far Easterners should fear . . . is the plundering of the RFE's natural resources by inventive Russians who market them to China, Japan, the US, South Korea, and other countries," writes Viktor Larin, hoping to inject some reason into the debate.[56]

Reform should also proceed with haste, because the window of opportunity for Russia to develop a processing industry that can compete with Chinese plants is closing rapidly. China is already the world's largest furniture exporter and will soon become the largest plywood exporter. Chinese manufacturers are now major producers of flooring products and a variety of engineered wood products. Giant Western firms, such as Wal-Mart, Home Depot, and IKEA, are fueling the Chinese expansion by providing investment and technology to their Chinese suppliers.

The danger is that Russian fears (real or perceived) of China's emerging economic dominance will stoke long-held Russian concerns about Chinese migration into the Russian Far East. Russian apprehensions could result in conflict that could be manifested in a variety of ways ranging from a general chilling of relations, to clamping down of borders by regional and federal authorities, to incidents of ethnic violence.

In a more optimistic scenario, the federal government could embrace the challenge and use timber-sector reform as a means to achieve larger geopolitical objectives. Economic prosperity, driven in part by an expanding processing sector, would discourage the two-decade-long out-migration that has drained the social and intellectual capital of the RFE. Reversing this trend would provide increased security and stability along Russia's eastern borders as China continues to grow.

It may be that the federal government lacks the capacity to push through reforms. Or that the Far East's forestry sector is so corrupt and decentralized that the Putin administration is not sure what can be done to reform it. But if it is a matter of political will, as I believe, then what is a required is a fundamental shift in how Moscow approaches the development of the Russian Far East.

## Notes

1 This theme pervades J. Thornton and T. Ziegler, eds., *Russia's Far East: A Region at Risk*, Seattle and London: National Bureau of Asian Research and University of Washington Press, 2002.

2 The most insightful history of the region remains J. Stephan, *The Russian Far East: A History*, Stanford, CA: Stanford University Press, 1994.

3 Some question the extent of the commercially viable resource base; see M. J. Bradshaw and N. J. Lynn, "Resource-based development in the Russian Far East: Problems and prospects," *Geoforum* 29, no. 4, 1998, pp. 375–392.

4 On this theme, see work by Mikhail Alekseev: M. N. Alekseev, *Globalization at the Edges of Insecurity: Migration, Interethnic Relations and International Economic Interactions in Russia's Border Regions*, Zurich: Center for Security Studies and

Conflict Research, 2002; and M. N. Alekseev, "Economic Valuations and Interethnic Fears: Perceptions of Chinese Migration in the Russian Far East," *Journal of Peace Research* 40, no. 1, 2003, pp. 85–102.

5 Large-scale infrastructure projects have long been used as a means to extend influence over the peripheries and to secure borders. The Trans-Siberian Railroad and the Baikal Amur Mainline (BAM) are two notable examples.

6 By most accounts, the fishing industry is the RFE's largest. Like the timber industry, it too has experienced tremendous fragmentation. International conflicts over access to marine resources in the Sea of Okhotsk have been marked by violence.

7 Moscow still maintains export controls over most of the RFE's precious metals.

8 Forest cover figures vary from 22 to 25 percent. For the higher figure, see Armin Rosencranz and Antony Scott, "Siberia's Threatened Forests," *Nature* 355, no. 6358, 1992, pp. 293–294. For the lower figure, see World Bank, *Project Appraisal Document on a Proposed Loan in the Amount of U.S. $6 million to the Russian Federation for a Sustainable Forestry Pilot Project*: Report 20144-RU, Washington, DC: World Bank, 2000.

9 Data are from 1995 and come from the Far Eastern Forestry Inventory Enterprise, based in Khabarovsk.

10 On 17 May 2000, Putin issued Decree 867, "On the Structure of the Federal Bodies of the Executive Authority," which handed over the functions of the Committee on Environmental Protection (*Goskomekologia*) to the Ministry of Natural Resources. The Forest Service was also folded into the ministry, but remains a distinct entity.

11 A. S. Sheingauz, V. P. Karakin, and V. A. Tyukalov, *Forest Sector of the Russian Far East: A Status Report*, Khabarovsk: Economic Research Institute, Far Eastern Branch of the Russian Academy of Science (FEBRAS), 1996, p. 48.

12 While reforms in the timber sector began as early as 1988, large-scale change really started with the first phase of privatization (1993–1996).

13 A. S. Sheingauz, *Developing a Forest Conservation Strategy in the Russian Far East*, Khabarovsk: Economic Research Institute, FEBRAS, 2003, p. 44.

14 Sheingauz, *Developing a Forest Conservation Strategy*, p. 44.

15 A. Lankin, *Status and Trends in Forest Product Exports from the Russian Far East and Siberia to China*, Vladivostok: Pacific Institute of Geography, 2004, p. 40.

16 Based on a rough tally of RFE production statistics, these firms account for between 70 and 85 per cent of total annual production.

17 A key early law was "The Fundamental Forestry Law of the Russian Federation" adopted in March 1993. The Russian government tried to codify the many laws and regulations (which often conflicted) by adopting the Russian Forest Code in 1997.

18 Sheingauz, *Developing a Forest Conservation Strategy*, p. 44.

19 Lankin, *Status and Trends in Forest Product Exports*, p. 40.

20 M. A. Alexseev, "Socioeconomic and Security Implications of Chinese Migration in the Russian Far East," *Post-Soviet Geography and Economics* 42, no. 2, 2001, pp. 122–141.

21 Sheingauz, *Developing a Forest Conservation Strategy*, p. 44.

22 J. Thornton, *The Exercise of Rights to Resources in the Russian Far East*, Discussion Paper from the University of Washington, Seattle, Department of Economics, 1999, pp. 1–53, here p. 30, econpapers.repec.org/paper/fthwasher/0058.htm.

23 J. Newell, *The Russian Far East: A Reference Guide for Conservation and Development*, McKinleyville, CA: Daniel & Daniel, 2004, p. 133.

24 Newell, *The Russian Far East*, p. 175.

25 The agreement with Rimbunan was made at the same time as the Malaysian government purchased jet fighters that were built at a defense factory in Komsolmolsk-on-Amur. This timing raises questions about whether the logging concession was awarded to Rimbunan on entirely fair terms.

26 M. Yamane and W. Lu, *Trends in China's Forest-Related Policies: From the Perspective of the Growing Timber Trade*, Tokyo: Institute of Global Environmental Strategies (IGES), 2002, p. 11.

27 A. Vasyenov, *Chinese Factor in RFE Economic and Business Development*, Khabarovsk: BISNIS, 2004, p. 6.

28 J. Newell, *The Russian Far East*, p. 71.

29 Useful compilations are the 1999 and 2000 editions of *Organized Crime and Corruption Watch*, published by the Transnational Crime and Corruption Center, American University, Washington, DC. See www.american.edu/traccc/Publications/OCWatch/v2n2_2000.pdf.

*30 Sheingauz, Developing a Forest Conservation Strategy, p. 44.*

31 S. Kuzmichenko, *Commercial News Update from the RFE*, Washington, DC: BISNIS, 2003, p. 4.

32 Alexander Sheingauz, interview by the author at the conference "Commercial Forestry in the Russian Far East," Yuzhno-Sakhalinsk, Russia, 18 September 2001.

33 World Wildlife Fund-RFE (WWF-RFE), *Implementation of the WWF Forest Strategy*, Vladivostok: WWF-RFE: Vladivostok, 2001, p. 11.

34 WWF-RFE, *Implementation*, p. 11.

35 The amount of timber that is simply smuggled out of the country without any form of documentation is actually quite small. While there are a number of land and river crossings along the Russian-Chinese border, most are small and have limited infrastructure on either side to handle significant amounts of timber. About 90 percent of all timber exported goes by train through three routes (Zabaikalsk-Manzhouli, Gorodekova–Suifenhe, and Naushki–Erlianhot). In the case of Japan and South Korea, timber moves by ship, which requires customs documents.

36 See Newell, *The Russian Far East*, pp. 72–73.

37 Such provisions are often a prerequisite for access to resources; a major factor when allocating large timber leases is the ability of the company to provide these services. However, this requirement has made the leasing process complex and subject to graft. It has meant other concessions by the state, such as a compromised ability to collect taxes and the loss of control over critical infrastructure. In the case of Terneiles, the concession is evident in the company's almost complete control over Plastun port.

38 M. A. Alexseev, "Socioeconomic and Security Implications."

39 Thornton, *The Exercise of Rights*, pp. 1–53.

40 A. S. Sheingauz, *Forest Industry of the Russian Far East: A Status Report*, Khabarovsk: Economic Research Institute, FEBRAS, 1999, p. 48.

41 Despite recent proclamations that the industry is rebounding, comparing the percentage of roundwood as a portion of total exports to the major markets for two periods, 1997 and 2002, reveals it has remained essentially the same for Japan and South Korea and deteriorated for China: Japan (88 percent and 86 percent), South Korea (95 percent and 94 percent), and China (74 percent and 90 percent).

42 This timber comes almost entirely from the southern RFE and southeastern Siberia.

43 S. Ziufang, *Meeting Chinese Demand for Forest Products*, Washington, DC: Forest Trends, 2004, p. 50.

44 No author, "China to Launch Largest Lumbering Project in Russia's Far East," *People's Daily* (Beijing), 7 July 2003, english.people.com.cn/200307/07/eng20030707_119621.shtml, (accessed 5 June 2005).

45 No author, "Russia: China is an Important Strategic Trade Partner," *People's Daily*, 25 September 2004, english.people.com.cn/200409/25/eng20040925_158265.html (accessed 5 June 2005).

46 A. Vasyenov, *Chinese Factor*, p. 6.

47 No author, "Quasi-free Trade Zone Being Built along Border," *People's Daily*, 20 June 2004, english.people.com.cn/200406/20/eng20040620_146948.html (accessed 5 June 2005).

48 G. Dieterle and A. Kuslin, *Key Challenges of Russian Forest Policy Reform*, Washington, DC: World Bank, 2004, p. 19.

49 Thornton, *The Exercise of Rights*, pp. 1–53.

50 USDA Foreign Agricultural Service, *Russian Federation Solid Wood Products, Annual Report (Report RS5012)*, Moscow: US Embassy, 2005.

51 UN Security Council, *Report of the Panel of Experts on the Illegal Exploitation of Natural Resources and Other Forms of Wealth of the Democratic Republic of the Congo*, New York: UN Security Council, 2001.

52 A. Kolesnikova, "Chinese Expansion to the Russian Far East as Covered by the Local and Central Press," in *International Studies*. Seattle: University of Washington, 2004, p. 109.

53 R. Eldashova, "Kitaiskii den' surka i kak s nim borotskaya," *Tikhookeanskaya Zvezda*, 11 May 2003, toz.khv.ru (accessed 5 June 2005).

54 As cited in O. Novak, "Dal'nii Vostok navstrechu resheniyam plenuma TsK KPK," *Tikhookeanskaya Zvezda*, 11 December 2003, toz.khv.ru, accessed 5 June 2005.

55 P. Bondarevskii, "Vnushitel'nyi ulov putiny," *Priamurskie Vedomosti*, 21 May 2003, toz.khv.ru (accessed 5 June 2005).

56 As cited in V. Kolesov, "Strategichesko partnerstvo," *Vladivostok*, 15 January 2004, toz.khv.ru (accessed 5 June 2005).

# Index

Abashidze, Aslan 223
Abkhaz crime group 229
Abkhazia 14, 89, 217, 218, 221; drugs 202; electricity 98; money laundering 190
Abramovich, Roman 31
Accounting Chamber 164
Adamov, Yevgenii 126
Adjaria 223
Aeroflot 30
Aerospace Equipment 162
AES electricity corporation 96, 98
Afghanistan 11, 14, 117; drugs 196, 197, 199, 208
Africa 163, 197
Aghazadeh, Gholamreza 129
AIDS 27, 197, 199–200
Akayev, Askar 34
Akhmetov, Daniyal 93–5
Al Hakim, Abdul Aziz 122
Alekperov, Vagit 31, 59; Iraq 119, 122, 123
Aleshin, Boris 162, 163
Alfa Group 24, 165
Allawi, Iyad 123
Almaz-Antei Air Defense 30
Al-Qaida 117
Alrosa 26, 33
Amnesty International 169
amphetamines 202
Angarsk 140, 142
Arco 144
Ardzinba, Levan 226
Ardzinba, Madina 228
Ardzinba, Vladislav 222, 226
Argentina 169
Armenia 33, 217, 218; oil 95; UES 96–8
Armenian crime group 229
arms 33
Asia 50

Asian financial crisis 134
Asia-Pacific region 133–54
Association of Russian Banks 179, 180–1, 193n18
Astrakhan 201–2
Astrakhansky, Yasha see Liudkov, Artur
Azerbaijan 33, 217; gas 92–3; LUKoil 102; oil 93, 95; smuggling 226, 230; trade 90, 91; Transneft 105; UES 96
Aziz, Tariq 119

Babaevskii 225
Bagapsh, Sergei 222, 229
Baikal Amur Mainline 257n5
Baku–Tbilisi–Ceyhan pipeline 89, 102, 106, 126
Baltic countries 199
Baltic Pipeline System 50
Baltic Shipyards 162, 165
Bank of Moscow 165
Bank of New York 188–91, 204
banks 24, 33
barter 160
Base Element 24
BASF 52
Batukaev, Aziz 206
Belarus 9–10, 18, 36, 38, 75–82; Gazprom 77–9, 81–4, 86n31; trade 90
Belarus–Russian Union 67, 75–6, 81
Beltransgaz 77–8, 86n35
Bendukidze, Kakha 220
black market 26
Blue Stream pipeline 50, 93, 137
Bondarevskii, Pavel 255–6
border guards 205, 241, 244, 248
Borsodchem 57
Brahmos antiship missile 168
Brazil 169
British Petroleum 25, 60, 144; Elvary Neftegas 148, 151; see also TNK-BP

Brownfield, William 168
Bulgaria 49
Bush, George W. 120, 121, 128–9
Bushehr 11, 125, 126–30
business: defined 4–5, 133

Calzolari, Giacomo 188
Cambodia 246
capital flight 27, 36, 188–9
Caspian Pipeline Consortium 105, 106, 107
Caspian Sea 89, 108, 126
Castro, Fidel 168
Caucasus 33, 38; drugs 197
Center for International Trade in Forest Products 251
Center for Strategic and International Studies 27
Center for the Analysis of Strategies and Technologies 164
Central Asia 33, 38, 230; drugs 197; Gazprom 98–101
Central Asia–Caucasus Institute 198
Central Bank of Russia 177–9, 180, 181, 184, 186, 187, 190–1
Chavez, Hugo 168–9
Chechen crime groups 206, 229
Chechnya 14, 197, 204, 205, 207–9, 217
Chelyabinsk 201
Chemezov, Sergei 161, 164, 165–6
Chernomyrdin, Viktor 180, 181, 229
Chevron 148
Chevron Caspian Pipeline Consortium Company 105
ChevronTexaco 105, 144
China 15, 20, 117, 133; arms sales 12, 13, 158–60, 163, 164, 167–8; conflict 152, 255; drugs 197, 199; electricity 95; energy demand 134, 135, 137–9; forestry 242, 246, 250–2, 252–3, 258n35, 258n41; gas 152; Japan 143; Kazakhstan 95; LUKoil 139; oil 95, 134; pipeline 141; Russian Far East 239; Sakhalin-1 147; Yukos 35, 139
China National Petroleum Corporation 141, 142, 147
Chita 252
Chubais, Anatoly 97–8, 180, 219
coal 135, 138
cocaine 199, 202–3, 230
Colombia 168, 169, 198, 209
Colombian crime groups 204–5, 206–7
Committee for Military and Technical Cooperation with Foreign Countries 161

Committee on Arms Trade with Foreign Countries 164
Committee on Environmental Protection 257n10
Common Economic Space 67
Commonwealth of Independent States 67, 89
Communist Party 34, 118
conflict 4–5, 17–19; arms trade 167–9; banks 185; drugs 207–9; energy 61–3, 72–4, 81–2, 107–8, 133; separatist regions 232–5; timber 255
Congo 255
ConocoPhillips 123, 124
contraband trade, defined 224
cooperation 16–17; energy 61–3, 72–4, 81–2, 107–8, 133
corruption 12–13, 14, 15, 25–6, 68, 170, 209; banking 175, 181–2; drugs 198; forestry 244, 248, 249–50; Gazprom 100
Council for Mutual Economic Assistance 49, 55
customs service 205, 241, 244, 248
Cyprus 25, 27, 58
Czechoslovakia 49

Dagestan 200
Dal'nevostochnyi Federal'nyi Okrug (newspaper) 255
Daqing 35, 142
Darfur 169
de Palacio del Valle-Lersundi, Loyola 51
Defense Ministry 165
Defense-Systems Invest 165
Denisov, Aleksandr 164
Dmitriev, Mikhail 161
drugs 27
Druzhba pipeline 49, 50
Duelfer report 118
Dugin, Aleksandr 219

Eberstadt, Nick 200
ecstasy 202
Ecuador 169
Eldashova, Raisa 255
Elvary Neftegaz 148, 151
Energy Dialogue 51, 61
ephedrine 199
Ergneti 226, 227
Estonia 36
Eural Trans Gas 70
Eurobank 190

European Aeronautical Defence and Space Company 163
European Energy Charter 50–1, 56
European Union 8, 16–17; China 160; drugs 197, 198; Gazprom 32, 35, 39, 86n32; Russia 70; South Caucasus 218–19; Ukraine 68–9, 73; WTO 188
ExxonMobil 144, 147, 148, 150

Fainberg, Ludwig 206
Far East 25; drugs 198
Federal Agency for Industry 167
Federal Energy Commission 81
Federal Forest Service 242, 244, 247–8, 254, 257n10
Federal Military and Technical Cooperation Service 161
Federal Security Service 205, 206, 208, 244
Federal Service for Financial Monitoring 189, 190
Federal Service for Oversight in Natural Resources 253–4
Federal Service for the Control of Narcotics 198
Fedotov, Yuri 121, 127
Felgenhauer, Pavel 164
Ferghana Valley 108
FIMACO (Financial Management Company) affair 190–1
Financial Action Task Force 189–90
Financial Monitoring Committee 189
Finland 95
Flora 253
foreign business (in Russia) 25, 133
foreign direct investment 48
Forest Code 253–4, 257n17
forestry 25
Fradkov, Mikhail 143
France 49, 50, 117, 121, 127, 130
Friedman, Robert 206
Frye, Timothy 180

Gaddy, Clifford 181
Gaidar, Yegor 24, 180
Galeotti, Mark 199
Gaon, Nessim 195n44
Gazexport 99
Gazprom 12, 18, 24, 26, 30; Abkhazia 228; banks 13, 184; Belarus 9, 77–9, 81–4, 86n31; Central Asia 10, 93, 98–101, 106–7; CIS 35; corruption 39, 68; EU 8, 56; European Energy Charter 51; Kazakhstan 99, 101; Kovyktinskoe

141–2, 151; Moldova 31; NE Asia 149, 151–2; Sakhalin-1 147; Sakhalin-2 146–7; Sakhalin-3 148; state 32, 133, 150; Turkmenistan 92, 99, 101; Ukraine 70–2, 73–4
Gazprombank 192n3
Gdansk refinery 58–9
Geogravionik 226
Georgia 10, 14, 25, 34, 217, 218; drugs 202; oil 95; Rose Revolution 39; trade 90; UES 33, 96–8
Gerashchenko, Viktor 179, 180, 187, 191, 193n13, 195n44
German Democratic Republic 49
Germany 27, 35, 74, 117, 121, 127, 130
Gilbertson, Brian 37
GKOs (government short-term bonds) 183
Gleason, Gregory 32
Glinkina, Svetlana 229
Golts, Aleksandr 166
Gorbachev, Mikhail 24
Great Britain 95
Gref, German 25
Group Alliance 26
Grupa Lotus 59
Gustafson, Thane 28
Guta-bank 178, 184

hashish 199, 230
heroin 199, 200, 230
Hezbollah 169
HIV *see* AIDS
Home Depot 256
human security 5
Hungary 49, 57
Hussein, Saddam 11, 116, 117
Hyundai 245

Ickes, Barry 181
Ignat'ev, Sergei 177, 179
IKEA 256
Il'yushin 162
India 12, 116–17, 152n1; arms 158–9, 160, 163, 168
Indian State Oil Company ONGC Videsh 144
Indonesia 160, 246, 254
Inkombank 183
International Accounting Standards 191
International Atomic Energy Agency 125, 126, 127
International Crisis Group 202, 208
International Finance Corporation 177
International Monetary Fund 188, 190, 191

Interros 140, 165, 183
Iran 11, 91, 92, 114–15, 125–30; drugs
198; UES 96–7
Iranian Atomic Energy Organization 128
Iraq 11, 115–25, 169; Lukoil 114, 115–16,
118–19
Irkut 160, 162, 163, 165
Irkutsk 200, 212n30
Irkutsk Oblast Administration 141
Ishaev, Viktor 243, 245, 252
Islamic Movement of Uzbekistan 201,
212n38
Israel 27, 160, 169
IST 165
Italy 27, 50; Kazakhstan 95
Itera 26, 65n26, 70
Ivankov, Vyacheslav 204
Ivanov, Igor 118, 121, 128, 129, 223
Ivanov, Viktor 30

Japan 20, 35, 133, 197; energy demand
135, 137–9; forestry 250–1, 252,
258n35, 258n41; LNG 136; Russian Far
East 239; Sakhalin-1 147; Siberian
pipeline 143; Soviet Union 134, 144

Kaldor, Mary 223
Kaliuzhny, Viktor 73
Kamynin, Mikhail 129
Kashmaria, Ruslan 225
Kasyanov, Mikhail 59
Kazakhstan 33, 36, 89; Chechen crime
groups 206; China 95; drugs 201;
Gazprom 99, 101; LUKoil 102; oil
93–5, 106; Russian FDI 95; trade 90–1;
Transneft 105
KazMunaiGaz 99
KazRosGaz 99
KBP Tula 169, 172n19
Khabarovsk Krai 140, 147, 204, 242, 243,
249
Khabarovskglavles 246
Khajimba, Raul 222
Kharazi, Kamal 128
Khodorkovsky, Mikhail 23, 29, 31, 37,
184
Kinakh, Anatoly 73
Kirienko, Sergei 228
Klebanov, Ilya 121, 160, 165
Klitgaard, Robert 26
Kogas 141
Kokoev, Eduard *see* Kokoity, Eduard
Kokoity, Eduard 222–3
Konsorcjum Gdanskie 59

*kooperativ* 24
Kovaliuk, Bogdan 246
Kovyktinskoe field 141–2, 147, 151
Krasnodar Krai 220–1, 227, 228
Kuchma, Leonid 69, 73
Kudrin, Aleksei 123
Kulczyk, Jan 59
Kurgan 201
Kurile Islands 143
Kuwait 116
Kuzyaev, Andrei 122
Kyoto Protocols 138
Kyrgyzstan 34, 90, 91; Chechen crime
groups 206; drugs 201; electricity 95;
gas 92; oil 95

Larin, Viktor 256
Latin America 197, 199
Latvia 36, 55
Lavrov, Sergei 124, 128, 129
Lebedev, Anatoly 246
Leningrad 25
Liberal Democratic Party of Russia 118
liquefied natural gas 135, 136
Lithuania 29–30, 55, 57, 221
Liudkov, Artur 231
Liuhto, Kari 104
loans-for-shares deals 182, 193n15,
194n24
lobbying 29–30, 179–80
Lobov, Oleg 180
Loranth, Gyongyi 180
LUKAgip 102
LukArco 105
Lukashenko, Aleksandr 9, 75–7, 80–1,
81–2
Lukianov, Anatoly 222
Lukin, Vladimir 119
LUKoil 10, 24, 26, 107; Abkhazia 228;
Azerbaijan 102–3; Belarus 79–80;
Caspian 101–6; China 139;
ConocoPhillips 123, 124; EU 53–5, 58;
Iraq 11, 114, 115–16, 118–19, 122, 124,
125; Kazakhstan 102; Lithuania 29–30,
60–1; Poland 57, 59; state 31, 32;
Ukraine 71, 74; Uzbekistan 102
Luzhkov, Yury 220–1

McDermott 144
Machine Building Scientific Production
Association 172n19
Machinery Design Bureau 172n19
Makiyenko, Konstantin 164–5
Malaysia 160, 257n25

Mamedov, Georgii 120
Marathon 144
marijuana 230
Mashinimport 119
Maskhadov, Aslan 207
Mazeiku Nafta 29–30, 57, 59–61
MDM 30 165
Medvedev, Dmitry 30
Menatep 184
Mexico 169, 205, 209
Mezhprombank 165, 175
Middle East 134, 163; energy source for
    Asia 135
MiG Russian Aircraft Corporation 162,
    169, 172n19
military 200, 205, 207–8, 208–9, 244
Miller, Alexei 38, 39, 70
Miller, Leszek 59
Ministry of Atomic Energy 228
Ministry of Defense 199, 208, 228
Ministry of Economic Development and
    Trade 150
Ministry of Internal Affairs 27, 198, 205,
    208, 244
Ministry of Natural Resources 150,
    257n10
Mirzoyev, Ghafor 201
Mitsubishi 144
Mitsui 144
Mobil 147–8
Mogilevich, Semyon 204
Moldova 31
money laundering 13, 26, 175, 188–91,
    197, 231
Morgoshina, Valery 230
Moscow City 220–1
Murmansk 35

Nafta Polska 59
Nagorno-Karabakh 14, 89, 217, 218
Nakhodka 142
National Energy Strategy 133
natural gas 138, 239; Asia 135; *see also*
    Gazprom
Nemtsov, Boris 74, 75–6
Netherlands 198, 199
Nicaragua 169
Nigerian crime groups 204–5
Niyazov, Saparmurat 101
Nogaideli, Zurab 220
Nomos 165
Norilsk Nickel 24, 33, 182, 183
North Atlantic Treaty Organization 49, 75,
    81, 117

North Korea 199
Norval, Chris 37
Novgorod 25
Novocherkassk City Bank 190
Novorossiisk 201
NPOmash 160
nuclear industry 11, 138; Iran 125–30
Nurgaliev, Rashid 26
Nye, Joseph 6

Oboronprom 162, 165–6
Odessa-Brody pipeline 71–2, 73, 85n14,
    106
oil 138, 183, 239
Oil for Food 118, 121, 123
Oneksimbank 182, 183
OPEC 123
Organization for Economic Co-operation
    and Development 135, 192
organized crime 246–8
Orttung, Robert 220, 221

Pakistan 197
Paoli, Letizia 203
Paris Club 122–3
Partnership and Cooperation Agreement
    51
Pegastar Consortium 147–8
Peru 169, 198
pipeline from East Siberia to Daqing or
    Nakhodka 142–3, 239
PKN Orlen 59
Poland 27, 49, 57, 73; drugs 199;
    electricity 95; LUKoil 104
police *see* Ministry of Internal Affairs
Poroshenko, Pyotr 86n23
Potanin, Vladimir 165, 183
Powell, Colin 121
Priamurskie vedomosti 255
PricewaterhouseCoopers 191, 195n45
Prikhodko, Sergei 30
Primorskii Krai 244, 247
production sharing agreement 144, 148–9,
    149–50
Promeksport 160–1
property rights 28–9, 166–7, 245, 248
Pugachev, Sergei 165
Pukhov, Ruslan 166
Pulikovsky, Konstantin 253, 255
Putin, Vladimir 3; arms 158; Caspian Sea
    89; Chechnya 208; drugs 209–10;
    energy 38; forestry 256; Iran 128, 130;
    Iraq 121–2; Pacific Russia 134;
    production sharing agreements 150;

Russian business 116; Sakhalin 146; South Ossetia 223; United States 120

railroad 30
refugees 232–3
Renova 33
Rice, Condoleezza 120
Rimbunan Hijau 245, 252, 257n25
Roksky tunnel 222, 227, 230
Rosbank 165, 183
Rosenberg, Dorothy 229
Rosneft 12, 30, 119, 191; BP 148, 151; Sakhalin-1 147; Sakhalin-2 144, 146; Sakhalin-3 148; state 133, 150
Rosoboroneksport 158, 160–1, 162, 164, 165
Rosprom 183, 184
Rossiya Association of Regional Banks 179, 193n18
Rosukrenergo 70
Rosvooruzhenie 160–1, 164, 165
Rotch Group 59
Rowhani, Hasan 127, 128, 129
Ruhrgas 52
Rumyantsev, Aleksandr 126–7, 128–9
Rusal Tour 229
RUS-Expert-Transit 163
Rusia Petroleum 141
Russian Aluminum 26, 33
Russian Atomic Energy Agency (Rosatom) 11, 125, 127, 130
Russian business, defined 23–6
Russian Far East 15
Russian Forestry Ministry (Rosleskhoz) 241, 242–3
Russian National Energy Strategy 149
Rutland, Peter 220

Saakashvili, Mikheil 98, 220
Saburi, Asadollah 128
St. Petersburg 200
Sakhalin 25, 134, 140, 144–9, 249
Sakhalin-1 140, 144, 147
Sakhalin-2 139, 144–7; Gazprom 146–7
Sakhalin-3 144, 147–8, 150–1
Sakhalin-4 144
Sakhalin-5 148
Sakhalin Energy Investment Company 144–7
Sakhalinmorenefgaz 144, 148
Sakhalin Oil Company 148
Salyut Moscow Machine-Building Production Enterprise 172n19
Sberbank 175, 177, 178, 180, 184

SBS-Agro 183
Schneider, Ben Ross 29
Sechin, Igor 30
Severstal 36
Severstaltrans 36
Shafranik, Yuri 118
Shah Deniz 93, 102
Shanghai Cooperation Organization 117
Shell 144, 146–7
Shenyang Heavy Machinery Corporation 253
Shevardnadze, Eduard 97–8, 220
Shingariev, Nikolai 127
Shuvalov, Igor 30
Siberia 12, 25; energy development 134, 140, 144
Sibneft 24, 31, 150
Silk Road Studies Program 198
siloviki 117
Slavneft 79–80
Slovakia 55
small business 24–5
Smolenskii, Aleksandr 183
Sodbiznesbank 178, 190
Solntsevo crime group 204
Soskovets, Oleg 180, 181
South Caucasus Pipeline 93
South Korea 20, 35, 133, 197; energy demand 135, 137–9; forestry 250, 258n35, 258n41; LNG 136; pipeline 141, 152; Russian Far East 239
South Ossetia 14, 89, 217, 218; electricity 98
Soyuzneftegaz 118
Spain 199
state 133, 151, 165, 220–1; banks 177–8, 182; business 32–7; coherent 38–9; drugs 205–6; energy 16, 17; lobbying 29, 30; sectors 37–40; weakness 18–19, 39–40, 197, 210, 248–9
State Duma 30, 117
statelets 217–18, 235n1
Stavropol 227
Stroyev, Yegor 118
SUAL 37
subsoil law 148
Sudan 169
Sukhoi Aviation Holding Company 162, 172n19
Sumitomo 245
Surkov, Vladislav 30
SVA Bank 165
Sverdlovsk 201

Svetlaia Timber Venture 245
Switzerland 27
synthetic drugs 199, 202
Syria 163, 169

Tactical Rocket Arms 162
Taishet 143
Taiwan 136, 160, 168
Tajikistan 32, 90, 91; drugs 196, 201, 205,
    208; electricity 95; gas 92; Iran 126; oil
    95
Tajiks 204
Taliban 126, 196, 197
Tatneft 71
Technowood 245
Tenet, George 32
Terneiles 245, 247, 248, 258n37
Terni, Steve 147
terrorist financing 27, 207
Texaco 147–8
Theede, Steven 37
thieves-in-law 203
Thornton, Judith 248, 254
Tikhookeanskaia zvezda 255
Tiumen 201
Tiumen Oil Company 25, 60
TNK-BP 71, 141–2, 147, 149, 151
trafficking in women 204
Transdniestria 31, 221, 235n3
Transnational Crime and Corruption
    Center 201, 227, 230
Transneft 18, 24, 31, 104–5, 107; Belarus
    79–80; China 143; Murmansk 35;
    Ukraine 72
Transnefteprodukt 30
Transparency International 25
Trans-Siberian Railway 140, 200, 257n5
Trutnev, Yuri 148, 151
Tupolev 162
Turkey 93, 137, 218–19; electricity 95;
    UES 96–7
Turkmenistan 70; drugs 202; Gazprom 92,
    99, 101, 107; oil 93, 95; trade 90–1
Turkmenneftegaz 99
TVEL 30
Tymoshenko, Yulia 74–5, 86n23

Ubaydollayev, Mahmadsaid 201
Ukraine 9, 34, 36, 38, 68–75; debt 52; EU
    68–9, 73; Gazprom 70–1, 73–4; Orange
    Revolution 39; trade 90
Ukrtransnafta 73
Unified Energy System 24, 26; banks 13,
    184; Central Asia 33, 95, 106; CIS 35;

EU 55–6; Georgia 10; reform 98; South
    Caucasus 96–8, 107
Union of Oil and Gas Producers 118
United Kingdom 50, 122, 127
United Nations: Iran 125; Iraq 117–18,
    120, 121; Oil for Food 118, 121, 123
United Nations Conference on Trade and
    Development 27, 48
United Russia political party 223
United States 11, 27, 50, 117; arms 163,
    169; Central Asia 89; China 168; energy
    135; Iran 127, 129; Iraq 115, 117–18,
    124; Kazakhstan 95; LUKoil 32;
    organized crime 26; Russia 70, 124–5;
    South Caucasus 218–19; Uzbekistan
    117; Venezuela 168; west coast 143;
    western Europe 49–50
Uralmash crime group 204
Uribe, Alvaro 168
Uzbekistan 32, 36, 90–1; drugs 200;
    Gazprom 92, 99; LUKoil 102; oil 95
Uzbekneftegaz 99, 102

Vahtra, Peeter 104
Vekselberg, Viktor 37
Venezuela 168, 169
Verkhnechonskoe field 142
Viakhirev, Rem 39, 70
Vietnam 160, 197
Vinogradov, Vladimir 183
Vladivostok 200, 206
Vladivostok (newspaper) 255
Vneshtorgbank 177, 180, 184
Volcker Commission report 118
Volgograd 201
Voloshin, Aleksandr 118, 120

Wal-Mart 256
Warsaw Pact 49
Weyerhaeuser 245
Williams International 29, 60
Wimm-Bill-Dann 186
Wintershall 52
World Health Organization 138
World Trade Organization 8, 51, 57, 70,
    76; banks 185, 187–8
World Wildlife Fund 246–7

Yabloko 34
Yakovenko, Aleksandr 127
Yakuza 248
Yamal pipeline 50, 74, 81
Yanukovich, Viktor 69, 72, 74–5
Yaponchik *see* Ivankov, Vyacheslav

Yastrzhembsky, Sergei 118
Yekaterinburg 200, 205–6
Yekhanurov, Yuri 86n24
Yeltsin, Boris 181
Yugankneftegaz 148, 150, 191
Yukos 24, 26, 150, 184, 191; China 35,
    139, 142–3; EU 53–5, 58; Lithuania
    29–30, 57, 60–1; opposition 34;
    production sharing agreements 150

Yushchenko, Viktor 69, 74–5, 86n23
Yusufov, Igor 121

Zarubezhneft 118, 119
Zebari, Hoshyar 122–3
Zhirinovsky, Vladimir 118
Zinchenko, Oleksandr 86n23
Zyuganov, Gennady 118